Quantum

ORGANIZATIONS

Other Books by
Ralph H. Kilmann
(as author, coauthor, coeditor)

The Management of Organization Design

Social Systems Design

Methodological Approaches to Social Science

Producing Useful Knowledge for Organizations

Corporate Tragedies

Beyond the Quick Fix

Gaining Control of the Corporate Culture

Corporate Transformation

Escaping the Quick Fix Trap

Managing Beyond the Quick Fix

Making Organizations Competitive

Workbook for Implementing the Tracks

Logistics Manual for Implementing the Tracks

Holographic Quality Management

Managing Ego Energy

Quantum
ORGANIZATIONS

A New Paradigm for
Achieving Organizational Success
and Personal Meaning

Ralph H. Kilmann

Davies-Black Publishing
Palo Alto, California

Published by Davies–Black Publishing, an imprint of Consulting Psychologists Press, Inc., 3803 East Bayshore Road, Palo Alto, CA 94303; 800-624-1765.

Special discounts on bulk quantities of Davies–Black books are available to corporations, professional associations, and other organizations. For details, contact the Director of Book Sales at Davies–Black Publishing, an imprint of Consulting Psychologists Press, Inc., 3803 East Bayshore Road, Palo Alto, CA 94303; 650-691-9123; FAX 650-623-9271.

Davies–Black and its colophon are registered trademarks of Consulting Psychologists Press, Inc. Culture-Gap® and MAPS Design Technology® are registered trademarks of Organizational Design Consultants. Holotropic Breathwork™ is the trademark of Grof Transpersonal Training, Inc. Knowledge Bridge™ is the trademark of ServiceWare, Inc.

Design, typography, illustrations, and index by Ralph H. Kilmann.

05 04 03 02 01   10 9 8 7 6 5 4 3 2 1
Printed in the United States of America

Library of Congress Cataloging-in-Publication Data
Kilmann, Ralph H.
      Quantum organizations: a new paradigm for achieving organizational success and personal meaning / Ralph H. Kilmann.
          p. cm.
      Includes bibliographical references and index.
      ISBN 0-89106-155-x
      1. Organizational change. 2. Quantum theory. 3. Consciousness. I. Title.
      HD58.8 .K5178 2001
      658.4'06–dc21
                                                                          00-065969

FIRST EDITION
First Printing 2001

CONTENTS

Illustrations

FIGURES IN CHAPTER 6 – CRITICAL SUCCESS FACTORS

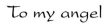

To my angel

PREFACE

During the past century, the great success of organizations in the Western world was achieved through extreme specialization. Experts could resolve well-structured problems within well-defined fields – and put a man on the moon. But the immense success of specialization has also resulted in a daunting progression of unintended consequences: *Specialization has created widespread fragmentation* – in people, organizations, and nations. Problems no longer fit within strict scientific specialties or traditional management functions but, instead, exist *in between* the specialties, fields, disciplines, and categories that evolved from prior centuries. Complex problems now swirl across – and encircle – the entire globe. The new millennium finds itself deeply entangled with the intermingling of all social, economic, political, biological, psychological, spiritual, and environmental problems.

It is rather ironic that innovations in information, communication, production, and transportation technologies, which were accomplished by extreme specialization, have so thoroughly interconnected all people and organizations – typified by the *World Wide Web*. Deregulation of industries, nations, and consortia of nations has also encouraged the merging of all aspects of business and life – worldwide. Biological and computer-based viruses and the increasing number of nations that can generate nuclear holocausts at the touch of a button have, in their own insidious way, also contributed to the intermingling of messy problems on a planetary scale. *Everything affects – and is affected by – everything else.*

What were once simple problems that could be solved by extreme specialization have become complex problems that challenge fragmented categories. To succeed in the new millennium, accordingly, requires *holistic categories* that will enable members and their organizations to (1) clearly *see* the flowing interconnections surrounding the globe, (2) consciously *think* about interconnected problems in comprehensive ways, and (3) purposely *behave* in a manner that stimulates the meaningfulness and coevolution of life and nature throughout the world and the expanding universe. *Seeing, thinking, and behaving with new – holistic – categories requires a mental revolution in self-aware consciousness.*

The members of business organizations (or other organizations) are intimately interconnected within the global ecosystem. Their success now depends on whether they are active participants in the holistic movement that is progressing toward self-aware consciousness. They can choose to ignore it and simply continue down the narrow course of specialization – with blinders in place. Or they can choose to embrace it – and transform the way they see, think, and behave. But one thing has become especially clear: Denying, ignoring, or avoiding what is already happening *in between* scientific spheres, management functions, and most other categories is not fully engaging with reality. *We live in an interconnected world yet suffer from acute fragmentation.*

The term *paradigm* defines the fundamental challenge that confronts humankind – as poignantly exposed by Kuhn (1962) several decades ago. The basis for a paradigmatic revolution, however, now involves all people and organizations – not just scientists. Briefly considered, a paradigm is a fairly rigid set of mental categories (and relationships among categories) for seeing, thinking, and behaving that is organically ingrained in every person's mind/brain. When challenging problems suit mental categories, people and organizations can be adaptive. But when mental categories no longer capture the nature of difficult problems, people and organizations become endangered. Remember the age-old problem of "hardening of the arteries" as a debilitating illness that endangers life? The new epidemic for both young and old is *hardening of the categories*. And a paradigm that is left to work its magic in the dark becomes, ultimately, the "mental illness" that prevents all other challenging problems in the universe from being seen – and then resolved.

Through the development of self-aware consciousness of one's own paradigm, however, the habitual blindness of one's seeing, thinking, and behaving can be brought to light. Consequently, paradigms are subject to revolutionary change – as long as people are able and willing to undergo self-reflection in an open-minded and determined manner. Simply stated, *self-aware consciousness* is first getting acquainted with your own paradigm (and how it differs from other paradigms) and then consciously changing it in order to see, think, and behave in a more successful and meaningful manner – for today's, not yesterday's, world. Conveniently, the process of *self-transformation* in organizations requires the continual development of self-aware consciousness in individuals. Indeed, it seems that a paradigm shift for organizations cannot occur without a corresponding shift in the paradigms of its members. "Know thyself" is the key to the universe.

The old paradigm that cultivates extreme specialization is called the *Cartesian-Newtonian Paradigm*. Basically, starting with Euclid's and Aristotle's notions of space and time, this paradigm became rigidified with Descartes' dualism (the forced split between mind and matter) and Newton's laws of motion (explaining the dynamics of inert objects – but excluding life and people). The Cartesian–Newtonian Paradigm has persuasively dominated Western society for several hundred years and remains deeply entrenched in everything we see and do. Indeed, this outdated paradigm continues to inhabit our minds/brains, since it has been incorporated into the formal systems and processes of our organizations and institutions.

By the early 1900s, however, Planck's insights into quantum action and Einstein's theories of relativity had already challenged the traditional principles of Newtonian reality – regarding the extreme separateness of light, space, time, mass, and energy and, hence, the extreme separateness of mind and matter. Eventually, a new worldview materialized from the pioneering insights and discoveries from quantum physics and relativity theory. The new paradigm, which I name the *Quantum-Relativistic Paradigm*, has been formulated by the "new" science – which incorporates quantum physics and relativity theory with recent developments in systems theory, chaos theory, cosmology, evolutionary theories, neuroscience, superstring theory, and mind/consciousness research. *This new paradigm explicitly includes mental categories for appreciating the dynamic interconnections of light, mass, energy, space, and time – and the coevolution of mind and matter throughout the universe.*

The classic problem of introducing revolutionary change, however, is evident: Since holistic categories in the new paradigm do not match the specialized categories in the old paradigm, it is rather difficult for Western people to comprehend – and assimilate – what appear to be incredulous theories and findings from quantum physics and relativity theory. Notice: If a person doesn't have a category for something, it doesn't exist. Yet by setting a process of self-transformation in motion for an organization, an assortment of powerful social forces are able to encourage all members to get thoroughly acquainted with their old paradigms while learning to see their world in a new light. Enabling self-transformation, therefore, brings about the much needed revolutionary shift in paradigms – even though members' specialized categories were not at first able to make much sense of the unfamiliar (holistic) challenges before them.

Albert Einstein was supposedly fond of saying: "A problem cannot be solved by the same consciousness that created it." The interconnected problems created by the organizational success of extreme specialization, therefore, cannot be solved with the same fragmented categories that still exist in the Cartesian–Newtonian Paradigm. A new *self-aware* consciousness is needed if we are to resolve the interconnected problems that now flow across all the old categories – problems which can now be witnessed and addressed by the Quantum–Relativistic Paradigm.

The distinctive purpose of my book is twofold: (1) to provide a deep understanding of the two dueling paradigms and (2) to offer an effective method for enabling self-aware consciousness and self-transformation in organizations. By applying these insights and approaches, it is possible to create *quantum organizations*. Although some organizations manifest one or more attributes of this new invention, despite a broad search I was unable to find a single example of a quantum organization – in which the thrust of transformation was enabling self-aware consciousness. There are many examples of piecemeal efforts at transformation or cases of organizational improvement imposed on members. But *self-transformation* – which enables members to examine unconscious paradigms, discover hidden forces, and self-design formal systems and processes – still remains to be seen.

There have been a couple of efforts to translate the new science into an organizational framework, particularly Margaret Wheatley's 1992 book, *Leadership and the New Science*, and Donah Zohar's 1997 contribution, *Rewiring the Corporate Brain*. While these two works introduce the reader to the new science, they go neither far enough nor deep enough into the primordial mystery of self-aware consciousness – and how to accelerate this mental revolution for members and their organizations. Even more to the point, these books do not offer change initiatives that empower organizations to transform themselves into the new paradigm. Readers of these beginning works are left on their own to figure out what to do with the exciting new knowledge that the new science offers. Consequently, I wrote my book to fill these noticeable gaps by examining self-aware consciousness in depth while presenting a *completely integrated program* that enables all members to achieve organizational success and personal meaning.

In this preface I discuss how all the material in the book is arranged into chapters – consistent with the dire need for holistic categories. After summarizing each chapter, I reveal the origin of this book, including the authors who stimulated the shift in my paradigm. The preface concludes with special acknowledgments to the people who actively supported my personal and professional development.

OVERVIEW OF CONTENTS

The material in this book is organized into Chapters 0 to 6. Realizing the extreme specialization that has dominated Western civilization, just think how easy it would have been to divide three hundred or more pages into many more chapters (between ten and fifteen), so that each chapter would be somewhere between twenty and thirty pages long. This is the standard for management books – which, incidentally, parallels the large number of extremely specialized departments that still exist in most organizations. Short chapters seem easier to absorb than long ones. When one's mental categories are suited for extreme specialization, what is most comfortable (or familiar) for our minds/brains, however, may not be best for deeply understanding – and then changing – our entrenched paradigms. A book composed of *many small chapters may seriously fragment holistic categories.*

Even if it is more demanding, therefore, to scrutinize a long chapter (between forty and seventy pages in length), holistic categories necessarily include a more encompassing piece of the whole puzzle. Moreover, these holistic categories (chapters) also embody the interfaces, interconnections, and interactions that generally fall in between specialized chapters (just as when some tasks are not clearly assigned to any unit in an organization, they tend to fall between the cracks). But organizations are changing their structures from management functions (extremely specialized) to business processes (holistic categories). The underlying structure of chapters in this book also reflects this movement toward wholeness.

Chapter 0 introduces the core theme of self–aware consciousness by using a story: *The Ultimate Encounter.* The reader will vicariously experience the deepest regrets of a person's unexamined life, which are reinforced by unconscious organizations. This story dramatically reveals the importance of knowing one's true essence (as early in life as possible) and using this self-knowledge to create organizations that encourage conscious living.

Chapter 1 describes *two dueling paradigms* – the Cartesian–Newtonian Paradigm and the Quantum–Relativistic Paradigm – summarized as seven diametrically opposed categories. Readers who can examine this material *before* proceeding with the subsequent chapters will attain a much deeper understanding of everything that follows. But if this forty–page chapter is too difficult to absorb as one *holistic* thought, move on to Chapter 2. Later, a greater depth of understanding can still be achieved by turning back to Chapter 1. *But I urge the reader to confront the mind-bending and paradigm-breaking discussion presented in Chapter 1 of this book — at one time or another.* It crystallizes the underlying worldview for achieving self-transformation.

Chapter 2 begins with a brief review of the key concepts of the new paradigm by making use of artwork. A series of figures graphically reveals the essence of seeing, thinking, and behaving in holistic ways. (For readers who may have skipped to this point from Chapter 1, these figures and the accompanying text will smooth the reentry.) Since the language of both paradigms was primarily developed from the physical sciences, Chapter 2 provides a translation of the salient terms into a vocabulary that is more appropriate to organizations. Using this *dictionary*, it is easy to distinguish a Newtonian organization from a quantum organization. Next, Chapter 2 describes the seven attributes of *the new organization* and then proposes the fundamental challenge: how to transform an old Newtonian organization into a new quantum organization. This chapter then switches to action by presenting an overview of self–transformation: (1) summarizing the three components of transformation – quantum infrastructures, formal systems, and process management; (2) deriving the completely integrated program of eight tracks – culture, skills, teams, strategy–structure, rewards, gradual process, radical process, and learning process; and (3) identifying the five stages of self–transformation.

Chapters 3, 4, and 5 cover the three components of transformation – quantum infrastructures, formal systems, and process management – each as a mini–book. Chapter 3 reviews the first three tracks of the completely integrated program, which develop *quantum infrastructures*. Most important, self–aware consciousness is noticeably enhanced by enabling members to manage cultural norms, implicit assumptions, and group process – topics that were rarely, if ever, discussed previously. As a result, members learn to confront these hidden forces consciously and purposefully. *Without first establishing quantum infrastructures, members will find it nearly impossible to engage in an effective dialogue about anything crucial and complex.*

Chapter 4 investigates the middle two tracks of self–transformation: strategy–structure and rewards. Building on the quantum infrastructures that were established, strategy first develops the architectural plan for the future and then determines short–term objectives for all strategic business units (SBUs); structure then arranges objectives, tasks, people, and all other resources into subunits within each SBU. Reward systems are developed to motivate members to provide strategically relevant behavior and results in exchange for intrinsic and extrinsic rewards. These three *formal systems* must be completely aligned and fully deployed – in order for members to spend the right amount of time on the right tasks according to the right strategic objectives. In fact, these systems should allow all members to see clearly which actions add the most economic value to their organization.

Chapter 5 presents the last three tracks of the completely integrated program – which presume quantum infrastructures and aligned systems. All members first learn to describe, control, and improve processes *within* their subunits. They then are ready to self-design new *horizontal* subunits around *holistic* business processes – supported by information technology. Once they have accomplished gradual and radical process improvement, members describe, control, and improve their learning processes: creating, acquiring, and sharing strategically relevant knowledge across all mental and organizational boundaries. Quantum organizations are thereby able to improve infrastructures, systems, and processes *faster and better* during all subsequent self-transformations, thus enabling self-aware consciousness, organizational success, and personal meaning *to accelerate and advance*.

The popular names for the material presented in Chapter 5 include total quality management (TQM), business process reengineering (BPR), and organizational learning (or knowledge management). Some of these terms have developed a negative connotation because of the high failure rate of implementing these improvement programs (which is greater than 75% for TQM and reengineering). Accordingly, these popularized improvement efforts are often dismissed as passing fads. The high failure rates, however, often resulted from ignoring weak infrastructures and misaligned systems, as opposed to any inherent flaws in the tools and techniques themselves. Basically, "the baby has been thrown out with the bathwater," which tends to discourage organizations from again trying to utilize these approaches. By making use of more neutral language (*gradual process*, *radical process*, and *learning process*), however, and by explicitly investigating *process management* within a larger context of quantum infrastructures and formal systems – perhaps the great concepts from TQM and reengineering can still be saved. Naturally, *any attempt* at improvement or transformation that does not take into account the crippling impact of poor infrastructures and misaligned systems is also doomed to fail, become a passing fad, and ultimately lose its potential contribution to organizations.

Chapter 6 concludes this book by summarizing twenty *critical success factors* that determine the key outcomes of self-transformation: self-aware consciousness, organizational success, and personal meaning. The topic of self-aware consciousness (including a mental revolution toward the new paradigm) has been the guiding light throughout our conversation up to this point. Additional material is provided to enhance this pivotal theme: Ego development (Freud) resolves the various psychological defenses and dysfunctional behavior that sidetrack ego energy; spiritual enlightenment (Buddha) reveals the highest stages of human evolution.

ORIGIN OF THE BOOK

Quantum Organizations includes most of the knowledge and experience that I have accumulated during the past thirty years of my professional career: essentially from the time I began the Ph.D. program in Behavioral Science at UCLA in 1970 until now. The bibliography lists some of my books that were important points along the way, notably, *Social Systems Design* in 1977, *Beyond the Quick Fix* in 1984, *Managing Beyond the Quick Fix* in 1989, *Workbook for Implementing the Tracks* in 1991, and *Holographic Quality Management* in 1993. The article that first organized the series of eight tracks into a completely integrated program was published in June 1995 as "A Holistic Program and Critical Success Factors of Corporate Transformation."

In mid-1995, however, I sensed that my approach to transformation was still missing something, but I didn't know what. Maybe I had become too acquainted with my own viewpoint, which made it impossible for me to break out of my familiar box and see something new. Because of what I was sensing, I refused to write another new book along the same lines as before – so I just started *reading*. I looked for books that epitomized areas that I always wanted to learn about, but never had the time (or took the time) to read – since I was preoccupied with my own perspective (the one I had learned at UCLA that had served me well for a quarter of a century). To make a long story short, there were several books that altered the way I see and think about organizations, which restructured my paradigm.

Leahey and Harris (1993) did a fantastic job of presenting and then integrating some basic material on learning and cognition, including how the mind/brain works. Then I switched to economics and thoroughly read and studied the brilliant work by Milgrom and Roberts (1992), which sets the stage for developing an economics of holism. From there I visited the evolution of consciousness in the universe – from the very first photon to the limits of human enlightenment: I learned how Young (1976) integrated physics, chemistry, biology, psychology, and spirituality via evolutionary theories. The consciousness theme then brought me to Grof (1993), whose insights awakened me. Transpersonal psychology (finding that people can consciously engage with past, present, and future life forms and matter in the cosmos) must be the utmost challenge to the current paradigm in the Western world. My mind was so stimulated by these ideas that I attended Grof's weeklong workshops. These transpersonal experiences changed my views about the links between mind/matter and psychology/physics. At this juncture, I had to learn about the beginning of time (and when time might end) and the creation of matter and consciousness in the universe.

The next stop on my nontraditional journey was quantum physics and cosmology – with a keen interest in universal consciousness. The new science was introduced to me by Wheatley (1992) and then Zohar (1997). I thoroughly enjoyed Goswami (1993), because he expanded on the theme of consciousness – which for me highlighted the real challenge to the old paradigm. Smolin's (1997) book on cosmological natural selection was just as challenging as Grof's work, suggesting that universes are evolving in a manner not unlike life forms on earth. Smolin also included stimulating discussion of Einstein's relativity theory and how it might be joined with quantum theory – sometime in the future. Smolin also introduced me to string theory, which led me to several additional works on this subject.

I next studied Shlain's (1991) book on art and physics. Not only did I learn the history of art (with doses of music and literature), but I learned how artists' creations anticipate later developments in physics (including the new science), by fifty to several hundred years. Linking right–brain art to left–brain physics (with a lag in between) provided an understanding of science that further challenged and changed my paradigm. Shlain's book also encouraged me to use artwork to illuminate science, which activates both halves of the human brain. (Indeed, the reader will encounter more than one hundred figures in this book.) Ken Wilber (1995) addressed both halves of the human brain by incorporating "all" history and philosophy across the Eastern and Western worlds. His penetrating insights extended my understanding of consciousness into spirituality. I had to read much more, of course, but these are the authors who transformed my mind.

Someday I would like to hold a creative, interactive workshop and invite these ingenious thinkers to attend: Goswami, Grof, Shlain, Smolin, Wheatley, Wilber, Young, Zohar. Imagine what could be generated – and learned – by having a distinguished group of paradigm breakers ponder the future for science and organizations. Energetic, divergent interaction is what all people need in order to break the old paradigm of specialization and begin living with the new paradigm of holism – and the evolution of self–aware consciousness. Until such a real–live setting can be arranged, I invite the reader to trust in my ability to understand and integrate what these and other authors have provided by their written word. I have tried to capture the essence of their provocative ideas and put them in a form that will enable self–transformation – and spiritual enlightenment.

One difficulty in writing a book that introduces a new paradigm for organizations is finding *real* examples. What if prototypes do not yet exist? Two forms of *initial* validation are useful to distinguish: (1) the proof is in the pudding and (2) the proof is in the experience.

The standard blueprint for management books is to propose a new theory or practice and supply plenty of business examples – revealing the best practices of that new approach to management. This blueprint recites the stories of companies that have been using this "new" approach – and what performance outcomes have apparently improved. It seems that the more companies that are cited along with demonstrative results, the more "proof" or credibility is attributed to the new approach. I call this process of knowledge validation: *the proof is in the pudding*. While this blueprint for validation has many positive features, it also has some serious drawbacks: It does not apply the principles of scientific research. But most perplexing is the "newness" paradox: The more companies that are already using the approach, the less it can really be new! If other organizations are waiting for this kind of proof before they try something new, they are relegating themselves to becoming followers to industry leaders who were somehow able to implement the new approach *first*, without any convincing "proof." Even though it helps to have some examples of what others have learned, the point is soon reached when an approach is no longer new.

At the other extreme is a different blueprint for management books, designated: *the proof is in the experience*. Now validation occurs if a book can shake up management thought and challenge prevailing practices – but there are very few examples that "prove" the effectiveness of this radical new approach to organizational improvement. Here the proposed theory and method must be judged by logic, emotion, intuition, past experience, conviction, and some amount of faith. Does the new approach stimulate dialogue, confrontation, and self–reflection? Can the new approach lead to change, improvement, and transformation *before* other organizations find the way? How does one become the popular example that will be cited in the future, which will thus demonstrate "proof" of the new approach? This blueprint is about stimulating contemplation, self–awareness, and action – rather than providing well-known examples about *others'* successes.

My book falls closer to *the proof is in the experience* than to *the proof is in the pudding*. While I have included many examples about various aspects of self-transformation and quantum organizations, I cannot point to any organization that incorporates all attributes of a quantum organization. Actually, my hope is that this book will challenge people to examine their own paradigms and those of their organizations. As people achieve both self–aware consciousness and self–transformation, they will create living proof of quantum organizations. At some point, we can then determine if *holistic categories with organized action can effectively heal the interconnected problems that encircle our globe.*

SPECIAL ACKNOWLEDGMENTS

Since this book has been in the works for thirty years, numerous people and organizations have played a key role in my personal and professional development. I would like to give special acknowledgment to those who have deeply affected my seeing, thinking, feeling – and mindfulness.

My father, Martin H. Kilmann, has always been my role model – for being inquisitive, scholarly, and open minded. He also taught me what it means to be a professional – and to conduct myself accordingly. His belief in me was unconditional when he was alive and his ever–present support now surrounds me after his passing. I know that he would have enjoyed (and does enjoy) this book very much.

My mother, Lilli Kilmann, taught me to believe in my abilities. She convinced me that I can accomplish whatever I set my mind/brain to do. She also taught me never to give up – no matter what. Her stubbornness has kept her alive for more than ninety–four years. She will probably live forever – just to make sure I have learned the value of determination.

My uncle, Morris Loeb, a very successful entrepreneur, gave me my first exposure to business when I worked for Liberty Hardware during my summers in college. He showed me all aspects of a business so I could see the big picture. He seeded my subsequent interest in organizations.

My formal education suited me well: At Carnegie Mellon University, I learned the quantitative approach to organizations – including statistics and mathematics. At the University of California at Los Angeles, I learned the qualitative aspects – including psychology and sociology. At Carnegie, if you didn't understand something, you were required to take additional courses in calculus. If the same predicament occurred at UCLA, you would be advised to seek additional sessions in psychotherapy. Striving to make sense out of these vastly different responses taught me to appreciate and synthesize diametrically opposed points of view. Special acknowledgment is given to Ken Mackenzie, Igor Ansoff, Herbert Simon, Ken Thomas, Dave Peters, Bill McKelvey, Tuck Taylor, Dave Jamieson, Kurt Motamedi, Harold Kelley, Bertram Raven, Harold Gerard.

In 1972 I joined the Graduate School of Business at the University of Pittsburgh – now named the Katz School. This was my very first full–time job and I've been there ever since. It has been a wonderful setting to grow personally and professionally – and I deeply appreciate the tremendous support that I have received for the past several decades. During this time, I have benefited greatly by my association with various faculty members at the Katz School and others I worked with at conferences, professional associations, and consulting projects. Special acknowledgment is given to Chris Argyris, Michael Beer, Warren Bennis, Colleen Carney, Pat Carr, Terry Deal, Stan Grof, Ed Lawler, Craig Lundberg, Ian Mitroff, Josephine Olson, Jeff Pfeffer, Lou Pondy, Ed Schein, Peter Senge, Jerry Zaltman, Jerry Zoffer. Several doctoral students have also contributed to my development: Rich Allen, Larry Boone, Dick Herden, Bernie Jaworski, Teresa Joyce, Bob Keim, Marjorie Lyles, Debbie MacInnis, Walter McGhee, Mary Saxton, Joe Seltzer, Louise Serafin, Betty Velthouse. Numerous executives have also supported my research: Vince Barabba, Joe Colosimo, Pedro Grau, Peter Mathias, Jim McIntyre, Bill Peace, José Renter, Roy Serpa, Kendra VanderMeulen.

My experience with Davies–Black has been awesome from the start: from Laura Simonds' first reaction to my new manuscript ("Wow!") to Alan Shrader's tactful challenge of my color palette. Jill Anderson–Wilson's eye for detail and Mark Ong's graphic arts knowledge filled in all the gaps.

Of all those acknowledged, Ian Mitroff has had the most profound influence on me – both personally and professionally. Since 1972, he and I have traveled many challenging roads together, jointly authored several articles and books, and pushed one another to self–aware consciousness – even when it hurt. He has been my deepest friend. Other friends who also have remained around for a long time and in a deep way include Jeanette and Dean Engel, Richard Pollens, Noreen Fennell, Richard MacDonald, Jeff Brown. Jeff entered into this distinguished support group just a few years ago by participating in my transpersonal journeys. He has become a deep friend in a short period of ordinary time. Two people have energized my spirit in *nonordinary* time: Nora Goetz and Father Walt.

My family is the center of my life – and my ultimate happiness. My son, Chris, is my perpetual Best Man and has the qualities that I admire in a person: He is honest, sincere, empathic, compassionate, warm, cheerful, helpful, humorous, and very insightful. By being actively involved in his growth and development, I have learned much about myself: Chris keeps me forever young. My angel, Twishy, is much beyond any person I could ever imagine. Yet she actually exists! The first moment I met her, I said to myself: "I could look at that face for the rest of my life." I soon discovered that her face is a natural reflection of her sweetness, warmth, wisdom, and zest for learning and growing. She has genuine confidence in herself and, therefore, can easily extend herself to others. She is also deeply committed to her own self–aware consciousness – and self–transformation. I therefore dedicate this book to my angel.

Quantum

ORGANIZATIONS

A book is a flexible mirror of the mind and the body. Its overall size and proportions, the color and texture of the paper, the sound it makes as the pages turn, and the smell of the paper, adhesive and ink, all blend with the size and form and placement of the type to reveal a little about the world in which it was made. If the book appears to be only a paper machine, produced at their own convenience by other machines, only machines will want to read it. – *Robert Bringhurst (1992, page 129)*

THE ULTIMATE ENCOUNTER

Getting Acquainted with Your Paradigm and Getting a Chance to Change It

People don't spend a lot of time examining their own behavior, thinking about their motives, and augmenting their self-knowledge. Although we hear about career and relationship changes all the time, these experiences don't necessarily mean that people have learned more about themselves. During most life changes, people automatically repeat their habitual ways of seeing, thinking, and behaving – and never look back. During personal crises or severe traumas, however, people are often forced to take a hard look at themselves and are thus given an opportunity to make significant improvements in their self–awareness. Undoubtedly, the most challenging crises are instigated by the appearance of death. Under these threatening circumstances, however, most people close down their minds and just live out what remains of their lives – especially when there is little time left to do anything else.

Wouldn't it be nice if the confrontational power of a deathbed crisis could be encountered much earlier in life – when there is more time (and desire) for people to reexamine their paradigms and consciously improve how they see, think, and behave? I ask the reader to intently reflect on the following story: It portrays a deathbed journey that confronts the deepest regrets of a senseless life – which unconscious organizations inadvertently create and perpetuate.

WHAT WOULD YOU DO DIFFERENTLY?

As I regained consciousness from what must have been a very deep sleep, I kept my eyes shut and didn't move. I heard the rain beating against the window. It was another dreary day in the city. I also heard the faint voices of my friends, but I didn't feel like talking. I had to figure out what I was experiencing. I had woken up with a peculiar feeling of dread throughout my body. I had never felt anything like it before. It was eerie. It was not of this world. Then, all of a sudden, it hit me: I wasn't going to get stronger. I wasn't going to recover. It was all downhill from here. I knew, without a doubt, I was going to die.

I was startled by my own morbid insight. I instinctively opened my eyes to dodge my coming fate. My two friends noticed that I was awake. Quickly they walked to my bedside. They didn't say anything, but I could read their faces. They also knew what was happening. Maybe the doctor told them or maybe they saw it in my eyes. They both forced a smile, but I could see their distress: They knew that death was approaching.

Peter seemed anxious. He said he was going to get something to eat. He looked at me as if he was trying to say something, but nothing came out. He turned slowly and left the room. Jeff, however, stayed at my side. He put aside his own feelings of discomfort and helped me face the end. I'm not certain what I would have said if I were in his shoes, but Jeff got right to the point: "Do you have any regrets?"

His blunt question caught me off guard. I didn't have an immediate answer. Maybe I was blocking. But after a brief pause, I was able to gather enough strength to ask: "What do you mean?" Jeff reworded his question: "If you could live your life all over again, what would you do differently? I really want to know."

I thought for a while and then started to talk. It's probably the most I ever reflected on my life. At this point, I had nothing to lose.

"Yes, I'm sure there are many things I would do differently. So much comes to mind. I wish I would have spent a lot more time with my kids. They grew up so fast. Before I knew it, they were off on their own. I guess that's what they're supposed to do. But I missed a lot of their growing up. I was always so busy with work and other things.

"I also would have spent more time with my wife. We had so many plans for 'someday.' But we didn't plan on her dying so suddenly. How do you get all those years back? How could anyone know?

"I spent most of my life working. After completing college, I worked for three companies for almost fifty years. That's a lot of time! Basically, I spent most of my waking hours doing things for someone else. That's one reason why I didn't have much time for family. And when I got home at night, I was tired. After dinner, I would go downstairs to my wood shop. Remember all those furniture pieces I used to make? I really enjoyed my hobby. It was the only time I felt I was doing something for me. Maybe if my full-time job had been more interesting, I wouldn't have retreated to my wood shop every weeknight and most weekends.

"In my wood shop, I was in my prime. I was doing something that came from deep inside me, something artistic, creative, lasting, timeless – something that made a significant difference. I got so much pleasure from creating furniture pieces for all my friends and family. I made tables and desks that people treasure. Some people still remind me about a furniture piece I made for them, way back when. They cherish what I made and are still using my creations. Remember the coffee table I made for your living room? You couldn't believe I spent so much time on that thing. But it was pure joy for me!

"At my job, I never experienced that pure joy. Sure, I had interesting assignments but, all in all, my work was rather empty. There wasn't much of a challenge. No, that's not really it. My work was difficult at times, often exhausting. The main problem, I think, is that there wasn't much of *me* in my job. I did what others expected of me. I had to please my boss and, in the process, I had to put up with so much foolishness. There was so much politics: everyone maneuvering for the next work assignment and all that in-fighting. There was so much time spent doing things that didn't make sense, that we knew was wrong or wasteful, that was definitely below our standards – just to get it out the door. We knew which customers would be back for rework. Sending the product out just bought us extra time. It was all about meeting deadlines that someone, who knew nothing about what work had to be done, promised someone else. On top of all that, we couldn't get the cooperation from other departments to keep our work on schedule. What's crazy is that departments were basically competing with one another! Can you imagine that? In the same company, people down the hallway wouldn't tell you when they would deliver what you needed. Or they would flat-out lie to you about what their own department was doing. How are you supposed to do a good job if you can't even count on what your own coworkers tell you?

"And the senior managers were completely in the dark about what was going on. How could they be so blind? They talked about quality and doing things right the first time, but not much happened as a result. They left everything up to our bosses. On so many occasions, we talked about doing things differently. But when we were in the thick of it again, it was business as usual. And I can remember how much money was wasted on those silly training programs. I spent hours and hours learning new stuff that never got used. We always used to say: 'Management should be here to learn this material. Why aren't *they* here? Why are *we* here? We can't do anything unless they get behind it'. So why did they make us go through all those training programs and useless exercises?

"No wonder I would come home at night frustrated and exhausted. But I could always escape to my wood shop. There, at least, I could make something special – and do it right. After I designed a desk for someone, I could order the materials I needed. I knew the best suppliers – and they knew me. They got me what I wanted when I wanted it. And once I began making a desk, I could stay focused on the friend I was making the desk for. I didn't have to wait for competing departments to do the cutting, the sanding, the staining, the sealing, the gluing, the polishing, the hardware, the packaging, the delivery, and the servicing. I could do all these tasks as needed. Let's compare this to my day job: Producing something as simple as a desk would have been a nightmare in scheduling and a headache in coordinating all the little empires that made up the company.

"Do you remember when I showed you all those different sketches for a coffee table? We created a style that blended with the other furniture in your living room. We had so much fun in coming up with the perfect design. We even changed it again when you saw the next set of drawings I put together. Remember when I finished that coffee table and brought it over to your home? You were so thrilled – and I was so proud. We started with an empty space and filled it with something beautiful.

"I never had that meaningful experience at work. I never felt I could create something worthwhile. I don't think anyone in the company really cared about our finished products – as long as the money kept rolling in. The company was about money. It was a numbers game. Work had little to do with pleasure or doing something special for someone else.

"As I now think about it, working in those organizations was a very negative aspect of my life. But the worst part is realizing how much of my life I gave to all those boring, senseless jobs. Not one of the organizations I worked for really got to know me, knew what I could give, what I could achieve – if I were given half a chance. They only wanted me to do what they thought I should be doing for them, even if it didn't make any sense. My hands were tied by all that ridiculous nonsense going on inside every department: all the games people played to take care of themselves, climb the corporate ladder, and get their paychecks. They never encouraged me to get seriously involved – so that I could put my true self into my work. *They wasted me!* I seriously doubt that any of my fellow employees felt they could contribute and truly be themselves. You always had to worry about how it would hurt your career if you spoke out and told the truth – and didn't go along with the silent crowd of defeated employees.

"Do you realize how many working hours were easily wasted by all those political games and useless procedures? After a while, I think I just turned myself off and switched over to autopilot. I would be at work, my body, that is, but I'd be dreaming about that furniture piece I could work on as soon as I got home at night. And if I got through the week without too much trouble, I would have enough energy left to work in my wood shop for most of the weekend."

That's when Jeff cut in: "So what would you do differently? You now know that you were alive in your wood shop and dead at your job."

"Okay, okay. I see what you're getting at. Well, I couldn't make any major changes in the companies I worked for. They were a tangled mess of competing departments, confusing policies, inefficient procedures, and remote executives anxious for retirement. Besides, most people there had already given up. Plus, I wasn't in charge of what went on. I had from ten to fifteen people reporting to me, at most. I was only a middle manager – stuck between those out–of–touch executives above and all the turned–off workers below. I wasn't ever going to be president, or anything like that. Actually, I'm not even sure what I would have done if I *had been* president. The companies I worked for were a complete mess. Even if I owned one of them, I'd probably sell it – and start all over again."

Jeff pushed me further along: "So you would sell the company and start over again. Now tell me something. What would you do so that you wouldn't re-create the same mess?"

Now I had to think even harder, yet I was getting tired. I don't even know how I got the strength to say what I did. Maybe I could keep going after a short nap. It's all I had left to do.

The next part is hard to recall. I know I continued talking with Jeff, but I'm not sure if it was a *real* conversation or if I just dreamed it. I know I fell asleep, but I don't remember waking *before* I started talking again.

Now that I think about it, I got out of bed and found myself by the window in my room, sitting in a chair across from Jeff. What's so weird is that I couldn't walk when I entered the hospital, so how did I get over to the chair? It's all rather vague, but I'll continue with my story anyway.

I looked Jeff straight in the eyes and said: "You asked me before if I had any regrets. Well, I was pretty happy during most of my life, at least what I knew at the time. But now, looking back, it's obvious that I wasted just about eighty percent of my waking life, which is, practically speaking, most of my whole life! That doesn't make me feel very good. Yes, I turned myself off. I just gave up trying to feel good about my job. It was useless trying to work around all those out–of–date manuals and cut through the bureaucratic red tape. I lost the best years of my life! At this moment, I'm not sure if it's better to leave this world ignorant but at least superficially happy or to die well informed but fully aware of my deepest regrets. You really opened up a can of worms for me, didn't you! Why *did* you raise all these doubts at the end of my life? Can't I just die in peace?"

Do you know what Jeff did next? He totally ignored what I just said and kept pushing with this stupid regrets stuff again by asking me what I would do differently, now that I know what I know. When was he going to stop this eleventh-hour, confrontational crap? Why didn't he just leave with Peter and get something to eat?

Yet, I had to admit, my conversation with Jeff felt unfinished to me. All my doubts and regrets were out there in the open. I couldn't pretend I didn't know what had just come out of my mouth; I couldn't bury it. So I just shrugged my shoulders, sank back into the soft chair, and continued to answer his damn questions.

"If I were fifty years younger, of course, I would do things differently. Since I wouldn't have been president of a company anyway, I'm not going to play that out. I'll just be myself, but this time being fully aware of what I was feeling and how I was living.

"I wouldn't have given up so readily. Maybe I wouldn't have given up at all. I would have kept bucking the system. I wouldn't have done it in a bad way. I would have challenged people to keep in touch with what was hurting the organization – and what could be done about it. I would have asked my coworkers to talk about their feelings, their experiences, their hopes, their dreams: 'How can we work together so that it all makes sense – and gets the job done for customers? How can we make our work lives meaningful? What can we do so that we all look forward to coming to work every single day?' I would keep questioning, keep pushing ahead. I wouldn't retreat into a shell. I wouldn't go on autopilot. I wouldn't give up all those years to a senseless existence.

"How long would I keep working within the same organization? It's hard to know. But I wouldn't stay for long if I couldn't succeed at bringing my soul into the workplace. That's too much frustration – and too much time – knocking your head against a brick wall. I would keep up the fight for about three to five years. After that, I would take a serious look at my job. And if I hadn't made much headway bringing my whole self into my work, I would start looking for another job. But this time, I would look for a company that deeply cared about its employees and genuinely wanted their true essence in the work; a company that knew how to bring out the very best in its people; *a company that didn't want its people to have all the regrets*

I am now having! I would try to find a company where I could experience the same excitement and meaning that I got from my wood shop. I would search for a while, and then I would take a job with a firm that seemed to understand these things. If I made a wrong choice, I would keep trying to bring out the truth – and not give up my soul. But if I couldn't find such a company or couldn't change one, I would create my own work life.

"I was very good at woodworking. I could have created a specialty furniture business. I could have hired people as the business grew. I could have really put my soul into this – if I had been aware of what I'm now seeing. I would have looked for people who also wanted to do something worthwhile. I would have hired people who understood themselves well enough to know what pure joy they could experience through their work. I would hire people who also could get pleasure from creating something special for others. I am not entirely sure how I would have done it, but I would have found people who still had a burning desire to do something meaningful – so they wouldn't have to be on their deathbed to discover their deepest regrets.

"But my biggest challenge would be creating a company that would actively nourish the radiant spirit inside people – and not squelch it. This has got to be the key: *I would create an organization that would further develop the self-awareness and consciousness of its people. This organization would also nourish its people with a healthy culture, coherent policies, and effective procedures – so they could give all of themselves to everything they do.*

"I know of no better way to create this company than to ask people outright for their help – and really listen. I would ask them to get together in groups. In a candid dialogue, we would figure out how to design and manage an organization that could appreciate and apply our inner selves. Because we would all be doing this work together, we would all share in the ownership and management of our organization. And yes, after every project or assignment, I would ask people what they would do differently next time – so they could further develop their self–awareness, heighten the personal meaning of their work, and achieve organizational success.

"This new brand of organization would produce things and provide services that we really care about. I would do everything in my power to encourage people to remain actively involved, say what they have to say, appreciate what others feel, and then figure out a way to make it all work. I wouldn't give up; I wouldn't quit. Expressing your soul at work is a vital aspect of living. Yes, I loved my wife deeply and always will. I deeply love my kids and want the best for them. *But I must also love my work!* I want to excel at both love and work.

"I couldn't be satisfied, anymore, just retreating to my wood shop. I couldn't let myself waste those forty hours a week, for fifty weeks a year, for nearly fifty years – by going through the motions at my job while I'm daydreaming about something else. I couldn't go through that again!

"If only my eyes had been open all along. If only I could have spent serious time figuring out my feelings. If only I hadn't waited until the last moment to confront my life, face to face, and realize what I was missing. If only I had known this fifty years ago, I could have saved myself. Chances are, I also might have saved my kids. What did I actually teach them? To put up with meaningless jobs – and deny their inner selves, their dreams, their desires? They have told me about their jobs. I know they're suffering, too. If only I could have seen then what I see now. I could have thought about things differently. I could have done things differently. But now it's too late. Why did I have to wait so long to wake up? For most of my life, I truly was in a very deep sleep."

That's the last thing I remember saying to myself as I woke up in a panic. My wife was shaking me: "Wake up, wake up! You're having a bad dream. Wake up. Everything's all right!" I opened my eyes and quickly sat up in bed. Just then, my wife and kids began singing, "Happy birthday to you, happy birthday to you… "

My God, it was only a dream! Or, more accurately, a dream within a dream. I'm alive! I didn't die! And I'm not going to die any time soon. I'm thirty years old today! I could hardly believe it. But then, all of a sudden, I realized that my wife and kids had just finished singing, "Happy birthday." I barely heard it. I had been too preoccupied with the sheer joy of being alive to give them my full attention.

My wife could see that I was still in a heightened state: "That must have been quite a nightmare. You look like you've seen a ghost! I realize you hit thirty today, but it's not like your life is over."

When the kids left our bedroom, I said to her: "It was a very intense experience: I dreamed that you had died, the kids had grown up and left, only Peter and Jeff were with me, and I was dying!"

"Oh my," she said, "that *was* a nightmare! Are you okay?"

"I think so. But I need some time to figure it out. Something tells me that my dream had to do with my birthday. I think I died but was given a second chance. Everything looks different. Everything has changed. Now I know what I must do. I know how to save myself. I know how I want to live. And I'm only thirty years old. My God, I'm so young. I have so much time. Let me think about it some more. I'll tell you everything, but I don't want to lose what I just experienced. I want to remember everything!"

My wife seemed a bit perplexed with my muddled description, but she still honored my wishes: "Just so you don't forget – Jeff will be here in about an hour."

"What? Jeff is coming here today?"

"Yes," she said, "don't you remember? He wants to wish you happy birthday and spend some time with you. He's also eager to see how much progress you've made on the end table – you know, the one to go with the coffee table you gave him last year. You promised to show it to him today. Don't you remember?"

I nodded my head as if I remembered, but I didn't. Wow, I must be really out of it. Or, just maybe, I'm finally "in it." I was so excited that Jeff would be here soon. He would help me remember my dream. After all, he was there!

Jeff and I talked for hours. It was great. Occasionally, I confused the *real* Jeff with the *mythical* Jeff, but he was very understanding – just as he had been in my dream.

In the days and weeks to come, I spent a lot of time thinking about my deathbed experience. I recorded everything I could remember, every word that I thought to myself or said to Jeff. I came to the realization that I had given myself the nicest birthday present anyone could ever give: the gift of self-awareness. It took the ultimate encounter with death, as real as it could ever be, to force me to take an honest look at myself: to see what deep regrets I might have had – if I had continued on my present course. And once I answered the questions that Jeff put to me, I faced my regrets with an open mind – and an open heart. The quintessential gift, however, was when I realized that the near–death encounter was just a sequence of dreams. I now have a lifetime to make sure that when my end does come, I will have made more conscious choices along the way – so there won't be much to regret.

In the years to come, it won't be easy: I will have to put myself on the line, time and time again, so I can be true to myself. I will have to risk my job and maybe my career. I will have to risk losing relationships and organizations – if my coworkers and bosses won't give me the freedom to be myself at work.

But here is the ultimate challenge: How to create an organization in which all members can express their true nature in everything they do – *where developing self-aware consciousness is recognized as being an essential journey for becoming a whole person and contributing to a worthwhile cause.* Just imagine what such a new organization of people could do for themselves and for others around the world!

A Challenge to the Reader

A person's struggle for self-aware consciousness is universal – if it hasn't been shattered by dysfunctional families, communities, organizations, and nations. Learning to see, think, and behave in increasingly adaptive ways is the essential path to survival, success, and evolution. The introductory story has illuminated a moral: The sooner people get in touch with their inner selves and their genuine desires, the more time they will have left to make better choices and live fuller lives. And then, when their deathbed experience is imminent, it will be a time for inner peace – not utter denial or helpless remorse over what might have been.

Chapters 1 and 2 provide a coherent framework for understanding and creating a quantum organization – an organization that is designed to nurture the true essence of who we are and what we can meaningfully provide for others. This conceptual material is not so much *difficult* as it is *foreign* to those who have been infused with the traditional ways of seeing, thinking, and behaving. In these two chapters, I present to you (1) a new paradigm and (2) how it can create a new type of organization. **If you give me your undivided attention for two chapters – and read this material with an open mind and an open heart – you will discover a new world of work without having to go through the ultimate encounter yourself.** In the process, you will deeply understand the crucial differences between viewing inert objects through the *Cartesian-Newtonian Paradigm* and viewing mindful people through the *Quantum-Relativistic Paradigm*. Additionally, you will deeply understand the essential distinctions between an unconscious *Newtonian organization* and a self-aware *quantum organization* – as portrayed throughout our story.

After you have read Chapters 1 and 2, you can learn the details for transforming a Newtonian organization into a quantum organization by reading Chapters 3, 4, and 5. Chapter 6 then returns to the vital theme of self-aware consciousness via ego energy, spiritual enlightenment, and the further evolution of people and their organizations.

CHAPTER 1

TWO DUELING PARADIGMS

The Essential Categories for Seeing, Thinking, and Behaving

> If we want to transform the structure and leadership of our organizations, we have to address change at the fundamental paradigmatic level. We have to change the thinking behind our thinking. Leaders who want to initiate real change processes must become aware that they have been acting out of a paradigm. They must see the origin and nature of this existing paradigm and its effect on their management. And they must get to a point where they can *feel* the reality of an alternative paradigm – or the creative excitement of standing at the edge between paradigms.
>
> *— Danah Zohar (1997, page 25)*

A *paradigm* is a coherent, internally consistent approach for making sense of the universe and coping with life: essentially, how one sees, thinks, and behaves. Similar terms that are often used interchangeably with paradigm include *archetype, gestalt, worldview, template, schema, mind-set, mental model,* and *conceptual/theoretical framework.* In its basic form, a paradigm is a fairly rigid set of categories that are organically infused within a human mind/brain: If a person does not have a category for seeing something, for all practical purposes it does not exist. Paradigms are deeply entrenched in unstated, untested, and unquestioned assumptions about the fundamental makeup of reality: light, space, time, energy, mass – and, particularly, the nature of life and human beings (Kuhn, 1962).

Organizational transformation represents a fundamental shift from one paradigm to another, since fundamental change, by definition, necessarily influences how all members of an organization see, think, and behave –

otherwise, a change initiative would be rather superficial and short lived, but not transformational or paradigmatic (Kilmann and Covin, 1988).

For most organizational transformations, fundamental change is not simply an exchange of one paradigm for another. It is more appropriately described as a shift from an old (inflexible, dysfunctional) worldview to a new (more adaptive, functional) worldview. Being adaptive and functional is usually judged relative to meeting the challenges that are posed by the organization's environment: What comprehensive approach is needed by an organization and its members to survive – and thrive – as a collective enterprise over an extended duration of time? Alternatively, defective and dysfunctional approaches block the organization from achieving both its individual and its collective goals.

For organizations today, most talk of transformation recognizes that the old ways are no longer working (old paradigm) and an altogether new approach (new paradigm) is required in order to succeed in an energetic, fast-paced, competitive, interconnected, global economy. While a variety of phrases have been used to underscore this old versus new approach, a powerful consensus is developing as to the essence of the transformation that is now required of more and more organizations. I find it most useful to refer to the outdated worldview as the *Cartesian-Newtonian Paradigm* and to the new worldview as the *Quantum-Relativistic Paradigm*.

As noted in the preface, there has been increasing attention devoted to the new science behind the new paradigm. But these discussions have not provided enough depth for illuminating (1) self-aware consciousness as the crucial ingredient for understanding and using the new paradigm and (2) a distinctive methodology for effectively helping people transform themselves and their enterprises into consciousness-generating quantum organizations. In this ambitious chapter, my purpose is to extract the most relevant aspects of the two paradigms in order to understand – in depth – their fundamental distinctions. Because transformation is usually moving away from the old paradigm and purposely shifting toward the new one, relatively more discussion will be provided for the Quantum-Relativistic Paradigm than for the Cartesian-Newtonian Paradigm. ***Basically, gaining a much deeper understanding of seven diametrically opposed categories that represent the two dueling paradigms will prepare organizational members to see, think, and behave in an adaptive manner and, thereby, transform themselves as well as their systems and processes***. Indeed, it is the intentional shift from the old paradigm to the new that characterizes self-aware consciousness and organizational transformation.

The Old Paradigm

The traditional Western view of the universe and life is usually traced to the vigorous ancient Greek civilization circa 400 BC and thereafter. Euclid and Aristotle are two significant figures who shaped the way we see and think about the universe. Euclid defined space in absolute terms, with an absolute point of origin. He built his elaborate geometry of space onto a perfectly flat surface, where the shortest distance between two points was a straight line – and two parallel lines could never touch. Aristotle, among his many other contributions, arranged linear time into past, present, and future – setting the stage for logical thinking and deterministic science. As a result, absolute space and absolute time became the basis for a rational approach to philosophy and science, actualized by an overriding belief in the existence of a linear, logical, and completely understandable universe (Euclid, 1956; Aristotle, 1958).

Leonard Shlain (1991, page 33), a surgeon and scholar, offers a cogent portrait of the impact of Greek culture on the Western mind:

> Euclidean space and Aristotelian time have formed the
> basis of a paradigm that has been remarkably enduring.
> This worldview has survived virtually unchanged since it
> was first proposed nearly twenty–five hundred years ago.
> Almost without exception everyone in Western society
> uses this ancient system. Euclid's *Elements* [of Geometry]
> is probably the second most widely read book in the
> history of the world. It is nearly impossible to grow up
> without being inculcated with Euclid's ideas at a very
> early age. Likewise, a tacit knowledge of Aristotle's logic
> is a prerequisite for every professional, technological,
> and literate position in sophisticated society.

Between 200 BC and 100 BC, the conquering Romans absorbed much of the Greek culture rather than revolutionizing philosophy (and science) on their own. Following the fall of the Roman Empire, circa AD 400, a long period of sleep, known as the Dark (or Middle) Ages, spread over Europe. The Catholic Church fully controlled the cultural landscape for centuries – concentrating solely on the disjointed spiritual perspective of space (Earth, heaven, hell) and time (surrounding the birth of Christ, during the life of Christ, achieving eternal life), while espousing the Son of God as the focal point of all worldly matters. During this process, the Church inadvertently stalled the progress of geometry, logic, and science (St. Augustine, 1958).

The period beginning around 1400, which has come to be known as the Renaissance, created revolutionary changes in the Western paradigm. Copernicus, Kepler, and Galileo acknowledged the sun (rather than Earth) as the orbital center of the solar system and also sensed that the physical expanse of the universe was much larger – and more complex – than had ever been thought previously (Motz and Weaver, 1989).

Two Dominating Patriarchs

Then, during the 1600s, came the renowned work of René Descartes and Sir Isaac Newton, who, apparently more than any others, articulated and formalized the old paradigm that was to dominate Western civilization for the next several hundred years (Descartes, 1969; Newton, 1934; 1960).

One of the most lingering principles that Descartes articulated was his view of the universe as a mechanical apparatus – as a large clocklike mechanism. This mechanistic perspective was further encouraged by his rigid split of the conscious mind inside the human body from the nature of the physical universe outside the body, which was termed *dualism*. The Church would continue to focus on the spiritual side, while philosophers and scientists could now be somewhat free from religious domination in order to examine the physical world. Dualism was a creative solution for this duration of time, when the boundaries between religion and science had to be carefully drawn and publicly respected. However, the rigid and artificial schism between the mind inside (consciousness) and the physical world outside (matter), even if useful in the short term, eventually led to a fragmented view of consciousness and matter.

In 1687, Isaac Newton additionally reinforced this dualistic approach when he published his framework of mathematical principles and laws to explain the motion of all physical objects in the universe – assuming that an objective reality existed completely independent of the human mind. Newton's theories, laws, and mathematics had no place for people or life. Much like Descartes, Newton portrayed a mechanical, clocklike universe – consisting of lifeless, inert physical objects – that conformed to all his laws of motion.

The physical objects that were in Newton's world – all matter from elementary atoms to solar systems – were also looked upon in a dualistic manner. All objects were seen as entirely independent of each other and thus could never penetrate one another: There was a hard and inflexible boundary that solidly delineated the mass, density, and identity of every object – in any space for any duration of time. The motion of all spheres (from atoms to solar systems) was similar to orbiting or colliding billiard balls in a three-dimensional playing field. Action and reaction were thus the only rules of interaction: Billiard balls couldn't combine or transform into anything else. Within Newton's system of motion, there weren't any "categories" for seeing interdependence, integration, or unification among separate physical objects. The whole of the universe was exactly the sum of its independently moving, orbiting, and colliding spheres.

Margaret Wheatley (1992, page 27) underscores how the Newtonian focus on separate pieces and parts has found its way into the structure of today's organizations – and most other realms of human endeavor:

> It is very interesting to note just how Newtonian most organizations are. The machine imagery of the spheres was captured by organizations in an emphasis on structure and parts. Responsibilities have been organized into functions. People have been organized into roles. Page after page of organizational charts depict the workings of the machine: the number of pieces, what fits where, who the big pieces are.… This reduction into parts and the proliferation of separations has characterized not just organizations, but everything in the world during the past three hundred years. Knowledge was broken into disciplines and subjects, engineering became a prized science, and people were fragmented – counseled to use different "parts" of themselves in different settings.

Seven Essential Categories in the Old Paradigm

The Cartesian–Newtonian Paradigm can be summarized by the following seven categories, which have strongly influenced (and continue to guide) how the Western world sees, thinks, and behaves:

1   **THE DUALISTIC SEPARATION OF CONSCIOUSNESS/MATTER** The physical world exists completely separate from and is unaffected by human beings (and all other varieties of life). The human mind and consciousness, therefore, have no effect whatsoever on the nature of physical reality. The universe – and the laws that explain it – would exist the same way whether there were human beings or not.

2 **THE UNIVERSE AS THE MOTION OF INERT MOLAR OBJECTS**
Matter is the building block of the universe. First, atoms consolidate into molecules, which compress into inert molar objects, which then are governed by Newton's laws of motion.

3 **THE SPACE BETWEEN MOLAR OBJECTS AS FLAT AND EMPTY**
Between all physical objects, space is always flat and empty. While planets have atmospheres, objects in motion still follow Newton's laws of motion for any mass at any speed – taking into account the effects of not being in a perfect vacuum: heat, humidity, barometric pressure, atmospheric pressure, wind, and so on. But in outer space, a vacuum of nothingness exists, within which the physical laws of motion apply perfectly to all objects.

4 **THE UNIQUE EXISTENCE OF ONLY ONE ABSOLUTE UNIVERSE**
There is only one universe, composed of three dimensions of space (length, width, and depth) and one dimension of time (from past to present into future). Space and time are absolute – the same for all observers and participants under all conditions. Therefore, the laws of physics are also absolute and eternal.

5 **THE DETERMINISTIC CERTAINTY OF INERT MOLAR OBJECTS**
Objects are inert and only external forces can move them – there is no self-motion. Thus objects in the universe are much like billiard balls: Position and momentum can be determined simultaneously and precisely, including the trajectory of any object, given the force and direction of some initial push and the invisible force of gravity. This universal force of gravity imposes an attraction between molar objects, based on their respective masses and the distance between them. But the creation and composition of this invisible force in the universe are entirely unknown.

6 **THE FUNDAMENTAL SEPARATION OF INERT MOLAR OBJECTS**
Inert objects are completely separate and distinct from one another. There is no force or bond between such objects separated in empty space – except for the invisible pull of gravity – even if these objects had prior contact or interaction.

7 **THE EVENTUAL DEATH OF THE ONE ABSOLUTE UNIVERSE** Since the inaugural push on our universe from the "big bang" or God, no other forces (except for gravity) have been acting on solar systems. Since no other pushes by God or anything else can be anticipated, all the galaxies, solar systems, stars, and planets will eventually be distributed randomly across the universe (entropy); simultaneously, the temperature of the universe will fall to absolute zero as the sun and stars burn out (thermal equilibrium). These dire predictions are based on Newton's laws of motion and the laws of *thermodynamics*.

The old paradigm, therefore, completely separates people from an outside, objective – existing on its own – material universe. All inert objects obey Newton's mathematical laws of motion. Between objects, there is nothing but the invisible force of gravity, which pulls objects together; space itself is flat, cold, and empty. Due to thermodynamics, the cosmic machine will eventually run out of heat, planetary orbits will atrophy, and the universe will become a random distribution of inert objects – void of heat, life, and movement. The universe, therefore, is doomed.

THE NEW PARADIGM

By 1800, the Cartesian–Newtonian approach to physical reality seemed to explain how virtually everything in the universe – which at that time did not include fundamental elements (such as atoms) or very large systems (such as galaxies) – moved. Tangible success with "medium–sized" objects is what endowed Newtonian science and its integral worldview with such an enduring influence on Western seeing, thinking, and behaving.

By the mid–1800s, however, research scientists equipped with better instruments and methodology used Newton's laws to examine the nature of light, heat, and the orbits of obscure planets more meticulously. It was these latter attempts to *generalize* Newton's laws of motion to the confusing qualities of light and heat that resulted in several puzzling gaps between predicted theories and experimental findings. These flaws in Newtonian-based theories formed troublesome "clouds" over the old paradigm.

By 1900, two distinctive clouds were most disturbing: (1) Why don't all wavelengths of light radiate at all levels of heat, which became known as the *ultraviolet catastrophe*; (2) Is light a wave or a particle – since it seems to behave in both ways? Confronting these two loopholes in Newtonian-derived theories led to the inception of quantum mechanics and relativity theory, both of which contradicted several fundamental aspects of the old paradigm. These theories, which were first made public in the early 1900s, are still referred to as the *new science*.

Discovering the Quantum Nature of Light

In 1900, Max Planck solved the first mystery of light. He recognized that the distribution of energy (radiated by a heat source) takes place not in a continuous manner, as thought previously, but in discrete units known as *quanta*. Only when a certain quantity of heat energy is generated will the next wavelength of light be radiated. Thus light is created in whole units, which suggests that action by light takes place in whole units as well. The previously continuous, smooth, linear functions that were used to explain the movement of matter and energy in the universe came to be regarded as quantum jumps and quanta of action (Planck, 1936).

Light has typically amazed and confused scientists, especially since light is accorded "first cause" in the creation of the universe and life itself. As proclaimed by God and published in Genesis: "Let there be light: and there was light." Recall that light, or *radiant energy*, covers the full range of James Maxwell's electromagnetic spectrum – from radio waves (very long waves) to gamma rays (very short waves). For humans, visible light resides within a rather small segment in the middle of the complete spectrum of radiant energy – from the color of red (which has the longest wavelength of visible light) to violet (which has the shortest wavelength).

Arthur Young (1976, pages xxvii and 10), a physicist and evolutionist, cogently summarizes why light (comprising the whole spectrum, not just what is visible to human beings) is entirely different from all other forms of matter and energy – and therefore should be accorded a supernatural essence in the creation of the universe:

> Objects can be at rest or move at a variety of speeds. Light, on the other hand, has but one speed (in any given medium) and cannot be at rest. Even space is a meaningless concept for light, since the passage of light through space is accomplished without any loss of energy whatsoever.... Light, itself without mass, can create photons and electrons which have mass. Light has no charge, yet the particles it creates do. Since light is without mass, it is nonphysical, of a different nature than physical particles. In fact, for the photon, a pulse of light, *time does not exist*: clocks stop at the speed of light. Thus mass and hence energy, as well as time, are born from the photon, from light, which is therefore the first kingdom, the first stage of the process that engenders the universe.

Discovering the Absolute Speed of Light

Before we address the core of Albert Einstein's revolutionary challenges to Newtonian mechanics and hence to the Cartesian–Newtonian Paradigm, it is first necessary to understand what is meant by a *law of nature*. Basically, if different observers, who are traveling at different velocities, in different places, and at different times from one another, determine different "laws" to explain the motion of objects, then no *general law* of nature can actually exist. By definition, a *law must generalize across all observers with different frames of reference*. Otherwise, one observer's particular experience with nature is a *unique* experience that offers no beneficial information whatsoever about what another observer might encounter. Only if different observers verify the same experience of nature – *regardless of their different motions, coordinates, or frames of reference* – can a law of nature, by this definition, be said to exist (Motz and Weaver, 1989). Now we return to our story.

Einstein was most puzzled by light, just like all the other scientists and philosophers who came before him. He took special notice, however, that James Maxwell's equations to unify electricity and magnetism within the electromagnetic theory included the speed of light (186,000 miles per second in a vacuum), since electromagnetic waves also travel at the speed of visible light. Einstein realized that if Maxwell's mathematical equations represented a general law of nature, and all previous experiments had in fact validated Maxwell's laws, *the motion of observers must be independent of the speed of light*. Otherwise, observers could make use of Maxwell's equations to identify their own particular movement – which would undermine the generalizability and hence the credibility of these mathematical equations as fundamental laws of nature. Using this compelling argument, Einstein appropriately concluded that light speed must be an absolute constant in the universe, no matter what an observer's speed happens to be.

Remarkably, by using the basic definition of what establishes a law of nature, Einstein's spectacular insight spearheaded a fundamental shift from Newtonian mechanics to *relativistic mechanics*. To appreciate the radical shift in science that resulted from this single insight, let's now contrast the Newtonian with the Einsteinian view of light speed.

Newton assumed that the speed of light, just like the speed of any object, was relative to the speed of an observer. Only if an observer were at absolute rest, with no motion at all, would the speed of light be 186,000 miles per second. If an observer were traveling at an imaginary speed of 100,000 miles per second, the speed of light moving in the same direction would measure only 86,000 miles per second relative to the speed of the observer (derived by subtracting the difference in velocities when the two entities are moving in the same straight line).

In sharp contrast, recall that Einstein concluded that light speed is absolute – regardless of the speed of the observer. Using this perspective, an observer journeying at 100,000 miles per second would measure light speed at 186,000 miles per second! How can this be? The answer is rather simple, but revolutionary: For Einstein's observer to measure light speed as 186,000 miles per second while he himself is speeding along at 100,000 miles per second in the identical direction, *his actual time would have to slow noticeably and his space (distance of travel) would have to shrink dramatically*. In the extreme case, as an imaginary observer approaches light speed, time stops completely and space compresses into a very thin line – so that absolute light speed remains at an everlasting 186,000 miles per second, no matter what. Thus at light speed, both time and space are frozen and compressed into one moment and one dimension – like a single length of motionless string of infinitesimal width. As a consequence of conducting a variety of such *thought experiments*, Einstein initiated a revolutionary – paradigmatic – shift in the nature of physical reality – including space, time, energy, mass, and light (Clark, 1971; Pais, 1982).

Recognizing absolute light speed as the speed limit of the universe necessitated that all Newton's laws of motion now had to incorporate this numerical value, indicated as a lowercase *c*, in all mathematical equations describing nature. These modifications to Newton's famous equations are especially relevant when attempting to predict the dynamics of particles that approach the speed of light – and to explain the nature of light in the cosmos. Furthermore, since the extension of space and the passage of time are determined by the speed of the observer, space and time are no longer absolute (which Newton had surmised), but are *relative* to the speed of the observer. Moreover, the manner in which space and time are interrelated with light speed moved Einstein to combine space and time into a fourth dimension of the universe, which Einstein's former mathematics professor Herman Minkowski later termed the *spacetime continuum* (Lorentz, Einstein, Minkowski, and Weyle, 1952).

Space and time were not the only previously independent qualities of reality that were interrelated by Einstein into a higher dimension. Mass and energy, which were similarly considered by Newton to be completely separate and distinct, were also combined by Einstein through his famous equation $E = mc^2$ (where E is energy, m is mass, and c is the speed of light). Consequently, the characteristics of mass and energy are interchangeable through absolute light speed.

Einstein's insights and reformulations of the laws of mechanics into relativistic mechanics were published in 1905 as his *special theory of relativity*. The term *relativity*, in this scientific context, means that the experience of spacetime (the shape of objects and the passage of time) is relative to the speed of the observer – whereas Newton had described space and time as absolute and thus independent of the observer. The term *special* is added since this theory of relativity is strictly limited: its laws apply only across observers who are moving at constant velocities in a straight line, referred to as *inertial observers*. In his special theory, therefore, Einstein's revisions to Newton's laws apply only to such inertial observers. Now recall that a true law of nature must be general across all observers, regardless of their type of motion – not just for a special class of moving observers. To correct this limitation, Einstein sought to extend his special theory into *a general theory of relativity* by establishing the laws of physical reality so they not only are relative to uniformly moving observers but also are relative to *accelerating observers* (Einstein, 1961; 1979; 1983; 1988; Mook and Vargish, 1987).

The Realization of a Relativistic Universe

Before we can appreciate another clear–cut but revolutionary insight that led Einstein to generalize his theory of nature across all types of moving observers, it is important to highlight another key distinction between the special and the general theories of relativity. Even with the addition of a four–dimensional spacetime continuum, Einstein's special theory included the long–standing convention of assuming space to be flat, homogeneous, and empty (just as Newton's laws had) and automatically used Euclidean geometry in the theory's mathematical expressions.

For his general theory, however, Einstein entertained new thought experiments about the spacetime continuum, which evidenced that space was not always flat and empty but could also be curved and compressed. Basically, Einstein mathematically demonstrated that spacetime becomes curved and compressed by the presence of an object. He was thus able to see that the larger and denser an object, the more curved and compressed the spacetime surrounding the object; further, the greater the speed of an object, the more the nearby spacetime becomes curved and compressed. Thus a high–velocity, highly dense object *severely distorts the surrounding space and dramatically slows the passage of time*. However, a slow, small object would enjoy a relatively flat spacetime in its immediate vicinity. Not surprisingly, Euclidean geometry is still appropriate for Einstein's general theory when spacetime remains flat. However, a non–Euclidean – curved – geometry is needed (*Riemannian* geometry) for accurately describing spacetime when a mass is traveling at or near light speed (Wheeler, 1990).

Most important, it is the curved and compressed spacetime around a large, moving mass, such as Earth, that then presses neighboring objects (including people) against its surface – as the spacetime continuum tries to revert back to an uncompressed, tensionless, flat state. This pressure, or force of gravity as Newton called it, is invisible, because we human beings cannot see four-dimensional spacetime, even if mathematics can describe it in great detail. It would seem that our minds/brains evolved so that we could survive on our planet; apparently, having the mental categories for experiencing three dimensions of conventional space (length, width, and depth) and one dimension of linear time (from past to present into future) was sufficient for us to endure our environmental challenges – at least up to this point in our human evolution.

Einstein's next great insight led to a revision of Newton's theory of gravity. Einstein imagined that the force keeping a person firmly planted on Earth's surface – as if it were *pulling* him down to the planet's center at 32.2 feet per second per second – would feel identical if that same person, instead, were traveling in a ship in outer space (away from a sizable mass) and the *acceleration* of the spaceship was the same 32.2 feet per second per second. Indeed, if the spaceship were either (1) sitting still on the surface of Earth or (2) traveling at this rate of acceleration in outer space – and if a person couldn't tell if he were situated on Earth or traveling in space – these two experiences would be exactly equivalent. Or said differently: In our conventional three-dimensional space, the Newtonian force of gravity (which was previously understood as *pulling* observers toward the center of Earth) is entirely an illusion created by three-dimensional beings who cannot see a four-dimensional universe. But in the abstract mathematics of four-dimensional spacetime, the hypothetical *pull* of gravity is actually the *push* of acceleration – due to the compression of spacetime geometry around Earth.

The *equivalence* of acceleration and gravity is precisely what enabled Einstein, in 1915, to reformulate and strengthen his special theory into his general theory of relativity. Recall: As long as neither a uniform-moving observer *nor an accelerating observer* can discover the prime causes of his own movement while applying a proposed theory in a particular circumstance, the proposed law does indeed generalize across different movements and coordinates of observers and, therefore, their different frames of reference. The *proposed* law thus becomes a *general* law of nature. It should be evident that all it really takes to prevent someone from discovering the nature of his own movement is to keep him in suspense with at least *two alternative explanations*. An observer being unable to tell whether a force is caused by (1) gravity on Earth or (2) acceleration in space – is sufficient to establish a general law of nature.

In sum, through Einstein's revolutionary insights about light, space, time, mass, and energy, he was able to substantiate (1) the absolute speed of light and thus the relative nature of space and time; (2) the coupling of space and time within the four-dimensional spacetime continuum; (3) the interchange between mass and energy via the absolute speed of light; (4) the curved and compressed geometry of spacetime that is determined by the mass and speed of an object or an observer; and (5) the equivalence of gravity on Earth and acceleration in space for generalizing the theories of relativity. Such was the reflective power of Einstein's thought experiments concerning what is absolute, what is relative, and what is a general law of nature (Einstein, 1988; Mook and Vargish, 1987).

Appreciating the important criteria of scientific value and practical significance, it should be noted that many of Einstein's counterintuitive predictions about physical reality have been subsequently proved correct (sometimes, decades later) using sophisticated research technologies and new methodologies. Stephen Hawking (1996, pages 31–34), a cosmological physicist, cogently summarizes just a sample of Einstein's many successful predictions:

> The mass of the sun curves spacetime in such a way that although the earth follows a straight path in four-dimensional spacetime, it appears to us to move along a circular orbit in three-dimensional space. In fact, the orbits of the planets predicted by general relativity are almost exactly the same as those predicted by the Newtonian theory of gravity. However, in the case of Mercury, which, being the nearest planet to the sun, feels the strongest gravitational effects, and has a rather elongated orbit, general relativity predicts that the long axis of the ellipse should rotate about the sun at a rate of about one degree in ten thousand years. Small though this effect is, it had been noticed before 1915 and served as one of the first confirmations of Einstein's theory. In recent years the even smaller deviations of the orbits of the other planets from the Newtonian predictions have been measured by radar and found to agree with the predictions of general relativity....

Another prediction of general relativity is that time should appear to run slower near a massive body like the earth.... This prediction was tested in 1962 using a pair of very accurate clocks mounted at the top and bottom of a water tower. The clock at the bottom, which was nearer the earth, was found to run slower, in exact agreement with general relativity. The difference in the speed of clocks at different heights above the earth is now of considerable practical importance, with the advent of very accurate navigation systems based on signals from satellites. If one ignored the predictions of general relativity, the position that one calculated would be wrong by several miles!

Superstrings as the Substance of Spacetime

There is still disagreement among physicists, however, regarding whether the pressure of compressed spacetime is composed of something physical and detectable. Even though Einstein's equations can successfully predict many effects of spacetime compression to a high degree of precision, what exactly is the substance of this invisible force?

One theory, which is gaining scientific interest, considers spacetime as being composed of *dark matter* that cannot be seen or measured as yet, which is why space *itself* (versus the materialization of matter/energy that resides within space) still appears to be vacuous (Genz, 1999). At the most fundamental structure of nature, however, this dark matter of spacetime might consist of infinitesimal stringlike particles that can spin, rotate, and vibrate. These enterprising strings could be as tiny as 10^{-33} centimeter for any known dimension but can form a multitude of open strands as well as closed loops – just as a flexible rubber band, either as an open strand or a closed loop, can become a number of different shapes (Greene, 1999; Gribbin, 1998; Peat, 1988). It should be noted that the infinitesimal size of these elementary strings is several orders of magnitude smaller than any apparatus or instrument can now detect – or will be able to detect in the foreseeable future. To put these very tiny strings into proper perspective, consider that the size of a person relative to an atom is about the size of an atom compared to a string.

String theory, or *superstring theory*, as it is now called, creates a dynamic portrayal of spacetime: spinning, rotating, and vibrating multidimensional strings. This spirited depiction of spacetime is thus radically different from the traditional view of empty space containing passive, zero–dimensional points. The creation and dynamics of the matter/energy in the universe, for example, might be fully explained by the breaking apart and joining together of elementary strings into distinctive configurations – including their various spins, twists, rotations, and vibrations (Peat, 1988).

Davies and Brown (1988, page 69) capture the immense excitement and challenge of superstring theory for explaining not only the substance of spacetime itself but all the various particles and forces that exist within the spacetime continuum:

> There is no doubt that string theory is extraordinarily compelling. Theorists speak eloquently of the incredible beauty and richness of the theory. But clearly another incentive for studying the subject derives from the fact that if superstring theory does eventually provide a quantitative explanation for all the particles and forces of nature, it will represent one of the greatest scientific triumphs in the history of mankind. Indeed, one might claim that it would be the culmination of reductionist science, because we would at last have identified the smallest entities from which the world is built and elucidated the fundamental principles on which the universe runs.

To get a sense of how string theory can provide a radically different depiction of spacetime itself, imagine for a moment how sound at various frequencies is carried through the atmosphere via invisible – vibrating – waves. Imagine what would occur if a large object were positioned in the immediate path of these vibrating sound waves. The shape and direction of the original waves would be modified due to the object's material and surface qualities via deflection or absorption. Or envision the traditional scientific demonstration that shows how iron filings scattered on a piece of paper quickly become organized into a wave pattern in the presence of an invisible electromagnetic field. However, introducing a noticeable mass within such a field (particularly if it has magnetic properties) would also change the geometry of the initial wave pattern. Another way to envision the dynamic nature of string theory is to remember what happens when a large, round object is dropped into a still pool of water: We see curved, rippling waves spreading across the surface of the water – strongest at the initial point of impact and then dissipating in space and time.

Now try to imagine the same type of effects on spacetime itself, due to the presence of a massive spherical object such as a planet: it displaces, compresses, and reshapes the geometry of vibrating strings surrounding its surface – resulting in a curved, non–Euclidean geometry of spacetime. Actually, the spherical mass in spacetime can be expected to generate a *resonating pressure* in the vicinity of its surface by compressing the vibrating strings that surround it. And most significant to our purposes here, *perhaps this resonating pressure surrounding the mass can only be eliminated when the strings expand back into their former, larger, volume* – thereby returning to a Euclidean geometry of flat spacetime. As long as the spherical mass remains in this spacetime region, the compacted strings will continue to press against its surface – thus requiring a non–Euclidean, *Riemannian* geometry to capture the movement of mass, energy, and light through curved spacetime.

On the surface of our planet Earth, the resonating pressure from the compressed strings of spacetime seems to be 32.2 feet per second squared. On a ship in space that is accelerating at this same rate, the surrounding spacetime strings would be compressed by an equivalent amount via the mass and speed of the spaceship. But to an observer, equivalent amounts of compressed strings and the resonating pressures that are generated by these vibrating strings (whether on Earth or in outer space) should appear exactly the same: thus gravity equals acceleration and superstring theory continues to evolve (Greene, 1999).

Rejecting the Separation of Mind and Matter

With the acceptance of Einstein's principles of relativity, the *observer*, whose conscious mind was previously identified as completely separate from the material universe, became an integral member of the physical world. Not too long after this historic blurring of the mind/matter distinction, it was recognized that the conscious mind of an observer actually plays an even more fundamental role in the cosmos than merely ensuring that different frames of reference do not result in different laws of nature. Maybe even more challenging to the old paradigm than Einstein's theories of relativity was the discovery that *an observer significantly affects what physical nature reveals.* Through further study of the wave and particle aspects of light, the long–standing Cartesian schism between mind and matter was not just blurred but rejected: The relatively passive observer in Einstein's universe became the absolutely *active participant* in the quantum universe (Schrödinger, 1969; Wolf, 1981; Herbert, 1987; Zuckav, 1979).

Peat (1987, page 4) recalls the comments of a noted physicist, John Wheeler, who colorfully described the significant transition that occurred when the passive observer became an active participant:

We had this old idea, that there was a universe out there, and here is man, the observer, safely protected from the universe by a six-inch slab of plate glass. Now we learn from the quantum world that even to observe so minuscule an object as an electron we have to shatter that plate glass; we have to reach in there.... So the old word *observer* simply has to be crossed off the books, and we must put in the new word *participator*. In this way we've come to realize that the universe is a participatory universe.

Incredible as it may seem, if a person – an active participant – sets up an experiment to measure the *wave* properties of light, a beam of light will cooperate and accurately reveal its wave properties. Alternatively, if a person sets up another experiment to measure the *particle* aspects of light, a beam of light will once again cooperate – this time representing itself as particles. Furthermore, if a light beam is not observed by anyone, it exists only in a wavelike form. Only when a light beam is observed specifically for its particle nature does its wave function collapse, so to speak, into a particle form, termed *photons*. Between these particle observations, a light beam apparently exists only as a wave of *potentia* (potential particles and possible locations). What accounts for these findings?

The identical quantum phenomenon (and perplexing question) also takes place for matter (and not only for light, which has no mass) during experiments with electrons (which do have mass). Specifically, an electron in orbit around an atom exists as a wave when there is no observation or between observations, but materializes into a distinctive electron particle in a particular location when it is observed by an active participant in the universe. Following the observation, if the electron is still intact its wave function is once again restored – instantly.

Now consider that the wave form, relative to the size of an electron particle, is spread out over immense distances. Yet at the exact moment of observation, this relatively huge wave collapses instantly into a very small particle. Because of the relative size of the wave compared to the particle, the collapse of the former into the latter must be occurring at a speed that is greater than light speed. How can this be? Nothing, especially matter, is supposed to be able to transcend this universal speed limit, according to Einstein's theories of relativity. What is going on here? Is there something that does not obey Newton's laws of motion and Einstein's speed limit of the spacetime continuum? Conceivably, there is an additional dimension to the universe beyond the three dimensions of traditional space, the one dimension of continuous time, the fourth-dimensional curved spacetime, or even the higher dimensions of *curled-up* spacetime – which, all together, could total eleven dimensions of physical space and time (Greene, 1999).

Nick Herbert (1993, pages 155–157), a physicist scholar, recounts how one of the outstanding mathematicians of the twentieth century, John von Neumann, resolved the "quantum measurement paradox" that couldn't be explained by anything in the physical world:

> In his magisterial tome *The Mathematical Foundations of Quantum Physics*, regarded by many scientists as "the bible of quantum theory," von Neumann exposed and boldly attacked the formidable quantum measurement problem, which most physicists had been too complacent or intimidated to confront.… To resolve the measurement problem in von Neumann's all-quantum world, something new must be added to "collapse the wave function," something that is capable of turning fuzzy quantum possibilities into definite actualities. But since von Neumann is forced to describe the entire physical world as possibilities, the process that turns some of these maybes into actual facts cannot be a physical process. To collapse the wave function, some new (actual not possible) process must enter the world from outside physics. Searching his mind for an appropriate actually existing nonphysical entity that could collapse the wave function, von Neumann reluctantly concluded that the only known entity fit for this task was consciousness. In von Neumann's interpretation, the world remains everywhere in a state of pure possibility except where some conscious mind decides to promote a portion of the world from its usual state of indefiniteness into a condition of actual existence.

Bringing Consciousness into the Cosmos

It is important to recognize that the old paradigm has always considered *matter* as the building block of the universe out there (outside the human mind). But the quantum worldview explicitly incorporates the additional dimension of *consciousness*: the completion of a process of measurement by a self-aware human being as the basis for whatever specific particles and objects are experienced in the material world. Although Newton had no place in his laws of motion for the human being, let alone life itself, the quantum view explicitly considers that *the world would not be there in material form were it not for a conscious mind to observe it* (Goswami, 1993; Herbert, 1987; Penrose, 1989; Zohar, 1990).

This quantum interpretation is strikingly contrary to the established Cartesian–Newtonian Paradigm to which we, in the Western world, have grown accustomed, if not indoctrinated. Even though quantum mechanics has been actively debated in the scientific community for more than half a century, most people are heavily steeped in the mind-set that matter is first, matter is all, and matter is independent of human consciousness. It is extremely difficult for most people to consider that if we humans did not exist to disseminate consciousness into the universe, the "actual" physical world "out there" would only be waves of potentia for particle and object locations – not separate material substances that exist exclusively on their own (Heisenberg, 1958; Schrödinger, 1969).

If this consciousness–reveals–matter interpretation were not radical enough, quantum mechanics goes even further beyond the materialistic assumptions of the Cartesian–Newtonian Paradigm. When an electron (a mass) is first observed as a particle in orbit around an atom, it is possible that the next observation will demonstrate that the electron has somehow jumped to another orbit surrounding the same atom – *but has not traveled through space to get there.* Instead, it has simply reappeared – instantly – in another orbit. How is this possible? As before: Is there another dimension in the universe through which the electron proceeds that is beyond space, time, and the many spacetime dimensions?

Even more revolutionary, consider the case in which two electrons are *correlated* with one another – when their respective spins are in accord, hence "bonded" following their interaction. These correlated electrons are then separated in space by a monumental distance (relative to the size of an electron particle). But at the particular moment that the spin of one of these electrons is changed and observed, *the other electron's spin, observed at the same moment, has already changed its spin to maintain its correlated relationship with its partner.* Because of the tremendous distance in space between these two electrons, some information or indication between them must have been transmitted (or somehow felt) – at a speed that would be far greater than light speed. This phenomenon is referred to as *action at a distance* or *nonlocal effects*, because it couldn't take place within the *local* spacetime continuum. As Einstein determined, nothing can travel through spacetime faster than the speed of light.

One reasonable answer to these paradigm-breaking experiments is that two electrons, once correlated, are forever bonded in a transcendent dimension of consciousness that does not exist, as such, within Newton's three dimensions of space and one dimension of time, or even Einstein's spacetime continuum. Furthermore, when an electron instantly appears in another orbit around the same atom, it has also in some form "traveled" through this higher dimension of consciousness. This does not reinforce either Newton's laws or Einstein's theories. Even the instant collapse of a sprawling wave packet into an infinitesimal electron particle at the instant of conscious observation appears to occur at a speed that is much beyond the theoretical limits of spacetime. These experiments confirm "action at a distance" – *nonlocality* – in the quantum world (Bohr, 1958).

These perplexing findings and mystical–seeming interpretations are exactly what makes quantum physics so hard to accept – especially when one has been conditioned to recognize only objective and physical truths, presumably not affected by subjective and intangible minds. Apparently, these incredulous explanations are what keeps the Newtonian worldview so deeply entrenched in our modern society.

Most people are truly uncomfortable with (if not frightened by) the possibility that a higher dimension of consciousness creates their physical world. It is also hard to entertain, let alone accept, that this transcendent dimension enables matter to disappear and reappear in other locations – without journeying through any physical space. And it may be even more difficult to accept that once two pieces of matter have interacted in some manner (just like two correlated electrons), they will forever be connected within a transcendent dimension of consciousness – a dimension beyond the conventional laws of physical motion.

You may ask: If a person's conscious observation of a wave function causes it to collapse into a particle, why then is there so much agreement about the physical world (the position and movement of objects) – given the existence of so many *very different people*, who may all be disseminating consciousness into the same universe?

Goswami (1993), a physicist and mystic, offers a poignant answer to this provocative question. He convincingly proposes that there is just *one universal consciousness that is shared among all human beings*. It is interesting to note that this growing view among physicists is entirely consistent with the philosopher William James' (1902) discussion of the *continuum of cosmic consciousness*; psychologist C. G. Jung's (1960) well–developed hypothesis of the *collective unconscious*; and theologian Pierre Teilhard de Chardin's (1965) idea of a *noosphere* (*noos* from the Greek word for *mind*): a meta–mind that embraces our planet (and the universe) as an "atmosphere" of awareness that surrounds the globe (in addition to air). Essentially, this one cosmic, collective mind incorporates all of the universe that ever was, is now, and perhaps will be – what David Bohm (1980) has designated *wholeness and the implicate order*. Moreover, every human mind allows holographic access to this universal consciousness (Jung and Pauli, 1955; Grof, 1993; Talbot, 1991; Peat, 1987; Sheldrake, 1981; 1988). Indeed, the *memory* of this universal mind continues to evolve as living systems (from superstrings to supergalaxies) dynamically interact with one another via positive – recurring – feedback loops (Schwartz and Russek, 1999).

Yet it is important to realize that the usual variations that different people see and report (variations from what would be the one universal consciousness) are attributed to each person's development. The divergent experiences that a person encounters in life create different psychological filters and thus somewhat different mental categories for seeing, thinking, and behaving. Consequently, there are *individual differences* in how this one universal consciousness affects – and is affected by – human beings.

Journeying into Consciousness

There are several reasons why most people remain extremely skeptical of the role of consciousness in materializing the physical world – including the transcendent dimension of consciousness itself. For one, much of their experience in living out the dualistic split between mind and matter *takes place in an unconscious manner*. Most people are not aware that the division between their inside mind and outside matter is a social construction (by René Descartes) and therefore merely an illusion. Nor would many people be consciously aware of universal consciousness, let alone be consciously aware of the processes by which their individual minds interlace with the universal mind (Jung, 1961; Singer, 1972).

For nearly all human beings, conscious life is enacting conditioned responses to external stimuli with a rather restricted amount of time and attention devoted to the "I," or "self," that is doing the seeing, thinking, and behaving. In familiar surroundings, people usually spend the majority of their conscious lives on "autopilot" as they continually perform their daily routines or, in some cases, make their life choices in a virtual "mental fog" without self-awareness or self-reflection. Declarations of the "self" such as "I think therefore I am" (René Descartes) – and the more recent versions: "I *feel* therefore I am, I *choose* therefore I am, I *know* that I know, I am *aware* that I am aware" – represent *ordinary states of consciousness*. But there is much more to consciousness than being locked on autopilot while occasionally acknowledging one's self-identity (Talbot, 1991; Herbert, 1993; Tart, 1975).

When people contemplate the experiences and functioning of their minds apart from the immediate moment, they often journey to the most traditional domain of self-awareness: the recall of biographical events as far away as the age of two or three years (which, for many people, is the time of their first vivid memory). Various forms of meditation (including spirituality and prayer) and schools of psychotherapy (including dreams and hypnosis) have been used to further elaborate a person's developing acceptance of self, refinement of the "I," and understanding (and working through) of significant historical events that have shaped the "I." Generally speaking, the focus of these approaches does not journey much past the biographical period. Yet even in this realm, the conscious mind can easily move back and forth from one location to another (space) and from one period to another (time) at a velocity that would be far greater than light speed – if the equivalent physical motion occurred within the spacetime continuum.

It is possible, however, to journey beyond the biographical mode of self-awareness and consciousness. Stanislav Grof (1993), a psychiatrist and mystic, has intently explored three *nonordinary states of consciousness*: (1) the postnatal state (after birth and into adulthood), which corresponds to the biographical recall of life events, (2) the perinatal state (just before, during, and after birth), which concentrates on the birth trauma (Rank, 1929), and (3) the transpersonal state, which encompasses out-of-body experiences, experiences within other people's lives, and experiences through animals, plants, substances, spirits, archetypes, and God – past, present, and indeed the hereafter (Jung and Pauli, 1955; Peat, 1987; Talbot, 1991; Ornstein, 1968; Wilber, 1979; 1980).

Apparently, the perinatal and transpersonal states of consciousness are the most challenging to our everyday experience. This is because they are concealed in the Western world, often denied or labeled as psychotic, and subject to considerable skepticism, if not ridicule. Grof (1993, page 18) summarizes the transpersonal territory and its revolutionary challenge to the entrenched principles of the Cartesian–Newtonian Paradigm:

> On occasion, we can reach far back in time and witness
> sequences from the lives of our human and animal ancestors,
> as well as events that involved people from other historical
> periods and cultures with whom we have no genetic
> connection whatsoever. Through our consciousness, we can
> transcend time and space, cross boundaries separating us
> from various animal species, experience processes in the

botanical kingdom and in the inorganic world, and even explore mythological and other realities that we previously did not know existed. We might discover that experiences of this kind will profoundly influence our life philosophy and worldview. We will very likely find it increasingly difficult to share the belief system dominating the industrial cultures and the philosophical assumptions of traditional Western science.

What sets Grof's approach apart from many other examinations of nonordinary states of consciousness is that he has also introduced a very engaging and effective methodology for journeying through the universal consciousness – which includes the use of rhythmic breathing, evocative music, body work, and symbolic expression. *Holotropic Breathwork™*, as it is called, allows people to journey into nonordinary states of consciousness without having to wait for a meaningful, near-death experience or to take psychedelic or psychoactive drugs. In these safe, expert-guided journeys, most participants experience their consciousness bringing them to spaces and times that they themselves have never previously seen or imagined (which is *beyond* biographical recall). Again we see how consciousness can instantly crisscross space and time in a way that is impossible within the physical dimensions of the universe. Perhaps Einstein's famous "thought experiments" became so unbelievably deep and intense that they enabled him to visit the inherent qualities of light, space, time, mass, and energy – *through nonordinary states of consciousness.*

Such transpersonal journeys demonstrate, rather convincingly, that there must be a transcendent dimension of universal consciousness which interconnects all matter and minds that ever existed. Only in those cases when experiences of nonordinary states of consciousness are deliberated strictly from within the archaic Cartesian–Newtonian Paradigm are people able to rapidly – and thus defensively – dismiss the reports of thousands, if not millions, of people who have already experienced the perinatal and transpersonal areas of universal consciousness. Many quantum physicists have acknowledged the fundamental role played by consciousness in the universe, as discussed previously. But most people who are not quantum physicists have not yet scrutinized their Cartesian–Newtonian worldview. Perhaps this is so because they still haven't been exposed to its limitations and inconsistencies.

To enable more people to see the underlying deficiencies in the old paradigm, Grof (1993, page 17) highlights the great irony behind the many "objective" principles of the Cartesian–Newtonian Paradigm:

The paradox is that René Descartes' *Discourse on Method*, the book that reformed the entire structure of Western knowledge and that provided the foundations for modern science, came to its author in three visionary dreams and a dream within a dream, which provided the key for interpreting the larger dream. What an irony it is that the entire edifice of rational reductionist, positivist science, which today rejects "subjective knowledge," was originally inspired by a revelation in a nonordinary state of consciousness!

The Evolution of Multiple Universes

What do journeys and experiences through transpersonal consciousness tell us about the origin and nature of the universe? Such accounts might provide relevant ideas for transforming people and their organizations. At the very least, a new paradigm that sees the interplay of mind and matter as explicitly involving consciousness is going to view transformation very differently than a paradigm that explains the origin of the universe as an initial push (or big bang) of material objects by some external force (God, for example) that, eventually – exactly like a mechanical clock – will wear down, stop working, and have all of its pieces randomly distributed across a flat, cold, empty space.

One abridged example of a transpersonal journey into the nature of the cosmos, by an experienced "consciousness traveler," is reproduced in Grof (1993, pages 165–166):

> The experience then changed into an extremely powerful and moving experience of the Cosmic Tree. The unified field of cosmic energy that I had experienced before now became a massive tree of radiant energy suspended in space. Larger than the largest galaxy, it was composed entirely of light.… I was taken around the tree and shown how to move from one person's experience to another and it was ridiculously easy. Different lives around the globe were simply different experiences the tree was having.…
>
> I was now actually experiencing the seamless flow of consciousness into crystallizations of embodiment. I was experiencing how consciousness manifests itself in separate forms while remaining unified. I knew that fundamentally there was only One Consciousness in the universe. From this

perspective my individual identity and everybody else's appeared temporary and almost trivial. To experience my true identity filled me with a profound sense of numinous encounter....

Though these experiences were amazing in their own right, the most poignant aspect of today's session for me was not the discovered dimensions of the universe themselves, but what my seeing and understanding them meant to the Consciousness I was with. It was so happy to have someone to show its work to. I felt that it had been waiting for billions of years for embodied consciousness to evolve to the point that someone could at last see, understand, and appreciate what it had accomplished.

Lee Smolin (1997), a physicist who is working to integrate quantum mechanics with relativity theory, provides a provocative – and plausible – rationale of the appearance and evolution of our own universe, including the evolution of the laws of physics themselves. His cosmological theory is totally consistent with what others have experienced on transpersonal journeys into the nature of the universe (Grof, 1993).

Using Charles Darwin's (1986) theory of natural selection applied to cosmology, called *cosmological natural selection*, Smolin provides convincing arguments and evidence that our universe (including its life forms) exists because it has descended from many preceding universes through a long evolutionary chain. Furthermore, the parameters for elementary particles (and the invisible forces acting on these particles) have evolved to enable the formation of stable atoms (particularly those that are essential for life, including hydrogen, oxygen, nitrogen, and carbon), supernovas, and black holes (Hawking, 1996; Taylor, 1973; Thorne, 1994).

Let's consider a *supernova*: first, a very large star burns out its nuclear fuel, then it collapses into a near–infinite dense mass by the monumental compression of spacetime strings, and finally it explodes from the intense pressure and heat. If there is a critical amount of mass remaining after the explosion, a black hole forms: an area of space where the density of mass is so extreme that even light can't escape from its surface (due to solidly compressed strings). Inside the hypothetical *event horizon* of this black hole, another explosion of astronomical proportions occurs, stemming from the immeasurable pressure and heat of the remaining, completely compacted, mass/energy/spacetime. Given these near–infinite scales of density, heat, and pressure, this mysterious explosion inside a black hole could possibly launch *the beginning of a new universe within a new spacetime continuum* (Frolov, Markov, and Mukhanov, 1989). Perhaps such a massive explosion within a black hole is the very same "big bang" that is believed to have created our universe about 15 billion years ago (Hawking, 1996).

Smolin (1997, page 88) conjectures what could unfold following this big-bang explosion and the creation of a new spacetime continuum:

> The expanding region may then develop much like our own universe. It may first of all go through a period of inflation and become very big. If conditions develop suitably, galaxies and stars may form, so that in time this new "universe" may become a copy of our world. Long after this, intelligent beings may evolve who, looking back, might be tempted to believe that they lived in a universe that was born in an infinitely dense singularity, before which there was no time. But in reality they would be living in a new region of space and time created by an explosion following the collapse of a star to a black hole in our part of the universe.

This newly created universe, however, would likely exhibit a slightly different construction of nature than its parent universe – due to normal random variation in the creation of waves, particles, and forces. If, at some later time, a supernova occurs in this new universe that also results in a new black hole and a subsequent big-bang explosion, another offspring universe will be created. As with the process of natural selection, however, only those universes that produce supernovas, black holes, and offspring will continue to survive and pass along their slightly modified parameters for nature. But as with life forms on this planet, if a particular universe is born whose parameters are not conducive to supernovas and black holes, it will not produce offspring (new universes): Its particular construction of nature, therefore, will not survive beyond its life cycle (Kauffman, 1993).

Let's take a look at our cosmic evolution in reverse – from what our universe is now to what it might have been, even preceding the big bang. Consider that our universe, by direct experience of its own existence, has likely survived a very large number of evolutionary cycles in the creation of new universes. It would seem, therefore, that the distinctive elementary particles we consciously observe and the universal forces that keep them together as stable atoms are, de facto, the most proficient arrangement of nature to sustain life in general and human life in particular. And just as universes evolve, so do the theories and equations that best describe the creation, motion, and self-transformation of all matter/energy/spacetime. Thus even theories in physics must evolve along with the waves, particles, and forces they attempt to explain.

In contrast to Newton's mechanical clocklike universe, Smolin thus describes a new view of our cosmos as a self-organizing, nonequilibrium system – *a universe that transforms itself*. Basically, energy/matter-filled space oscillating throughout the universe has evolved so that heat transfers and exchanges can take place at all levels of analysis – known as *fractals* – from fundamental particles to atoms to stars to galaxies to clusters of galaxies up to supergalaxies (Briggs and Peat; 1984; 1989). *Space is not cold and empty*. Space is filled with energy and heat – with temperatures maintained, via various feedback processes, well above absolute zero. Space is also filled with matter: approximately 90% of all matter in the universe consists of dark – invisible – matter in space, which does not appear as large masses such as planets (Genz, 1999). Solar winds, molecular clouds, carbon dust, and a variety of chemical and nuclear processes all regulate the life cycles of galaxies – so they continue to procreate supernovas, black holes, and new universes (Jantsch, 1980; Kauffman, 1993; Thorne, 1994; Wolf, 1988).

It is absolutely essential to stress that in order for galactic systems to continue evolving while maintaining the necessary conditions to support life, *they must remain in a state of thermal nonequilibrium*. As Smolin (1997, page 125) explains, the fact that our universe regulates itself to maintain a state of thermal nonequilibrium is entirely at odds with the old paradigm:

> The image of the warm living Earth in the depth of cold empty space is thus not only misleading … it is simply wrong. Most of the volume of the galactic disk is taken up by a medium which, although it is incredibly dilute, is hot, much hotter than it is here on Earth! To appreciate this, and the processes that heat the medium and govern its properties, is to begin to glimpse the huge system of the galaxy that we live inside of

Such "aliveness" in the cosmos is best illustrated by our own planet, Earth, which, for some time now, has been viewed as a living system in its own right – the *Gaia Theory*, which is named after Mother Earth (Lovelock, 1979; 1988). Many agree that the planet Earth (along with its atmosphere) regulates the spread of temperature on the planet, the amount of oxygen in the air, the amount of salt in the oceans, and other chemical-biological processes via the coevolution of living beings – *despite steadily decreasing heat energy from our sun.* Certainly, the clever control of such complex functions using a composite of regulatory–feedback and information–management processes convincingly demonstrates the existence of life and intelligence on a planetary scale (Bateson, 1979).

Grof (1993, page 110) documents a transpersonal journey that lends support to the growing appreciation that the Earth – as a whole – is both alive and intelligent:

> While the objective evidence for the Gaia Theory might not be sufficient to convince hardcore scientists, it is certainly supported by the existence of transpersonal experiences that are fully congruent with it. For example, in one of our five–day workshops in Holotropic Breathwork™, a young German woman had a persuasive experience of becoming the archetypal Great Mother Goddess. Then the experience developed further and she felt herself becoming planet Earth (Mother Earth). She reported that she felt no question at all that she had merged with and had become the consciousness of the Earth. She experienced herself as the Earth, as a living, breathing organism with an intelligence, an organism that was evolving toward a still higher level of awareness.
>
> As the Earth consciousness she felt that the metals and minerals that were a part of her constituted her skeleton. Similarly, the biosphere, all forms of life, was her flesh. She experienced within herself the circulation of water from the oceans to the clouds, from there into creeks and rivers and finally to the great seas. The water system was her blood and the meteorological changes, such as evaporation, air currents, and rainfall, ensured its circulation, the transport of nourishment, and cleansing. The communication between all living things, large and small, constituted her nervous system and brain.

While it remains to be seen whether other sections in the universe contain living forms that also regulate their biospheres in the accentuated manner represented by this account of Earth's consciousness, it should be apparent that our universe is fundamentally different from anything that can be formulated from the Cartesian–Newtonian Paradigm. Our universe is not heading toward the random distribution of matter and an eventual heat death. On the contrary, our universe is apparently able to maintain, transform, and reorganize itself. As such, it can also become much better at *creating and spreading life forms throughout its galaxies* (Davies, 1999).

With this invigorated, more magnificent image of our universe, it is important to keep in mind the radical findings from quantum mechanics: Without self-aware conscious entities, universes will not exist in material form to manifest their scintillating display of sophisticated organizational structures – and life forms – arranging spacetime and matter/energy from superstrings to supergalaxies (Gell-Mann, 1994; Greene, 1999).

The Relevance of Quantum Mechanics

When medium-sized objects – from molecules to moons – are the focus of interest, their bigger-than-quantum size may lead one to conclude that Newtonian science is adequate for explaining and predicting movement. Of course, various aspects of Newtonian mechanics have been revised by Einstein's relativistic mechanics to take into account the effects of absolute light speed, the curved geometry of spacetime, and the interrelationships among mass, energy, space, and time. Some people, however, still dismiss the relevance of quantum mechanics for anything but nuclear particles.

The typical reason for applying quantum mechanics only to nuclear particles is based on the premise that molar objects are always there: they don't revert back to wave functions if no human being is watching them. When you look away from the moon and then look back, it appears to be in the same location as before. Presumably it didn't evaporate through a transcendent dimension of consciousness and then suddenly reappear in an altogether different location. Actually, the mathematical equations for quantum mechanics simplify to Newtonian equations for masses that are equal to or greater than atoms (Bohr, 1958). Although big objects (such as the moon) do have a wave function, it is infinitesimal (Kaufman and Rock, 1982). Between conscious measurements, however, the wave function of a photon or an electron spreads out over a vast space relative to the size of the particle form. Consequently, from one observation to another (even in a very short instant of time), a photon's or electron's position can change dramatically.

A core question to address: Why should we concern ourselves with applying quantum-based principles to medium-sized objects – including people and organizations? Why not simply use the Cartesian-Newtonian Paradigm for the particular objects that we can see using our own eyes – rather than wondering what really happens to submicroscopic electrons and photons or supermacroscopic stars and galaxies? The main question: When does it make the most sense to use the Newtonian or the quantum approach – especially for organizations and their transformations?

REGARDING THE SELF-MOTION OF PARTICLES AND PEOPLE One easy way to discover which paradigm is best for which problem makes use of Young's (1976) pivotal distinction of inert molar objects versus self–motion monads. The movement of inert objects is determined solely by external forces and therefore is thoroughly explained by Newtonian mechanics – particularly for molar objects that are neither composed of exceptionally large mass nor traveling near light speed. But entities that are capable of self-motion are better explained by quantum mechanics. The term *monad* designates a spark of life: an entity that decides for itself what it is, when and how it will move, and why.

Young (1976, page 7) simplifies the fundamental distinction between inert molar objects and self–motion monads – a distinction that relates to the question of when it is best to apply which of the two paradigms:

> In science we discover that *the evolution of matter itself is a "fall."* By fall we mean loss of freedom, increase of constraint. This occurs in steps: first the condensing of the original energy of the photon into mass to form a charged particle, then the joining of opposite charges to constitute a neutral atom, then of atoms to form molecules, and finally the compaction of molecules into inert objects. In this declension the original freedom is lost: the free motion of one particle is canceled by the free motion of another, so that where billions of particles are compacted, there results an *inert object*, which, having no self motion, responds to exact laws....
>
> The world of fundamental particles is quite different from that of predictable billiard balls. From the point of view of predictability, it is like that of human beings. Its creatures have a life of their own.

Both nuclear particles and human beings are monads, because they choose their direction and motion all by themselves: they do not require external forces to move them. Similar to human beings, nuclear particles seem to have the freedom of going here and there and even transforming themselves into a variety of other forms and meanings – which generates uncertainty (Heisenberg, 1958; 1971). Further, nuclear particles appear to be aware, as discussed earlier, of whether they are being observed by another conscious being and, as a result, these monads can change back and forth between a wave function and an actual particle. Perhaps nuclear particles are not as self-aware as human beings, but they do seem to crisscross the transcendent dimension of consciousness, since they stay connected with correlated partners across huge distances.

Young's insightful distinction of inert molar objects (appropriate for Newtonian mechanics) and self-motion monads (appropriate for quantum mechanics) makes the main point that *size or mass itself is not what determines whether to make use of the Newtonian versus the quantum worldview.* Photons and people are of vastly different sizes, but both are proficient at self-motion. Molecules and moons are of enormously different scales, too, yet both are inert in their own way. Consequently, when observing and facilitating the potentia of self-motion people in organizations, we must make use of the modern Quantum-Relativistic Paradigm – *regardless of the molar size of people.* Instead, if we use the old Cartesian-Newtonian Paradigm for self-motion people, we will surely perpetuate the behavior of human beings as inert objects. Moreover, since the universe is a self-organizing, nonequilibrium, *self-motion* system in its own right, the structure of the universe itself (as a whole) might provide significant insights for people-based collectives on Earth that also have great potential for self-motion, self-organization, and self-transformation (Jantsch, 1980; Peat, 1991; Prigogine and Stenger, 1984). Hence, the quantum worldview has relevance for organizational life.

REGARDING THE QUANTUM BRAIN AND SELF-AWARE MIND   Another angle to the current question of when to use Newtonian versus quantum mechanics concerns the nature of the human brain. Recall that Newton's mathematical principles to explain motion in the external physical world had no interest in people, let alone their brains. Since Newton's time (the 1600s), however, much has been discovered about the coevolution of life (Darwin, 1986; Kauffman, 1993); during this past century, much has been learned about the dynamic functioning of the human brain (Eccles, 1966; Hooper and Teresi, 1986; Searle, 1984; Chopra, 1989; Horgan, 1999).

Herbert (1993, pages 93–94) provides a fascinating description of the dynamic functioning of our mental organ yet also acknowledges that we still have much more to learn about the brain's role in self-awareness and consciousness:

> The human brain has been described as the most complex
> object in the universe. Certainly a lot goes on in this warm

fist-sized ball of meat. Various exotic fluids pour, soak, and trickle through its channels and crevices. A veritable drugstore of chemical substances is synthesized there, put to strange uses, then broken down and recycled for future use. Legions of brain cells are born (in the early months of life), connect up to other cells, and carry out their mysterious cellular tasks in various neural communities before they die. Trillions of electric signals travel through the brain's wet electrical networks, each impulse inducing a weak electrical and magnetic field that races across the cranium at the speed of light. Torrents of electrically charged ions escape through suddenly opened cellular gates only to be captured one by one and sequestered again inside a brain cell. In addition, if the [mystics] are right, certain special brain processes act in unknown ways to send and receive messages from the spirit world. With so much activity going on all at once, it is difficult to tell which brain functions are important, which irrelevant, for producing the phenomenon known as ordinary awareness.

MacLean (1985), a neuroscientist, anatomizes our human brain into three functional layers, termed the *triune brain*, that follow the evolution of brains for all species. As summarized by the surgeon philosopher Leonard Shlain (1991), the oldest, deepest, most primitive layer in the human brain, the *reptilian brain*, is only capable of instinctual responses that derive from genetic transmission and alterations. No choices are accessible, except *See! Act!* The next layer, the *paleomammalian brain*, is primarily capable of strong emotions and stimulus/response learning – which can be modified after birth through experiences in adapting to the external environment. A few choices are possible with multiple stimuli that provide several alternative responses. The most recent addition to the human brain, the *cerebral cortex*, lying right on top of the earlier limbic system – enables human beings to be both imaginative and intelligent, to create both art and physics. Many more choices are possible with a cerebral cortex – including free will and the self-aware capability to override behavioral conditioning and atavistic instincts (Carter, 1998).

The cerebral cortex is subdivided into two halves, known simply as the *left and right hemispheres* (or left brain and right brain), which are joined together by way of the *corpus callosum* (Hooper and Teresi, 1986). It is now well documented that the left brain's functioning incorporates a person's conscious, serial mental processes that are applied to language, logic, and mathematics (one–at–a–time sequences via neural tracks). The right brain's functioning, in contrast, subsumes a person's unconscious, parallel mental processes that are necessary for recognizing whole images – as used in art and music – including patterns and rhythms (all–at–once experiences via neural networks).

Of particular interest, Zohar (1997), a physicist, equates the left brain with the particle aspects of physical nature (addressed one at a time in a linear fashion), while the right brain represents the wave aspects (treated as one holistic experience). Zohar speculates that rapid oscillations across the corpus callosum integrate the left and right brain functions. She labels this *quantum thinking*. In this context, quantum thinking is apparent when a person is faced with a fairly intense, unexpected, unfamiliar experience. Attempting to make sense out of such an experience immediately causes the rapid, chaotic firing of neurons across a person's left and right brains. These cross–hemisphere–firing neurons serve to integrate the particle (left brain) and wave (right brain) aspects of reality into a new – holographic – understanding.

Quantum thinking, according to Zohar (1997, page 21), is expected to be the foundation for all transdisciplinary creativity, paradigm shifts, and organizational transformation:

> The essence of quantum thinking is that it is the thinking
> that precedes categories, structures, and accepted patterns of
> thought, or mind–sets. It is with quantum thinking that we
> create our categories, change our structures, and transform
> our patterns of thought. Quantum thinking is vital to
> creative thinking and leadership in organizations. It is the
> key to any genuine organizational transformation. It is the
> key to shifting our paradigm. Quantum thinking is the link
> between the brain's creativity, organizational transformation
> and leadership, and the ideas found in the new science.

Further considering the quantum functioning of the brain, there is increasing speculation that (1) a wave function across the whole brain is capable of rapidly collapsing into a single thought or idea – much like the immediate collapse of a sprawling wave in spacetime into an infinitesimal electron; (2) neural firings jump from one section of the brain to the other without a trace – analogous to an electron jumping from one orbit in an atom to another without journeying through spacetime; and (3) complex neural patterns materialize from correlated, firing neurons that somehow know how to respond to one another when replaying an old memory or forming a new one – consistent with correlated electrons that continue to influence one another at extreme distances within the higher dimension of universal consciousness (Eccles, 1989; Wigner, 1967; Herbert, 1993).

In particular, rapid oscillations of firing neurons across the integral mind/brain (via the neural pathways in the corpus callosum) apparently propagate a *strange attractor*, or a *chaotic attractor* (Briggs and Peat, 1984; 1989; Gleick, 1987). Basically, a strange attractor is a rhythmic wave pattern that emerges from recurring particle locations – equivalent to a diagram of the quantum dance of a honeybee (Frank, 1997). Especially relevant, a strange attractor that emanates in the mind/brain is a multidimensional image of a meaningful thought, category, or paradigm (Barton, 1994; Horgan, 1994). After the formation of a strange attractor, new neural tracks and networks are "hard wired" into the organic structures of the brain to store the wave pattern (and what it represents) for later use. The next time an analogous situation is apparent, the familiar wave pattern will first be remembered, retrieved from storage, then compared and contrasted, and subsequently stored again – but always in some evolved form, depending on what was experienced (Levy, 1994).

It should not be surprising to learn that neural firings oscillate at a particular frequency, approximately 40 cycles each second (Horgan, 1994), which might resonate *at the same frequency with the vibrating strings of spacetime*. These elementary strings constitute the spacetime that lies in between the much larger cells in the brain. Indeed, these vibrating strings of spacetime might be the mysterious medium that allows firing neurons to propagate strange attractors inside the mind/brain – which we call seeing, thinking, and behaving.

Goswami (1993, page 132) reviews a highly intriguing research study that strongly supports the quantum nature of the human mind/brain by explicitly demonstrating that nonlocal behavior takes place among *people* as well as electrons and photons:

> A recent experiment by the Mexican neurophysiologist
> Jacobo Grinberg–Zylberbaum and his collaborators directly
> supports the idea of nonlocality in human brain/minds....
> Two subjects are instructed to interact for a period of
> thirty or forty minutes until they start feeling a "direct
> communication." They then enter separate Faraday cages
> (metallic enclosures that block all electromagnetic signals).

Unknown to his or her partner, one of the subjects is now shown a flickering light signal that produces an evoked potential (an electrophysiological response produced by a sensory stimulus and measured by an EEG) in the light-stimulated brain. But amazingly, as long as the partners in the experiment maintain their direct communication, the unstimulated brain also shows an electrophysiological activity, called a transfer potential, quite similar in shape and strength to the evoked potential of the stimulated brain. (In contrast, control subjects do not show any transfer potential.) The straightforward explanation is quantum nonlocality: The two brain/minds act as a nonlocally correlated system – the correlation established and maintained through nonlocal consciousness – by virtue of the quantum nature of the brains.

Self-aware consciousness and quantum functioning are now known qualities of the human mind/brain. But where in the human brain is this self-aware consciousness located and how does it go about its quantum functioning? Or asked a bit differently, how does the electrochemical soup of energy/matter in the brain encourage a self-aware mind to say to itself: "I know that I know; I am aware that I am aware"? Briefly considered, the new paradigm would presuppose quantum waves of consciousness to be spread across a person's brain. However, a specific perception, thought, or behavior (particle) would only be revealed to the "self" when a completed observation by the "self" collapsed one or more wave functions. But how does this happen?

My own best guess about "where consciousness is located" takes us back to the intriguing split of the brain into two mini-brains. Specifically, I wonder if an observation of the "self" by the "self" is a performance that necessarily requires the two hemispheres of the brain. Perhaps the human experience of self-awareness and consciousness is nothing more than one hemisphere of the brain consciously observing its counterpart – thereby collapsing the wave of potentia into the particle state: "The subject is me (via the left brain *conducting* the observation) and I know it (via the right brain *receiving* the observation)." Maybe the evolution of the human brain into two separate functioning hemispheres (correlated, originally, via the corpus callosum), may be exactly the process that enables human beings to recognize their self-aware consciousness. Instead of the "consciousness mechanism" being located inside a particular organic region in the brain, *the consciousness experience may be a participative process whereby the two separately functioning halves of the human brain engage in an ongoing dialogue with each other.* If this guess turns out to be the case, it should be apparent that without two mini–brains existing within the whole human brain, and without the two hemispheres being integrated through the transcendent dimension of consciousness, there would be no self–awareness and thus no capacity for knowing or engaging the one universal consciousness.

Seven Essential Categories in the New Paradigm

The main reasons for using the Quantum–Relativistic Paradigm for other than nuclear particles should now be transparent: When people and their organizations are the subject of study, the Cartesian–Newtonian Paradigm simply cannot handle the uncertainty of movement to their next position or state of being – including each person's next perception, thought, and behavior. Therefore, human evolution and organizational transformation involve much more than a single push from an external source of energy. Besides being self–motion monads with a mind of their own, people can know several nonordinary states of consciousness; self–aware people can assimilate and disseminate the accumulated knowledge contained within the one universal consciousness. As people become even more self–aware and conscious, *both hemispheres of their mental organ* will play an increasingly crucial role in self–motion, self–development, and thus quantum thinking. Understanding human behavior in organizations (and elsewhere) is thus radically different from predicting the motion of billiard balls.

The new Quantum–Relativistic Paradigm can be seen through seven essential categories – which are diametrically different from the similarly numbered categories in the old paradigm. But it is these categories in the new paradigm that explain – much more realistically – how self–motion monads see, think, and behave:

1   THE MONISTIC UNIFICATION OF CONSCIOUSNESS WITH MATTER
    The physical world exists via the active participation of self–aware, conscious people. The physical world and the laws that describe it are thus intimately intertwined with life – especially human beings.

2   UNIVERSES AS MATERIALIZED BY CONSCIOUS PARTICIPATION
    Consciousness is the ultimate building block of our entire universe. Self–aware, conscious participation causes the collapse of quantum waves into materialized particles – commencing from the vibrating

strings of spacetime to supergalaxies of matter/energy. Integrating relativity theory and quantum mechanics with cosmological natural selection and consciousness into superstring theory will, hopefully, be able to explain the creation and evolution of all universes.

3   **SPACETIME AS CURVED AND FILLED WITH MATTER/ENERGY**
The geometry of spacetime is curved or warped if mass and energy are nearby; otherwise it is flat. But space is never empty (even if no mass or energy exists); instead, spacetime is composed of oscillating string–potential waves and vibrating string–loop particles. The mass and speed of an object compress fundamental waves and particles; consequently, an object warps its surrounding spacetime geometry. Both mass and speed thus interact with space and time. Actually, in the spacetime continuum, mass, energy, time, space, and light are all interactive and interchangeable. Moreover, the higher dimension of universal consciousness is far beyond Newton's laws of motion and Einstein's theories of relativity – and is not constrained by the speed limit of light. Consciousness obeys its own holographic geometry.

4   **THE NATURAL SELECTION OF MANY RELATIVISTIC UNIVERSES**
There may be many potential universes, each comprising numerous dimensions, including three dimensions of conventional space, one dimension of linear time, the added dimensions of spacetime, and the transcendent dimension of universal consciousness. Very likely, our universe has evolved from a long evolutionary chain that has procreated self–organizing, nonequilibrium, complex systems. These systems are capable of reproducing offspring universes with slightly modified waves, particles, and forces. As these universes evolve, the laws of physics evolve as well: there are no absolute theories. Space and time are not absolute, either, but are relative to the speed of an observer. In the physical cosmos, only light speed is absolute for all observers (regardless of their particular movement) and defines the upper speed limit of the spacetime continuum.

5   **THE PROBABILISTIC UNCERTAINTY OF SELF-MOTION MONADS**
Nuclear particles and human beings are self–motion monads. There is always uncertainty while trying to pinpoint both the position and movement of these quantum phenomena: They move by their own intentions as well as being affected by external forces – the curved geometry and string compression of spacetime. Consciousness itself

may be assimilated and disseminated by forces that simply do not exist in the spacetime continuum – but can be explored via various transpersonal journeys into nonordinary domains of consciousness. To actualize the self-motion of human beings through ordinary and nonordinary aspects of consciousness (including quantum thinking and self-observation) requires that we examine the mind/brain and how the right/left hemispheres interact via the corpus callosum.

6   THE ETERNAL CONNECTIONS AMONG SELF-MOTION MONADS
Once nuclear particles – or human beings – have bonded, they are forever connected in the unity of universal consciousness. Affecting any of these correlated, self-motion monads immediately affects all others – without any delay due to time or space. The transcendent dimension of universal consciousness threads the cosmos into one intertwined fabric of harmonious string-based waves and particles.

7   THE ETERNAL SELF-ORGANIZATION OF RELATIVISTIC UNIVERSES
The cosmos itself is a quantum system in that it embodies universal consciousness and perpetually self-organizes its diversity of forms – from superstrings to supergalaxies. In lieu of assuming an eventual heat death due to the Newtonian-based laws of increasing entropy and thermal equilibrium, the universe will regularly transform itself at every level of structure and will create new universes.

Recall that the Cartesian-Newtonian Paradigm was entirely based on the insular development of Western philosophy and science, initiated during the ancient Greek civilization, from about 400 BC to 100 BC. But hundreds of years earlier, between 1000 BC and 500 BC, several ancient civilizations throughout Asia were already developing a different paradigm of nature, life, and the universe. This old Eastern worldview, however, has typically seemed strange to Westerners, if not primitive or backward – particularly when judged according to the Newtonian-derived assessments of material production and economic wealth. In retrospect, however, we can now see that ancient Eastern philosophies had recognized the quantum principles of self-awareness and universal consciousness *several thousands of years ago* – whereas they were not effectively introduced into the Western worldview until the twentieth century.

Capra (1991, pages 23–24) offers a glimpse into the ancient paradigm developed in the Eastern world (further discussed in Chapter 6) – which is remarkably compatible with the Quantum-Relativistic Paradigm:

Although the various schools of Eastern mysticism differ in many details, they all emphasize the basic unity of the universe which is the central feature of their teachings. The highest aim of their followers – whether they are Hindus, Buddhists or Taoists – is to become aware of the unity and mutual interrelation of all things, to transcend the notion of an isolated individual self and to identify themselves with the ultimate reality. The emergence of this awareness – known as "enlightenment" – is not only an intellectual act but is an experience which involves the whole person and is religious in its ultimate nature.… In the Eastern view, then, the division of nature into separate objects is not fundamental and any such objects have a fluid and ever–changing character. The Eastern world view is therefore intrinsically dynamic and contains time and change as essential features. The cosmos is seen as one inseparable reality – forever in motion, alive, organic; spiritual and material at the same time.

THE CHALLENGE OF TRANSFORMATION

It should be rather clear by now that the differences between the old and new paradigms are like night and day, death and life. The *old paradigm* is derived from the dualistic separation of mind and matter along with the physical separation of all material objects by empty space; it also predicts the ultimate heat death of the universe. The *new paradigm* is based on the interconnection of mind and matter throughout the universe along with the inclusion of multidimensional spacetime and universal consciousness; it ensures eternal life via a self–organizing, self–transforming universe that continues to create additional variety, complexity, and life.

Most organizations have undoubtedly been created and maintained according to the old Cartesian–Newtonian Paradigm. These organizations have recruited, trained, and rewarded members for seeing, thinking, and behaving according to the categories in the old paradigm. As a result, the employees of these organizations have become (and were destined to be) no more than inert molar objects – controlled by external reinforcement and coercion. These Newtonian organizations will most certainly become even more inefficient and ineffective in facing the increasing challenges of a living, self–organizing, global economy – epitomized by Mother Earth as an intelligent, living system.

The principal challenge to the survival and evolution of our highly organized society is to reverse the growing discord between inert-object organizations and the self-motion global community. To accomplish such a self-transformation requires *quantum infrastructures* so that organizational members, who currently may be functioning as frustrated human objects, can develop self-aware consciousness and thus become fully functioning, self-motion monads. These enlightened participants would then generate *quantum thinking*, which is the basis for self-designing, implementing, and improving *formal systems and value-added processes*. As members enhance their innate capabilities for creativity, collaboration, and commitment, they will perpetually transform themselves and their organizations. This evolution will further enhance self-aware consciousness, organizational success, and personal meaning.

Keep this in mind: The transformation of inert-object people into self-motion monads mandates the establishment of effective quantum infrastructures before self-transformation of systems and processes can possibly succeed. Failure to honor this commandment is the prime reason change initiatives fail at shifting paradigms and achieving transformation.

The remainder of this book will illuminate how transformation to a quantum organization can truly be realized for a Newtonian organization. We will frequently return to the seven essential categories that define the new paradigm (versus the old) with the purpose of deeply understanding *why* we are moving in a particular direction and, therefore, *how* we can get there. During this journey, the guiding light for consciously exploring the underlying distinctions between the two dueling paradigms will become even more apparent than it is now.

CHAPTER 2

THE NEW ORGANIZATION

From Essential Categories to Achieving Self-Transformation

To incorporate relativity and quantum mechanics into our mind–sets seems at first inconvenient but it has become imperative if we are to continue to evolve consciously. In order to take advantage of the new discoveries in the field of physics, we will have to begin integrating the two hemispheric functions [of our human brain]. It will be a prodigious task: The gulf that divides the right hemisphere from the left in Western culture is very wide.... Perhaps the answer lies with the synthesis of art and physics. Once these two endeavors can be seen as being inextricably linked, the ensuing reinforcement across the corpus callosum between the right and left hemispheres will enrich all who are able to see one in the terms of the other.

— Leonard Shlain (1991, pages 431, 434)

For many readers, it may be tough to absorb the nontraditional concepts, categories, and paradigms that we experienced in the preceding chapter – particularly if you haven't been exposed to them previously. Because this material is so vital for understanding how to transform an old Newtonian organization into a new quantum organization, however, let's reexamine some of the more complicated material through the medium of symbolic figures. In fact, the geometric depiction of spacetime waves and particles harmonized in this colorful artwork will be spotted throughout the rest of this book whenever additional graphics are used to highlight the relevant principles of self–transformation. Incidentally, I have used these identical figures for stimulating executives and other members of organizations to understand the stages of transformation – before, during, and after their own journeys. Since "a picture is worth a thousand words," it should not be surprising that *entrusting art to illuminate physics* is exceedingly useful for deeply appreciating the intricacies and subtleties of the new paradigm for organizational transformation.

It is also important to remember that the essential categories in the two dueling paradigms were developed from scientific studies of physical nature in general (within the fields of physics, philosophy, neuroscience, consciousness, and chemistry). While these paradigms make use of either passive observers or active participants, the fundamental categories were never intended for understanding and managing people in organizational settings. Even the term *organizational transformation*, for example, was rarely heard prior to the 1980s. The nomenclature of the two dueling paradigms, therefore, must be translated into useful terms that speak the language of contemporary organizations.

Following the careful rewording of the dueling paradigms, we will focus our attention on outlining the key attributes of the *new organization*. This quantum organization is still quite unfamiliar to most people, since the new paradigm from which it is derived is still largely unknown in the Western world. But clearly perceiving the underlying distinctions between the Newtonian organization and the quantum organization will prove to be essential for confronting the quintessential problem: *how to transform an old organization into a new one.*

Lastly, this chapter presents a grand overview of the transformation process – a big–picture summary of all the material we will cover in the remainder of the book. This overview will begin by summarizing the *three transformational components* that will subsequently be discussed in detail in inclusive chapters: (1) quantum infrastructures, (2) formal systems, and (3) process management. These three components assimilate the *eight tracks of self-transformation* – which must be implemented in a prescribed sequence, since the early tracks create the necessary groundwork for the later tracks to achieve their specialized objectives. Ignoring any of the eight tracks or implementing them out of the prescribed sequence can severely limit the potential of self-transformation.

In sum, after a brief pictorial journey into the Quantum–Relativistic Paradigm, the two antagonistic paradigms will be translated especially for people and their organizations. Next I illuminate the seven attributes of a quantum organization. Lastly, I summarize the requisite sequence of eight tracks that generates a *completely integrated program* for transforming an old Newtonian organization into a new quantum organization.

PICTURING THE NEW PARADIGM

To get a better sense of the new paradigm, I will use a series of symbolic pictures. Figure 2.1 illustrates string–based quantum waves that make up the substance of curved (and flat) spacetime. Because a two–dimensional drawing cannot possibly capture multidimensional spacetime, this figure is only meant to depict the idea of dark matter as comprising elementary waves that materialize into very tiny strings when observed by self–aware, conscious human beings. Perhaps as many as eleven dimensions of space and time define spacetime (Greene, 1999).

FIGURE 2.1
Spacetime as String-Based Waves and Particles

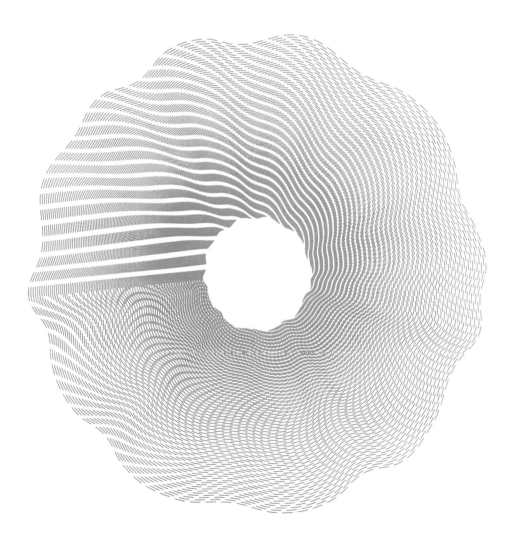

Consider the first moment of light in the universe, emanating from the big bang. Try to picture oscillating, stringlike waves radiating energy across the ever expanding cosmos at the absolute speed of light. Figure 2.2 portrays *light* – which appears in a finite amount of time after an amazing explosion (inside a black hole?). But we three–dimensional human beings can only see (and assume) a continuous emptiness in flat space – because of our inability to experience the infinitesimal quantum scales of discrete, curved spacetime. We must, therefore, *imagine* this vibrating geometry of spacetime that unifies all light, mass, and energy into universal – living – memory (Schwartz and Russek, 1999).

FIGURE 2.2
Radiating Energy Through Vibrating Spacetime

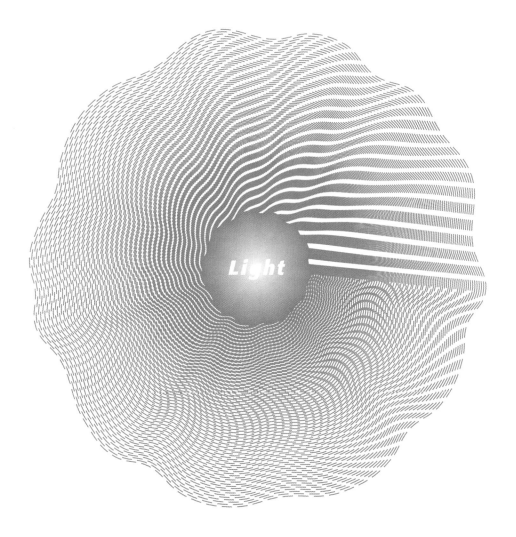

In Figure 2.3, we can appreciate that these same string–based waves and particles engender all the other forms and forces in the universe – by strings breaking apart and joining together into different configurations, which also include different spins, twists, rotations, and vibrations among multidimensional strings. These stringlike waves, particles, and forces then create atoms, molecules, and all other macrosystems, up to and including supergalaxies. Remember, however, that the *creation of matter* (visible forms) is possible via *universal consciousness* (invisible forces) – which is assimilated and disseminated by self–aware, conscious human beings. Be sure to take note of the unfolding shape – the emergence – of both forces and forms.

FIGURE 2.3
Creating Forces and Forms via Superstrings

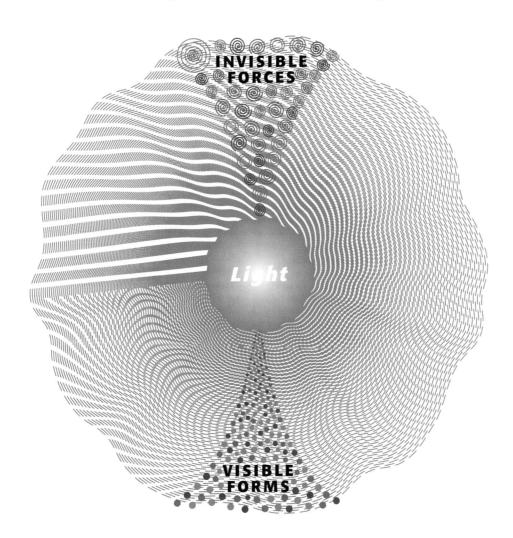

To explore the transcendent dimension of universal consciousness, Figure 2.4 displays the three *nonordinary* states of consciousness. Postnatal consciousness – the recall of biographical events – is the easiest to access and thus closest in position to the human form. Perinatal consciousness – the recall of the birth experience – is usually a lot more difficult to access. Transpersonal consciousness circulates deep within the "collective soul" of the universe and thus is portrayed nearest to universal consciousness, the ultimate *invisible force*. Remember that human beings are themselves *visible forms* which are derived from the same stringlike waves and particles that create all other forms in the universe.

FIGURE 2.4
Nonordinary States of Consciousness

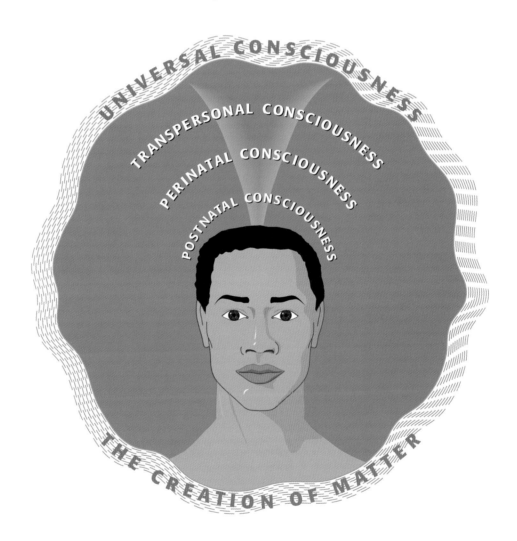

Let's consider the *ordinary* states of consciousness by which human beings, as active participants, materialize the physical universe. Figure 2.5 reminds us of the everyday functions of sensation, perception, attention, recognition, and language. But another illuminating aspect of this figure is the important inclusion of the *mind/brain* of human beings: the mental organ that assimilates and disseminates universal consciousness. Further, it personalizes ordinary and nonordinary states of consciousness. A *brain*, incidentally, also contains the concepts, categories, and paradigms in the *mind* – making use of the neural tracks, networks, and pathways by which a person sees, thinks, and behaves.

FIGURE 2.5
Ordinary States of Consciousness

The next four figures investigate the essential mind/brain of human beings. Figure 2.6 reveals the remarkable three–pound organ that enables all varieties of consciousness. Indeed, the human brain may very well be the principal form in the universe, since it allows the universe to become materialized into visible forms as well as invisible forces. Note the loosely articulated split between the right and left hemispheres that emerges from this transverse view of the brain. Recall: It is the rapid oscillations of firing neurons across these two hemispheres (via the corpus callosum) that not only enables quantum thinking, but also promotes the inner dialogue for self–observation and self–aware consciousness.

FIGURE 2.6
The Two Hemispheres of the Human Brain

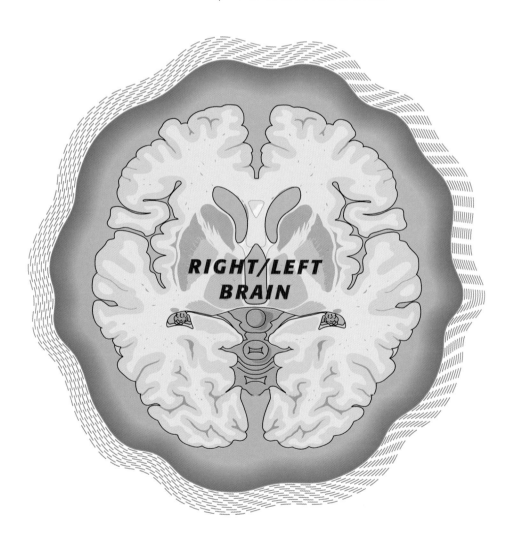

Quantum thinking, it will be recalled, materializes the potential of human ingenuity, which includes paradigm breaking and making sense out of new, unfamiliar, often intense experiences. Once a *strange attractor* is elaborated (by an oscillating pattern of firing neurons that demonstrates a repeatable and, hence, recognizable form), additional neural pathways are hard wired into the organic tissues in the brain. Figure 2.7 shows one way in which these neural pathways can be modified: by weakening or losing neural connections – also termed *unlearning*. Notice two types of synapses that connect a neural track with a neuron: one stimulates the neuron into firing (●), while the other inhibits the neuron from firing (■).

FIGURE 2.7
Weakening/Losing Connections in the Brain

Besides weakening or losing neural connections, another aspect of learning involves strengthening existing connections or actually creating new ones, as shown in Figure 2.8. (These new connections are hard wired into the brain.) Changing paradigms, of course, encompasses both losing and adding neural connections. Or expressed more dramatically, shifting paradigms is like tearing out old connections while sewing in new ones – a rather distasteful image/experience. Perhaps that is why transformation, which by definition incorporates a shift from one paradigm to another, is so hard to achieve: Self-transformation for people and their organizations may feel like radical brain surgery!

FIGURE 2.8
Strengthening/Adding Connections in the Brain

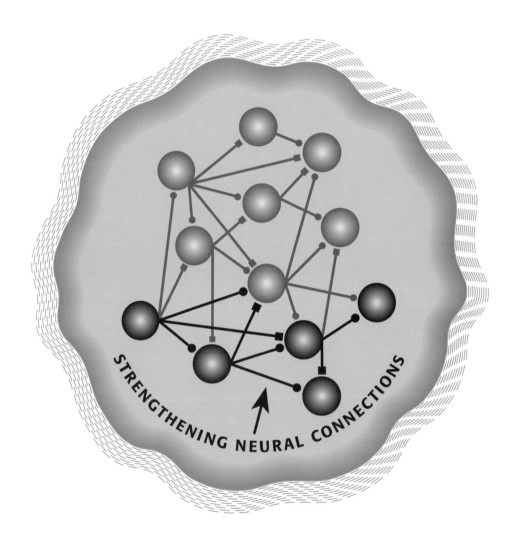

Rather than simply picturing neural connections in the *organic brain*, Figure 2.9 illustrates a *mental schema* itself – as a set of categories and their interrelationships. Recall: If a person doesn't have a category for knowing something, for all intents and purposes, it doesn't exist. It should also be mentioned that each category in a schema/paradigm does not represent a one–to–one correspondence with a neural connection or an organic part in the brain. It is nevertheless convenient to illustrate a paradigm as a set of categories (nodes) and the potential relationships between them (lines), which include causes, effects, sequences, associations, and expectations of one category versus another, as the *evolving* mind.

FIGURE 2.9
The Evolving Paradigm in the Mind

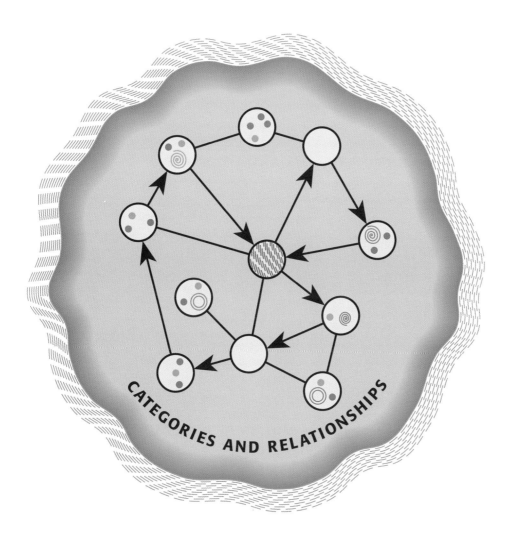

As illustrated in Figure 2.9, a category may be "empty" if no current sensory data – or past memory or thought experiment – fits its purview. Furthermore, if a category identifies matter as separate particles, that is all that will be apparent. But if an existing category includes the elementary waves and particles that create all the matter/energy in spacetime, these quantum ingredients will be available for seeing, thinking, and behaving. Moreover, a *paradigm shift* means that altogether new categories are being invented for seeing what was not seen earlier, preexisting categories that are no longer practical or accurate are being erased – and, consequently, the relationships between the old and new categories must be redefined (and redrawn) as well. *A human mind evolves through these paradigm shifts.*

The symbolic description of a paradigm displayed in Figure 2.9 can also represent a *phase* between the categories in the old paradigm versus the categories in the new paradigm. On the one hand, such an ambivalent worldview might persevere *at the edge of chaos* between these two dueling paradigms. On the other hand, if we use quantum thinking, this puzzling solution might eventually self-organize into an unusual integration of the two paradigms – into an entirely new *strange attractor*. But either way, being very explicit about the categories of the paradigm in the mind enhances self-aware consciousness, self-transformation, and human evolution.

PARADIGMS FOR ORGANIZATIONS

The seven essential categories that define the old and new paradigms are appropriate not only to physical objects but also to human beings. These categories, however, need to be explicitly translated for people working in organizations – in a language that does not use the scientific terminology originally selected for describing the motion of objects and particles. For the sake of convenience, only the titles for the divergent categories in the two dueling paradigms are reproduced here; the reader is referred back to Chapter 1, pages 17–19 and 48–50, for the unabridged versions.

1   THE DUALISTIC SEPARATION OF CONSCIOUSNESS/MATTER –
     THE MONISTIC UNIFICATION OF CONSCIOUSNESS WITH MATTER

2   THE UNIVERSE AS THE MOTION OF INERT MOLAR OBJECTS –
     UNIVERSES AS MATERIALIZED BY CONSCIOUS PARTICIPATION

3   THE SPACE BETWEEN MOLAR OBJECTS AS FLAT AND EMPTY –
     SPACETIME AS CURVED AND FILLED WITH MATTER/ENERGY

4   THE UNIQUE EXISTENCE OF ONLY ONE ABSOLUTE UNIVERSE —
    THE NATURAL SELECTION OF MANY RELATIVISTIC UNIVERSES

5   THE DETERMINISTIC CERTAINTY OF INERT MOLAR OBJECTS —
    THE PROBABILISTIC UNCERTAINTY OF SELF-MOTION MONADS

6   THE FUNDAMENTAL SEPARATION OF INERT MOLAR OBJECTS —
    THE ETERNAL CONNECTIONS AMONG SELF-MOTION MONADS

7   THE EVENTUAL DEATH OF THE ONE ABSOLUTE UNIVERSE —
    THE ETERNAL SELF-ORGANIZATION OF RELATIVISTIC UNIVERSES

Although they are subjective, here are proposed translations of key words from the physical sciences into analogous terms that are particular and relevant to organizations:

dualistic separation	=	exclusion of consciousness
monistic unification	=	inclusion of consciousness
matter/consciousness	=	design of formal systems
matter with consciousness	=	self-designing systems
unique existence	=	unconscious administration
natural selection	=	conscious self-management
universe	=	organization
absolute	=	rigidly structured
relativistic	=	flexibly designed
inert molar objects	=	passive jobholders
self-motion monads	=	active participants
motion of objects	=	following official procedures
materialized consciously	=	self-designing processes
space	=	white space in formal systems
spacetime	=	cross-boundary processes
flat and empty	=	implicitly ignored
curved and filled	=	explicitly addressed
filled with matter/energy	=	infused with information
deterministic certainty	=	external control
probabilistic uncertainty	=	internal commitment
fundamental separation	=	enforced segregation
timeless connections	=	empowered relations
death	=	self-destruction
self-organization	=	self-transformation

The seven contradictory categories for the two dueling paradigms – *rewritten exclusively for organizational settings* – are represented below. For the purpose of achieving clarity, however, first I list the essential categories for the Newtonian organization (numbered N1 to N7) and then later I list the essential categories for the quantum organization (numbered Q1 to Q7).

The Newtonian Organization

N1   THE EXCLUSION OF CONSCIOUSNESS IN THE DESIGN OF FORMAL SYSTEMS

N2   THE ORGANIZATION AS PASSIVE JOBHOLDERS FOLLOWING OFFICIAL PROCEDURES

N3   THE WHITE SPACE BETWEEN PASSIVE JOBHOLDERS AS IMPLICITLY IGNORED

N4   THE UNCONSCIOUS ADMINISTRATION OF A RIGIDLY STRUCTURED ORGANIZATION

N5   THE EXTERNAL CONTROL OF PASSIVE JOBHOLDERS

N6   THE ENFORCED SEGREGATION OF PASSIVE JOBHOLDERS

N7   THE EVENTUAL SELF-DESTRUCTION OF A RIGIDLY STRUCTURED ORGANIZATION

As a total set, these seven categories describe the root of what has often been defined as *bureaucratic* or *mechanistic organizations*. These qualities summarize why such organizations would be challenged by a fast-paced, competitive, interconnected, global economy. A Newtonian organization is designed to be perfectly rigid and completely structured; its jobholders sooner or later become passive from being externally controlled by their unconscious administrators. These jobholders are commanded to exactly follow official procedures without any concern for connections with other jobs or departments in the organization. Employees blindly perform their roles with little self-awareness or consciousness. In the extreme, the entire organization remains locked on autopilot. The likelihood of monitoring and then adapting to a challenging environment, therefore, is quite low. Eventually, the Newtonian organization self-destructs.

Figure 2.10 reveals the classical organization chart that has become the trademark of our bureaucratic, mechanistic, Newtonian organizations. Each *shaded box* on the chart designates a formal department or the official office of jobholders. These formal departments have specific, well-defined charters outlining the scope of their tasks and objectives. The jobholders associated with each shaded box are assigned official, exact, detailed job descriptions and standard operating procedures. The chain of command or lines of authority are shown by the *solid lines* between the boxes: who reports to whom and who is in charge of which department or job. Most often, there are several levels in this command–and–control, *administrative and management hierarchy*. Note: The empty space between departments and between jobs is the *white space* on the organization's chart – whatever task or problem does not belong within any department's responsibility and, therefore, "falls between the cracks." Essentially, the shaded boxes and the solid lines are the key categories and relationships, respectively, of the old paradigm by which jobholders see, think, and behave.

FIGURE 2.10
The Newtonian Organization

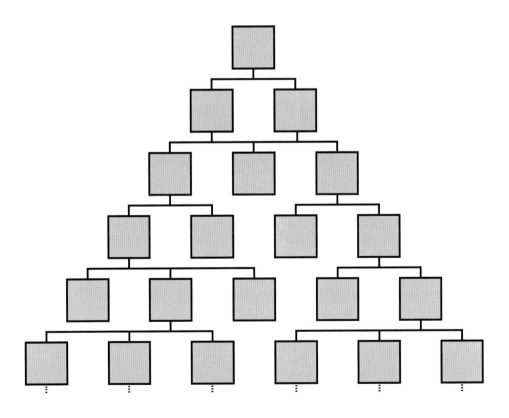

Shortly, we will itemize and describe the attributes of the quantum organization. But first let's experience an image of this new organization and see how different it looks from the Newtonian one. Figure 2.11 gives a symbolic portrayal of this radically new kind of organization among the quantum waves and particles that incorporate spacetime. As can be seen, shaded boxes (blinders) are replaced by clear (self–aware) circles; the solid lines characterizing hierarchy are replaced with dotted lines representing interrelationships and interconnections; the white space is converted into the living, breathing global economy: Mother Earth. *The structure of this new organization is the evolving paradigm in the mind* (see Figure 2.9, page 63).

FIGURE 2.11
The Quantum Organization

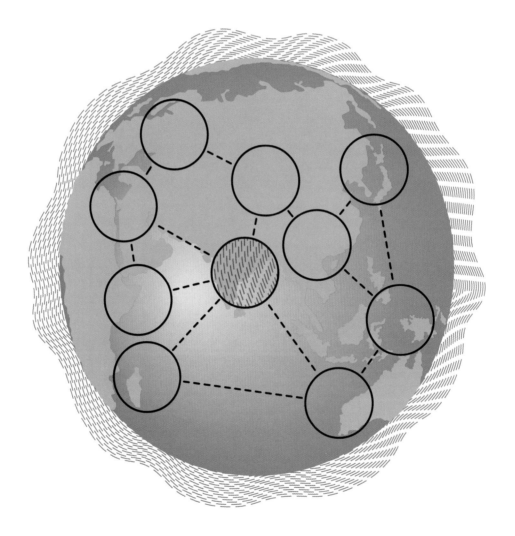

CHAPTER 2

The Quantum Organization

Q1   THE INCLUSION OF CONSCIOUSNESS IN SELF-DESIGNING SYSTEMS

Q2   ORGANIZATIONS AS CONSCIOUS PARTICIPANTS ACTIVELY INVOLVED IN SELF-DESIGNING PROCESSES

Q3   CROSS-BOUNDARY PROCESSES AS EXPLICITLY ADDRESSED AND INFUSED WITH INFORMATION

Q4   THE CONSCIOUS SELF-MANAGEMENT OF A FLEXIBLY DESIGNED ORGANIZATION

Q5   THE INTERNAL COMMITMENT OF ACTIVE PARTICIPANTS

Q6   THE EMPOWERED RELATIONS AMONG ACTIVE PARTICIPANTS

Q7   THE ETERNAL SELF-TRANSFORMATION OF FLEXIBLY DESIGNED ORGANIZATIONS

As a total set, these seven categories represent a revolutionary, new organization – one that is organically matched with a living, competitive, global economy. Numerous phrasings have been proposed to define this new type of organization: the empowered organization, organic–adaptive organization, network organization, horizontal organization, knowledge-creating organization, and learning organization. Presumably because of its newness, there is little consensus concerning what this organization is really like or what to call it. It is not at all clear, for example, whether any existing organizations can serve as useful prototypes. Yet it is worthwhile to describe the potential attributes of this radically new organization.

Q1   THE INCLUSION OF CONSCIOUSNESS IN SELF-DESIGNING SYSTEMS
All employed members of a quantum organization would be energetically involved in the design of their formal systems (which includes strategy, structure, and reward systems) – which might also incorporate the active participation of prime external stakeholders (suppliers and customers, for example). This widespread participation means that members' hands–on knowledge regarding their work in the organization (including their skills, interests, and experiences) will affect how strategy, structure, and reward

systems are designed – and aligned – with one another. And when these designed systems are put into practice, these members will be in the best position to understand the daily context of implementation and thereby how to make their formal systems work. They also will be more likely to *accept* the design of the systems as well as the process of implementation (and therefore be committed to its success) if their insights and experience have been respected, represented, and genuinely used from beginning to end. Naturally, if other relevant stakeholders have also been included in the design and implementation process, formal systems are more likely to be aligned with their needs and wants. *This proactive, widespread, participative approach to the redesign of formal systems makes the best use of the self-awareness and consciousness of members and other key stakeholders – which is the premier attribute of a quantum organization.*

The ordinary approach is for members to design formal systems on autopilot – with limited insight, reflection, and creativity. These and other uniquely human qualities can only deliver their tremendous potential via self-aware consciousness. What often occurs in Newtonian organizations, however, may be even worse: Here, formal systems are typically designed by higher-level senior managers with meager participation by lower-level jobholders who will determine the success or failure of implementation. Perhaps even more incomprehensible, however, is when these uninvolved jobholders are then required to follow all official procedures to the letter even though they don't understand them.

Q2 ORGANIZATIONS AS CONSCIOUS PARTICIPANTS ACTIVELY INVOLVED IN SELF-DESIGNING PROCESSES Actively involved members of a quantum organization would also use their self-aware consciousness for designing value-added processes (which would include strategic, management, and business processes that can be described, controlled, and improved). The conscious participation by all relevant internal and external stakeholders would help ensure that the organization's core processes will satisfy the needs and requirements of all its constituencies – which complements the same widespread participation in self-designing formal systems.

Through greater self-awareness and consciousness, members would also be more reflective about their self-processes. Aside from performing, members would be internally motivated to get in touch with their *learning processes* – to study ways to *improve their improvement processes*. This concept of organizational learning will be investigated in more detail later. For now, it is enough to appreciate that a key element of organizational learning is *self-reflection* about how members acquire and use knowledge. This positive focus on learning in a quantum organization is in significant contrast to Newtonian organizations, in which attention is concentrated on following well-established procedures – not attempting to improve them per se, let alone considering how to achieve better (and faster) improvement during the next cycle.

Q3 CROSS-BOUNDARY PROCESSES AS EXPLICITLY ADDRESSED AND INFUSED WITH INFORMATION Another valuable attribute is further based on the self-aware consciousness of members (and other key stakeholders). Continuous, conscious, focused attention would be directed to what flows "between the cracks" – whether processes, information, responsibilities, or behavior and attitudes. A cooperative effort would have been undertaken to self-design and then implement formal systems and processes so that members can focus all their wisdom and energy on the most strategically valued work. In our interconnected global marketplace, however, it is just not possible to organize work into perfectly contained, independent work units (whether jobs, departments, or whole organizations). *Some vital work, therefore, will always be flowing across formal boundaries at all levels – fractals – in an organization.*

A quantum organization, therefore, examines all its cross-boundary processes to manage these "cracks" in the most efficient and effective way possible. Declarations such as "it's not my problem," "it's not my job," and "it's not my department's responsibility" would rarely, if ever, be heard in a quantum organization. Instead, the *filled space* on the organization chart would be regarded as presenting new possibilities for integrating systems and processes as well as entirely new ways to solve old problems – which previously were addressed separately and, thus, incompletely.

Equally significant, members and other key stakeholders would also be consciously aware of early-warning signals that could identify when a redesign of their current systems and processes is justified. Since the most *interdependent* decisions and tasks can best be performed by members who work collaboratively within the same subunit, *it is necessary to know when to redesign cross-boundary processes into within-subunit processes.* In fact, the required information that is needed to make the right decision on structure resides *between* the formal work units in an organization. Members and other key stakeholders, therefore, must see, think, and behave not just according to the well-defined fragments on an organization chart but also in tune with the ill-defined connections – and essential information – that is invisibly infused in the filled space between subunits. *What happens behind the scenes, between the lines, and below the surface must be managed explicitly.*

Q4 THE CONSCIOUS SELF-MANAGEMENT OF A FLEXIBLY DESIGNED ORGANIZATION All members of a quantum organization would be active participants in self-managing their systems and processes just as soon as they have been designed and implemented. Of course, the inputs and the active involvement of other prime stakeholders would also be included in self-managing the quantum organization. Thus, as opposed to high–level managers taking charge of daily planning, decision making, monitoring, evaluating, and changing, the members of subunits themselves would be responsible for these management functions. Recruiting, hiring, training, educating, developing, retaining, and promoting members would also be the responsibility of the subunit itself. And as circumstances change, the members of these work units would likewise be actively involved in both formulating and implementing improvements in systems and processes. As such, the subunits in a quantum organization would remain especially resilient so that they could easily be redesigned as needed. Keep in mind, however, that self-managing each subunit must necessarily occur within the existing paradigm; therefore, it is not transformational (paradigmatic) change. Transformation can only be achieved by all members *self-designing* (and not just self-managing) their systems and processes.

Self-management does not flourish in the Newtonian organization. Virtually all the traditional management functions (planning, controlling, organizing, budgeting, recruiting, and evaluating) take place top down – *external* to formal work units – with virtually zero input from jobholders. Similar to the familiar effects of an autocratic design of formal systems or management processes, jobholders remain passive, uninvolved, and thus uninformed about the management of their own subunits.

Q5 THE INTERNAL COMMITMENT OF ACTIVE PARTICIPANTS Members of a quantum organization are passionately committed to the additional enhancement of their self-awareness and consciousness – as the primary ingredient of long–term organizational success. Naturally, such profound changes in the mind also bring about corresponding organic changes in the brain. Members would be not only entirely conscious of this but also receptive to new opportunities for mental and organic improvements – in order to enhance their *quantum thinking*. Consequently, avenues inside and outside the organization would be made accessible so all members could continuously enhance their minds/brains. During educational programs, members would actively encourage themselves (and their stakeholders) to scrutinize their *self-knowledge* – in order to foster self-identity, self-esteem, and self-worth. By attempting to pinpoint and improve these underlying aspects of self–awareness and consciousness, members will be capable of focusing their time and energy on the important problems and processes of the organization – instead of being drained by psychological defense mechanisms or self–defeating interpersonal solutions (for the purpose of *protecting* rather than *applying* the self). Therefore, a *deep internal commitment to self-discovery* prepares all members to contribute to something larger than themselves: a complicated undertaking that can only be accomplished by a collaborative effort among self–aware participants.

Not surprisingly, Newtonian organizations have no reason or place for self–awareness and consciousness. Such topics are considered strictly private matters: to take place far away from the job and to be kept there. Only those "hired parts" of jobholders that specifically pertain to official procedures are accepted as under the jurisdiction – and control – of an organization. Indeed, in a Newtonian organization, it would be regarded as highly inappropriate and possibly unethical to command jobholders to enhance their self-knowledge regarding how they see, think, and behave. And Newtonian jobholders would be unlikely to explicitly question their implicit assumptions – the old paradigm – underneath the rigid systems and inflexible procedures that guide their daily work.

Q6 THE EMPOWERED RELATIONS AMONG ACTIVE PARTICIPANTS The members in a quantum organization would maintain their relationships with all the other members they have ever worked with before, including members in other subunits and external stakeholders – notwithstanding transfers, promotions, restructurings, reorganizations, and consolidations. Forming, developing, and sustaining both within–group and across–group relationships empowers organization–wide commitment and thus fosters a greater potential for systemwide collaboration. Furthermore, preserving cross-boundary connections permits members to proactively manage the filled space between formal systems and processes. Consequently, rather than identifying this in–between space as *white space, empty space, open space,* or *someone else's space*, it is essential that members retain mutual ownership of what lies between them – so they will be committed to self–managing whatever flows across the boundaries.

Incidentally, nurturing human connections across the whole planet is precisely what encourages the effective functioning of a *global* quantum organization – in which relationships across *national* boundaries become the basis for holistic missions that one organization, on its own, could not possibly realize. Many of our planet's most complex social, political, and economic problems – which disjointed Newtonian institutions have been unable to manage successfully – can perhaps be resolved more effectively by a collaborative network of quantum organizations. All the connections among these entities is what allows them to self-organize into innovative arrangements for *collective action.* This global, collective action would be the apotheosis of Max Planck's pioneering concept of *quanta of action,* which he created to explain the ultraviolet catastrophe (see pages 19–20). Currently, the evolution of our planet to higher forms of consciousness necessitates that we resolve these other, potentially more devastating, catastrophes as well – with collaborative networks of quantum organizations.

Q7 THE ETERNAL SELF-TRANSFORMATION OF FLEXIBLY DESIGNED ORGANIZATIONS The members of a quantum organization would surely embrace the unmistakable need to *continually transform themselves along with their systems and processes.* Cycles of self-transformation would preserve the organization's life – although its transformed missions and forms might not be recognizable from its preceding incarnations. As an alternative to Newtonian organizations dying a disturbing death (resulting in job loss, hostile feelings, and eroding trust in the community of future members), the evolving organization deliberately maintains and nourishes the trust, commitment, and creativity of its past, present, and prospective members. These *transpersonal connections* are precisely what allows current members to focus their quantum thinking on complex problems and processes, rather than being impeded by ignorance, mistrust, or inexperience. The evolved organization's former cultural heroes, for example, would provide current members with eternal links to the useful knowledge and best practices of the past – instead of abruptly eliminating the history of the organization with its premature self-destruction. Transforming into renewed/reformed organizations via creative mergers, acquisitions, joint ventures, and global networks thus preserves and builds upon the vast reservoir of knowledge and experience of past and present members. *Ultimately, this significant gain in useful knowledge about self-transformation adds to the greater reservoir of universal consciousness – and human evolution.*

Now that I have described the attributes of a quantum organization, a challenging question arises: how to transform a Newtonian organization (whose members see, think, and behave in concert with the old paradigm) into a quantum organization (whose members thrive harmoniously with the new paradigm). If we don't answer this question, the seven attributes of a quantum organization will remain as mere rhetoric, with little chance of achieving self-transformation. *So let's move on to action.*

An Overview of Self-Transformation

During the past several decades, a diversity of methods has been used for improving and transforming organizations. The popular approaches have been designated as follows: strategic change, repositioning, consolidating, restructuring, reorganizing, delayering, downsizing, rightsizing, employee training and development, management education, incentive and reward systems, cultural change, climate building, team building, customer focus, market orientation, product innovation, total quality management (TQM), business process reengineering (BPR), and organizational learning.

Often these terms are used synonymously with transformation. But an important distinction must be made: If a change initiative is intended to improve an organization *within the existing paradigm*, then it cannot be a transformational effort. Only if an explicit attempt is made to first identify the existing paradigm, next delineate the new paradigm, and then switch from the old to the new paradigm by restructuring how all members see, think, and behave can a change initiative be transformational in nature. And if there's no mention of old versus new paradigm, it is probably safe to assume that no transformational change was ever anticipated or likely to occur.

When managers are first exposed to the inflexible and demoralizing attributes of the Newtonian organization, they usually proclaim that their organizations are not like that – particularly if they come from the higher levels of the management hierarchy. They proceed to describe the various change initiatives they have already implemented in their organizations during the past years (identical to the ones listed above) and then assume they must be moving toward the new paradigm. They also profess several attributes of a quantum organization to support their position (including participative management, employee involvement, and cross–functional teams). Yet they acknowledge that several of these quantum attributes are foreign to them or suggest "maybe it's just semantics."

As soon as the same kind of discussion is held with the lower–level jobholders, however, these frontline employees steadfastly assert that the attributes of the Newtonian organization are alive and well in their own organization! They provide many examples to illustrate rigidly structured systems, meaningless procedures, and unconscious administrators. When they are asked about the separate change initiatives that have supposedly been implemented, these jobholders promptly respond: "It's pretty ironic, isn't it? The more things they try to change (using a top–down approach), the more they keep things the same (the Newtonian organization)."

Figure 2.12 shows the starting point for genuinely proceeding with transformation: explicitly describing the deficiencies of the old paradigm (what is) versus the potential for the new paradigm (what should be) and then identifying the gap between them. Transformation is thus planning and implementing change initiatives to close this gap – so that members can see, think, and behave according to a new organizational reality. This gap, incidentally, pertains to all members and other key stakeholders, not just to top management. For everyone, *the categories in the mind and the neural networks in the brain must be restructured/rewired* – by adding categories, erasing others, and then redefining the relationships between them.

FIGURE 2.12
Identifying the Transformation Gap

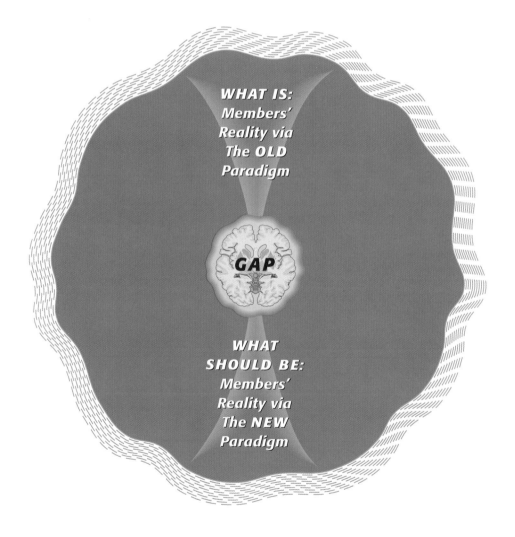

Probably the most misunderstood and inadvertently self–defeating aspects of transformation are (1) deciding which change initiatives to use and (2) deciding on the sequence in which the chosen change efforts will be implemented in an organization. Many approaches have been used for making these two significant decisions. *The adhoc approach* is definitely the most prevalent. In this case, each change initiative is chosen primarily by happenstance: who introduced it, which other organizations are using it, and what people have read about it. If this one change initiative doesn't lead to satisfactory outcomes (and we will see momentarily why a single effort cannot possibly succeed at modifying how all members see, think, and behave), then another change initiative is attempted – also based on who happened to propose it, what other organizations have tried it, and what managers have learned about it. This self–defeating cycle of *quick-fix* change programs is well known and has been documented extensively: It is activated by unconscious administrators who are pressed for time, need immediate results, and unconsciously view the change process and their organization from strictly within the Cartesian–Newtonian Paradigm.

Another approach for deciding which change efforts to implement in what order has been termed the *shotgun approach*. In this latter case, the organization implements several if not many change activities all at once, expecting that the whole set will somehow address the root causes of "the problem." The theory behind this approach is quite simple: If one change program doesn't have the right result, maybe another one (implemented simultaneously) will. It is rather universal for organizational members to confess that a great variety of change initiatives are currently underway. But the most likely outcome for these shotgun activities is confusion and frustration. In most cases, these multiple change efforts are implemented separately from one another – thus leading to mixed signals (as to which change effort is actually the number one priority), conflicted signals (one change initiative, if taken very seriously, contradicts what another change effort requires of members), and duplicated activities (members partake in repeated conversations on the same issues within several different change programs). Not surprisingly, the shotgun approach gives the appearance that the organization is really trying to improve things, but it most often backfires – because of all the confusion it creates by mixed and conflicted messages and the frustration it causes when members continue to discuss meaningful issues in different programs but to no avail.

The third approach for deciding which change efforts to implement in what sequence requires a deep understanding of how to bring about a genuine paradigm shift and hence real transformational change: starting with jobholders who are currently functioning as inert molar objects in a Newtonian organization and concluding with transformed members who have evolved into self-motion monads in a quantum organization. This approach utilizes a diversity of change initiatives that cover a wide range of dimensions – all integrated into a well-planned, carefully orchestrated sequence of change activities. Referred to as a *completely integrated program,* this approach is fundamentally different from the adhoc and the shotgun approaches for choosing and sequencing change initiatives.

As an alternative to a repeat cycle of singular quick fixes or a bunch of all-at-once stabs with many change initiatives, a completely integrated program explicitly considers (1) the interrelationship of the key attributes of an organization that shape how people see, think, and behave – which includes all formal systems as well as value-added processes; (2) the root, underlying cultural waves of an organization that have to be functioning effectively *before* systems and processes can be fundamentally improved – which recognizes that the foundational infrastructures of an organization must first be prepared for creating and implementing change in systems and processes; (3) the change initiatives that must be conducted together because they are highly interrelated and therefore must be aligned with, and reinforce, one another – which include, for example, how structure must support the strategic objectives of the organization, which must also be sanctioned by the reward system; and (4) that the process of planning and implementing transformation is guided by a clear understanding of the consequential gap between the old paradigm and the new paradigm. This latter point stresses that the change process must be implemented so that jobholders can purposely evolve to become self-motion monads who are consistently supported by the legitimate authority in the organization. This vital support from the traditional powers-that-be must be sustained in sufficient magnitude even as the source of authority shifts from *external control* by leaders, managers, and administrators to the *internal commitment* of self-managing subunits throughout the organization.

The *guiding light* for helping old Newtonian organizations transform into new quantum organizations shows that only a completely integrated program can possibly achieve self-transformation. At best, the adhoc and shotgun approaches can bring about only evolutionary change *within the existing paradigm.* At their worst, the two shot-in-the-dark approaches will undermine the credibility of senior management and the capacity of the organization to succeed at transformation: When members witness either one failed attempt after another or experience a barrage of disorganized change efforts, they lose faith in others – and in themselves.

It should now be apparent that utilizing only one or a few change initiatives is not likely to accomplish *real* transformation – even under the best of circumstances. Since behavior in all organizations is influenced by infrastructures, systems, and processes, an integrated – holistic – approach is needed to significantly change the minds/brains of members: how they see, think, and behave. Figure 2.13 displays *three transformational components* under the full control of an organization that exist within a *global context*, which is not under immediate control. The three components include the entire complex of attributes that shape organizational behavior – which is essential for developing a completely integrated program.

FIGURE 2.13
The Components and Context of Transformation

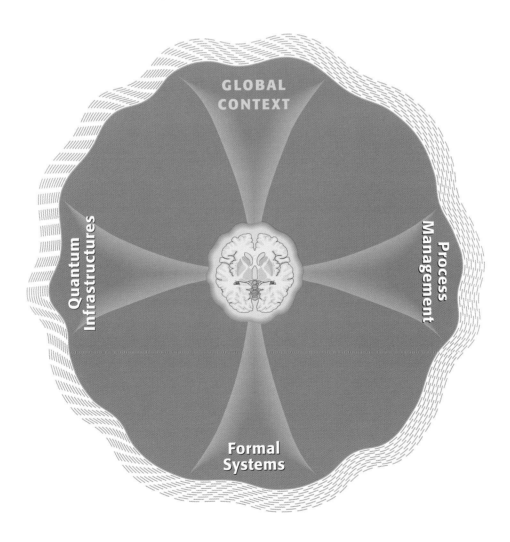

Figure 2.14 arranges change initiatives into the three components of transformation. Quantum infrastructures expand the belief that members can learn to interact with one another as self-motion monads – who are capable of self-awareness and self-managing their *culture, skills, and teams.* Formal systems examine the documents that pinpoint direction, how all resources are organized into action, and what incentives are available for all members: *strategy, structure, and rewards.* Process management focuses on *gradual process improvement* within the existing formation of subunits, *radical process improvement* by redesigning structure around processes, and *learning process improvement* for better and faster improvement thereafter.

FIGURE 2.14
Organizing Change Initiatives

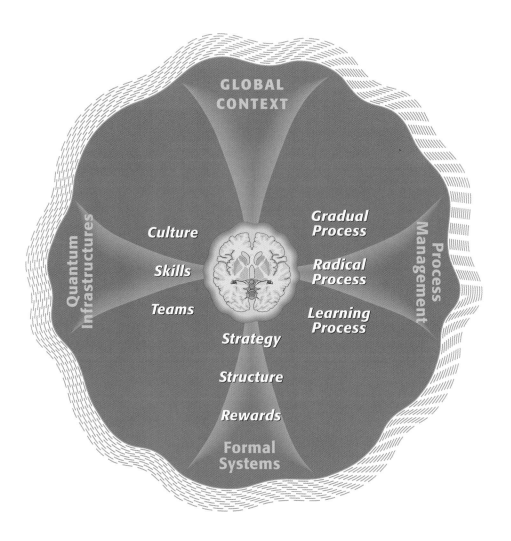

The remaining question is how to sequence the three components of transformation into one completely integrated program. Young's (1976) integration of the evolution of universal consciousness into a *sequential arc* provides a powerful framework for organizing change initiatives to attain self–aware consciousness in organizations. Figure 2.15 summarizes Young's sequential arc, which originates with light, which creates nuclear particles, which form atoms, which become two types of molecules. *Organic molecules* then evolve into plants, which evolve into animals, which further evolve into people. Young's theory effectively describes *the fall* from free light into inert matter and then *the rise* from living matter to human enlightenment.

FIGURE 2.15
The Evolution of Consciousness

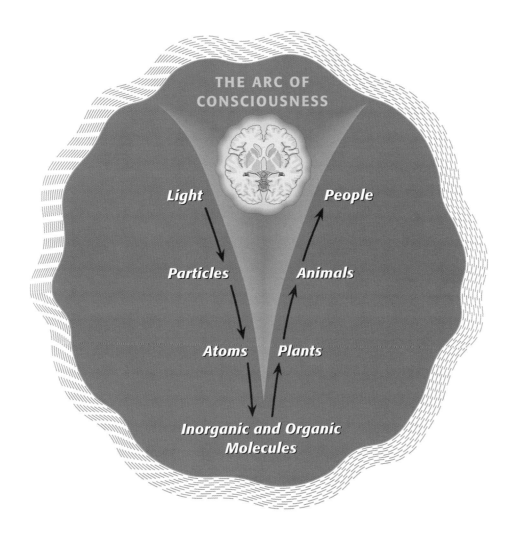

As shown in Figure 2.16, the fall from light (complete freedom) into atoms (constrained choice) thus becomes the *infrastructure* for organic and inorganic entities in nature. Inert molar objects – as compacted *systems* of molecules – embody the least amount of freedom and, therefore, can be completely explained, predicted, and controlled. The sequential arc then outlines the rise from molecules to plants (with more freedom than inert objects) all the way up to people (who can potentially create self-motion *processes* analogous to photons and nuclear particles). People also have the potential to attain higher forms of self-awareness and consciousness via quantum thinking in their minds/brains.

FIGURE 2.16
Sequencing the Evolution of Consciousness

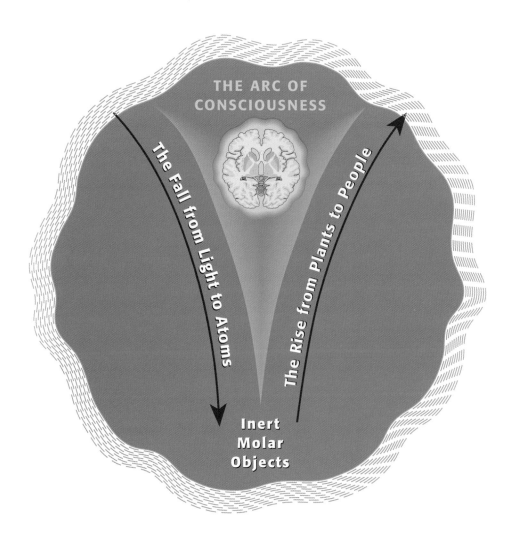

Figure 2.17 introduces the *arc of transformation* for sequencing all the change initiatives that sort into the three components of transformation. When applied to members in organizations, according to the evolution of human consciousness, *quantum infrastructures* should first be established in order to generate self–aware consciousness for all members and other key stakeholders. Drawing upon their self–awareness, quantum thinking, and collaborative teamwork, members would then be able to self–design their *formal systems*. When these reformulated systems have been implemented successfully, members can further enhance performance, self–knowledge, and enlightenment by consciously improving *process management*.

FIGURE 2.17
Sequencing the Components of Transformation

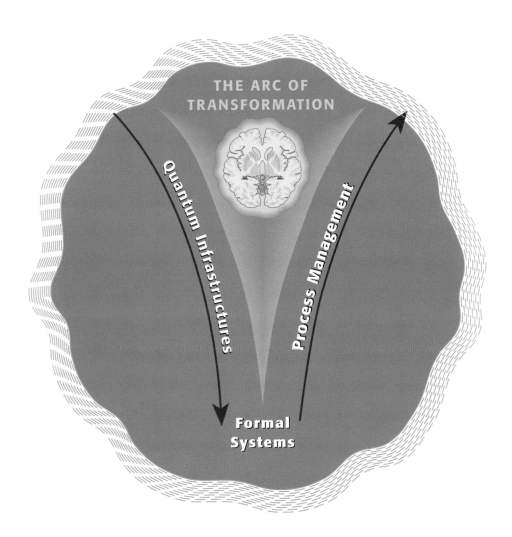

Figure 2.18 presents the arc according to a particular sequencing of change initiatives, or tracks, as we will refer to them. Simply put, a *track* is a well–orchestrated set of change activities that allow members and other key stakeholders to self–transform their organization. Initially the culture, skills, and team tracks, in sequence, produce *the fall* to the formal systems and documents in an organization (corresponding to molar objects in the physical universe). Then the gradual process, radical process, and learning process tracks create *the rise* to the quintessence of human enlightenment: self–knowledge, self–renewal, and continuously enhancing consciousness. *The eight tracks — in sequence — are the embodiment of self-transformation.*

FIGURE 2.18
The Eight Tracks to Self-Transformation

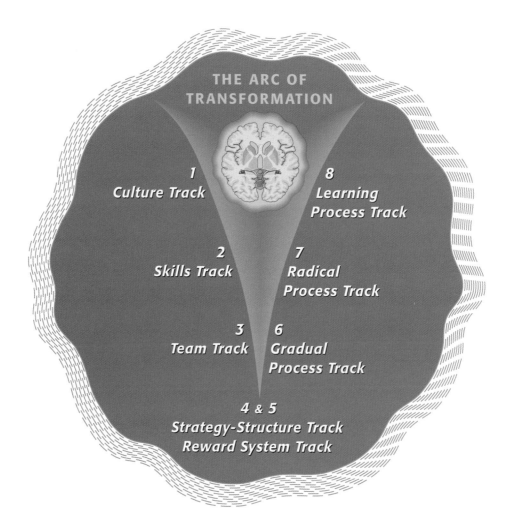

THE ARC OF
TRANSFORMATION

1
Culture Track

8
Learning
Process Track

2
Skills Track

7
Radical
Process Track

3
Team Track

6
Gradual
Process Track

4 & 5
Strategy-Structure Track
Reward System Track

Summarizing the Eight Tracks

The eight tracks are actually designed to address the three components of transformation: The first three tracks (culture, skills, and team tracks) are conducted to establish well-functioning *quantum infrastructures* in subunits all around an organization. The middle two tracks (strategy–structure and reward system tracks) are implemented to redesign the *formal systems* in an organization. The last three tracks (gradual process, radical process, and learning process tracks) are administered in order to describe, control, and improve value-added processes – which is called *process management*.

Consider the first three tracks of the completely integrated program: The *culture track* nurtures trust, communication, information sharing, and a willingness to change among all members: the conditions that must exist before any other change initiatives can succeed. The *skills track* provides all members with improved ways of engaging with people and problems. In particular, all members learn how to work effectively with diverse people, complex problems, and implicit assumptions and, thereby, learn quantum thinking. The *team track* ingrains the new culture and enhanced skills into every work unit within the organization – transferring what is learned in relatively safe workshop settings thoroughly into the everyday workplace. Note: Everyone in the organization must actively participate in these first three tracks – to establish quantum infrastructures that empower all other aspects of self-transformation.

Consider the middle two tracks (effectively building on the recently achieved organization-wide quantum infrastructures). The *strategy–structure track* first creates either a new or an improved strategic architecture for the organization. Second, it restructures divisions, departments, work groups, and jobs – including all necessary resources – in order to achieve strategic objectives. The *reward system track* proceeds to design a performance-based reward system that will sustain all improvements by formally sanctioning a healthy culture, the use of enhanced skills, and cooperative team efforts within and across all work units. Besides metrics that capture individual, subunit, and organizational performance, the reward system track further develops metrics to assess individual and group contributions to process improvements (which pinpoints the rate of organizational learning) once the process tracks are underway. Note: Two cross-boundary task forces of roughly twenty-five members each, which represent all areas, levels, and locations in the existing (or newly formed) structure, are appointed to the strategy–structure and reward system tracks (one task force for each track) to self-design the new quantum organization.

The last three tracks provide steps for gradual process improvement (also known as *total quality management*), radical process improvement (also defined as *business process reengineering*), and learning process improvement (for becoming a *learning organization*). These three tracks are heavily rooted in a process view of work: since the process *determines* the results, the best way to improve results is to improve the underlying process. In addition, increasing the rate at which an organization can gradually and radically improve its core processes defines the goal of organizational learning.

The *gradual process track* provides monthly workshop sessions for all members to master how to describe, control, and improve core processes within their subunits – often with process flowcharts (diagrams), statistical process control, and an ample assortment of quality tools. Once everyone in an organization is accustomed to seeing and improving their work as a process, the *radical process track* commissions cross-boundary task forces to describe, control, and improve major business processes – which includes the possibility of restructuring work units into a horizontal organization (while collaborating with the strategy-structure track). Most important, if members have become accustomed to *gradual* process improvement and understand the value of process management *within their subunits*, they are more likely to deeply understand – and accept – the rationale for radically redesigning structures around value-added processes.

Once an organization has moved through a number of cycles – and successes – at gradual and radical process improvement, the *learning process track* pinpoints and then spreads useful knowledge about what has been learned throughout the organization. With this track, monthly workshop sessions provide all members with the primary concepts and methods for effective learning *before* they are capable of improving learning processes by themselves. For purposes of definition, a *learning organization* explicitly describes, controls, and improves the core processes by which knowledge is acquired, distributed, stored, retrieved, and used – within and across all subunits – in order to achieve organizational success.

While the customary focus of process improvement is on workflow (which occurs *between* members and their work units), it is also important to accept the mental/emotional processes that occur *within* each member. Continual pressure for gradual and radical improvement can take a great toll on the human mind, because most people experience change as loss – and as a major threat to who they are and what they have accomplished. One feature of the learning process track, therefore, is helping members to improve their minds/brains. In the process, they will be able to cope with change – better and faster – with more confidence and self-awareness.

Sequencing the Eight Tracks

The sequence of eight tracks is one of the most fundamental principles of self-transformation to understand – and honor. Even though it might be tempting to try to improve things by first modifying the formal aspects of the organization (strategy–structure and the reward system), this approach inevitably results in a failed outcome. *Changing formal systems on paper cannot possibly result in genuine change on the job – unless members are willing and able to change how they see, think, and behave.* Indeed, if there is widespread mistrust, defensive communication, a withholding of information, inadequate skills for solving complex problems, and little cooperation across departments (the traditional attributes of a Newtonian organization), then better formal systems can be neither designed nor implemented.

Just reflect on the frequent group discussions in which members are asked to express their real opinions about the need for change in general or a proposed change initiative in particular. In the public setting of such a meeting, members declare the politically correct responses – or they say little or nothing at all. But when the meeting concludes and members go their separate ways, they chitchat about their real opinions and feelings: "This discussion of change is a joke! We go through this nonsense every time the numbers don't look good. When will they [the executives] realize that everyone is going to have a good laugh as soon as they hear about the *fourth program of the year?*"

Now consider the increasing role that cross–boundary task forces or project teams have in most organizations today. Although the design of a cross–functional group might look good on paper (as a listing of talented and diverse members from a number of work units in the organization), the anticipated collaboration may never materialize when these members meet face to face. Why? Mistrust, a withholding of information, defensive communication, suppressing disagreements in open meetings, and lack of cooperation or teamwork (determined by a dysfunctional infrastructure) frustrate the needed exchanges across boundaries. *Before* cross–functional teams are formed and mobilized into action, therefore, the culture, skills, and team tracks should be implemented so that all members can use their diverse abilities and energies to serve the interests of the organization and its external stakeholders – instead of their self-protection.

Further, what if all members are not crystal clear about the strategic architecture of their organization and how strategic objectives have been operationalized into objectives for their subunits and goals for their jobs? Under such circumstances, what does it actually mean to expect members to concentrate on the value-added processes in their organization? What constitutes value-added processes can only be determined by prioritizing strategic objectives and *explicitly translating these priorities into performance goals* (which would be primarily addressed during the strategy-structure track). Moreover, if the existing reward system does not assess the performance of members with respect to the *full range* of their contributions to strategic objectives (which would be investigated by the reward system track), it is again highly unlikely that members will apply their abundant energy and talent on performing, let alone improving, the right strategic processes for the right customers at the right times. In this all too familiar predicament, TQM and reengineering will be inappropriate attempts that are doomed to fail – unless the quantum infrastructures and formal systems are already functioning well and moving the organization in a productive direction. Or consider the futility of this typical scenario: If an organization has not been successful with *gradual* process improvement (via TQM), what sense does it make to attempt *radical* process improvement (via reengineering)?

In addition, since several of these tracks are highly interconnected, implementing some of them simultaneously makes it considerably easier to coordinate their efforts. Let's consider, as one example, how the reward system must be designed to measure a variety of member contributions, so that employees will be motivated to achieve what each track offers for long-term organizational success. An ongoing dialogue across several task forces and workshop sessions can significantly help with operationalizing the criteria for job performance and in establishing a valid – acceptable – process of performance appraisal.

The reward system must effectively assess and reward (1) behavior that nurtures an adaptive culture, the use of enhanced skills, and effective teamwork within and across work units (culture, skills, and team tracks); (2) behavior that leads to the achievement of strategic objectives via valid measures/criteria for performance (strategy-structure track); (3) behavior that successfully administers the performance review system to augment member development and corporate performance (reward system track); (4) behavior that improves value-added business processes – both within and across subunits – and thus fosters customer satisfaction (gradual and radical process tracks); and (5) behavior that initially speeds up the rate of process improvement and then disperses this knowledge throughout the organization (learning process track). *But if the reward system is not designed to support the explicit purposes of all eight tracks (and, hence, all interrelated attributes of a quantum organization), it will unintentionally motivate jobholders to contribute only passive, narrowly focused, and misdirected behavior.*

Besides appreciating the sequence of eight tracks, it is also helpful to consider the expected time frame for each track. In most instances, a track does not have to be "completed" before the next track can begin. In fact, some tracks should be implemented simultaneously, since they should be coordinated with one another: the strategy–structure and reward system tracks, for example. Employing the metaphor of *railroad tracks*, Figure 2.19 summarizes a time schedule that is reasonably accurate for the first three tracks (for quantum infrastructures). The times for the subsequent tracks, however, are more difficult to predict because they concern very complex problems that are significantly affected by external stakeholders.

FIGURE 2.19
Scheduling the Eight Tracks

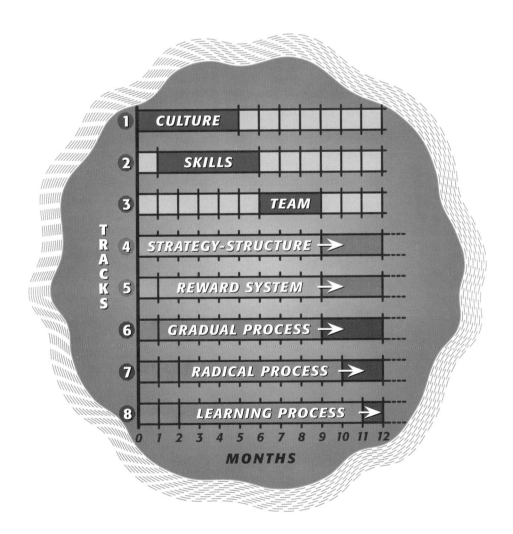

The railroad track metaphor might appear too precise or structured for self-transformation. But, as illustrated in Figure 2.20, the tracks should be considered as *quantum channels* through which all change initiatives are conducted – with considerable flexibility and ongoing responsiveness to the self-motion monads who are actively participating in the completely integrated program. Further, without the eight tracks members would not see – or understand – the crucial links among the many change activities, which could result in confusion and frustration. Keeping this *big picture of transformation* in everyone's mind will break the sad history of adhoc and shotgun approaches – and thus keep everyone *on track*.

FIGURE 2.20
The Eight Tracks as Quantum Channels

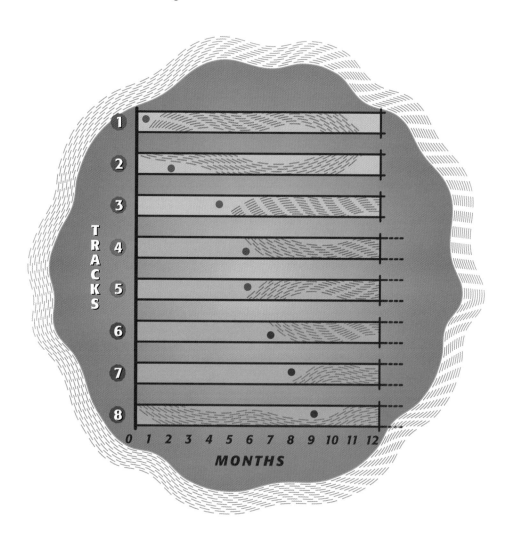

To highlight the value of *seeing the big picture* and transforming an old Newtonian organization into a new quantum organization, let me share with you a workshop I conducted for the fifty senior executives of a large division of a *Fortune* 100 company. Before these top executives decided to proceed with transformation, they wanted to explore the philosophy of a completely integrated program and the change activities in each track.

On the last day of this three–day workshop, after considerable time had already been spent on discussing why the integrated sequence of the eight tracks is fundamentally different from the prevalent cycle of adhoc, quick–fix approaches, the chief financial officer (CFO) of the firm raised his hand and proclaimed: "I now understand what you have done. When you get right down to it, your integrated program is a quick fix!"

I was shocked at this obvious lack of understanding, but I tried not to show it. Instead, I asked the CFO: "Please tell me more about what you have on your mind. I don't think I really understand what you just said." The CFO responded in a way I will never forget:

> Sure, I'll be glad to explain what I mean. I've been working for this company for over twenty years now. I've seen every improvement plan come and go: quality circles, participative management, teaming, matrix management, empowerment, employee involvement, and recently TQM. You name it, we've done it! But hardly anything around here that really matters has actually changed at all. Yes, we have new charts, job titles, buildings, products, people, and all kinds of fancy computers – but we still make decisions in the same old way. We still put one another down in the same old way. We still exclude certain people from key meetings because we don't want to hear different points of view. And we continue to blacklist people if they didn't support our pet projects.
>
> But you're telling us that by going through a sequence of eight tracks and doing first things first and getting it right before you go on – which includes explicitly facing our root dysfunctions at the start and gradually proceeding to change our invisible infrastructures and align our formal systems, month by month, before we try quality management and reengineering again – *we can transform our organization in just a couple of years*. Well, your program *is* a quick fix compared to what we've been through for the past twenty years!

Summarizing the Stages of Transformation

The foregoing has provided the rationale for implementing eight tracks in a particular sequence. But it is essential to appreciate that implementation is just one stage of transformation. First, a completely integrated program must be properly initiated. Second, problems – gaps – must be diagnosed. Third, the eight tracks must be scheduled. Fourth, this schedule must then be implemented. Fifth, key results must be evaluated. Figure 2.21 shows all five stages, which are intended to close the gap between the old paradigm and the new one – in the minds/brains of all organizational members.

FIGURE 2.21
Closing the Transformation Gap

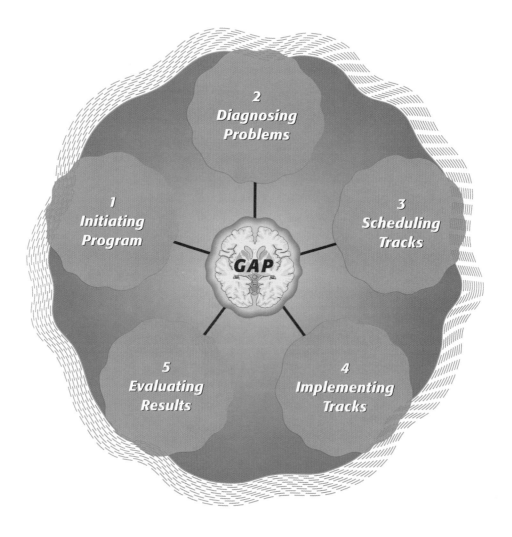

Briefly, the *initiating stage* consists of activating senior management support and deeply understanding what a completely integrated program requires of everybody's time, commitment, and resources. This stage then mobilizes a single task force – the *shadow track*, made up of representatives throughout the organization – whose purpose is to monitor the evolution of the program and do whatever is necessary to move the program along. The *diagnosing stage* involves uncovering the old paradigm that is behind seeing, thinking, and behaving in the organization and thus pinpointing the various dysfunctions in quantum infrastructures, formal systems, and process management. The difference between the old paradigm (including its dysfunctions) and the new paradigm (including the seven attributes of a quantum organization) identifies the gap. This diagnosis of dysfunctions also continually reminds members why transformation must be achieved. *Scheduling and implementing tracks* takes into account what is learned during the diagnosis, as well as what takes place as the program is underway, by remaining adaptable and responsive to members and other stakeholders. Lastly, *evaluating results* compares various measures to the initial diagnosis and other key indicators of organizational success. Depending on what is learned during evaluation, further activities are designed, scheduled, and implemented – which might include revisiting previous segments of the eight tracks. Parenthetically, evaluation is not only carried out during the last stage, because the shadow track has been monitoring the progress of the program from its inception. This last stage of transformation, however, develops a more comprehensive evaluation than any steering committee or task force can conduct on its own.

The five stages of transformation must be guided with special care and commitment. Ideally, all stages are conducted in a collaborative and participative manner among members and other stakeholders – including expert consultants. At the very least, internal/external consultants should fully participate in the diagnostic stage in order to derive an independent assessment of the current paradigm (and its dysfunctions) and, thereby, a clear indication of the transformation gap that must be closed (regardless of what members may have uncovered on their own). Moreover, the eight tracks must be scheduled and implemented in an integrated manner with flexibility and adaptability. Quick–fixing a completely integrated program would do the members and their key stakeholders a great disservice. The meticulous reader is referred to my previous books for the details on all stages of corporate transformation, including case studies of organizations that have journeyed through these five stages successfully (Kilmann, 1984; 1989a; 1989b).

The following three chapters offer the primary change initiatives for achieving self-transformation, systematized into the three components of self-transformation: quantum infrastructures, formal systems, and process management (Chapters 3, 4, and 5, respectively). While various aspects of the other stages of self-transformation are incorporated as necessary, our primary focus in the next three chapters will be on the change activities, experiences, and learning that take place while implementing the eight tracks. But even here, it is just not possible to document all the detail and depth that implementation deserves. Consequently, the reader is referred to my workbooks on implementing the tracks to examine the voluminous activities, instruments, exercises, and discussions that take place during a completely integrated program (Kilmann, 1991; 1992; 1993).

CHAPTER 3

QUANTUM INFRASTRUCTURES

Generating the Potential for Achieving Self-Transformation

> The quantum organization will have infrastructures that
> encourage and build relationships between leaders and
> employees, between employees and their colleagues,
> between divisions and functional groups, between structures
> themselves.... *The infrastructures of the quantum organization must*
> *nourish human and organizational creativity.* They must enhance
> inner mobility and personal responsibility and facilitate the
> free flow of information and ideas. There must be spaces in
> the organization without boundaries, relationships without
> fear. The parts (whether individuals, teams, functions, or
> divisions) must be free to rearrange themselves.
>
> — *Danah Zohar (1997, pages 123, 125)*

During the first three tracks of self–transformation (the culture, skills, and team tracks), members are asked to discuss topics that they rarely, if ever, have spoken about previously: (1) *cultural norms* that control how they see, think, and behave; (2) *implicit assumptions* that conceal how they define and solve their complex problems; and (3) *group processes* that confuse how they conduct their group meetings – both within their formal subunits and as members of cross–boundary teams and project groups. Within Newtonian organizations, cultural norms, implicit assumptions, and group processes remain mostly unconscious among passive jobholders and, consequently, undermine change efforts. Only the members of a quantum organization, therefore, can understand the nature of these *invisible forces* and then make them conscious for self-transformation. Bringing quantum infrastructures into the spotlight generates a *vital threshold of self-aware consciousness.*

This chapter begins with the *culture track* by examining an invisible force that is based on silent rules for seeing, thinking, and behaving. But these elaborate quantum waves can be materialized and self-managed by intentionally surfacing negative (dysfunctional) cultural norms – and then consciously establishing positive (favorable) norms. Since a description of cultural norms is so essential for characterizing a Newtonian organization, special attention will be given to the actual process of uncovering cultural norms (which takes place during the diagnosing stage of transformation – presented in Chapter 2 on pages 92–93). The case of a disguised company, American Gas & Electric (AGE), is then used to illustrate the dysfunctional cultural norms that can be uncovered when members are offered a secure forum in which to speak the unspeakable. This diagnostic report provides a compelling glimpse into the Newtonian AGE.

Second, our attention will advance to the *skills track* by considering another invisible but powerful force that affects all members: the life cycle of complex problems swirling around with hidden, implicit assumptions. These problematic waves, which arise from our quantum cosmos, require members to become intensely aware of the different minds/brains – and thus the various mental categories – that diverse experts bring to complex situations. It is essential for all members to learn the five crucial steps for managing complex problems – so they can avoid making five debilitating errors. The skills track also involves the further development of quantum thinking: all members learn how to surface and then revise out-of-date, inaccurate assumptions regarding how internal and external stakeholders see, think, and behave. As always, it is only by explicitly examining what previously was kept silent that members can attain consciousness.

Third, we will highlight the *team track*, which ensures that what was learned within a relatively safe workshop setting during the previous two tracks will translate directly into the riskier, more challenging workplace. Besides using intact work groups to ensure that this *transfer of learning* does indeed take place, all members also learn how to work effectively in any group facing crucial, complex problems (which includes cross-boundary teams, steering committees, and project groups). However, since complex problems, by definition, cannot be deciphered by utilizing the knowledge, experience, and commitment of only one or a few experts, members must learn to work interactively with dissimilar others (who may have radically different perspectives, expertise, and knowledge). By carefully monitoring and modifying the quality of their group process, however, members can learn to encourage *collective quantum thinking* among different minds/brains for all complex problems.

As we will recognize, *establishing quantum infrastructures* in all subunits throughout an organization (by encouraging adaptive/functional cultures, maintaining accurate/up–to–date assumptions, and conducting synergistic group meetings) is absolutely essential for realizing the inherent potential of all subsequent tracks of the completely integrated program – and thus for achieving transformation. Henceforth, *sustaining quantum infrastructures* will be equally important for addressing all the other complex challenges that are likely to materialize in a quantum universe.

① THE CULTURE TRACK

In the most comprehensive review of organizational culture to date, Trice and Beyer (1993, page 33) delineate culture as "shared, interrelated sets of beliefs about how things work; values that indicate what's worth having or doing; and norms that tell people how they should behave." Although beliefs and values help us understand many relevant aspects of this core concept, it is *cultural norms* – the unspoken, unwritten rules of the game – that offer the most practical approach by which to diagnose dysfunctional infrastructures so they can self–transform into quantum infrastructures.

All organizations have unwritten rules that influence how members interact with each other and how the work gets done. Generally speaking, these below–the–surface cultural norms are so ingrained that employees, especially those who have been members of the organization for several years, do not even question them anymore: "It's just the way we do things around here." New members must learn these unwritten rules for seeing, thinking, and behaving – otherwise, they will not receive support in their work group. It seems that every person's primitive need to be accepted by social groups – family, friends, coworkers, neighbors – is essentially what gives a group leverage to demand compliance with its unwritten rules. If people didn't care about being accepted, a group would have little hold, other than formal sanctions, over members. In actuality, social pressure is applied to "deviants" so they follow the accepted modus operandi and do not question the wisdom or rules of the past. The nonconformists and the mavericks who defy pressures to adhere to cultural norms always do so at a considerable price. In fact, any deviant who ignores the unwritten rules may be severely punished and eventually banished from the tribe.

When an organization finds itself facing a fundamentally different and unfamiliar environmental challenge, however, dysfunctional cultural norms can diminish performance and morale. The traditional ways – the unwritten rules – no longer lead to satisfactory outcomes. At some critical juncture when a Newtonian organization's survival is at stake, it becomes essential to examine the existing norms: the tried–and–true "rules of the road." By seeing them face to face – in a proactive, participatory manner – members have an opportunity to deliberate what cultural norms are still functional and thus should be retained versus what aspects of the culture are dysfunctional and therefore should be discarded or transformed. The whole process of seeing and discussing cultural norms for the first time is a somewhat painful experience – since it necessarily involves a significant rewiring of members' minds/brains.

Diagnosing Cultural Norms

Many organizations make use of numerous employee–opinion surveys to learn what members think about their jobs, their department, and even the well–being of the whole organization. While the information gathered from questionnaires is simple to quantify and tabulate, research suggests that this approach provides limited insight into the underlying dynamics that determine decisions, actions, and results (Harrison, 1987). Experience demonstrates that only a face–to–face interaction can hope to disclose the breadth and depth of cultural norms that leave an imprint on members. Similarly, face–to–face interviews help to foster the candid exploration of complex relationships among various organizational attributes, which are necessarily inaccessible on structured questionnaires or surveys (Beer and Spector, 1993). And should it ever seem more efficient to interview groups of members rather than separate individuals, it is important to remember that people will not voice their actual feelings in front of others unless the organization has already established an open and trusting culture.

Expert consultants – internal to the organization, external, or both – with the cooperation of managers (who have access to organization charts and job positions) formulate a plan to gather diagnostic information from members throughout the organization. The core mission is to sample each level in the hierarchy across every division, department, and work group in order to obtain a representative, unbiased sample of the membership. If there are more than 10,000 employees in an organization, interviewing approximately 350 should provide sufficient information to diagnose the organization's cultural norms (based on the "law of large numbers" along with stratified random sampling). With respect to smaller organizations or strategic business units, holding 50 to 150 interviews should be enough – since most members will have internalized their organization's culture via interpersonal interactions and internal "mental dialogues" (Harris, 1994).

When conducting a one-on-one interview with each representative member, the consultant initiates the diagnostic process by reviewing the background and expectations of the meeting. He or she outlines the range of questions that he or she will be asking and indicates what will be done with the responses. Then the essence of the interview proceeds:

> Can you suggest some of the unwritten rules that reveal how things get done around here? How do you get ahead? How do you stay out of trouble? What do you get rewarded for? What does the boss really want? What have you learned by living here and surviving here all these years?

During the interview process, storytelling seems to be a natural way of describing daily life in an organization. Stories also help the consultant to understand organizational practices that are difficult for an interviewee to define. If a member is having a tough time knowing what is relevant to discuss, the consultant might say: "Why don't you just tell me what life is like here. Try to give me instances of what led up to someone (1) getting angry or mad, (2) voluntarily leaving the organization, (3) getting fired, (4) being deceived or given faulty information, (5) becoming embarrassed or being humiliated, (6) working very hard but still not being successful, (7) not satisfying a major customer, or, instead, (8) feeling like celebrating or having a party because something great happened. Try to remember the people involved and the series of events that led to such experiences."

The consultant can also uncover insidious cultural norms by posing this challenging question to the interviewee:

> If I were your favorite sister or brother and let you know that I plan to get a job here, what would you tell me about what life is really like, so I won't be surprised or disappointed later? And remember, if you mislead me in any way, you're going to hear about it for the rest of your life! Give me some information: Whom can I trust? (Why? What happened?) What department (or people) should I stay away from? (Why? What happened?) What topics should I not discuss with others, especially my boss? How should I approach my job? What can I expect during performance appraisals and when I apply for a promotion? Remember: I'm counting on you to tell me the truth about what really goes on here, and what I should do to survive and how I can get ahead.

A great variety of descriptions and stories are accumulated from the one–on–one consultant/member interviews. The richness of such cultural revelations is best illustrated with a detailed, exhaustive diagnosis from a real organization. Essentially, a diagnostic report composed as an intricate narrative (instead of an abbreviated listing) is needed to illustrate the *deep quantum waves of dysfunctional norms* that usually are swirling around an old Newtonian organization. After studying the relevant history of a disguised utility company, American Gas & Electric (AGE), we will see the damaging cultural norms that were revealed during one–on–one interviews between external consultants and representative members – whose joint, conscious observation caused the instantaneous collapse of invisible cultural waves into materialized (spoken and written) cultural norms.

The Case of American Gas & Electric

AGE, an old established company in the utility industry, provides gas and electrical power to various urban and rural communities. Back in 1975, it expanded its operations by merging with two smaller utilities in the state that were providing equivalent services to other townships. AGE employs about a thousand people.

As a Newtonian organization existing in a Newtonian environment, AGE enjoyed all the advantages of being in a very regulated and protected industry: secure jobs, excellent salaries and fringe benefits, and not much pressure to improve. Employees expected (and actually received) lifelong employment. There was a healthy family spirit: The company took care of its people and the people were loyal to the company.

Then, of course, almost everything changed – or at least the external environment became more deregulated and competitive, which put a lot of pressure on the company and its employees to change their traditional ways of doing things. "Do more with less" became the battle cry, although the troops did not accept, let alone understand, what that phrase meant. And management was similarly bewildered about what to do differently. After all, they had been successful via their traditional, autocratic style of controlling the organization.

For almost a decade, starting around 1980, management attempted one new remedy after another to get everyone to be more cost, customer, and safety conscious in addition to becoming more innovative. Speeches were made on productivity improvement, newsletters were distributed on valuing the customer, and discussions were held on the need to empower employees by moving decision making downward.

When nothing of much consequence had actually improved, senior management began conducting employee surveys to determine what was really going on down below. The results were always neatly tabulated, but senior executives did not know what steps to take next. So they collected additional data, established task forces to examine the results, and hoped that their recurring problems would eventually be addressed.

The process of surveying employees, tabulating their responses, and organizing special task forces took place year after year. Yet nothing was being done differently where it really counted: on the job. Finally, senior management came to the disturbing conclusion that it just did not know much about changing – transforming – an old, traditional company into a new, market-driven organization. Senior management only knew how to provide gas and electricity the way it always had done.

With continued complaining by the employees (as documented by the latest opinion surveys), management decided to proceed with a more systematic – and integrated – approach for revitalizing their organization. After studying numerous methods and talking to several consultants, they decided on a completely integrated program for self-transformation.

The cultural diagnosis for AGE is summarized below. (The full report also noted other serious problems in AGE's systems and processes.) It was developed by having six outside consultants interview about 150 people (one-on-one for an hour or so each) who represented all areas, levels, and locations in the thousand-member company. During these interviews, it was not very difficult to probe employees to find out "what really goes on around here." From their numerous descriptions and stories, the following twelve norms – in the form of ironic imperatives – are offered as a way of capturing the experience of working in the Newtonian AGE.

1 **DO NOT TRUST ACROSS THE BOUNDARIES** There exist numerous cliques, turfs, empires, and kingdoms in AGE (choose your favorite term) that make it exceedingly difficult for people, groups, and departments to work together – in a collaborative fashion – on cross-boundary problems. The kingdoms include union employees, nonunion employees, temporary employees, contracted workers, marketing, finance, accounting, personnel, technical, information systems, sections, home office, regions, supervisors, managers, customers, new, old, young, women, men, minorities, members from Merger #1, people from Merger #2, and so on. Within each faction, members mostly take care of themselves at the expense of the company. These factions are encouraged and reinforced by several cultural norms: Do not trust anyone who is not in your group. Second-guess any decision

made by another group – they probably made the wrong decision. If you are part of a decision–making group that includes several of these "other" members or groups, pretend to go along with their decision in public but kill it behind the scenes. Express animosity toward the members of other groups. Stereotype each group in disparaging ways: Marketing people are arrogant, finance people are silly bean counters, human resources people are against all the employees, technical people don't respect the customer, union people want to take the company for a ride, and management only takes care of itself. Moreover, don't expect any member within any group to be different or capable of changing. And you can't learn anything from those other groups: If something wasn't invented in your group, it doesn't apply and shouldn't be used.

2 **REFUSE TO SEE THE BIG PICTURE** There is a widespread practice that seems to permeate all levels and areas in the company. Rather than knowing what other people do, most members take a rather narrow view of what leads to overall organizational success. While some of the satellite locations must, by necessity, take a more general view of their job, even here there is a propensity to underestimate the value of the home office. Thus, employees see the company with self–serving blinders and, in fact, devalue and negate the important – but different – roles that other people and their departments play in the larger scheme of things. Of course, the refusal to trust across the boundaries only reinforces the inclination to see just a small piece of the whole company.

3 **PICK YOUR FAVORITES AND PROMOTE THEM** Many employees perceive that at least 95% of all personnel decisions pertaining to hiring, job transfers, promotions, and performance assessments are determined by favoritism. It's *who* you know, not what you know. Employees describe many situations in which they experienced the impact of being favored (or not) by management owing to criteria other than performance. These criteria not only influence promotion decisions but induce "self–fulfilling prophecies" that predispose subsequent promotions and other rewards – unfairly. For example, it has been claimed that senior management has its favorites. They are usually assigned the interesting and challenging work, while others, who undoubtedly are able to do the same quality work, are not offered the same opportunity. Then, over time, the favorite ones have the relevant job experience to meet additional challenges (for subsequent transfers and promotions), while the others are at a clear disadvantage. As a result, the favorites get richer while the nonfavorites get poorer – quite

literally – in AGE. While supervisors and managers are in the best position to pick their favorites, employees are in the best position to partake in the action. It is conceivable that employees have intentionally (but sometimes unknowingly) tried to become the favorite one, rather than concentrating on the job itself and letting their performance do the talking. Employees, in fact, gave many examples of creative strategies to become more visible to their managers – such as generating many internal memos, joining the right committees, belonging to the right clubs, laughing at the right jokes, participating in certain sports, and arguing for the boss's opinion in order to wear the prized halo.

4 PLAY THE JOB-POSTING GAME Several managers appear to have developed a covert procedure to ensure they get their favorites promoted or transferred while appearing to follow the accepted procedures for job posting and the laws for equal opportunity employment. Abbreviated, the covert scheme proceeds something like this: First choose the winner (your favorite), prepare a job posting to fit perfectly with the talent, experience, and attributes of that person, go through the motions of welcoming and then interviewing a suitable variety of applicants (to support affirmative action policies), and finally announce your previously selected candidate. (Because you are so confident of the legitimacy of this approach, you can send out the letters of rejection before their interviews have taken place!) Regardless of how the job–posting process was designed to function, the culture has slanted the selection process to promote favoritism.

5 DO NOT CONFRONT POOR PERFORMANCE There appears to be a cultural habit of not confronting performance problems and not replacing consistently poor performers. Perhaps this sensitive issue is avoided since management cannot defend the personnel selections that were made and must now try to cover for its mistakes. Numerous members have stated: "Management just cannot admit that it placed the wrong person in that job." On a continuing basis, therefore, performance problems weaken the culture of the organization and reduce the satisfaction of the members. It is not just managers, however, who nurture this cultural norm. In many cases, employees themselves cover for low performers in their group for all kinds of reasons: comradeship and loyalty among union members, us (employees) versus them (management), don't tell mom or dad, don't be a tattletale, don't be a traitor, don't fraternize with our enemies, don't break rank, don't talk with strangers, and "I'll cover for you, if you'll do the same for me."

6 MAKE DECISIONS IN A TOTAL VACUUM This old cultural norm, undoubtedly ingrained from decades of autocratic management, suggests that people should make decisions about things they know little about: Why let a lack of information or knowledge get in the way of making a decision? Managers, for example, sometimes make decisions without even getting input from the most knowledgeable people in the organization: the employees who are living the problem daily! Instead of gaining their valued input, management proceeds to operate in a perfect vacuum. Then senior managers wonder why morale is so low and why their employees complain about the working conditions. As several employees have said: "Management appears to spend more time trying to make people happy after some incident than working with them *ahead of time* so they don't get mad in the first place." In the worst cases, employees see management as totally out of touch with reality and living in an ivory tower. The problem of making decisions in a vacuum, however, is not exclusive to managers. Over the years, it has spread throughout the organization. Employees do not bother to consider – beforehand – the potential consequences of their decisions on their fellow employees in other departments and work units: Even when employees are picked for a committee assignment to represent their coworkers, they automatically go ahead and make decisions without first seeking information from the people they are assigned to represent!

7 DO NOT LISTEN ACROSS THE BOUNDARIES Many employees have brought important problems to management through various discussions and surveys. Management hears (a physical process) but does not listen (a cultural process). It seems acceptable in AGE to go through the motions of getting some input from others, planned or not, but then no real response is given to persons who have taken the trouble to provide the input. This generally leads to frustration, anger, apathy, and, eventually, passivity. At some point, management will simply not be told of some critical problem because no one expects management to listen. Even if there are excellent reasons for not acting on a comment or suggestion, employees – like most people – expect some acknowledgment that they exist and their message has been received. Otherwise, they will probably assume the worst – that their good ideas fall on deaf ears – which is reinforced by the lack of trust across the management hierarchy. And employees do not always listen to their fellow employees, either: Numerous employees, in fact, admitted that they regularly ignore requests from other departments, do not get back to their coworkers as promised, and, on occasion, do not return phone calls for weeks or at all.

8 AVOID THE TOUGH PROBLEMS AT ALL COSTS This cultural norm adds to the previous one and offers one more reason why employees do not receive an adequate response to their questions or suggestions. There appears to be a high avoidance tendency operating in AGE. It is, perhaps, consistent with individual propensities to shy away from uncomfortable situations and is endorsed by these cultural norms: Don't take risks, don't stick your neck out, don't assume responsibility, and don't take the chance of being caught with a mistake. Even if managers really do listen to what employees say, the collective avoidance mode encourages them to ignore problems, especially the controversial problems that might get them into trouble. So they listen – somewhat – but avoid any decision or action on the topic, hoping that the whole thing will just go away of its own accord. Similarly, employees usually find it easier (and safer) to avoid confronting their bosses when questionable decisions are made – especially decisions that, ironically, are most important to the success of the organization.

9 BLAME OTHERS WHEN THINGS GO WRONG One scheme to avoid problems is to deflect attention toward someone else – preferably another group inside the company or, ideally, a remote group outside. In fact, the further the problem can be removed from the person, the better. Because most problems today are extremely complex and have roots that spread across the artificial boundaries in the organization, it is relatively easy to deflect such complex problems onto others. Harboring low levels of trust toward other work units and a desire not to be the victim of any mistake either, most managers and employees are very quick to blame others well in advance of discovering the true nature of the problem. To be "quick on the draw" in AGE is to give the problem to others – right after refusing to see the big picture, making decisions in a total vacuum, not listening, and avoiding the problem as long as possible – and then blame *them* as soon as anything goes wrong. Since so many people have removed themselves from the problem, it is only a matter of time before something important *will* be overlooked, which makes it easier to blame others.

10 PUNISH OTHERS EVERY CHANCE YOU GET If you can incriminate another person, group, or department for making a bad decision, seize the opportunity to punish them. Ridicule them whenever you have a chance, but *do it nicely*. And then remind them of their error every chance you get. If you are successful at punishing people and groups for making mistakes, perhaps they'll never attempt an inventive solution again. Perhaps they'll continue to do things the same old way – conservatively and according to all the other cultural rules. Better yet, if you can punish others enough so that they'll try to maintain the status quo, all the pressure will be off your back to change and improve!

11 DO NOT COMMUNICATE TO EMPLOYEES Several managers seem to behave as if they do not owe employees any explanation, rationale, or reason for a decision: "Just do as you're told! You don't have to know why. If you don't like what I'm telling you to do, then look for another job." If employees were just tools or children, such unacceptable communication might be more understandable. But in today's world, employees prefer to be treated as adults – responsible adults – and it is difficult for them to understand why this rather obvious preference is not recognized by their management. Employees are certain that management has been informed about this ineffective communication through one forum or another. But somehow they have not listened, or maybe they have simply avoided the problem. Or, ironically, maybe they do understand but somehow forget to communicate this back to the employees. Regarding the worst cases, some employees are sure that they have been deceived on numerous occasions when management was asked to explain some incident. Sometimes, they disclosed their private feelings to management and discovered afterward that the promise of confidentiality was definitely violated. Such deceptive, condescending, or unethical behavior by anyone in the organization will continue to erode trust and make it even more difficult to heal the varied fractures in AGE's culture.

12 KEEP WOUNDS OPEN The former merger of AGE with two other utilities is still a living part of the company's *internal* environment. But by avoiding the problem, management and employees have not empowered the organization to address the issue directly, understand and accept what happened, undo whatever can still be undone, mourn any injustices that cannot be undone, feel sad about what happened, and then definitely put the matter to rest. Many years after the merger, employees are still labeled according to their previous affiliation – which continues to interfere with trusting, sharing, cooperating, and getting the work done.

SUMMARIZING AGE'S DYSFUNCTIONAL CULTURAL NORMS The twelve foregoing cultural norms engender widespread ineffectiveness as well as dissatisfaction throughout AGE. Being far removed from the organization's problems, seeing only small pieces of the problems anyway, not listening to those who do know something about the unique aspects and dynamics of the problems, avoiding the problems besides, not trusting other people to support you (except, of course, your favorites), blaming and punishing others for having created these problems in the first place, and then not explaining why various solutions were chosen in the end – such cultural norms are unquestionably dysfunctional for mental health as well as for organizational success. Without belaboring the point, it should be evident that AGE is caught in a self-inflicting cultural mess. If this mess is allowed to continue by perpetuating its old norms unconsciously and habitually, trust and confidence will further erode – making it ever more difficult to transform the organization. The prospects for achieving long-term success will become doubtful as well: Without an adaptive, positive culture, there is little hope of overcoming environmental threats and challenges.

Step One: Surfacing Actual Norms

Once the diagnostic report has been delivered and discussed throughout the organization, a sequence of distinctive workshops for the culture track should be customized and then scheduled. In half–day to full–day off–site meetings, members have the opportunity to see and discuss the particular dysfunctional norms that are alive and well within their own intact work groups. Attended only by peer groups, gathering without any immediate managers present, the first step in the culture track is for members to list the cultural norms that currently regulate their behavior and attitudes. In order to get the process started, most times it is helpful to remind group members of the ironic imperatives that were addressed in the diagnostic report (which were developed for the organization as a whole, not for any specific work unit). On other occasions, it just takes a little prodding and a few illustrations to get the discussion going. But once it begins, members are quick to suggest many cultural norms. In fact, they seem to delight in being able to unearth what previously was never stated in any document and rarely mentioned in any conversation.

For an organization whose culture is clearly dysfunctional, some of the cultural norms members may list for their own work group are: Look busy even when you are not; don't be the first to disagree; don't step on the toes of senior management; laugh at those who suggest new ways of doing things; complain a lot; don't be the bearer of bad news; shoot the messenger who brings bad news; don't trust anyone who seems sincere; ridicule the work of other groups. Ironically, there is one norm that must be violated so that such a list can be developed in the first place: *Remain unconscious: Don't make norms explicit!*

Step Two: Establishing Desired Norms

The second step in the culture track requests all group members to list the desired norms that would lead to organizational success. At this point, the members usually recognize the impact that unwritten rules have had on their behavior. They already experience some relief as a new way of life is considered. They realize that they no longer have to pressure one another to behave in dysfunctional ways. The members can create a new cultural agreement within their own work groups and organization. Part of this sense of relief comes from recognizing that their dissatisfaction is not the outcome of their being incompetent or bad individuals. It is much easier, psychologically, for people *to blame the invisible force called culture*, as long as they take responsibility for uncovering and improving it.

Some of the new cultural norms are often listed in order to help an organization confront today's quantum challenges: Be willing to take on responsibility; introduce changes to improve performance; treat everyone with respect and as a potential source of valuable wisdom and expertise; congratulate those who suggest new ideas and new ways of doing things; enjoy your work and express your enthusiasm for a job well done; speak with pride about your work group; be helpful and supportive of the other groups in your organization. Perhaps the most important desired norm is: *Become conscious: Make norms explicit!*

Step Three: Identifying Culture-Gaps®

The difference between the desired norms identified in Step Two and the actual norms identified in Step One is termed a *culture-gap*.

Do all members in an organization perceive the same culture–gaps? Apparently not. The smallest culture–gaps are usually found at the top of the hierarchy in a Newtonian organization. Executives believe their own publicity: As a classic example, they say that they reward creativity and innovation – as "demonstrated" by the widely distributed brochures on the company's new innovation program – but do not recognize that their actions speak much louder than their words. Culture–gaps are largest at the lower levels, where jobholders experience the various inconsistencies that have trickled down the hierarchy. Using the identical example of the innovation program, employees usually regard it as a joke: "Innovation? You've got to be kidding. Nobody around here even remembers the last time when someone was rewarded for a new idea. If someone *did* propose something new, they wouldn't be around long enough to talk about it!"

Just as the *size* of culture-gaps can vary according to the structure of the Newtonian pyramid (the organization chart), the *type* of culture-gaps can differ group–by–group within the same organization. Divisions have different histories, critical incidents, strategies, markets, and managers. A special problem emerges, however, when each subunit of an organization has very different norms. Communications and conflicts across divisions are much more difficult and time–consuming to manage when work units have different jargons, values, work habits, and attitudes. If subunits need to share information, technology, personnel, and other resources, different cultural norms will get in the way of cooperative efforts.

But there is a universal rule that can resolve this cultural dilemma: Allow each work unit to create the subculture that is conducive to its own high performance and satisfaction, but encourage each subunit to adopt those organization–wide norms that promote organizational success. The latter include norms that encourage cooperation and coordination across subunit boundaries that define the white space on the organization chart: Help other departments whenever possible; look at the problem from the other member's point of view; remember that we all work for the same organization.

Step Four: Closing Culture-Gaps®

When members and their organization are at least receptive to change, it is miraculous how making lists of desired norms affects the members of a work group. Sometimes, significant change can be brought about just by listing new cultural norms because members start acting out these norms immediately after they are discussed.

When the members and their culture are cynical and depressed – as is often the case with a Newtonian organization – the reaction to listings of desired norms is very different. Even when large culture–gaps exist, the members are usually apathetic and passive. Members respond by saying that their work units are unable to change for the better until the level of management directly above them and the rest of the organization change first. Members believe that their organization is keeping them down.

When the culture-gap conversation occurs at the next–highest level, the very same arguments are heard again: "We have no power to change; we have to wait for the next level to let us change; *they* have the power." It is astonishing to find the top management group experiencing the same feelings of helplessness. Here top management is waiting for the economy to change! In reality, it is the organization–wide culture that is prescribing:

Don't take on responsibility; protect yourself (CYA); don't change – at least not until everyone else has changed; don't lead the way; if you ignore the problem, it will go away. Or presented in technical language: Continue to see, think, and behave as a passive jobholder (as an inert molar object) in a Newtonian organization.

A worthwhile lesson to learn from organizational cultures that have notably improved – especially from cultures that were dysfunctional – is that people do not have to feel they are powerless and inept. If managers and members decide that cultural change should occur, then change can be brought about. Power and control are more a participatory, quantum reality than an independent, physical reality. Many times individuals and organizations have achieved great success when everyone else "knew" this was impossible.

Merely listing the desired norms, however, is not sufficient to instill them in an organization. Each work unit must design a *sanctioning system* that monitors and then reinforces the desired norms. *If there are no penalties for persisting in the old ways and no reward for engaging in new behavior, why would anyone want to change?* Before the reward system – reformulated during the fifth track in the program – provides formal incentives to all members for behaving according to the desired norms, an *informal* reward (sanctioning) system is developed and used within every work group.

Specifically, each work group is asked to reach a consensus on what exactly will be done if any member acts out an old norm (referred to as a *violation*) or behaves in the desired manner (referred to as a *victory*). Typical negative sanctions that are delivered for violations include stares, frowns, and groans; verbal reprimands; assignment of unpleasant work; financial penalties; public ridicule. The usual positive sanctions applied to victories include smiles, cheers, and applause; compliments and praise; assignment of valued work; financial bonuses; peer recognition. For example, suppose the retired norm is "arrive at meetings whenever you feel like it," while the desired norm is "arrive at meetings on time." Generally, the first infraction results in subtle reminders – as when members conspicuously glimpse at their wristwatches whenever latecomers arrive at a meeting. Subsequent infractions incur stronger sanctions – such as placing someone's habitual lateness on the formal meeting agenda or displaying a brief description of the violation on the organization's bulletin boards. In addition, members who regularly set the best example of timely arrivals for all meetings are treated to a lavish dinner by those who have violated the norm! In these ways, the point is rather clear: Get used to the new norms, or it will cost you (and benefit others).

As long as each sanctioning system is both ethical and legal, groups can be encouraged to be as creative as possible in generously rewarding desired behavior while penalizing outmoded habits. If every sanctioning system also involves some gentle humor, the cultural change will not be as difficult as might first be expected. Bringing the traditional sanctioning system to the attention of all group members generally motivates them to establish a workable system that is sympathetic and equitable. Self-aware consciousness, therefore, is significantly enhanced not only by every work unit surfacing and reforming its previously unwritten, unspoken cultural norms, but also by self-managing its own sanctioning system in order to encourage all members to see, think, and behave in more productive and satisfying ways.

❷ THE SKILLS TRACK

Once the members have pinpointed the culture-gaps in their work units and proceeded to close them by effectively using their specially designed sanctioning systems (within the workplace as well as workshop sessions), they are ready to materialize two intertwined waves in their organization: complex problems and implicit assumptions.

In a Newtonian organization, jobholders are assigned well-defined tasks and well-structured problems. In both cases, the subject has already been defined by an external authority such as the next higher level in the management hierarchy. Furthermore, jobholders are not permitted much discretion in interpreting policies or implementing action: Their responses to these *simple problems* are prescribed in considerable detail via standard operating procedures, which have previously been formulated to address all foreseeable situations and contingencies. Any uncertainty in applying these well-formulated guidelines is simply redirected to the "higher-ups" for resolution. In principle, as long as a Newtonian organization exists in a *Newtonian world*, jobholders remain skilled in managing simple problems by simply using prescribed bureaucratic procedures.

But a Newtonian organization in a quantum world (consisting of a fast-paced, dynamic, global environment), painfully finds out – again and again – that standard operating procedures cannot adequately cope with *complex problems*. To begin with, most problems in a global context cannot be anticipated; rather, they must first be sensed – and defined – by active participation among members before viable solutions can be derived and implemented. Furthermore, one person, by himself, cannot possibly solve a complex problem, because one person's knowledge and information are decidedly limited by the *specialized mental categories that exist in one mind/brain*. Thus complex problems generally require a group of diverse experts with different categories and interrelationships (schemas) in their minds/brains to define the major causes of a complex problem *before* deriving solutions. And implementing solutions in our quantum world is not a simple matter either. Instead, any solution, once implemented, necessarily affects a wide variety of internal and external stakeholders who may have very different needs and expectations. Actually, the multi–stakeholder environment for implementing a solution to a complex problem further elaborates what is meant by *complexity*. An additional aspect to this already complicated mess is the quagmire that emerges when an implemented solution fails to solve the initial problem: What might have gone wrong during any or all of the previous steps of problem management?

Moreover, to succeed at managing complex problems in a quantum world, it is not enough for members to learn the skills for conducting the different steps. Members must also learn how to manage another related quantum wave swirling around complex problems: the *implicit assumptions* they make – in an unconscious manner – which define the root causes of a complex problem and how to implement chosen solutions. But if any of their implicit assumptions are incorrect, members will fail at resolving the problem. Only by discovering how to *materialize* their implicit assumptions behind any proposed problem definitions and implementation plans will members have a chance to revise false assumptions and thus successfully manage complexity in a quantum cosmos (Mason and Mitroff, 1981).

The best place to learn the techniques of problem management and assumptional analysis is in a workshop setting. There all participants are removed from the daily pressures of their jobs and from the authority of their immediate supervisors. During several workshop sessions, members learn new skills by practicing with cases and exercises before tackling real problems – within their intact work groups. For the various details about planning and scheduling these workshop sessions as well as the particular materials that are used to learn the concepts of problem management and assumptional analysis, the reader is referred to Kilmann (1991; 1992; 1993). Here I abbreviate these two parts of the skills track – managing complex problems and implicit assumptions – to acquaint the reader with the core concepts. After these topics in the skills track, we will close the chapter on quantum infrastructures by summarizing the chief purpose and methods of the team track. In the following chapters, we will focus our attention on formal systems and process management – both of which require healthy quantum infrastructures throughout an organization.

Managing Complex Problems

Figure 3.1 displays the five steps of problem management. Members learn that this cycle begins when someone senses that something is wrong. As with a transformation gap (Figure 2.12, page 76), a problem can be said to exist if there is a gap between *what is* and *what should be.* Specifically, if this gap is beyond a certain threshold (usually derived from past experiences, expectations, or goals), a problem is sensed. Notice: During the five steps of problem management, it is the minds/brains of the involved members that determine which mental categories are used for managing problems.

(Figure 2.12, page 76)

FIGURE 3.1
The Five Steps of Problem Management

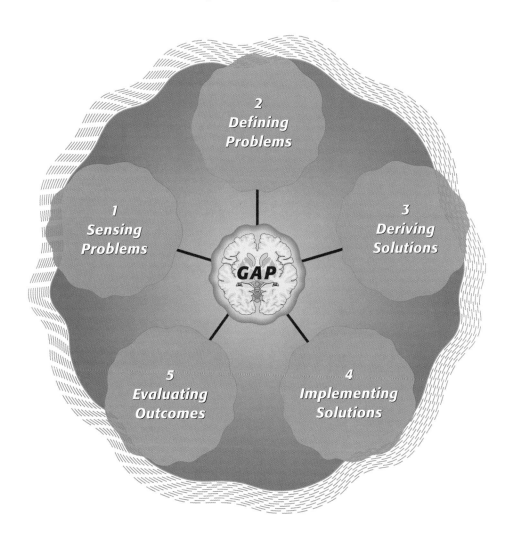

Figure 3.2 illustrates the five errors of problem management: *sensing errors* (ignoring the existence of large gaps or being too sensitive to small gaps); *defining errors* (describing obvious symptoms instead of pinpointing root causes or working on an incidental problem or the wrong problem); *solving errors* (choosing solution A when solution B is in fact better or vice versa); *implementing errors* (ignoring egos, fear, anxiety, culture, and politics while implementing derived solutions or assuming that quality solutions will automatically be accepted and then used); and *evaluating errors* (falsely appraising whether a problem still exists and thereby continuing to work on a nonproblem or, alternatively, ceasing to work on a crucial problem).

FIGURE 3.2
The Five Errors of Problem Management

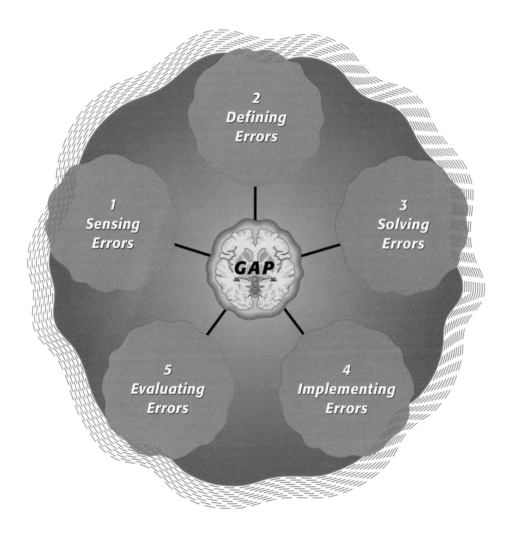

Essentially, unless the five basic errors of problem management are avoided, members will waste their time and energy by repeatedly cycling through the steps of problem management – without success. At an early point in the skills track, members usually wonder just who is responsible for sensing their organization's problems: Does their organization identify problems in a purposeful and systematic way? When they realize, as they typically do, that problem sensing has been conducted haphazardly and unconsciously, members begin to suggest specific means for ensuring that important problems are not being overlooked or denied simply because everyone believes that someone else, somehow, must be addressing them.

How do members define problems – once they have been sensed? Typically, they automatically assume that their worldview (their specialty) defines the essence of the problem. This selective perception is natural for any person who has received extensive skills training. Professionals wear blinders in order to become specialists, which includes having specialized categories wired into their minds/brains: A finance person sees a financial world; a marketing person sees a marketing world; a social scientist sees a universe of human relationships. This biasing effect is reinforced by one's personality (the traits and abilities that incline one to pursue a specialty in the first place) and by one's work group (which puts cultural pressure on its members to see problems a particular way). *Any* problem definition arrived at through such tunnel vision will likely result in a defining error, which negates all the remaining steps of problem management.

How can you choose among alternative solutions? By making use of decision theory, you formulate a *decision tree*, with the problem definition as the trunk and the alternative solutions as the branches. Alongside each branch are associated costs, benefits, and probabilities leading to a desired outcome. Then an *expected* cost/benefit analysis can be performed for each series of branches so the decision maker can choose the best solution.

Consider this crucial distinction: Choosing one decision tree versus another is an example of making a potential *defining error* (in choosing the wrong decision tree). But once the problem has been defined, selecting a weak solution with regard to cost/benefit considerations is an example of a *solving error* (in choosing the wrong branch on a particular decision tree). But it is far better to choose a weak solution from the correct decision tree than the best solution from the wrong decision tree! Shortly, we will learn how to choose among numerous decision trees (or even create a new tree) by first surfacing and then revising the out–of–date, incorrect assumptions underneath each tree in the *quantum forest*. First, however, let's clarify some of these vital distinctions by using graphics and symbols.

Figure 3.3 displays a cosmic decision tree for a simple problem. The trunk or base of the tree represents the definition of the problem that, for a simple problem, has already been determined (either unconsciously or deliberately) through a single specialty. The branches on the tree express alternative solutions (which assumes that the definition of the problem is correct). Smaller branches heading off from the larger branches represent additional steps or substages of any given solution. Since the problem is already defined, all attention is focused on selecting the best solution (and its subbranches) for the members and other prime stakeholders. A solving error would be picking the wrong branch on the tree.

FIGURE 3.3
A Single Decision Tree for a Simple Problem

Figure 3.4 shows several decision trees – including their respective branches – that may exist for every complex problem. Although decision trees generally are drawn from left to right as if they were lying on their sides, I find it more sensible to draw them from the ground up – alive and growing. In this manner, not only are trees directly observable above the surface of experience, but each decision tree is rooted – grounded – in its below–the–surface assumptions. As all the members in the skills track will learn, before you can truly appreciate why diverse experts define complex problems according to different trees, it is essential to expose their tangled roots below the surface.

FIGURE 3.4
Multiple Trees for Complex Problems

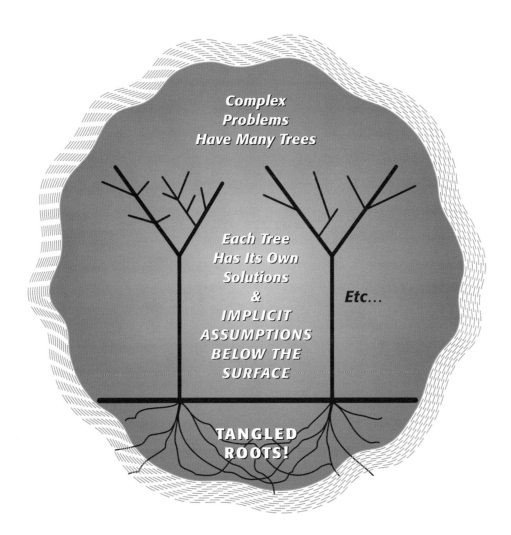

Figure 3.5 shows what happens when the roots of several different decision trees are untangled by uncovering their assumptions: It becomes possible to create an altogether new decision tree in the forest. This new tree represents the height of *quantum thinking:* creating a new definition of a complex problem that no single expert was able to detect previously. At the same time, the branches on this new tree present solutions that were never before available on other trees. As members struggle to make sense of this new tree and its new branches, new categories (and relationships) are created in their minds and new neural tracks (and networks) are wired into their brains. *New paradigms are born of this quantum process.*

FIGURE 3.5
Creating New Decision Trees and Mental Categories

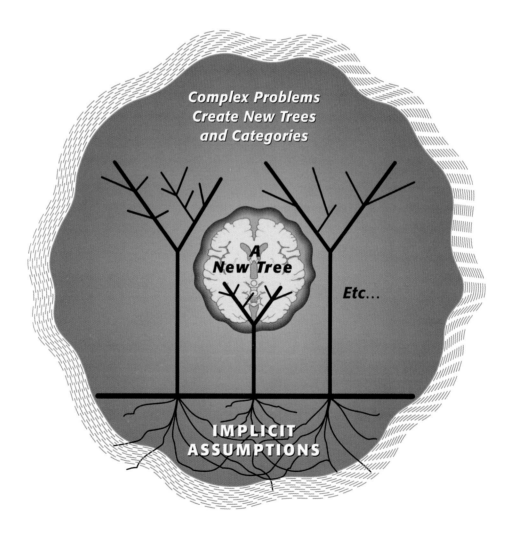

At this point it might help to give an example showing the different decision trees that are, in actuality, cultivated by experts and how each is rooted in a different specialty: Our planet faces incredibly complex social, political, economic, and environmental problems that can be satisfactorily solved only through healthy and adaptive – transformed – organizations. But effectively transforming an organization is itself a supremely complex problem. *Undoubtedly, how to achieve transformation may be the most complex and important problem facing our planet today – since we must depend on organizations and institutions to address all our other global problems!*

During the course of three decades, I have collaborated with diverse experts to thoroughly understand the complex problem of organizational transformation. These experts, as is the case in most arenas, are specialists in what they do and therefore articulate their own specialized categories for transforming organizations. The dominant decision trees in this forest include experts who argue that the best way to transform an organization is to (1) restructure the tall, vertical departments into self-managed work groups; (2) teach team-building skills to all work units and, in the process, improve the culture within the organization; (3) implement total quality management throughout all existing work units; (4) generate and analyze strategic alternatives in order to reposition the organization in a redefined industry; (5) enhance the existing reward system to include 360° feedback from customers, suppliers, direct reports, supervisors, and peers, which is then explicitly tied to both intrinsic and extrinsic rewards; (6) reengineer the organization to create process-based units that make use of the latest advances in information technology; (7) teach all members how to acquire and use their knowledge and then how to rapidly spread this knowledge across all organizational boundaries; (8) provide extensive skills training for managing people, problems, time, resources, and projects.

Each of these decision trees has been used as the primary definition of how to transform an organization. The branches on each tree represent different ways of restructuring, repositioning, redesigning, reengineering, teaching, and, in general, bringing the defined change target to members inside the organization. A *defining error*, of course, is choosing one tree to bring about transformation versus what another tree would define as the primary target of transformation. A *solving error* is choosing a less effective way to introduce change (top down) versus a more effective way (bottom up). As we will see in a moment, each decision tree is based on a number of implicit assumptions about the other trees in the forest – assumptions that may not be true. Each tree also includes assumptions, which may be false as well, about various internal and external stakeholders.

Thus for complex problems that arise in a quantum world, there is potentially a large forest of trees available by which to define root causes of any problem – including the respective branches from which to choose novel solutions to implement. Figure 3.6 represents the *quantum forest.* Note the distribution of trees: The one in the middle is the most obvious tree to consider, based on the history of the organization. The central area depicts the accepted, mainstream grove of trees, which the majority of specialists are able to see and endorse. But the outer edge of the forest, closest to the quantum waves, depicts the most radical views. These revolutionary trees can be materialized if quantum infrastructures enable their formation.

FIGURE 3.6
The Quantum Forest of Decision Trees

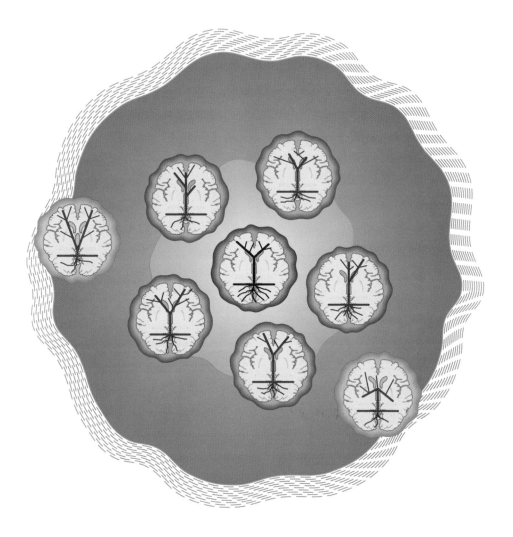

Managing Implicit Assumptions

Assumptional analysis is a systematic and engaging method for tackling the most complex steps of problem management: defining problems and implementing solutions. This method not only pinpoints all the trees that are potentially relevant to problem definitions and implementation plans; it also probes below the surface of each decision tree to reveal its roots – the *implicit assumptions* that keep each tree alive and well. It is through the use of all the relevant areas of expertise from both inside and outside an organization that a synthesis of different decision trees and their roots can be developed – as members originate a new tree in their quantum forest. Using assumptional analysis is a superb illustration of quantum thinking: Both the right and left hemispheres of every participating mind/brain are actively involved in creating a new tree in the forest, providing altogether *new categories and relationships* for resolving a complex problem.

It must be stressed, however, that if a problem is defined incorrectly, all the subsequent steps of problem management are not only irrelevant but possibly harmful. Similarly, failing to implement the selected solution immediately invalidates all the previous steps and has its own frustrations and damaging consequences. It is therefore imperative that members take deliberate action to minimize the defining errors and implementing errors for the most important challenges facing their organization. Incidentally, sensing problems and evaluating outcomes are the least complex steps of problem management, since they require either "go" or "no go" decisions: Is there a significant gap that deserves our attention? The step of deriving solutions is not that complex either, since there are numerous cost/benefit methods for choosing among alternative solutions.

Assumptional analysis enables all members to develop self-aware consciousness about the validity of their proposed problem definitions and implementation plans. The basic premise is simple: Whenever someone concludes that his definition of the problem is correct, his arguments are valid only if their underlying assumptions are accurate. We define *assumptions* as all the things you have to take for granted as true (including human nature, mother nature, father time, and lady luck) in order to argue convincingly that the conclusion, as stated, is correct. Generally speaking, an *initial conclusion* is anything that is argued for or against: most often, a problem definition or implementation plan. These conclusions are termed *initial* since they will certainly undergo change as their underlying assumptions are analyzed and revised. Initial conclusions are just a way to initiate the process – a way of getting at the tried–and–true but potentially false (or uncertain) assumptions.

The assumptions underlying a conclusion can be surfaced by listing all the possible stakeholders – those inside and outside the organization – who are associated with the *initial conclusion* and therefore have a stake in what takes place. The essential reason for identifying stakeholders is not to list people for the sake of listing them, but to surface assumptions. The objective is not to miss *any* relevant individual, group, or organization. As represented in Figure 3.7, members make assumptions about what various stakeholders want, believe, expect, and value. Stated differently, any initial conclusion is a set of mental categories (and relationships) that implicitly assumes how stakeholders see, think, and behave.

FIGURE 3.7
Stakeholders for an Initial Conclusion

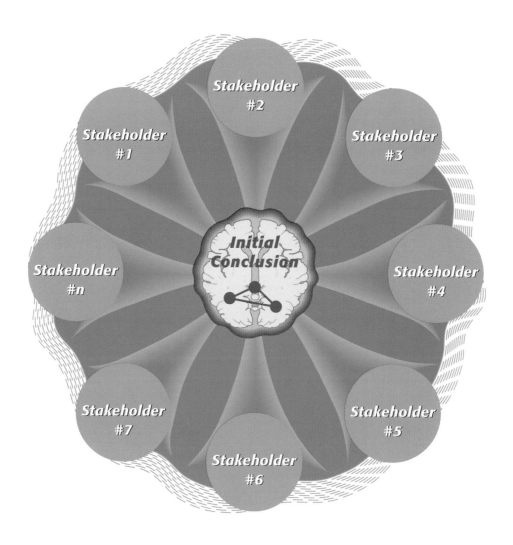

Figure 3.8 shows an initial conclusion concerning strategic change – surrounded by some of the typical stakeholders that would be affected by a change in strategic direction. Thereafter, these same stakeholders could also determine whether the strategic change will eventually be achieved. Thus, there is a two-way relationship between the initial conclusion and each potential stakeholder. Notice that each initial conclusion represents a schema/paradigm that views the problem from a limited perspective: as a single decision tree with branches. (Naturally, there are a number of other significant stakeholders besides those illustrated in eight circles here, such as other nations, future employees, family members, and best friends.)

FIGURE 3.8
Stakeholders for Strategic Change

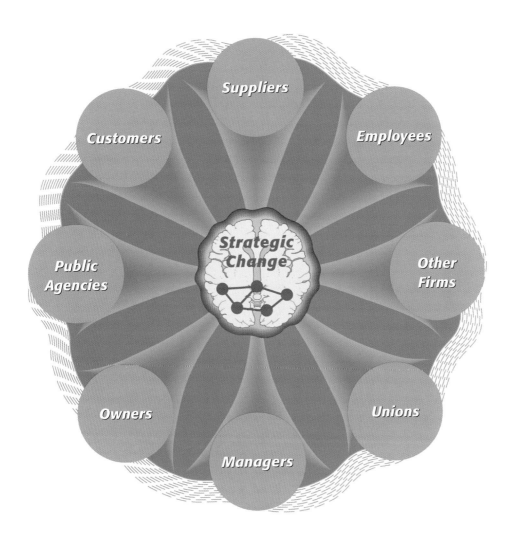

For each stakeholder, members list their assumptions: What would have to be true about any and all aspects of a given stakeholder in order to argue, most convincingly, that the conclusion, as stated, is true? Indeed, each assumption is written in a form intended to maximize this support, despite how credible, obvious, or, instead, how ridiculous the assumption may appear. The "truth" of each assumption will be investigated later. As Figure 3.9 reveals, members can now see the implicit assumptions behind their initial conclusions. Just as with surfacing cultural norms, people may experience delight as they materialize the quantum waves that have been unconscious in their organization – and underneath their decision trees.

FIGURE 3.9
Surfacing Assumptions for Each Stakeholder

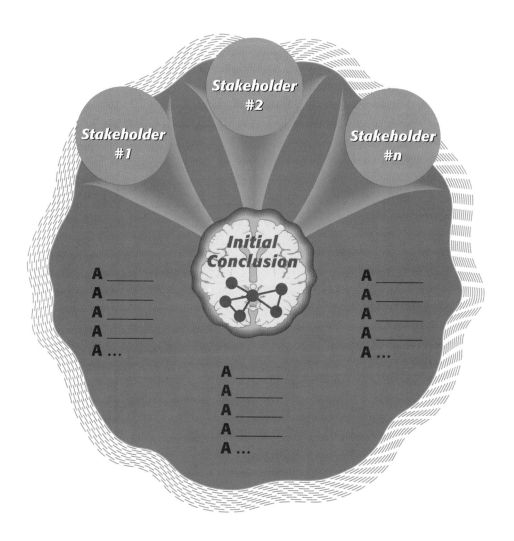

Now members must attempt to figure out the tens if not hundreds of implicit assumptions they have surfaced. Not surprisingly, we introduce several new categories for our minds/brains. First, are all assumptions of equal importance? There are always several *least important assumptions* that, even if they are false, do not prevent you from arguing forcefully for your conclusion. But there are ordinarily some *most important assumptions* that, if they turn out to be false, would greatly undermine your entire argument. In this case, you can no longer argue for the conclusion when the fallacy of such a basic assumption has been revealed. The distinction is shown in Figure 3.10 as a simplified either/or classification.

FIGURE 3.10
Distinguishing Assumptions by Their Importance

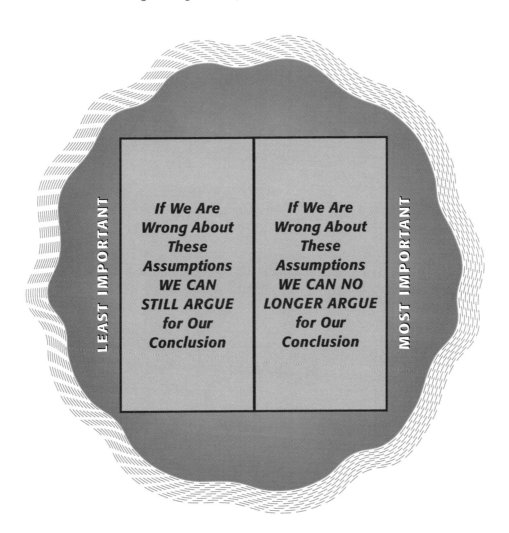

Here is an additional category for the mind/brain that helps people make sense of all their implicit assumptions: Are all assumptions of equal certainty? It seems that some assumptions are more certain (or uncertain) than others. On the one hand, a fact is an assumption that is expected to be true – or false – with complete certainty (100%). On the other hand, an assumption has great uncertainty when nobody can predict or control its eventual truth. In this situation, the certainty of the assumption is a 50/50 proposition: It is just as likely to be true as it is false. Figure 3.11 illustrates the certainty distinction: Here the top line is 100% certain and the bottom line is 50/50, while any assumption in the middle is 75% certain.

FIGURE 3.11
Distinguishing Assumptions by Their Certainty

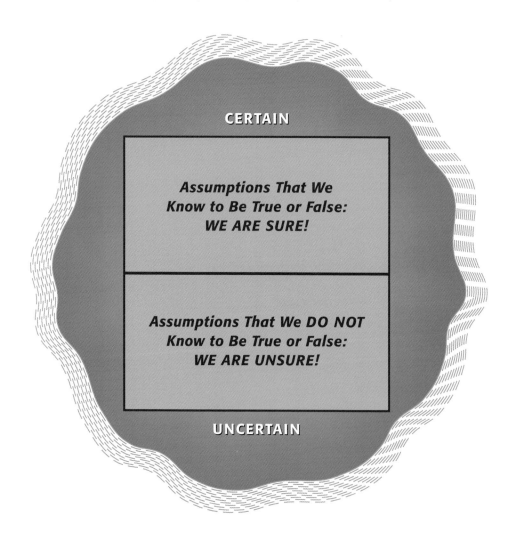

CERTAIN

Assumptions That We Know to Be True or False: WE ARE SURE!

Assumptions That We DO NOT Know to Be True or False: WE ARE UNSURE!

UNCERTAIN

Figure 3.12 portrays the *assumption matrix* for classifying assumptions according to their importance to the initial conclusion and also according to their certainty. Is the assumption, practically speaking, most important to arguing for your conclusion or is it least important? Is the assumption, as stated, fairly certain to be true (or certain to be false), or is its truth (or falsity) uncertain? Combining the two distinctions creates four categories of assumptions: (1) certain, least important, (2) certain, most important, (3) uncertain, least important, (4) uncertain, most important. This assumption matrix enables members to untangle the roots behind all the trees in their quantum forest by explicitly classifying implicit assumptions.

FIGURE 3.12
The Assumption Matrix for Classifying Assumptions

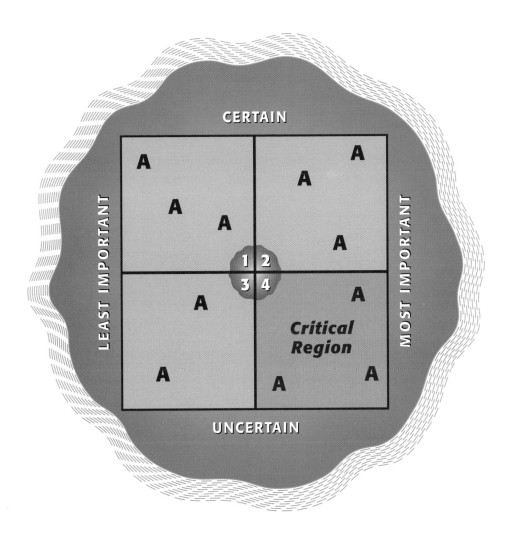

The first category (certain/least important assumptions) represents trivia – highly certain facts that have little bearing on the subject at hand. The second category (certain/most important) represents important facts; if we *know* them to be true, these assumptions do not contribute anything new. In this second category, however, it might be astonishing to discover that some central assumptions behind our favorite conclusion – now that these assumptions have been surfaced for examination – are clearly false, when all along we were assuming exactly the opposite. The third category (uncertain/least important) shows what is not fully known to be true (or false), but these issues are not primary to the arguments being presented. The fourth category (uncertain/most important) emphasizes the principal reason for surfacing and classifying assumptions. This revealing category highlights assumptions that are most important to the initial conclusion (if you're wrong about any of these assumptions, all your arguments fail), yet there is considerable uncertainty regarding the truth or falsity of these assumptions. As suggested earlier, maximum uncertainty presents a 50/50 split: These most important assumptions, as stated, are just as likely to be false as they are to be true.

The fourth category is named the *critical region*. This area is where the ultimate challenge to any argument will be focused. Too often, this critical region not only is neglected but is deliberately repressed. Individuals and groups arguing strongly for their conclusions do not want to expose their Achilles' heel: Others would see the weakness of their arguments. In short, building a problem definition or implementation plan on assumptions in the critical region is like building a house on a foundation of quicksand.

The second category is very meaningful when it presents members with their biggest surprise ever: when one or more of the most important assumptions that support the initial conclusion are actually false without any doubt whatsoever. Yet people have been making decisions according to these false assumptions for a very long time. Only by having surfaced their implicit assumptions, however, are the members able to confront – face to face – the false assumptions that have guided how they see, think, and behave. But finally they have the opportunity to do something about it: They now can revise these false assumptions by writing them to reflect what they know is true and, thereby, augment their consciousness.

The emphasis of assumptional analysis next shifts to examining the assumptions that were classified into the two most important cells of the matrix (the right-hand side of Figure 3.12). Regarding the critical region, it is worthwhile to collect information from people, books, newspapers, and the Internet to discover the actual "truth" of these assumptions.

Figure 3.13 reveals how reversing assumptions that were known to be false into statements that are known to be true creates revisions in the assumption matrix (**A**). Further, new information may transfer previously uncertain assumptions to the certain region, although these might have to be rewritten in order to assimilate what was learned. But the advantage of removing uncertain assumptions from this critical region is that you can then argue for the conclusion with much more confidence. While the least important assumptions are not investigated for the moment, they should be monitored from this time forward. What was once least important may become most important at any time.

FIGURE 3.13
Revising the Assumption Matrix

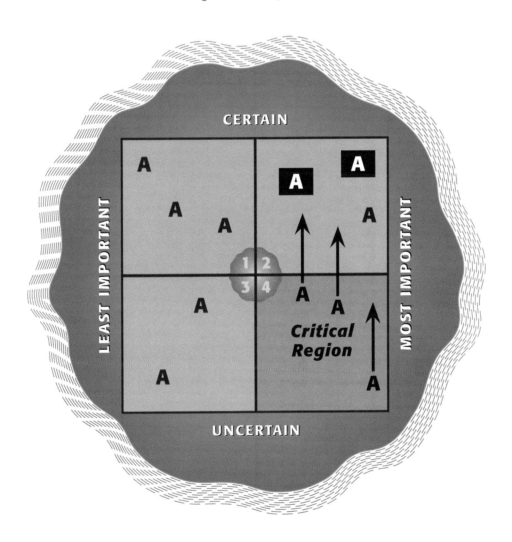

The revised assumption matrix, adjusted for new information, now becomes the basis for deducing a *new conclusion*, as shown in Figure 3.14. In essence: What new conclusion derives logically from all the assumptions plotted in the matrix – particularly those in the two most important cells? In order to deduce a new conclusion, the members often realize that they do not have to consider their assumptions as fixed. As a result of having mastered assumptional analysis, the enlightened members develop a new assumption about *assumptions themselves:* Assumptions are the attributes of stakeholders; if members influence these attributes, any conclusion that is desired can become true! *This insight epitomizes quantum thinking.*

FIGURE 3.14
Deducing the New Conclusion

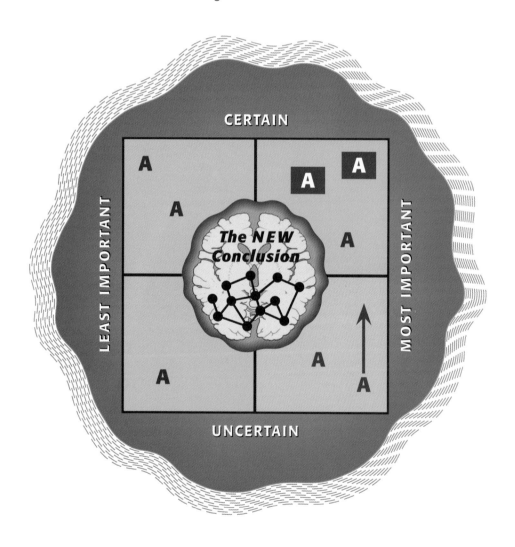

Figure 3.15 exhibits a pictorial summary of assumptional analysis: It should now be apparent that in order to minimize the errors of problem management, it is essential to *surface assumptions* (write them out explicitly), *classify assumptions* (according to their relative importance and certainty of being true/false), and *synthesize assumptions* (collect additional information about the validity of the most important/uncertain assumptions and then revise how the problem is sensed, defined, solved, and so forth – based on these revised, up–to–date assumptions). Most members eventually realize that assumptional analysis supplies them with a deeper – more accurate – approach for managing complex problems in their quantum world.

FIGURE 3.15
A Summary of Assumptional Analysis

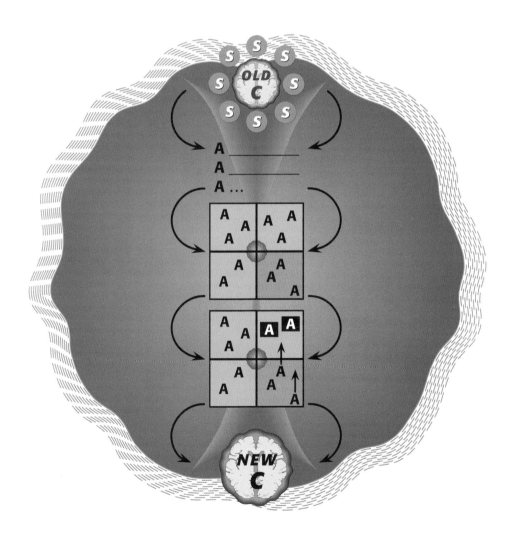

During the discussion on problem management, I offered a specific example to show that different specialists on the topic of transformation can be regarded as different decision trees in a large forest. Furthermore, below each decision tree lies (1) implicit assumptions about all the other trees in the forest and (2) implicit assumptions about the key internal and external stakeholders who will be impacted by a change initiative and, in return, will ultimately affect the success of transformation. Now I want to expand on this example to highlight key aspects of assumptional analysis.

A long time ago, I assembled twenty illustrious professionals in the field of change management for a nine-hour workshop. After expounding the basic technique of assumptional analysis, I organized them into three groups representing three divergent approaches to organizational change and improvement. The C-groups – short for *initial conclusion groups* – were delineated as human resources, organizational design, and organizational development. Each C-group was asked to formulate a list of stakeholders that would directly pertain to this initial conclusion: "Organizations that seriously desire to improve their overall performance and morale can best be served by implementing change initiatives that are generally affiliated with human resources (or organizational development or organizational design)." It was interesting to discover that the overlap in the three lists of stakeholders was roughly 95%. Specifically, all three C-groups pinpointed these prime stakeholders: shareholders, customers, suppliers, competitors, financial institutions, government agencies, the surrounding community, union organizations, prospective (future) employees, existing employees, senior managers, middle managers, supervisors, union members, families of employees, and prospective customers.

Before they were asked to list their assumptions, the C-groups first spelled out the change initiatives that define their specialty. The C-group composed mostly of human resources specialists quickly agreed that they are preoccupied with the match between individuals and designated jobs, now – and in the future. This match includes the functions of acquisition, allocation, utilization, maintenance, and development of people assigned to jobs. Thus, the *people/job interfaces* are the natural targets for most change initiatives among human resources experts.

The C-group made up of all organizational development specialists, however, was concerned with the quality of interpersonal relationships in the organization, the culture of the organization, and the establishment of trust, motivation, and commitment among members (and their subunits). Thus, culture and the *people/people interfaces* (including members-to-groups) are the prime targets for organizational development experts.

The C-group of specialists in organizational design took a different approach: The members of this C-group were primarily concerned about the formal structure of an organization's departments and divisions and the prime methods of governance (for example, management hierarchies or self-managing teams). The focus for organizational design, therefore, is typically the *subunit/subunit interfaces* and the mode of coordination among these subunits.

Next each C-group proceeded to untangle its implicit assumptions about stakeholders and then presented them to the entire community of change experts. Even though every C-group knew, intellectually, that the three specialties were vastly different from one another, they still seemed very surprised to hear, in a live forum, just how different they really were. What concerned one C-group was dismissed or overlooked by the other two C-groups! Gradually, however, each C-group began to appreciate that the numerous attributes that they routinely disregard in their specialized approach *have a dramatic impact on organizational success.*

Two representatives from each C-group were then asked to form an integrated group, called a *synthesis group*, or S-group for short. The mission of the six-member S-group was to formulate an integrated assessment of the key assumptions underneath all three initial conclusions (which had been surfaced independently by each of the three C-groups) and then to propose a synthesis (a new conclusion) to this question: What integrated approach to transformation would help most organizations significantly improve their overall performance and morale? I now want to feature the fundamental assumptions that guided the S-group's discussion and then summarize the "new tree" that was created within this quantum forest.

The S-group proclaimed that each specialty assumes that the other two specialties have already consulted with the organization in question and thus have already accomplished their change objectives. Specifically, human resources assumes that (1) the culture of the organization and the trust, motivation, and commitment of its members are already conducive to obtaining accurate assessments of people/job interfaces throughout the organization; (2) these cultural as well as people-to-people attributes have already attracted the most competent people (and will continue to retain these people) in the marketplace; (3) the current design of subunits in the organization (strategic business units, divisions, departments, and groups) is the most effective and efficient way of managing all the organization's resources (including the mechanisms used to coordinate these work units) and these subunits have been operationalized into clear jobs throughout the organization. The S-group could see that these assumptions are most important – but highly uncertain for change initiatives within the human resources specialty.

The S-group also proclaimed similar uncertain assumptions when focusing on either organizational development or organizational design: The former approach assumes that the proper design and coordination of subunits have already formed the best jobs for the present and the future; the latter approach assumes that the culture and members' relationships are already adaptive, healthy, and receptive to change and improvement. Both approaches assume that the best people have already been attracted, rewarded appropriately, and retained by the organization.

When the S-group proceeded to synthesize the three specialties into one comprehensive approach (after revising and rewording many of the most important assumptions), a startling paradox caught their attention: How can each specialty justify its sweeping assumptions about the other two approaches when so many reports of failed efforts at transformation indicate that all the other attributes of the organization (addressed by the other two specialties) were also in dire need of change and improvement? As a result of struggling with this dilemma, the S-group began to realize that *all three approaches to transformation are needed all of the time!*

The new tree that the S-group firmly planted in the forest contained several branches emphasizing the sequence by which all three specialties should be brought into an organization: Should all three be implemented simultaneously? The S-group named this solution the *shotgun approach*. Or should all three specialties be brought into the organization, one after the other, depending upon who made the request and which consultant was available? The S-group characterized this solution as the *adhoc approach*. Or should the three specialties proceed harmoniously, right from the start, in designing and implementing a coherent, well-designed, well-orchestrated solution to change and improvement? The S-group considered this fertile branch a *completely integrated program*.

Recall: The adhoc, shotgun, and completely integrated program are the same three approaches to transformation that were introduced earlier (pages 77–78). It can now be revealed that the roots of these useful insights about how to sequence change initiatives were initially suggested by this community of specialists in organizational change (Kilmann, Benecki, and Shkop, 1979). These experts made use of assumptional analysis to examine the implicit assumptions that were below their professionally grown trees (Kilmann, 1983a). Then, after an intense debate and negotiation took place across the three C-groups, a representative S-group was formed to resolve the remaining differences and deduce a new conclusion to the problem of transformation. During this process, members of the S–group clearly saw the obvious limitations of the specialized categories that were instilled in their minds/brains. But through a creative interchange, they were able to derive a synthesis that not only made sense to them but also confirmed their extensive experience in change management. They also encountered intense contradictions in their professional paradigms, but they were able to create new categories in their minds and rewired their brains as well. While I don't have the traditional scientific results to support this claim, I am convinced that these twenty experts fundamentally changed the way they see, think, and behave about organizational transformation. I surely know that I have: *The eight tracks became one subbranch on that new tree.*

③ THE TEAM TRACK

Much of the interaction and work that goes on in today's organizations takes place in groups – which include intact work units, cross–functional teams, task forces, and steering committees. The paramount reason for all this group–based and project–based functioning is that organizations are increasingly facing complex problems that need varied perspectives and commitment from diverse experts representing both internal and external stakeholders. This rationale should be reason enough for organizations to use groups extensively – but never indiscriminately.

Also germane, the invisible force of cultural norms and sanctioning systems is applied most effectively inside groups. Most people are affected more directly by their intimate group than by an impersonal organization of thousands or a much larger community of millions. Furthermore, intact groups provide the immediate feedback to help members learn and cope with new problems. Therefore, having work groups attend all workshop sessions together during the first two tracks of the completely integrated program helps members learn and rehearse new skills. Similarly, when it is time for work groups to apply what they've learned to the riskier, more challenging workplace, the intact unit furnishes members with emotional support and effective feedback (as supported by adaptive cultural norms and new behavioral skills for giving/receiving feedback) for making the necessary transition from learning to doing.

During the early workshops for the team track, members learn (and confirm) that one of the biggest time wasters in their organizational lives is ineffective group meetings. Often members have been so frustrated by dysfunctional groups, let alone repeated useless meetings, that they have almost given up on the notion that groups can actually be effective. But if they search their collective memories, they can usually recall some group experience in which the collective mission was achieved and everyone felt good about the process. Of course, members usually attribute such group effectiveness to luck and leadership, or the group's size and composition. But rarely do members possess a deep understanding of the fundamental processes that occur in group meetings that determine success or failure. The basic objective of the team track, therefore, is to open everyone's eyes to the unconscious processes that affect every meeting.

Teaching the underlying principles of group process and providing numerous opportunities to give and receive feedback (on how well each member was able to apply these key principles of group process) enables group members to become fully conscious of this potent feature of their quantum infrastructures. Subsequently, whatever new groups are formed, whether newly redesigned work units, cross–boundary teams, or project groups, members from all previous departments, levels, and areas in the organization will be able to become a capable team – quickly and easily. Since more has been documented about groups/teams than perhaps any other topics on organizational change, improvement, and transformation, I will not summarize what is already available through numerous sources. But I will highlight what I have found to be the most fundamental aspects of group process that every member in an organization should know and practice in all group settings (Dyer, 1977; McGrath, 1984; Parker, 1990).

At the beginning of each group meeting, every member should be fully aware of the objectives of the meeting. Group members should plan their time wisely and determine the priority of their agenda items before they discuss any subject at length. They should agree to address the most important issues first and the less important issues last. Group members also should plan how each agenda item will be approached and whether it can be subdivided into several manageable pieces (and subgroups), so that a project's complexity does not immobilize them. Naturally, spending a little time planning these matters *before* proceeding usually saves a lot of time later. As soon as a plan is developed, the assumptions underlying all subsequent discussions should be illuminated – not only to minimize the likelihood of committing serious errors in problem management, but also to reduce the occurrence of circular, repetitive, and superficial discussions (which might also be based on false assumptions).

Furthermore, the more talkative members should make a concerted effort to bring the less talkative members into every discussion to ensure that all perspectives are heard and all available information can be used. (This is particularly meaningful if any international members feel shy or hesitant to speak, since the host language is not their native tongue; they might still be trying to figure out the cultural norms and customs of the host country.) Even more to the point, group members should regularly assess whether their cultural norms continue to support new, bizarre, and provocative ideas. All communications should be courteous – respecting every person's ego and treating everyone with dignity. Only one member in a meeting should be speaking at one moment; everyone else should be listening. A collaborative spirit, not a competitive one (fighting to talk the most and trying to win the final argument), must be applied on complex problems in order to make full use of everyone's knowledge in a creative way for the best *group* outcome (Thomas and Kilmann, 1974). Occasionally, members should take a break from the discussion on content and inquire about the *process:* How are we doing as a group? Are we applying the key principles and skills? If not, what should we be doing differently?

When it comes to ensuring that members will actually apply these principles and be able to improve their group process, it is most beneficial to appoint one member as a "process observer" at the start of every group meeting. This person is entirely responsible for monitoring how well the principles guide the group's discussions. At the end of each meeting, the process observer summarizes what the group did particularly well and in what ways the group fell short. A plan is then formulated regarding what to do differently during the group's next meeting – and how to make this newly developed knowledge readily available to other work groups in the organization. Moreover, a different member should be appointed to this role every time the group meets. Consequently, during a period of several weeks or months, every member of the group will have the opportunity to develop sharp observation skills and practice giving effective feedback. In the future, it will no longer be necessary to appoint a process observer; the responsibility for monitoring and improving the group's process will have become shared among all group members.

After the first session of the team track, *every* group meeting should make convenient use of a process observer by following these guidelines. Members will therefore become familiar with – and skilled at – describing group process and proposing ways to improve it. As a result, they become more conscious of one more invisible force that significantly affects how they see, think, and behave. Further, members will have been introduced to a *process view* of work. This view will be indispensable when they must examine all the other processes that take place within their organization – during the last three tracks of the completely integrated program. This is when members self–design/self–manage their value–added processes.

Becoming a quantum organization therefore mandates that all members become consciously aware of the distressing (dysfunctional) *cultural norms* they have been imposing on one another in an unconscious manner. By specifically discussing these invisible forces in open forums, they have an opportunity to establish favorable (functional) norms that will strengthen trust, goodwill, and mutuality within and across all subunits.

Becoming a quantum organization also mandates that all members discover the inherent causes of their *complex problems* before implementing solutions. Accepting and clearly understanding this maxim will minimize the most incapacitating errors of problem management. Moreover, instead of blindly making decisions and solving problems according to outdated and invalid assumptions (as is usually the case with passive jobholders on perpetual autopilot in Newtonian organizations), members of a quantum organization must explicitly analyze the *implicit assumptions* underneath all their crucial decisions and actions. As a result, they have an opportunity to bring their assumptions in sync with the expectations of their internal and external stakeholders – thereby cultivating the effectiveness of their subsequent decisions and actions.

Becoming a quantum organization also requires that members be consciously aware of what processes will enable them to fully utilize the special wisdom and knowledge in every member's mind/brain: During all meetings, they must closely monitor the below–the–surface *group processes* and make mid–course corrections as needed. At the end of each meeting, members must then consider ways to improve their group functioning for their next scheduled meeting – and rapidly circulate this newly acquired knowledge throughout the organization. In these ways, the effectiveness of collective action (within and across subunit boundaries) will continue to evolve to higher forms of dialogue, debate, creativity, and synthesis.

This learning in the culture, skills, and team tracks will inseminate self-awareness – and consciousness – into all the quantum infrastructures throughout an organization. Thereafter, whenever members interact with one another, either within their work units or across subunit boundaries, they will be supported by the invisible but *conscious* forces that engender organizational success: seeing, thinking, and behaving in an enlightened manner. Establishing quantum infrastructures is especially important for members self-designing their formal systems and value–added processes during the remaining tracks of the completely integrated program. And so is the case for self-managing all other complex problems.

FORMAL SYSTEMS

Managing Strategy-Structure and Rewards with Quantum Thinking

The identity of an organization, then, is a holistic image, often vague and implicit, of the continuing nature of the organization as it moves through social space and time. Those at the strategic apex of the organization who hold this image must translate it into something more practical, into an integrated operational model – a design that brings together a desired strategy, structure, and [reward system] of the organization into a coherent whole.

— *David Limerick and Bert Cunnington*
(1993, page 170)

For a quantum organization, *strategy* must not only maintain and increase market share in an already existing industry. It must also create a strategic architecture for materializing the new industries, markets, products, and services for the future. Likewise, *structure* must not only allocate resources, efficiently and effectively, to accomplish short–term strategic objectives. It must also leverage these resources to capture global market share for the yet–to–be–transformed industries of tomorrow. Additionally, *rewards* must be intrinsically experienced and extrinsically presented so that members will remain self-motivated and devote their skills, knowledge, and energy toward achieving their self-designed strategy through their self-designed structure – across social space and time. Aligning and deploying all these elaborate aspects of strategy, structure, and rewards are enabled through quantum thinking supported by quantum infrastructures. Establishing an organization's formal systems for a quantum world, therefore, represents the epitome of complex problems.

This chapter presents the problem management organization (PMO) as a social methodology for addressing the most complex problems that impact the whole organization. As we shall see, PMOs make considerable use of quantum thinking in order to minimize the most disastrous errors of problem management: defining problems and implementing solutions. The very first use of a PMO, incidentally, is to constitute a special steering committee – referred to as the *shadow track* – that is fully responsible for orchestrating the implementation of the completely integrated program. Shortly after the diagnostic report has pinpointed the transformation gaps (and hence, defined the problems), about twenty-five representatives from all levels, areas, and locations in the organization are carefully selected to be members of this steering group for the duration of the program.

The second use of a PMO is to analyze and redesign the strategy and structure of the organization via the strategy–structure track. This PMO is composed of a different set of twenty-five members – but also represents all levels, areas, and locations in the current organization. The third use of a PMO is to provide a new organization–wide, performance–based reward system via the reward system track. This PMO is composed of another set of about twenty-five members, who again represent all levels, areas, and locations in the organization. Thereafter, additional PMOs are utilized for both radical process improvement and learning process improvement via the last two tracks of the program – and for ensuing problems that affect the entire organization.

Such active participation among so many representatives (and their ongoing communication with those they represent) *helps ensure the creation of a self-designing, self-managing quantum organization.* Quantum infrastructures throughout the organization (via the first three tracks) have already been established for successfully analyzing and implementing transformational changes in systems and processes. To recapitulate, only if an organization has already developed a healthy culture, only if its members have learned the skills for managing complex problems and implicit assumptions, and only if a cooperative team spirit has been activated within and across all subunits – only then will all members have achieved a vital threshold of self–aware consciousness and learned the skills for self-transforming their systems and processes.

This chapter next presents a new *holistic image* – a model for aligning the three systems (strategy, structure, and rewards) through three levels of deployment (from *integrated architecture* to *sequenced implementation* and then to *subsequent improvement*). Even though the three formal systems and their deployment are generally treated in a piecemeal manner in a Newtonian organization, a quantum organization thoroughly understands that these formal systems must be completely aligned and fully deployed if they are to guide self–motion monads toward organizational success: Inconsistent strategic architecture, structural forms, and reward practices will certainly confuse the membership. Not translating integrated plans for these formal systems into desired behavior renders them wasteful and useless.

The chapter also covers the material discussed with the participants of the strategy–structure PMO: how to generate a strategic architecture for a quantum organization and how to harmonize this strategic architecture with structural forms and the coordination of self–managed subunits. The chapter then tackles the overriding issues confronting the reward system PMO: What is motivation? What is a reward? What is performance? What is measurement? How can an organization motivate high performance – measured accurately – with its extrinsic and intrinsic rewards? If reward practices are instituted with a deep understanding of self–motion monads (while also being aligned and deployed with strategy–structure), members will be able – and willing – to achieve success for their organization and personal meaning for themselves.

In summary, after a brief introduction to the problem management organization, this chapter presents a holistic model for managing strategy, structure, and rewards – from redesigning these systems to implementing them to subsequently improving them. Finally, the chapter elaborates the various concepts and methods that participants in the strategy–structure and reward system tracks use to align and deploy all their formal systems: to create a self–designing/self–managing quantum organization.

The Problem Management Organization (PMO)

The PMO is an effective way to assemble a diverse collection of members – from all areas, levels, and locations in the organization (including external stakeholders) – in order to manage complex, organization–wide problems. This technique for problem management has also been called a parallel or collateral organization (Bushe and Shani, 1991; Zand, 1981). The members in this unique arrangement spend two to ten hours per week working on complex problems; the remainder of their time is spent back in the formal operational structure. The PMO continues to exist for as long as it takes to bring the identified problems within an acceptable threshold or gap. Once this takes place, the members are disbanded and return to other activities, which might include other PMO assignments. (Indeed, most members can expect to participate in a PMO assignment at least once a year.)

The top portion of Figure 4.1 represents the *operational* (day–to–day) structure of an organization. The vertical bars characterize the traditional functions (operations, marketing, finance), while the horizontal bars show cross–boundary task flow. The roof of this "Newtonian house" portrays the management hierarchy, which coordinates the functions within subunits and what flows across subunits. The PMO is created by forming a *collateral* structure of C–groups and one S–group. Note: C–groups can refer to either *cross-boundary groups* for the PMO or *conclusion groups* for doing assumptional analysis. An S–group is either the *steering group* for the PMO or the *synthesis group* during assumptional analysis. Flexible designs are vital to PMOs.

FIGURE 4.1
Defining the Problem Management Organization

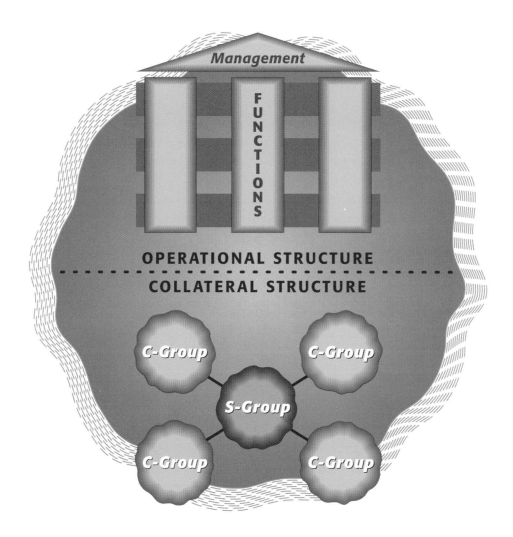

     CHAPTER 4

Figure 4.2 captures the diverse members (●) that form the C–groups and one S–group – from all areas, levels, and locations in the operational structure. The fundamental reason for using these parallel structures with overlapping cross–memberships in the PMO is to increase the probability that creative/effective solutions to complex problems will be derived and implemented. A collateral structure allows diverse members to be directly involved in defining and solving complex problems; these same members are then directly responsible for implementing their solutions back in the operational structure, *thus becoming a self-designing, self-managing organization.* Note: The S–group consists of at least one member from each C–group.

FIGURE 4.2
Forming the Problem Management Organization

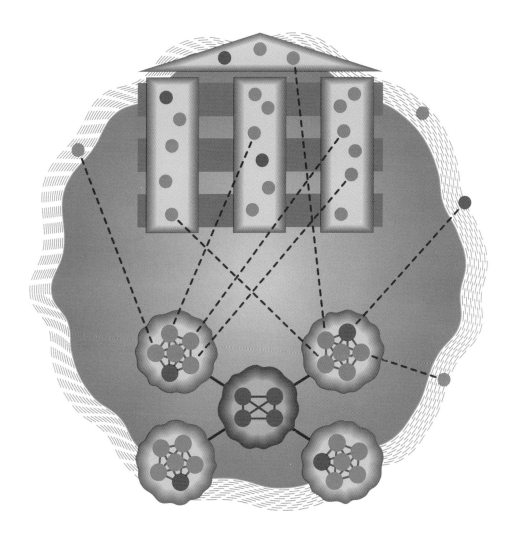

Figure 4.3 illustrates the usual process for conducting assumptional analysis in the PMO: (1) several alternative (radical) initial conclusions are generated by all PMO participants; (2) a different C–group is composed to surface and classify the assumptions underneath each initial conclusion; (3) each C–group, in turn, shares and debates its assumption matrix with the other C-groups – thus identifying fundamental differences in both the importance and certainty of implicit assumptions; (4) an S-group is then formed to resolve any remaining differences – usually by collecting more information, followed by additional dialogue and debate; (5) the S-group deduces a new conclusion based on its revised assumptions.

FIGURE 4.3
C-Groups and an S-Group in a PMO

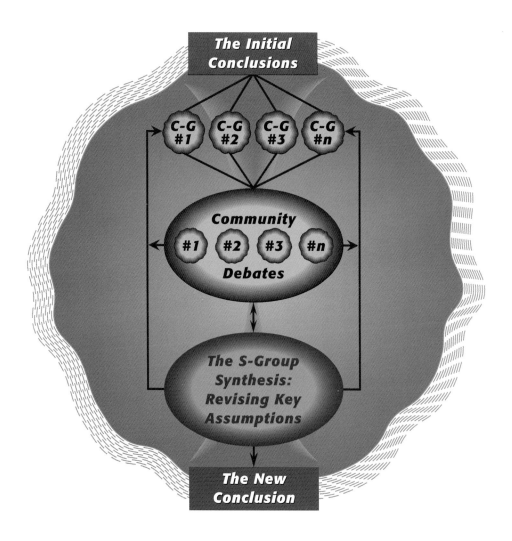

Figure 4.4 shows the sequence of C–group and S–group activities in a PMO – alongside the formal steps of assumptional analysis. This intricate group process using assumptional analysis is a practical way to minimize the defining and implementing errors for the complex issues confronting an organization (such as strategy–structure and reward systems). However, the first three tracks should precede the formation of a collateral structure in a PMO – to create organization–wide quantum infrastructures. Without favorable norms, enlightened skills, and cooperative teamwork within the *operational* structure, we could hardly expect much sharing of information and experience in the *collateral* structure.

FIGURE 4.4
Analysis and Action in a PMO

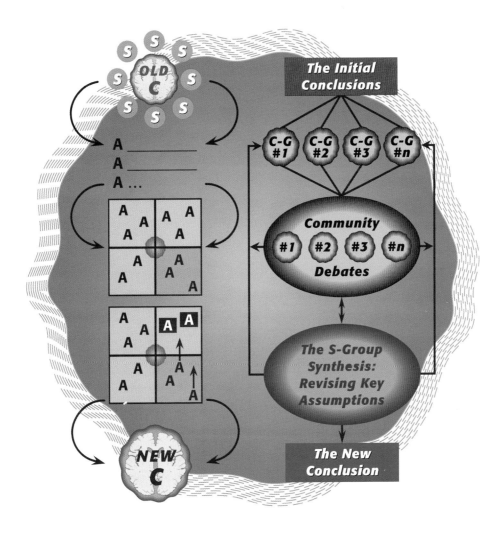

Mobilizing the Shadow Track

Regarding the first application of a PMO, full responsibility for managing the completely integrated program is neither delegated to some external consultant nor assigned to any staff group. Instead, a *shadow track* (running parallel to all eight tracks) is established right after the diagnostic report is distributed and discussed. This special track oversees the implementation and evaluation of the whole program. Its members – consisting of senior executives and an equal number of members who represent all levels and areas in the organization – are selected by the senior management group. (The number of shadow track members is somewhere around twenty–five, depending on the size of the organization in question.) Knowing that the membership will certainly be judging the fairness of the selection process always seems to motivate the senior executives to use a process that they can defend – easily, rationally, and publicly.

Usually an engaging all–day workshop is conducted for the purpose of getting the shadow track off to a good start by establishing functional norms and engendering a team spirit. Basically, the difficulty involved in getting off to a good start is that the organization, as might be expected, is still operating according to all the dysfunctions that were pinpointed in the diagnostic report (since members have not yet created their quantum infrastructures). The shadow track, consequently, is still engrossed with its Newtonian environment. But by being exposed, early on, to a discussion on cultural norms and participating in team–building activities (including the regular use of process observers), perhaps the shadow track can stay at least one month ahead of the rest of the organization and thus acquire credibility while performing its task. (See Kilmann, 1991, pages 2•45–2•55, for detailed procedures for establishing the shadow track.) Eventually, of course, the shadow track and the entire organization will fully internalize all the principles and practices of the completely integrated program.

After their all–day workshop, the participants in the shadow track meet regularly (at least several hours every month) to monitor the impact of the program on the organization and to find approaches for improving the process of implementation: They are asked to be as imaginative and proactive as possible to guarantee that the program continually promotes self–transformation. Typically, the shadow trackers are expected to keep in regular contact with the work units they are representing throughout the organization. They also develop and utilize a special–purpose information system so that unfavorable attitudes, feelings, and any difficulties with the program can surface. With this input, the shadow track (taking advantage of the expert knowledge and experience of the consultants) has a basis for adjusting its efforts in order to manage the evolving needs and problems of the organization and its members.

When positive events or interim results signal the desired direction of transformation, it is very important to share such critical incidents with the whole organization. While accounts of what other organizations have experienced with a transformational program may inspire some members to try improved ways of doing things, no exemplar is ever as powerful as discovering how a subunit in the *very same organization* has actively applied the principles and practices of the program. Sometimes the shadow track develops its own newsletter or makes use of an existing publication and electronic bulletin boards to publicize significant improvements and serve as a public forum for ongoing question–and–answer dialogue. Essentially, the consultants and the participants in the shadow track meet regularly to consider all the various ways in which stakeholder needs can be satisfied and positive changes can be celebrated.

Mobilizing the Strategy-Structure Track

When the organization is ready to begin work on the complex problems of strategy and structure, the shadow trackers then choose approximately twenty–five participants for the strategy–structure track. In most cases, the selection process includes a request for nominations to this track (by self or others) and may entail an elaborate job–posting process – including a job description for the track, materials to support the applicants, letters of reference, and formal interviews. Regardless of which approach is taken, the selected participants should fairly represent all areas and levels in the organization; they should also exemplify the positive norms and the use of problem management skills, as evidenced through their behavior and attitudes at the workplace; they should be viewed as formal and informal leaders and team players. When the rest of the membership examines the roster of persons chosen to participate in the strategy–structure track, the response should be: "These are the right people to tackle our problems."

Once all the participants in the strategy–structure track have been brought together for an inaugural one–day meeting, some time should be spent on getting acquainted and developing a team spirit (especially since members come from different regions in the organization and may never have met one another before). Thereafter, the most important ingredients of strategy and structure are presented and debated, including (1) visions, dreams, missions, purposes, goals, objectives, tasks; (2) corporate strategy, competitive strategies, core competencies, information and communication technologies, electronic markets, and creating altogether new markets and industries; (3) work processes and task flow, forming subunit boundaries, different approaches for coordinating subunits, vertical versus horizontal organizations, and global network (knowledge or learning) organizations. Consultants, external or internal, are often recruited to teach participants the knowledge they need in order to address strategy–structure problems. The objective is that all participants in the strategy–structure track have a working knowledge of the pertinent concepts and methods (as discussed later in this chapter). Next the participants examine the diagnostic results that were discussed several months ago. After having been exposed to the latest theories for determining an organization's strategic direction and its structural arrangement of resources, the strategy–structure problems that were identified become much more meaningful.

Following these educational sessions, the participants are prepared to address their organization's strategy–structure problems with all their knowledge and experience. And because of all the progress with the prior tracks, they will be particularly aware of the consequences of committing various problem management errors. They know that if a *defining* error is committed while reshaping strategic directions or restructuring resources, all subsequent attempts at transformation will be wasted. And even if an effective strategic plan and operational structure have been designed, the latent potential of the organization cannot be achieved if an *implementing* error is committed. Although other mistakes of problem management can undermine the overall success of the strategy–structure track, the defining and implementing errors are the most devastating of all.

Mobilizing the Reward System Track

Motivating self–motion monads to first attain high performance and then equitably distributing rewards according to their performance generate a most complex problem. Thus another version of the PMO should be used for the reward system track in order to minimize all the errors of problem management. Just as soon as the strategy–structure track has formulated the organization's *operational* structure, the *collateral* structure for the PMO can be formed to represent this new arrangement of members and other resources. Thus even if members are spending most of their time in their old work groups as the new design of subunits is being implemented, the new reward system should be in sync with the most recent alignment of strategy and structure.

Again it is the shadow track (consisting of executives and additional members who are coordinating the completely integrated program) that selects about twenty-five participants to address reward system problems (this is a different sample of participants from those who are still involved with implementing strategic architecture and structural forms). The same criteria, however, are used for selection: The participants should represent all areas and levels in the organization (which in this situation would be the newly designed subunits); they also should exemplify (1) the desired cultural norms, (2) the successful use of problem management skills, and (3) cooperation and teamwork.

Once the members of the reward system track have been brought together for their inaugural one-day workshop, adequate time should be spent on getting acquainted and developing a team spirit. Then material is presented on such topics as motivation, intrinsic and extrinsic rewards, reliable and valid measures of performance, evaluation and feedback, job design, goal setting, and legal issues in the design and administration of reward systems. Moreover, alternative reward systems are examined that combine some of the following distinctions: piece rate versus hourly rate; hourly rate versus salary; skill-based pay versus job-based pay; monetary bonuses; gain sharing versus profit sharing; ownership options; and fixed versus flexible fringe benefits. Most often, both external consultants and internal human resources experts provide the participants with a working knowledge of the purposes, designs, and functioning of reward systems. During this first work session, the participants also review the diagnostic report that was presented at the early stages of the program. After having been exposed to the recent knowledge on *motivation*, participants find new meaning in the reward system problems that were pinpointed during the diagnostic stage of transformation.

In subsequent work sessions, the participants in the reward system track meet with their associates in the strategy-structure track to discuss their progress to date. Such *cross-track* interaction continues throughout the implementation of the renewed strategy-structure and reward systems. In addition, these PMOs also keep current with the work taking place in the last two tracks of the program (the radical process track and the learning process track), which would have already begun. This ongoing exchange of ideas and knowledge helps to *align all the formal systems and processes in the organization*. Similarly, all the participants in the various PMOs are required to maintain two-way communication with the rest of the membership – a process that fosters organization-wide understanding and commitment to all implemented solutions.

ALIGNING AND DEPLOYING ALL SYSTEMS

Figure 4.5 demonstrates a holistic image for designing, implementing, and improving formal systems – as an arrangement of strategy, structure, and rewards. These three dominions have generally received isolated attention (in specialized books on strategic management, organizational design, and human resources), but have rarely been contemplated as *three interconnected ingredients* – each supplying a symbiotic function for directing, organizing, and rewarding the behavior of self–motion monads. But this integration is precisely what is needed for transformation (Mackenzie, 1991).

FIGURE 4.5
Aligning All Systems

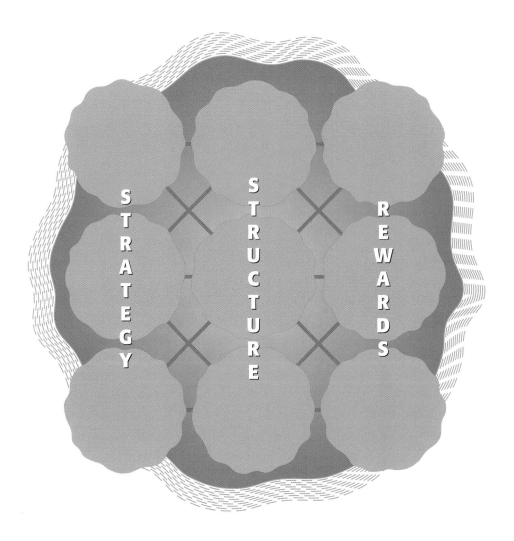

Another key dimension of a holistic approach is illustrated in Figure 4.6, where special attention is devoted to the role of deployment: from the creation of an *integrated architecture* to the *sequenced implementation* of planned action steps, and, finally, to the continuous process of *subsequently improving* the formal systems once they have been implemented. All too often, plans for strategy, structure, or rewards remain on paper but are not effectively translated – and operationalized – into clear job guidelines and processes for every member in the organization. Or, equally ineffective, once formal systems are implemented, they become inflexible – since they are seldom monitored, evaluated, and improved.

FIGURE 4.6
Deploying All Systems

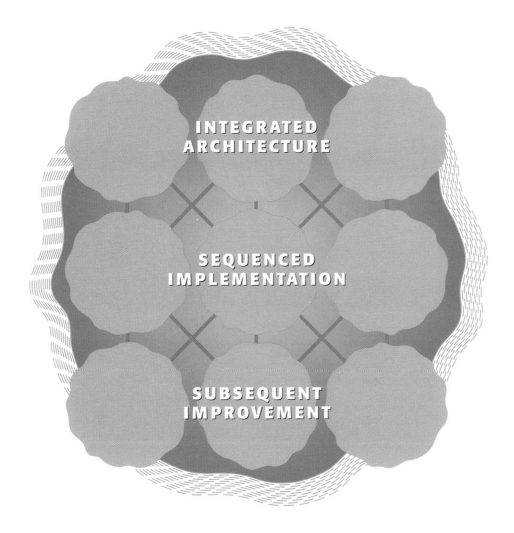

The detailed model shown in Figure 4.7 reveals *nine interrelated waves to materialize formal systems*. Recall: There are scores of books that argue for one piece or another (one cell at a time) or one interface or another (two cells at a time). And yet Figures 4.5, 4.6, and 4.7 imply that the problem of establishing formal systems is far more complicated than most members, consultants, and scholars like to believe. Besides neglecting the quantum infrastructures, during piecemeal efforts at transformation, one or more of these interfaces concerning alignment or deployment are also overlooked as management proceeds to address only one formal system at a time or does not effectively deploy its formal systems.

FIGURE 4.7
A Holistic Model of Formal Systems

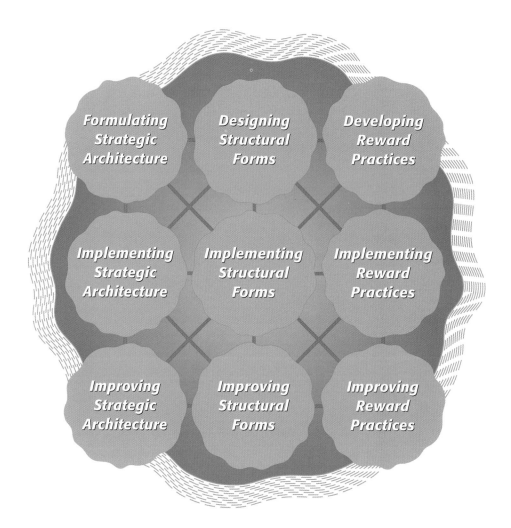

To thoroughly appreciate the integrated makeup of formal systems, consider the case in which the strategic direction of a firm is significantly changed (for instance, entering global markets with new products for new customers), yet its divisional structure and reward systems remain rooted in the previous domestic marketplace. Or consider when the structure is redesigned into horizontal units in order to support business processes, yet the link between business processes and strategic objectives remains vague and ill-defined – and changes in the reward system are ignored as well. Or consider when reward systems are revamped – yet new metrics for measuring performance are difficult to corroborate due to overlapping functional areas or an outdated strategic direction. A holistic approach, in contrast, *always* considers the interfaces of strategy, structure, and rewards while attempting to improve – let alone transform – an organization.

Essentially, the holistic model requires that all three formal systems be aligned and coordinated in every instance – to deliver one integrated message to every organizational member. For this to be accomplished in actuality, the makeup of the three formal systems must be translated and communicated to all members – through job expectations, processes, and job descriptions. Then, over time, as the needs and wants of internal and external stakeholders change (or as the prevailing integrated architecture can be translated and communicated more effectively), efforts should be directed at *improving* formal systems – incrementally or radically. Thus the work of the strategy–structure and reward system tracks does not end as such, even if other members or forums (subsequent PMOs) are assigned to monitor, evaluate, and improve the interconnected formal systems.

It is tempting to argue that all formal systems should be designed and implemented within one PMO – so that all the crucial interfaces for aligning and deploying the three systems are addressed explicitly. Or one might argue that each system should be managed by a separate PMO – to include more representatives in self-designing the formal systems (just as separate C-groups are composed for different initial conclusions). In this latter case, however, the three PMOs must integrate their efforts along the way (just like the S-group must incorporate the numerous contributions of the different C-groups). I always find that the most viable approach is to arrange for two PMOs: the first PMO for all strategy–structure interfaces, because the direction of an organization and its composition of subunits are so intertwined (and structure, in essence, implements strategy) – and a second PMO for all reward system problems, because certain technical and legal aspects of measuring performance and distributing rewards require very specialized knowledge that is not needed for strategy–structure on a regular basis. Additionally, having two PMOs offers opportunities for more members to be vigorously involved in self-designing their formal systems than if only one PMO were mobilized for all three systems. But remember: The strategy–structure and reward system tracks must *coordinate* the design and implementation of their respective systems in order to make sure that strategy, structure, and rewards are completely aligned and fully deployed throughout the organization (Mackenzie, 1991).

④ THE STRATEGY-STRUCTURE TRACK

Numerous terms have been used to describe the intended direction of an organization – often called *ends* as distinguished from the *means* of getting there. Some of the many terms used to denote ends include *dreams, visions, missions, aspirations, ambitions, intentions, expectations, targets, goals,* and *objectives.* The various means for achieving ends include structural arrangements of people, tasks, technologies, money, materials, information, and documents (organization charts, group charters, policies, guidelines, procedures, rules, regulations, and job descriptions).

The term *strategy* is generally meant to describe a top-management-driven, systematically derived selection of organization ends. But also, by necessity, the word has evolved to include the means for achieving these ends: hence the hyphenated term *strategy-structure.* Two related transitions during the latter part of the twentieth century, however, have significantly challenged the traditional concept of strategy–structure: (1) the evolution toward a fast–paced, competitive, interconnected, global, living economy and (2) the evolution toward further self–aware consciousness in people, organizations, and institutions. Both of these major developments require greater member participation and involvement in the formulation as well as the implementation of strategy–structure – because these topics evoke very complex problems that can effectively be addressed only by making use of the diverse minds/brains of an organization's internal and external stakeholders.

In the following two sections, I provide the basic material presented to all the participants in the strategy–structure track – *before* they proceed with assumptional analysis of radically different strategies–structures. The action steps include formulating and deploying strategic architecture and then designing and deploying structural forms. In both cases, the reader is referred to Figures 4.5 through 4.7 for the holistic model that furnishes an interconnected approach for managing strategy, structure, and rewards – so that we keep in mind *the big picture* of these formal systems.

Formulating and Deploying Strategic Architecture

It is essential to see the distinctions between the Newtonian and quantum approaches to strategy. Each is rooted in very different assumptions about an organization's environment (as either one absolute universe or many relativistic ones) and its members and other prime stakeholders (as either inert molar objects or self-motion monads). As we will see, however, only a quantum organization has the capabilities for achieving organizational success in the *future* while at the same time performing the necessary tasks to ensure success in the *present*.

The Newtonian approach to strategy (as presented in most accounts of business policy, long-range planning, strategic planning, and strategic management) considers the organization as a collection of independent business units (or strategic business units or, simply, sbus), each of which is organized into the typical functional subunits (marketing, sales, finance, operations, design, engineering, service, and so forth). Consistent with the Cartesian–Newtonian Paradigm, this classic approach to strategy assumes a fairly stable environment or, at most, a steadily changing environment – whose trajectory can therefore be predicted with considerable accuracy. Therefore, jobholders within every Newtonian sbu see, think, and behave according to all the established categories of a well-defined industry with well-defined markets containing well-defined customers.

The strategic focus of each Newtonian sbu is only a matter of how to position the price, cost, and differentiated features of its products and services (including the choice of market segments, distribution channels, and sales/service packages) in order to compete with its sbu counterparts in other organizations. *Strategy in the Cartesian-Newtonian Paradigm is correctly positioning each independent business unit within fixed industry boundaries to satisfy existing customers.* Only within the Cartesian–Newtonian Paradigm is there one absolute universe (marketplace) whose laws are fixed and eternal for all time (as in rules and principles for retaining and gaining market share within a well-structured economy). The old paradigm views the economy as consisting of independent, passive individuals: the *invisible hand*. Indeed, the passive customers in a Newtonian economy are moved (motivated) to consume products or services by the pressure of external forces – such as advertisements, promotions, or simply the *price*.

Regarding a longer time perspective, industry structure is expected to remain stable and reasonably predictable in a Newtonian marketplace. *Competition for the future*, therefore, consists of each sbu striving to achieve incremental improvements to its present mix of product/service features (which include reducing cycle time, lowering process costs, and increasing customer satisfaction) in order to maintain or increase its future market share in the *same industry*. Under these conditions, the traditional theories of industrial economics and firm behavior (Schmalensee and Willig, 1989) and the well-established methods of industry–structure analysis and firm performance (Porter, 1980) consistently explain and predict the impacts of different competitive strategies on SBU performance. For the convenience of accounting systems and investment decisions, the performance of the whole organization is simply the sum of the performance contributions of its independent SBUs – as a portfolio of distinctive businesses in different industries. Investing in incrementally better tools, technologies, products, and services within traditional markets, for example, is greatly facilitated by the well–accepted methods of discounted cash flow (DCF) and present value analysis (PVA) of alternative investment opportunities.

The quantum approach to strategy is fundamentally different – and still unfamiliar to most contemporary organizations. Hamel and Prahalad (1994) present the most compelling discussion of this recently emerging paradigmatic shift within the arena of strategic management. While their treatise is not couched in a Newtonian versus a quantum worldview, it is evident that these authors intuitively understand the quantum dynamics of self–motion, self–organizing, and self–transforming systems – and how these consciousness–based attributes require a fundamental change from the historically limited approaches of strategy and structure. In particular, Hamel and Prahalad argue that the conventional boundaries of markets, industries, SBUs, subunits, and product or service offerings are entirely a previous creation by the minds/brains of human beings through cultural evolution. These economic categories are thus not cast in stone – but are, instead, rooted in antiquated Newtonian assumptions. Furthermore, while current customer needs and current products/services determine current returns on capital investments, the future success of the organization may be determined by entirely different categories of industries, technologies, products, services, and customers. Indeed, it is an organization's capacity to self–transform from one set of mental categories to another (including the speed and cost of undergoing this paradigm shift) that will ultimately determine its long–term success in a quantum world.

There is a dire need for balance, however, between the present and the future, since net cash flow in the short term provides the resources for creating the long term. A quantum organization *leverages* its resources by applying them rapidly and creatively in new and inventive ways; people, technologies, finances, materials, information, and all other resources are not simply taken as fixed – once they have been allocated to a particular subunit. Instead, all resources in a quantum organization (currently being used in the operational structure) are also leveraged for the generation of new industries, markets, products, and services (through numerous PMOs that include particular experts across SBUs). In sharp contrast, the SBUs in a Newtonian organization mostly hoard/hide "their" people, technologies, and knowledge in order to focus exclusively on short–term profitability – even if it means sacrificing organization–wide success for the future. Nor have Newtonian organizations developed either the quantum thinking or the quantum infrastructures to consider that (1) the future will likely be fundamentally different from the present and (2) the present allocation of resources must simultaneously be leveraged in order to create this future. The Newtonian organization, therefore, is doomed to play the perpetual game of catch–up to any quantum organization that rethinks and reforms the future categories of industries, markets, products, and services.

Let me articulate the quantum approach to strategic management – especially how to materialize a dramatically different future. I will rely on several of Hamel and Prahalad's (1994) concepts, which I have transcribed explicitly into the language of the new paradigm. Categorically, their key concepts of *strategic architecture* and *core competencies* – which are the basis for transforming industries while transforming an organization's products or services – punctuate the underlying distinctions between a new quantum strategy and an old Newtonian strategy.

Consistent with the quantum view, Hamel and Prahalad's concepts shatter the traditional notion that there is a linear path to the future from the present – thereby challenging the Newtonian theory of absolute space and time along with Euclid's geometry of flat, empty, homogeneous space. Instead, *discontinuities* on the way to the future (including deregulation of markets and nations, new information and communication technologies, breakthroughs in science, political upheaval, and rapid changes in social values and corresponding consumer tastes) *may turn the future upside down relative to the present* – in much the same way that Einstein's view of relative, curved, and compressed spacetime revolutionized Newtonian mechanics. In reality, these quantum discontinuities can be consciously generated by human action – just as self–aware, conscious beings, through their active participation in the universe, materialize quantum waves into discernible forms. Within the Quantum–Relativistic Paradigm, therefore, members (as self–motion monads) can materialize a great variety of potential industry boundaries, customer needs, and scientific innovations (as with numerous relativistic universes). In the new paradigm, moreover, customers are also approached as self-motion monads who can dramatically shift their needs and desires as they self-design different possibilities for living within their quantum world.

The *action steps* for generating new industries for the future consist of an organization first uncovering and then developing its *core competencies:* a set of underlying skills and technologies that are usually spread across its existing SBUs. These core competencies (typically implicit and hidden and sometimes hoarded within self-protecting SBUs) are the primary skills and technologies that are now being used to create, produce, and distribute an organization's portfolio of products/services. Rather than an organization being considered as simply the sum of its independent business units (the Newtonian view), a quantum organization can best be appreciated as an *evolving portfolio of interconnected core competencies.*

By way of example, Canon is often cited as a classic case of having evolved a coherent set of core competencies that make a strong platform for the generation of existing – and futuristic – industries, products, and services. Four of Canon's core competencies are precision mechanics, fine optics, microelectronics, and electronic imaging. These are the underlying skills and technologies for its current line of products: still cameras (both film and electronic), video cameras, laser printers, bubble-jet printers, fax machines, copiers, cell analyzers, and so forth (Hamel and Prahalad, 1994). The future for Canon will undoubtedly include many new combinations of its current four core competencies plus additional core competencies – either developed internally or acquired externally. Furthermore, each core competency can also be improved as an organization further invests for the future. NEC, as an example, is strategically focused on computers and communications as its major core competencies. Its skills with computers are developing from central processing to artificial intelligence processing, while its communication technologies are developing from simple digital transmission into totally integrated communication networks (Hamel and Prahalad, 1994). Thus NEC's capacity to provide new products and services is continually being enhanced by a concerted, strategically focused effort to improve its future platform of core competencies. Additional examples of core competencies include miniaturizing technologies (Sony), logistics management (Federal Express), engines (Honda), imaging (Kodak), change management (Andersen Consulting), wireless communications (Motorola), organizational learning (General Electric), measurement (Hewlett-Packard), customer service (Ritz Carlton), and network management (Corning).

It is worth repeating: Combining core competencies from different SBUs in unconventional ways (and also combining them with additional, soon-to-be developed or acquired core competencies) is doubtlessly what provides an organization with *platforms* for creating new products/services in transformed industries for tomorrow's customers around the globe. The new economics of intramarket *interdependence* (versus the old economics of *independent* suppliers, producers, and consumers) provides the underlying theory for investing in core competencies – especially when technologies, industries, and products have not yet materialized (Milgrom and Roberts, 1992). Perhaps this is the most striking feature of a quantum organization: an organization investing in the future development of core competencies and complex capabilities (quantum infrastructures, as a suitable example), even though the traditional discounted–cash–flow methods of accounting and finance would have nullified the necessary expenditure of corporate funds. Traditional capital budgeting procedures do not recognize implicit, interconnected core competencies (or quantum infrastructures), since it is not possible to document a specific cause–and–effect cash stream of future income arising from imaginary products, services, markets, and customers (Baldwin and Clark, 1992). Despite all the difficulties involved in precisely documenting and justifying (inventing) future cash streams to support its investment decisions, a quantum organization nevertheless invests for the future. Yet an organization should not take unnecessary, unwarranted, or dangerous risks. Instead, a quantum organization confronts the numerous risks of investing for the future by purposely and consciously engaging in well–planned action steps – while effectively learning as it proceeds on its bold journey into the distant future.

With regard to risk management, a quantum organization not only generates and maintains an inventory of its core competencies across all its SBUs but also formulates a strategic plan to create a coherent variety of core competencies that are fertile in their potential – new – combinations for the future. Furthermore, a quantum organization plans specific action steps (and the learning processes that will enable mid–course corrections) *to translate these new combinations of core competencies into new products and services.* And creating these new products and services takes place simultaneously with careful preparations for producing and distributing them around the world – by forming strategic alliances, joint ventures, and networks with other organizations and nations.

Of course, such proactive, future–creating behavior has never been forthcoming within an SBU's operational structure (which, by its nature, is largely focused on competing for the present, not for the future). Indeed, Hamel and Prahalad expect that the strategic management process, when viewed as identifying, building, and combining core competencies across the entire organization, mandates a planning outlook of between ten and twenty-five years! Obviously, this means having a time frame far beyond the familiar sbu horizon of only one to five years – hence the crucial need for mobilizing a pmo in the strategy-structure track.

The three stages of formulating and deploying strategic architecture are restated here (and seen in Figure 4.7, page 152, as the *left* three waves):

FORMULATING STRATEGIC ARCHITECTURE This initial phase involves conducting a thorough identification and assessment of an organization's existing set of *core competencies* – including potential *discontinuities* in future developments and their implications for new products and services. These assessments and their various implications must also be developed into a well-conceived strategic plan to improve the coherence and variety of an organization's core competencies. Specifically, an original, coherent set of core competencies will become a new foundation for materializing future industries, markets, products, and services.

This first stage of formulating strategic architecture would probably not be seen or seriously considered by a Newtonian organization – since this initial stage requires members to systematically uncover the implicit assumptions underlying the historical perspectives of their industries, the future needs of their customers (including *unknown* future customers), and all the other *economic categories* in their minds/brains. Also improbable in a Newtonian organization, members would have to be skillful in quantum thinking while surrounded by a quantum infrastructure – otherwise, sbus would neither reveal nor share the core competencies they are currently using to conceive, produce, and deliver existing products/services within their firmly established, and relatively safe, industries.

IMPLEMENTING STRATEGIC ARCHITECTURE Deploying a new strategic foundation for the future also requires well-conceived, sequenced action steps that operationalize unique combinations of core competencies into new products and services – via the evolution and improvement of skills, technologies, and product/service platforms. Also essential for effectively deploying this strategic architecture are additional actions for establishing new organizational networks and international arrangements in order to promptly produce the soon-to-be-created products/services and deliver them to brand-new global markets. Complementing efficient production processes and rapid distribution channels while developing new products and services will enable the focal organization to capture a major share of the emerging market.

This second stage of strategic architecture, therefore, clearly requires a focus on the short term – once new industries have been established. In particular, collective action would be directed toward achieving a large share of the emerging global market. Even here, however, the Newtonian approach is primarily focused on maintaining a given market share and making only incremental improvements to its products or services within a taken–for–granted *paradigm* – rather than capturing global market share in new industries for the very first time. The latter activity clearly involves entrepreneurial behavior that is unlikely to be forthcoming within an old, traditional Newtonian organization made up of passive jobholders with a dysfunctional infrastructure from the past.

IMPROVING STRATEGIC ARCHITECTURE Regardless of how effectively the strategic architecture has been implemented, however, there are likely many opportunities for improvement – which will become a competitive advantage to any organization that can implement strategic change more efficiently and effectively than its competitors. As a result, it is important to establish a well–conceived plan for reviewing and then improving the entire strategic management process from pinpointing core competencies to capturing market share – so that all subsequent efforts at formulating and implementing strategic architecture will take place better and faster during the next cycle. Moreover, rather than waiting many years before a "final" review is conducted, a quantum organization appreciates the need for continuous monitoring and learning – so that mid–course corrections can be made throughout the long cycle of strategic management.

This third stage of deploying strategic architecture also requires that an organization already incorporate most of the primary attributes of the Quantum–Relativistic Paradigm: How else would members have available to them the prerequisite cultures, skills, teams, systems, and processes to learn deeply from all their perplexing experiences and then rapidly apply this recently extracted knowledge to generate their future? Improving the deployment process (let alone the improvement process itself) will occur only if members have already established a vital threshold of self–aware consciousness. Members must also be skilled in examining their learning processes across all SBUs and across other boundaries in the organization. And most important, the members of all subunits must be committed to the strategic architecture of the organization and be willing to share their experiences of deploying this architecture with one another – openly and candidly. *No boundaries, either surrounding subunits or within minds/brains, should stand in the way of organization-wide learning and improving.*

I can recall an intriguing example of how an assumptional analysis on a company's strategic architecture led to an innovative new tree in the quantum forest. This tree had the potential of radically repositioning the firm's products and services for its future customers – and fundamentally reshaping the emerging industry. But to take full advantage of this newly discovered core competency, this firm, which we will call "InfoTech," had to confront the shortcomings of its paradigm and recognize the need for its own transformation before it could possibly transform its industry.

InfoTech, as its name implies, exists in the dynamic industry known as computer and information technology. It provides industrial customers with custom computer hardware/software and services all these products. InfoTech manufactures all its products in geographically dispersed plants. With regard to design, marketing, and sales, there are numerous SBUs that assemble combinations of hardware and software products for industrial markets. In particular, a number of SBUs offer computer-based systems for automating manufacturing processes in the industrial sector and delivery processes in the financial services industry. Additionally, in the process of developing these computer systems for its present and future customers, *InfoTech applies its computer hardware and software products to itself.* After all, if the firm is to maintain its competitive position in the industry, it must use the best manufacturing and delivery processes currently available – including its own computer systems.

 For several decades, however, InfoTech had been painfully aware of the difficult problems of implementing change. While upgrading its own operations from one generation of computer systems to another, InfoTech encountered the many roadblocks that exist in a Newtonian organization: dysfunctional infrastructures as well as misaligned/underdeployed formal systems. While change did take place, it was a slow, agonizing experience that made it tough to realize the full potential of InfoTech's well-designed computer products.

When several of InfoTech's SBUs – but not the whole organization – proceeded to transform themselves with a completely integrated program, the seeds for growing new perspectives began to take root. After one year of implementing the first three tracks, about twenty-five participants were selected for the strategy-structure track. To make a long story short, it was during an involving assumptional analysis on strategic alternatives when one C-group unearthed this major fallacy: InfoTech, as a highly successful, technical firm, was practically blind to the human aspects of technological change – even though it had been struggling for decades to implement its own systems in its own (very human) organization!

It was never possible to identify which particular member first saw the light. But when this particle of bright light materialized, the effect was profound: All C–group members sat in utter silence as they slowly began to appreciate the false assumptions that had dominated the industry for decades. They eventually pinpointed two most important (yet completely false) assumptions: (1) The best technically devised computer systems will be used efficiently and effectively no matter what dysfunctions exist in a client organization; (2) the more complex the information system and the more enhancements it can offer to customers, the more irrelevant are the dysfunctions in both the supplier's and the user's organizations.

The S–group deduced that a new core competency should be either acquired or developed: *the capability to transform organizations with a completely integrated program so they can actualize the full potential of InfoTech's computer-based systems.* If quantum infrastructures did not exist in customer organizations and their formal systems were not fully aligned/deployed, InfoTech would collaborate with these customers to bring about self–transformations. As a result of combining these core competencies, InfoTech's computer systems could be implemented better (and faster) than if dysfunctions were either ignored or assumed away.

This new strategic vision was much broader than merely providing the best computer systems. And it was more rational than assuming that industrial clients were ready for massive technological change – or would proceed with their own transformation. InfoTech had already learned that other companies in the industry (1) do not have this core competency, (2) are still operating as old Newtonian organizations, and (3) tend to assume that progressive computer systems, per se, will save them. But by the time other companies in the industry learned these important lessons, InfoTech would have acquired its core competency in transformation; its members would already have rewired their minds/brains to see, think, and behave according to the new paradigm. The industry would have been redefined and transformed to provide the marketplace with integrated (human and technological) systems – and not just Newtonian boxes.

But this strategic architecture never saw the light of day. Apparently, when corporate management took one more look at what was happening with its maverick SBUs, it concluded that this approach was far too radical for its primary business: providing and servicing computer hardware and software products. Transforming organizations was another topic, another industry, and an altogether different specialty. InfoTech would stick to its knitting and focus on what it knew best. In other words: the future of the industry would be determined by someone else.

As a brief review, let us examine the concept of core competencies using the symbol for defining and solving complex problems in general. Figure 4.8 presents the familiar decision tree. Instead of the underground, implicit assumptions below each problem definition (Figure 3.4, page 117), we see the underlying core competencies that enable an organization to conceive, produce, and deliver end products and services to its customers. Notice that the trunk of each tree now represents intermediate platforms, components, and core products that make up the primary ingredients of all end products and services. Further observe that the core competencies are entangled and spread across all the SBUs in an organization.

FIGURE 4.8
Core Competencies and Decision Trees

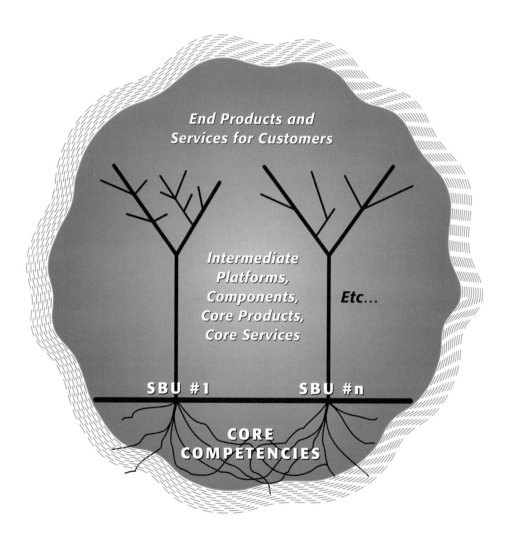

As shown in Figure 4.9, between the trees in the quantum forest are the open spaces of potentia. Just as synthesizing the implicit assumptions underneath current problem definitions generates a new tree in the forest (Figure 3.5, page 118), consolidating a set of core competencies underneath existing SBUs in unique ways creates altogether new SBUs – and thus new products and services for future customers. Only a quantum organization, however, has the essential attributes for materializing such new industries in everyone's mind/brain. And only a quantum organization realizes that the present allocation of resources must also be leveraged for the future: A viable balance of present/future enhances long–term success.

FIGURE 4.9
Core Competencies and New Industries

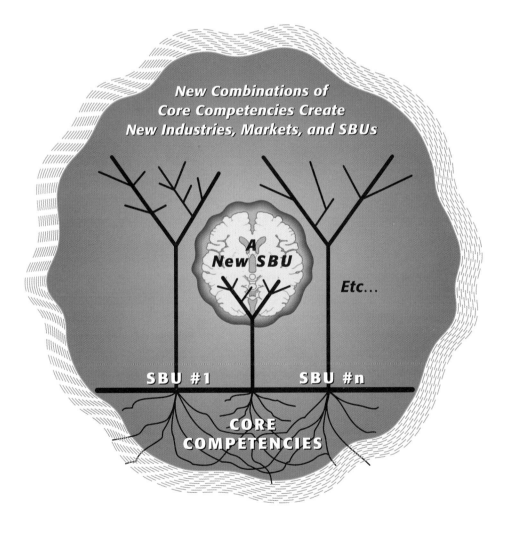

As illustrated in Figure 4.10, a PMO's two parallel structures enable a quantum organization to maintain the required balance between present and future. Recall: A PMO is used for mobilizing and then conducting the strategy–structure track. Specifically, short–term success in the present is managed through an operational structure, whereas success for the future is created through a collateral structure (whose members are drawn from all SBUs). This collateral structure (1) derives the *future ends* by formulating strategic architecture, (2) determines the *present ends* by deploying strategic architecture into short–term objectives, and (3) redesigns the operational structure in order to organize *all the means* for achieving these objectives.

FIGURE 4.10
Balancing the Present and the Future

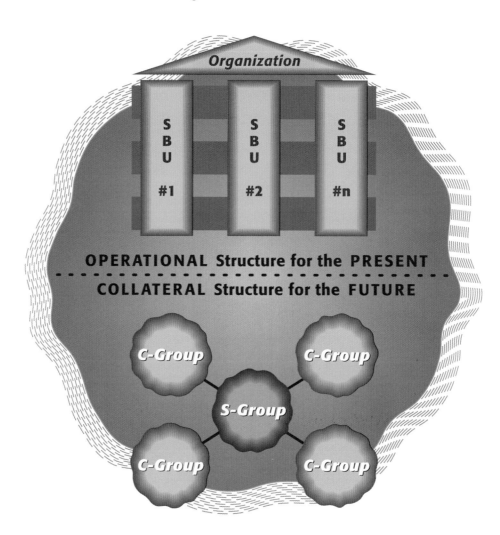

We do not have the necessary space or time in this book to present a full account of the detailed workings of the PMO that manages the three points above. But it should be evident by now that the participants in the strategy–structure track would do these kinds of things: first, list radically different combinations of core competencies – as soon as the existing core competencies have been identified as well as assessed; second, subdivide into three to five C–groups in order to perform an assumptional analysis on each radically different *initial conclusion:* "This particular combination of *core competencies* will shape the new industries of tomorrow – based on the *discontinuities* that will likely materialize during the next ten to twenty–five years." Once a strategic architecture is formulated by an S–group, the focus would switch to deploying this architecture for the *present* by establishing short–term (between one and five years) strategic objectives. (If significant differences are detected in these discussions, however, a group decision is made whether to rely on assumptional analysis for synthesizing radically different deployment plans.) Regardless of how the plan is established for deploying strategic architecture, the organization's *strategic objectives* are the basis for designing its *structural forms* – including the operational structure of SBUs and subsequent PMOs (which are formed from these SBUs).

Designing and Deploying Structural Forms

If an organization's short–term, strategic objectives are to be achieved, all members must have an operational structure to guide their time, wisdom, and energy. I define *structure* as (1) objectives to be pursued, (2) tasks to be performed, (3) the design of objectives and tasks into subunits, and (4) the management processes that coordinate subunits into a functioning whole. Making organizational structure *operational* means that the members who are assigned to work units must have the mandatory resources (financial, technical, material, and informational resources, for example) allocated or available to them in order to convert the latent potential of their structure into collective action. Naturally, a Newtonian and a quantum organization differ significantly on how these various features of operational structure are designed and implemented. Recall: The two structural forms were first introduced in Figures 2.10 and 2.11, pages 67 and 68, respectively.

The structural form for a Newtonian organization is represented by the traditional functional boxes coordinated by a management hierarchy. The strategic objectives for this structural form are derived from a precise, linear extrapolation – much like drawing a straight line on a flat, uniform surface from the past into the future. Furthermore, choosing the particular objectives, tasks, and people (and all other resources) that are assigned to each functional unit is done according to historical precedence – allowing only minor deviations from the usual management functions. And even if more fundamental changes were documented on paper (with the official organization chart), the everyday tasks and activities of passive jobholders would still be governed primarily by an *informal organization* reinforced by a Newtonian infrastructure and an equally out-of-date reward system. In addition, the numerous management processes for coordinating subunits are organized within a conventional management hierarchy: a pyramid of managers – *external* to the units themselves – who coordinate one or more work units. In sum, Newtonian work units are neither self-managed nor self-designed – especially the configuration of SBUs and the arrangement of functional subunits that make up each SBU.

The structural form of a quantum organization is also composed of objectives, tasks, and people arranged into subunits. But for this new form of organization, (1) objectives are consciously linked to a comprehensively formulated strategic architecture, (2) tasks are consciously self-designed to achieve these short-term objectives, and (3) people are active participants who are able and willing to perform tasks to achieve objectives. Moreover, the subunits in a quantum organization are *self-designed to be self-managed* by the members themselves – instead of being managed and coordinated by "external forces." Actually, the coordination of subunits into a functioning whole is addressed by designing subunits to be self-sufficient as much as possible – depending on how well *task flow* can be contained *within* versus *between* subunit boundaries (to be investigated shortly). Any task flow that still cuts across subunit boundaries, however, would be coordinated with cultural norms, member skills, and systemwide teamwork – hence by the quantum infrastructures throughout the organization (established during the first three tracks of the completely integrated program). Furthermore, aligned and deployed reward practices (addressed via the reward system track) would help focus members' attention on managing the white space between subunits. But any meaningful task flow across subunits that was not successfully coordinated by these means could be explicitly addressed by a PMO that would be formed to manage the remaining white space on the organization chart (Rummler and Brache, 1990).

Through a series of figures, I will illustrate the essence of designing structural forms, a process that is often ignored in the rush to restructure organizations by fabricating new organization charts and job descriptions. Just as our own universe is self-organized into fractals – from superstrings to supergalaxies – so, too, is the social invention we call *organization*.

The essence of structural forms is revealed in Figure 4.11, where all the short–term objectives that were derived from a strategic architecture, including the tasks that members must perform in order to achieve these objectives, are subdivided into two or more subunits. The broadest cluster of subunits might be two or more SBUs. Each SBU, in turn, is then further subdivided into two or more functional subunits (for example, operations, marketing, sales, finance, technical, and service) or two or more horizontal subunits (including order fulfillment, performance management, product development). Eventually, the narrowest cluster of subunits will consist of two or more groups – each with aligned *objectives, tasks, and people.*

FIGURE 4.11
Designing Structural Forms

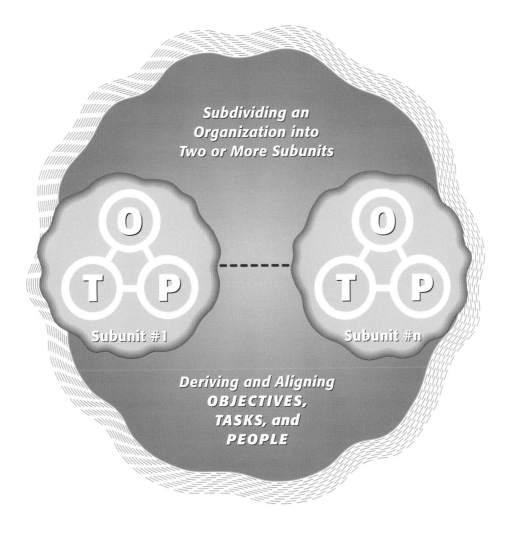

Every subunit in the organization, at any level (SBU, department, or group), involves many *interactions* by which people perform tasks in order to achieve objectives. As Figure 4.12 illustrates, these interactions include exchanges *between* subunits (inputs, outputs, feedback) and *within* subunits (including value–added processes and mid–course corrections). *Value-added* is when people perform only those tasks that achieve strategic objectives. Now for the main question: *What is the basis for choosing which combinations of objectives, tasks, and people become subunits in an organization?* Thompson's (1967) insights into task flow – how the performance of one task depends on the results of another – are still the most useful for answering this question.

FIGURE 4.12
Subunit Interactions and Processes

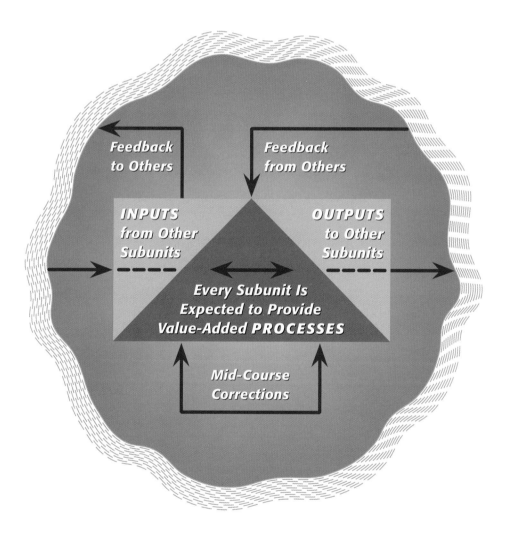

Thompson defines three types of task flow: pooled, sequential, and reciprocal. *Pooled* flows occur when two or more people can perform tasks independently of one another and then, at some later time, the results can be added together to produce useful output. *Sequential* flows occur when, in order to generate meaningful output, a task needs to be completed by one person before another person can complete his or her assigned task. *Reciprocal* flows occur when frequent interactions and exchanges must take place among people in order to provide desired results. Figure 4.13 shows the three types of flow: pooled flows are dotted lines, sequential flows are single arrows, and reciprocal flows are double arrows.

FIGURE 4.13
Three Types of Task Flow

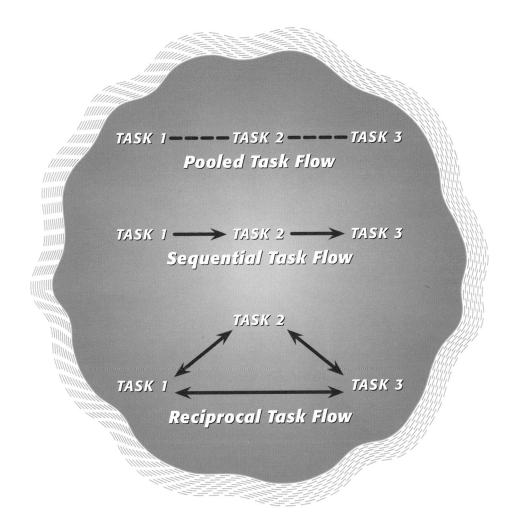

Figure 4.14 shows the best way to design structural forms – from the architecture of jobs to work groups, to departments and divisions, to sbus, and to clusters of sbus (similar to the structural entities we materialize in the universe – from superstrings to supergalaxies). Here we use only two subunits to illustrate the overriding design principle: Each subunit should be formed to contain all the reciprocal and sequential task flow *within* its boundary, thereby allowing pooled task flow to fall between its boundary and that of other subunits. This *containment of task flow* is what enables each work unit to self-manage – since members can perform the relevant tasks to achieve strategic objectives *within their own subunit.*

FIGURE 4.14
The Best Structural Form

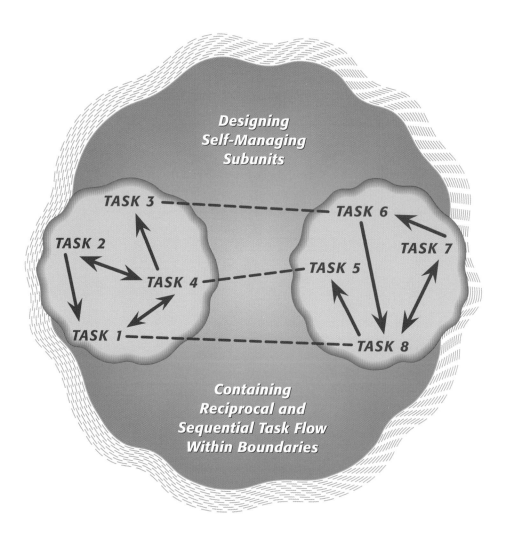

Figure 4.15 shows the worst way to design structural forms: leaving the reciprocal and sequential task flow *between* subunits, while pooled task flow is now contained within subunits. Here members would not be able to self-manage their own subunit – since their time and energy would be spent *interacting with members in other subunits* so that the necessary resources would be available (information, materials, finances, personnel) to achieve strategic objectives. This worst–case design is the typical source of a classic Newtonian nightmare: being held fully accountable for performing tasks and achieving objectives, yet not being in control of the resources that are needed for success – since these are located in *someone else's* subunit!

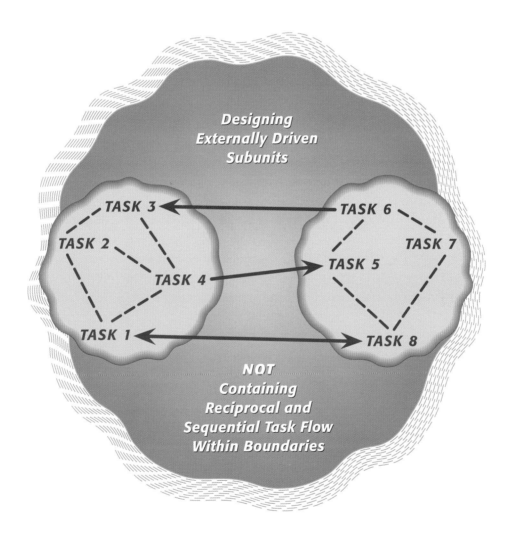

FIGURE 4.15
The Worst Structural Form

Each type of task flow differs in the cost of managing it – which is determined primarily by the amount of time spent in coordinating related activities. Pooled flows are the least costly to manage, simply because the outputs of different tasks can be combined rather quickly by simple rules and procedures. Sequential flows are more costly to manage than pooled flows, since more time for planning and scheduling is required to ensure the prescribed sequence of activity. Reciprocal flows are the most costly to manage, since considerable time is spent on back–and–forth adjustments among people as each one influences, and is influenced by, the other.

The closer an organization's subunits are to the best case, however, the lower the costs of managing all the work. Basically, coordinating task flows *within* a subunit is enabled by the physical proximity of its members (via face–to–face conversations), informal peer–group pressures (according to cultural norms and sanctioning systems), and the formal reward system that is administered primarily within the subunit (augmented by intrinsic and extrinsic rewards). The closer subunits are to the worst case, however, the greater the costs of coordination and integration: It is more involving and time–consuming for members to exchange information and materials when they are assigned to different work units (which may be housed in different buildings in different cities in different nations). While electronic forums (e–mail and groupware) can overcome many of these difficulties, face–to–face interaction is vital for complex problems and for deepening the psychological bonds among team members.

To understand the important implications of different task flows for designing subunits, we must further consider two related components of organizational performance: effectiveness and efficiency. *Effectiveness* means maximizing the chances for long–term survival by adapting to the needs of both external and internal stakeholders. What is considered ineffective? Members may have formulated the wrong strategic architecture for their organization (based on a limited set of stakeholders and an inaccurate set of assumptions), thus resulting in the wrong strategic objectives. *Efficiency* means maximizing the likelihood for short–time productivity by working without wasting time, effort, or resources. What is considered inefficient? Members may (1) spend time on the wrong tasks – those that do not link to short–term objectives, (2) not spend sufficient time on the right tasks – those that do actualize objectives, and (3) not be able to work on the right tasks – those that have been assigned to some other subunit. It should be evident that efficiency can be improved by shifting the time spent on the wrong tasks – or the wrong time spent on the right tasks – to the right time on the right tasks (Kilmann, 1983b: Mackenzie, 1986).

It is now possible to pull together most of the foregoing discussion on strategy, structure, efficiency, and effectiveness. Figure 4.16 shows how an operational structure must be deployed at three interfaces – from the strategic interface through the structural interface to the job interface. The *strategic interface* considers how well an organization's strategic architecture has been both formulated and translated into short-term objectives and tasks. The *structural interface* considers how well the most costly task flows have been placed within – rather than between – subunits. The *job interface* considers how well each subunit is self-managing its efforts to spend the right amount of time on the right tasks according to the right objectives.

FIGURE 4.16
Deploying Structural Forms at Three Interfaces

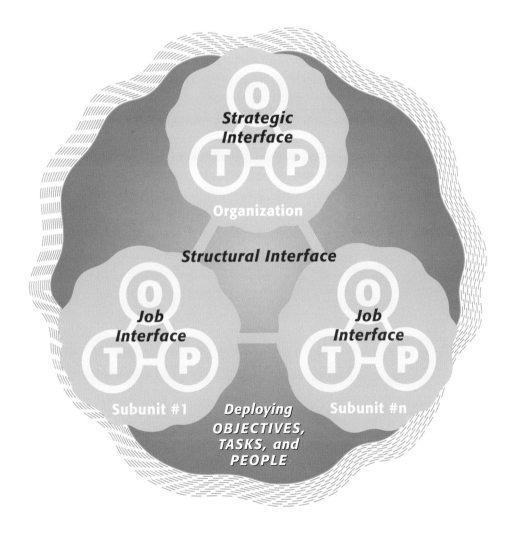

If the strategic interface is not managed properly, the remaining two interfaces are irrelevant. For this case, the structural interface is allocating the *wrong* objectives, tasks, and people into every subunit – which renders members' attempts to allocate their efforts inconsequential. Efficiency has little meaning unless a minimum level of effectiveness is being generated. Alternatively, if the strategic interface is managed properly (and therefore effective performance *can* be generated) but the structural interface is not, the job interface still cannot be deployed for efficiency. Here members in every work unit are restricted in their efforts to perform well by the tasks they do not directly control (since these tasks and the necessary resources have been allocated to another subunit). Lastly, even if both the strategic interface and the structural interface are managed properly, each subunit must still distribute every member's time on the right tasks with the right objectives – if the job interface is to be fully deployed. But since members now have the right objectives, tasks, and people immediately within their subunit, *both effectiveness and efficiency – via self-management – can be achieved.*

When the participants in the strategy–structure track discuss all the numerous implications of Figure 4.16 for their organization, they begin to understand the powerful impact that the design of subunits has had on performance and satisfaction. Now they fully comprehend *why* members' biggest frustration is to be held responsible for their performance without having direct control over all the crucial tasks and resources. These tasks, because of reciprocal and sequential task flows, are thus located in other subunits. The members in one subunit, of course, have no authority to tell members of other subunits how to spend their time and effort. Therefore, members are forced to beg, borrow, or steal so that these other work units complete their work on time (or adjust what they are doing) so that their subunit can complete its job on time. All this added time for negotiation and persuasion represents inefficiency: spending time on the wrong tasks rather than performing the principal work of the organization. Even after successful completion of the first three tracks of the program, sometimes as much as 80% of members' time is drained by negotiating with those in other subunits, while as little as 20% of their time is devoted to tasks that have officially been allocated to their own subunit.

Fully deploying the operational structure via these three interfaces (strategic, structural, job), puts more control of the work in the hands and minds of organizational members. What previously appeared out of reach (and therefore was perceived as *external* control), can be transformed into *internal* control by giving members direct access to the tasks and resources that are essential for the performance of *value-added processes.*

The participants in the strategy–structure track will be coordinating their efforts with those in the process tracks. Consequently, they must all learn that *task flow* is just another way of talking about the core processes within and between work units – with a clear focus on *value-added processes*. Figure 4.17 makes this important translation explicit by showing how the containment of task flow is precisely what brings value–added processes under the direct control of the members of every subunit. The essence of radical process improvement (reengineering) is designing the operational structure around an organization's business processes (P), subsuming the flow of inputs (I) from suppliers and the flow of outputs (O) to customers.

FIGURE 4.17
Translating Task Flow into Process Management

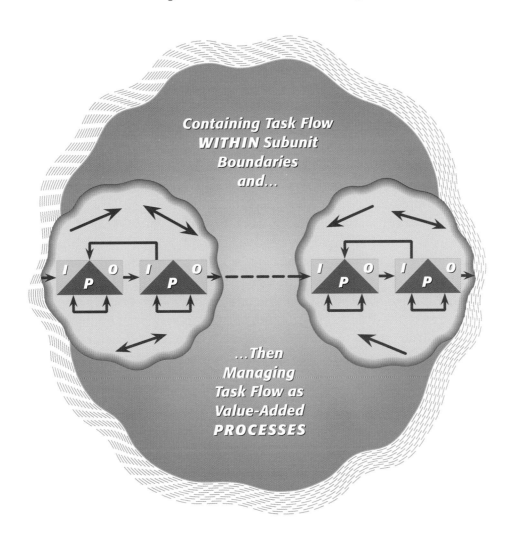

At this juncture, the participants in the strategy–structure track are struck by a revelation: Subunit boundaries are not cast in stone; they are cast in outdated assumptions about how to organize task flows. Now the participants are eager to consider alternative ways for designing subunits. In fact, they are anxious to begin devising alternative "initial" conclusions about radically different structural forms, whose implicit assumptions can be surfaced, classified, and then synthesized. With assumptional analysis, therefore, the participants proceed to design a new structure of subunits – one that will improve the alignment/deployment of strategy–structure.

Next, the participants in the strategy–structure track must recognize the absurdity of trying to implement change by announcing that the new structure – on paper – will be in effect on a certain date. Rather, it is only when members' behavior is focused on the new strategic objectives that the proposed structure will be fully operational. Actually, implementing a structural solution represents a complex problem in its own right, since such a change involves a difficult adjustment for most people. Disbanding old work groups and forming new ones is a dramatic switch that disrupts familiarities, traditions, and relationships in the organization.

Now the participants in this track are asked to develop alternative plans for implementing the new structure. Each proposed plan addresses several fundamental questions: What is meant by implementation? How long does it take? How do you know when it is complete? Is it ever really complete? In their different C-groups, the participants surface and classify their assumptions in order to support their proposed plan. Following the debate of implicit assumptions across all C-groups, an S-group is formed to resolve any remaining differences on assumptions.

By way of example, the S-group usually agrees to these synthesized assumptions: (1) members regard the idea of strategy–structure change as a threat to their self-esteem and identity; (2) members need to know, in advance, exactly what to expect during the various steps of implementing the new structure; (3) members are more likely to *accept* structural change if the new situation can be anticipated as an *improved situation* – from their point of view; and (4) members' minds/brains *will* be rewired along with the operational structure – as long as ample time, emotional support, and developmental activities are provided.

Based on these revised assumptions, the S-group deduces a "final" implementation plan that usually includes these characteristics: First, the conversion from the old to the new structure should take place gradually (over several months to perhaps one year), so that members have time to adjust – mentally and emotionally – to the new structure. Thus there is a rhythm and pace of change that can be nudged but not rushed. Too much change too quickly results in resistance; too little change too slowly leads to resignation.

Second, during the transition, participants in the strategy–structure track should continue to assess members' experiences and feelings about the new structure. As a result of these assessments, information about the process and content of change can be provided regularly – according to members' needs. How are other work units proceeding? What progress is being made in work units that are undergoing radical structural change? Honest answers to these questions will help put the emotional aspects of structural change in a realistic perspective. If members are uninformed or misinformed, however, they could assume the worst.

Third, participation should be extensive during the entire process of structural change so that members have a chance to improve and accept the new structure. For example, each new subunit of members can meet regularly to develop their objectives and tasks into formal charters. These meetings can take place in a collateral arrangement (just like a PMO), since most of the members' time is still being spent in the current operational structure. Moreover, members can be actively involved in designing new planning, control, and budgeting systems or adapting current systems to give them the strategic and operating information they need for effective self-management in their subunit. (Participants in the strategy–structure track can be involved in designing or adapting the centralized systems for the whole organization.) Furthermore, the members in each subunit can be given an opportunity to participate in the self-design of their jobs: The more that each job is defined by the same criteria that govern the design of each subunit – that is, containment of a complete piece of work so that internal control is further augmented – the more each job will maximize its potential for high performance in a quantum world. In order to realize this potential, each job should enable a self-motion monad to spend the right amount of time on the right tasks according to the right objectives.

And fourth, the more that each subunit has changed – in terms of different objectives, tasks, and people – the more that certain segments of the earlier tracks must be deliberated again. For example, the members in each new work unit can be assembled for additional meetings to agree on the cultural norms for their new subunit, since every member may have created a somewhat different culture in the previous structure. Additional skills training (management *and* technical) can also be arranged to prepare members for their new situation. Discussion on group process would also help each new subunit enhance its synergy and teamwork.

I recall a consulting project that revealed the benefits of conducting a thorough analysis of task flows for overcoming mental – and physical – walls that place ineffective boundaries around subunits. As we shall see, it occasionally takes a radically different approach to free members from all their self-imposed categories and walls – so they can create more sensible subunits for themselves and their organization.

Our story involves a large company in the foods industry, which we will name "Good Foods." In one of its large divisions that was responsible for all basic research, marketing research, and new product development, steady growth in personnel over many years resulted in placing people in offices, floors, and buildings based on what physical space was available at the time, instead of how office location affected task flow. In fact, by the mid-1980s, four different office buildings, spread across a large downtown area, housed five hundred employees in a haphazard manner.

Over time, complaints about the cramped facilities increased, as did the obstructions in scheduling face-to-face meetings with members of the same work group. Complaints from internal customers in other divisions increased as well, due to the long delays in tracking work in progress and receiving contracted work on time. It seemed that people, paper, and vital information got bogged down in travel time between buildings, walking time between floors, and meeting times between offices. While electronic communications sought to overcome these physical barriers, the creative processes that were so essential in this division were highly dependent on spontaneous face-to-face discussions throughout the workday.

Just when management was deciding to lease additional space in a new office complex (which would have become the *fifth* building to house the division) and possibly rearrange all office assignments among all five buildings according to traditional functional boundaries, the participants in the strategy–structure track surfaced their implicit assumptions about structural forms. The participants not only questioned the reasons behind the functional form of the division's subunits. They also asked whether it was possible for all divisional members to be relocated to the new office complex downtown. Since the senior managers were prepared to relocate all members anyway – and the new building had surplus capacity – they agreed to move all offices into the new building.

The strategy–structure track proceeded to investigate the task flows among all members in the division by making use of a design technology called MAPS – multivariate analysis, participation, and structure (Kilmann, 1977). This systematic procedure takes advantage of computer technology for performing the most computationally demanding aspects of designing subunits: (1) identifying all work flows for tens of objectives, hundreds of tasks, and thousands of people and (2) designing structures to contain the sequential and reciprocal flows within subunit boundaries.

According to the MAPS Design Technology®, the participants in the strategy–structure track first developed an objectives dictionary and a task dictionary. The objectives dictionary listed all the strategic objectives (with definitions) that the division must accomplish in order to realize its part of the firm's strategic architecture; the task dictionary listed all the tasks (also with definitions) that must be performed in order to accomplish the division's strategic objectives. It took the participants about two weeks to finish their initial draft of these two dictionaries. Members throughout the current operational structure were then given an opportunity to examine and modify the proposed items (and their definitions). Eventually, the two dictionaries comprised items that were well understood by all members (no jargon or ambiguities) and convincingly operationalized the division's strategic architecture into strategic objectives and tasks for people.

This is not the place to elaborate how the two MAPS dictionaries are developed into questionnaires and the way in which members are asked to indicate on a seven–point rating scale their ability to accomplish each objective and their need to perform (or be aware of) each task. Nor is this the place to show how members' responses to these MAPS questionnaires are used to design operational structures by using multivariate statistics. The meticulous reader is referred to another source for a comprehensive presentation of this social technology (Kilmann, 1977).

For Good Foods, the MAPS analysis revealed structural alternatives for subunits that were not based on physical buildings, floors, and offices, but on *task flows* for achieving strategic objectives. Nor were the subunits created for functions, since this form of specialization no longer captured the critical task flows for creating new products from market research and scientific research. Thus new subunits were designed to resolve structural interface problems that could not be resolved previously. Some scientific research tasks, for example, were combined with several market research tasks and with other product design tasks – to form several new subunits: New Product Research and Design for Market "X." After the participants in the strategy–structure track had time to reflect on this new arrangement, they recognized how much time had been spent trying to coordinate new product introductions: R&D had been conducting studies that were too far removed from potential new product concepts according to the rest of the organization; marketing had been distracted with supporting short–term sales objectives instead of researching consumer trends and possibilities;

product design had resisted making any changes to its standard operating procedures for developing new product plans.

After completing the steps of assumptional analysis, the participants in the strategy–structure track presented a formal proposal to the relevant top managers. This proposal became the blueprint not only for designing and implementing a new operational structure for their division, but also for developing an action plan for locating members in the new building. Many physical walls and mental categories were restructured and rewired during this task analysis. (See Mackenzie, 1986, for a related approach.)

Here is a summation of the three stages of designing and deploying structural forms (shown as the *center* three waves in Figure 4.7, page 152):

DESIGNING STRUCTURAL FORMS Short–term objectives are extracted from the organization's strategic architecture, including the tasks, people, and other resources needed to achieve these objectives. Based on implicit assumptions about task flow (reciprocal, sequential, and pooled), radically different operational structures are formed that subdivide and then align objectives, tasks, and people into two or more subunits. Following debates among the different C–groups, the S–group derives a synthesized structure (supported by a revised set of assumptions) regarding strategic objectives, task flows, self–managing subunits, and value–added processes. Naturally, this new operational structure has also been shaped by the deliberations occurring in the three process tracks – especially what it means to design subunits around *business processes* versus *management functions*.

IMPLEMENTING STRUCTURAL FORMS This next stage determines how to translate the operational structure – on paper – into manifest behavior. Now attention shifts to deploying objectives, tasks, and people from the strategic interface through the structural interface to the job interface – so that all members can clearly see the link between their subunit jobs and the strategic architecture. First, radically different plans for implementing structural change are proposed, debated, and synthesized – making use of C–groups and an S–group. The members of each new work unit then meet regularly to further design the processes and self–managing systems that will channel their energies in the new operational structure. In most cases, members revisit and reformulate cultural norms and sanctioning systems, reaffirm their understanding of problem management and assumptional analysis, and reconsider how to make effective use of a process observer during all group meetings. In these ways, members will self–manage their quantum infrastructures to support their operational structure.

IMPROVING STRUCTURAL FORMS When all work–associated activities are occurring within the new arrangement of subunits, the first round of implementation is complete. Now the strategy–structure track must assess how well the new structure is actually helping members achieve strategic objectives – effectively and efficiently – and to what extent the alignment or deployment of objectives, tasks, and people can be improved. Subunits can be asked to verify any troublesome task flows that still cut across the boundaries – requiring members to spend excess time with those in other subunits. In these cases, it is sometimes possible to reassign objectives or tasks from one subunit to another – in order to improve the containment of task flows within boundaries. If many of these task flow problems are identified, however, it might be necessary to undertake a more thorough reexamination of the operational design. During the process of improving this structural design for achieving the organization's short–term strategic objectives, opportunities for improving collateral structures should not be overlooked. Thus the strategy–structure track should also improve the use of C–groups and S–groups in all current and future PMOs. These subgroup designs must fully utilize the creative talent in the organization – whether the topic is strategic architecture, reward systems, reengineering, learning, or any complex problem. How to organize issues, subgroups, debates, and dialogues among diverse experts directly pertains to containing task flow, defining boundaries, and coordinating subunits. Once the participants in the strategy–structure track are connoisseurs in designing, implementing, and improving operational structures, it will be easy for them to improve collateral structures as well.

Even if strategy–structure has been effectively aligned and deployed, an organization must not only attract and retain the best people. It must also motivate them to apply their energy, wisdom, and time on the right tasks according to the right objectives. First, members (as representatives) must be *motivated* to formulate a long–term strategic architecture for their organization via the C–groups and S–group of a collateral structure. Next, these members must be *motivated* to derive short–term strategic objectives, pinpoint the important tasks, and then determine task flow – so they can self–design their operational structures. Subsequently, all members must be *motivated* to achieve their strategic objectives within their self–managed subunits. When examined as a *holistic image*, designing, implementing, and improving reward practices so that members are continually motivated to design – and use – their strategy–structures will unify the alignment and deployment of all formal systems.

⑤ THE REWARD SYSTEM TRACK

Organizations offer people various rewards in exchange for the behavior they provide and the results they produce. All rewards can be categorized into two basic types: intrinsic and extrinsic. *Intrinsic rewards* are the positive feelings a person gets while performing a job. If the work is meaningful, captivating, and challenging, for example, a member experiences pleasure just by doing what the work entails. *Extrinsic rewards* are given formally by the organization instead of occurring naturally in the work setting. Salary, bonuses, vacations, fringe benefits, office furnishings, promotions, awards, celebrations – all come to members from the organization rather than the job itself.

To receive all the intrinsic and extrinsic rewards that organizations may offer, members have to provide strategically desirable behavior and produce accurately measured results – commonly termed *high performance*. As discussed before (page 88), all behavior and results that constitute high performance in a quantum organization can easily be categorized into the eight tracks of the completely integrated program: (1) behavior that fosters an adaptive culture, the use of problem management skills, and effective teamwork within and between subunits (culture, skills, and team tracks); (2) behavior that achieves strategic objectives – *evaluated by accurate measures of results* – and behavior that contributes to part-time collateral structures (strategy-structure track); (3) behavior that administers the agreed-upon reward practices – by assessing subunit as well as individual performance, distributing equitable rewards according to performance, and presenting feedback to improve performance for the next work cycle (reward system track); (4) behavior that improves core processes both within and across subunits – *evaluated by accurate assessments of economic value-added contributions as well as measures of customer satisfaction* (gradual and radical process tracks); and (5) behavior that first speeds up the rate of process improvement and then spreads this useful knowledge throughout the organization (learning process track).

A basic point: The great majority of these performance dimensions are directed toward providing *behavior* versus producing *results* (even if the latter can be measured more accurately). This ratio of behavior/results, as a generic "performance formula" for a quantum organization, should not be surprising given the makeup of a fast-paced, interconnected – living – global economy. In particular, if high performance is determined more by short-term results than long-term behavior (or is basically more restricted than what is represented by all eight tracks and, hence, all interconnected attributes of a quantum organization), exchanging rewards for such *limited* performance will sooner or later steer all members' behavior off track and undermine an organization's future survival and success.

A key principle: *A performance-based reward system is essential for achieving success in a quantum world.* Consider for a moment this probable scenario for a non–performance–based reward system: Inherently, the high performers are the most dissatisfied members in an organization – since they do not receive significantly more rewards than the low performers. Meanwhile, the low performers are generally the most satisfied members – since they receive almost the same rewards as the high performers for doing much less work. But the high performers (due to their greater accomplishments) have more job alternatives than the low performers. As a result, the high performers (the more dissatisfied members with several job opportunities) are more inclined to leave the organization, while the low performers (the satisfied ones with few available options) remain behind. This migration of personnel neither represents a desirable human resources strategy nor supports long-term success. Alternatively, designing and implementing a well–functioning, performance–based reward system not only attracts and retains high performers but also motivates them to excel (Lawler, 1990).

Now consider the most perplexing questions that must be answered in the reward system track: What intrinsic and extrinsic rewards motivate members to demonstrate all the behavior and results that will accomplish short–term strategic objectives – and ultimately materialize the long–term strategic architecture? What rewards will first attract and then employ the high–performing members? Fundamentally, what reward practices should an organization develop and deploy in order to motivate – and sustain – high performance in a quantum world?

Motivation, Rewards, and Performance

The question of what motivates members to high performance (either as individuals or as groups) is rooted in the Newtonian/quantum distinction between passive jobholders and self-motion monads. The corresponding question of what attracts and retains members is also based on this major distinction, but the subject of motivation is paramount. Consider this: An organization that primarily makes use of *external* reward practices (such as pay and fringe benefits) in order to push its members toward maintaining existing work procedures will surely attract and retain passive jobholders. Alternatively, an organization that predominantly relies on *internal* reward practices (self-designing and self-managing systems, for example) in order to motivate its members toward high performance will likely attract and retain self-motion monads. Moreover, an organization that recognizes the quantum potential of human beings (including self-aware consciousness) will also strive to continually improve the inherent capacity of its human resources. Unquestionably, an organization's investment in expanding its members' minds/brains will attract and retain people who are specifically motivated to learn, grow, develop, and evolve.

In a Newtonian organization, *motivation* (which is derived from the Latin word *movere*, meaning "to move") is addressed by applying external forces on passive jobholders – mandates, rules, threats, demands, appeals, and directives spring forth from bosses and are imposed on subordinates. Newtonian reward systems also offer money and other extrinsic rewards to motivate (move) employees to do their very best. But these jobholders could not attain high performance even if they desired, because they are obviously constrained and confused by dysfunctional infrastructures and an incompletely aligned and deployed strategy–structure. In a Newtonian organization, the most that one could expect from passive jobholders is for them to *keep doing what appears to be the right job.* Even with the very best intentions, however, these members could not devote the right amount of time on the right tasks according to the right objectives, because needed information and other resources have been assigned to *other* subunits. The lack of systemwide teamwork and cooperation – based on dysfunctional infrastructures – contributes to the ineffective and inefficient completion of work assignments for all the tasks that flow across subunit boundaries. Worse yet, continually blocking people from successfully completing their work assignments results in more frustration – and eventual resignation. Ultimately, passive jobholders only put forth the minimum effort required to remain in the organization until something better comes along.

In a quantum organization, however, there is a strategic interest in fully activating the internal motivation of all members in order to realize the potential of human beings (which, for many quantum organizations, becomes one of their core competencies). Ideally, a quantum organization first recruits people who desire growthful, participatory, and challenging work settings and who have already developed a threshold of self-aware consciousness. Since a quantum organization would already have created quantum infrastructures, members can continually enjoy healthy cultural norms and conscientious sanctioning systems, well-functioning skills for problem management and assumptional analysis, and effective teamwork within and across subunits. *These quantum attributes epitomize some of the most salient intrinsic rewards that are passionately desired by enlightened human beings.*

A quantum organization also provides its members with numerous opportunities to self–design and self–manage their systems and processes (including their participation in various organization–wide PMOs). Prior to self–designing the reward system, a quantum organization would already have aligned and deployed its strategy–structure – so that every member can definitely see the link between short–term strategic objectives and the long–term strategic architecture. Furthermore, the principle for designing structural forms is to contain the essential task flows within (as opposed to between) subunit boundaries, which enhances members' responsibility, self–sufficiency, and self–identity. This design principle is applied not only to operational structures, but also to collateral structures. *These opportunities for active participation in designing formal systems – which not only focus the present but also materialize the future – provide members with highly prized intrinsic rewards: meaning, purpose, self–expression, fulfillment, and a legacy for the next generation of an organization's key stakeholders.*

Besides all these *intrinsic rewards* that emerge naturally from existing quantum infrastructures and from members self–managing their systems, a quantum organization also offers *extrinsic rewards* for achieving strategic objectives. Most convenient for a quantum organization, *active participation in self–designing and self–managing reward practices transforms extrinsic rewards into additional internal feelings of meaning and purpose.* Only when extrinsic rewards are established and distributed by external forces do members experience an external push instead of their own internal pull.

The participants in the reward system track examine an assortment of behavioral concepts to help them appreciate motivation in a quantum organization. (They are also informed, of course, of the technical and legal requirements of reward systems, including federal, state, and local laws.) The following sections summarize how developing and deploying reward practices is enabled by (1) completing the earlier tracks of the completely integrated program, (2) designing jobs especially for self–motion monads, and (3) accurately measuring behavior in a quantum world. During these discussions, primary attention will be devoted to *extrinsic rewards*, since we have already highlighted how intrinsic rewards flow naturally from active participation in a quantum organization.

THE PREREQUISITES FOR SUCCESSFUL REWARD PRACTICES Without sufficient progress in the prior tracks, it would be most difficult to develop successful reward practices for self–motion monads. Essentially, the prior tracks do much more than simply provide intrinsic rewards for members: Developing quantum infrastructures and then aligning strategy–structure improve the likelihood of attaining strategic objectives. Further, the more that members and their subunits achieve strategic objectives, the more an organization accumulates extrinsic rewards that can be distributed to its members (via bonuses, gainsharing, and profit sharing). At the same time, achieving strategic objectives further adds to an organization's resources, which can then be leveraged for the future – toward realizing its strategic architecture. But the existence of dysfunctional infrastructures combined with a confusing strategy–structure makes it very difficult for members to achieve anything – since resources are squandered instead of reallocated in the present and leveraged for the future.

Without an adaptive culture that encourages trust, openness, and information sharing, members have little reason to believe that achieving high performance today will bring them extrinsic rewards tomorrow – let alone that reward practices are honest and fair. In a dysfunctional culture, members believe (perhaps rightly so) that rewards are primarily based on favoritism and politics, not on performance. Making matters even worse, *organizations often keep their members in the dark by not giving them the information they need to decide for themselves whether rewards are actually based on performance – and whether reward practices are fair to all individuals, groups, and larger work units.* How does completing the culture track help members and their subunits decide that it is advantageous for them to work hard (motivation) and do well (achieve strategic objectives)? Consider the following.

It appears that a person's decision about how hard and how well to work derives from a deliberate thought process – until cultural forces take over. First we examine the situation to determine if there are any extrinsic rewards available that satisfy our needs. If there are none, we either leave the situation or do the minimum to remain as a member until we have a better alternative. But if there *are* rewards that suit our needs and wants, we then determine the probability that we can do what it takes to receive them. Basically, we consider what the job genuinely requires, whether we have the ability to do the work, whether we can control the activities that will lead to success, and how much time and effort we must put forth in order to achieve high performance. As long as we *believe* that worthwhile rewards will be forthcoming after we achieve a level of performance that we can control, we will employ our effort and talent in the right direction (Porter and Lawler, 1968; Vroom, 1964).

Where do such beliefs about rewards following performance come from? *The formation of beliefs about a reward system is affected more by cultural forces than by an expected value analysis conducted by each individual member.* If members do not receive the extrinsic rewards they feel they deserve (based on their performance), the reward system loses credibility. As members proceed to share these bad experiences with one another, they revise their collective beliefs (cultural norms) about the reward system: "Don't believe what top management says. In this organization, performance appraisal is *personal* appraisal." Even if the formal documents indicate that the distribution of rewards is determined by performance, members rely on critical incidents and stories when they decide who or what to believe. Consequently, there may be a big difference – a reward system gap – between what is written on paper for all to see and what the membership believes to be the actual reward practice. How can this gap be closed? There must be trustworthy information. If information is not obtainable, people will surely invent it. This becomes an extremely dangerous situation that almost always results in distortions that negatively affect motivation and performance.

Does the current reward system give members the information they need to judge its credibility? The participants in the reward system track are often surprised when they realize that crucial information about their own reward system is held in complete secrecy. Although the participants appreciate that many people consider wages and salaries as personal and confidential, they also recognize that there is a lot of room for variation between complete secrecy and full disclosure. Even if individual salaries are kept secret, most members would prefer to know the salary ranges of different jobs, the ranges of various bonuses, and the average percentage of salary increases. Moreover, it may be useful to make available – every year – the performance ratings of every subunit, including the ratings of individual members, along with the actual amount of increases in salaries and bonuses or only the percentage change in both. Such information is absolutely vital for judging whether the distribution of extrinsic rewards is based on performance. It is seldom necessary to reveal each member's actual salary, however, because that is determined by variables other than current performance: the demand/supply conditions for the job at time of entry, education, experience, and the previous levels of performance that have resulted in accumulated increases in base salary.

Porter, Lawler, and Hackman (1975, pages 354–355) succinctly express the dilemma of secretive versus open compensation systems:

> Secrecy about … pay rates seems to be an accepted practice
> in many organizations. However, organizations typically
> do not keep secret how other extrinsic rewards are
> administered. They do not keep promotions or who gets
> certain status symbols secret; in fact, they publicize these

things. Why then do they keep salaries secret, and what are the effects of keeping them secret? It is usually argued that the pay of individuals is kept secret in order to increase pay satisfaction. Presumably secrecy increases satisfaction because if employees knew what other employees were earning, they would be more dissatisfied with their own pay. This may in fact be true in organizations where the pay system is chaotic and cannot be rationally defended, but it is not clear that it is better to keep pay information secret when it is being well administered. In fact, there is evidence that keeping it secret may increase dissatisfaction and make it more difficult to use it as a motivator.

With further discussion on this controversial subject of open versus secretive reward practices, the participants realize how the cultural track has already prepared the membership for a more open reward system. In fact, by the time the organization has progressed to this fifth track, almost all work units have developed norms that encourage the open sharing of information that pertains to complex business problems and the financial performance of the organization itself. Extending these norms to the open display of reward and performance information is not a tough adjustment in most cases. Since the culture track has nurtured open information and exchanges about everything else taking place, it would be hypocritical to keep members in the dark while they decide whether to risk their efforts for the promise of extrinsic rewards. Moreover, participants often discover an added benefit that derives from establishing an open reward system: It helps keep everybody honest. When information is made available about performance evaluations and the accompanying distribution of extrinsic rewards, gross inequities and questionable practices become transparent. Thus all subunits are more likely to administer an open reward system in a fair and equitable manner – which further promotes organization-wide trust and thus provides members with additional intrinsic rewards.

Regarding the skills track, it would be most difficult to achieve high performance – and therefore receive extrinsic rewards – if members could not address and resolve the many complex problems that come their way. By being able to surface and revise implicit assumptions behind different problem definitions and implementation plans, not only will self-motion monads experience intrinsic rewards, but they are also more prepared to sidestep the errors that would diminish their performance. Not achieving strategic objectives, for example, could certainly result from having made false assumptions about what suppliers were willing to provide and what customers actually wanted. Or deriving a solution to a product or service problem but then failing to anticipate the customer's unique use of that solution – its implementation – will also fail to achieve the desired results. But if all members are skilled in problem management and assumptional analysis, they are more likely to prevent such errors before any damage is done. As a result, members will be able to specify the precise inputs they need from their suppliers *before* they proceed with their own value–added processes. Members will also be able to determine the precise mid–course corrections to make in order to ensure quality products and services – so they don't send flawed outputs downstream to their customers.

Regarding the team track, experiencing an effective group process is not only intrinsically satisfying to organizational members; it is the ideal way to define and solve complex problems. Instead of relying on just one or a few decision trees in the quantum forest, members can explore many divergent viewpoints – and thus see old problems from new perspectives. But this extensive (and satisfying) use of problem management can only occur if effective group process allows members to take full advantage of all the wisdom in their subunits. Ironically, when an operational structure is specifically designed to contain the sequential and reciprocal task flows within subunit boundaries, high performance for the subunit is especially dependent on each member consistently demonstrating the behavior and results needed by other subunit members – just as a chain is no stronger than its weakest link. Such *interdependence* is conspicuous when a subunit's output must be combined in a particular sequence – with hand–offs from one member to the next (value–added processes) – and requires ongoing relationships and adjustments among members (mid–course corrections). High interdependence among members of the same work unit, therefore, demands effective group process. *This is one reason why the team track precedes the strategy-structure track – so that highly interdependent members of newly designed subunits can achieve high performance and thus receive extrinsic rewards.*

The strategy–structure track does additional things for the benefit of the reward system track. It should now be evident that the notion of high performance, including effectiveness and efficiency, is basically pointless if the strategic interface has not been properly addressed. High performance is based on the important assumption that the right objectives are being pursued: to satisfy – and delight – customers and other key stakeholders. Certainly, the painstaking process of conducting assumptional analysis in a PMO helps ensure that the right long–term strategic architecture has first been formulated and then translated into short–term strategic objectives.

In fact, the strategic, structural, and job interfaces must all be successfully managed in order for members to achieve high performance within their subunits – and then receive the extrinsic rewards they desire and deserve.

Also confronted in the strategy–structure track is the dilemma that pay and other extrinsic rewards cannot be correctly distributed according to performance *if results cannot be measured accurately*. An accurate measure – in the form of a numerical score – is composed of two essential qualities: reliability and validity. Reliability concerns whether the same number is obtained by independent raters. Validity considers whether the number incorporates the true and complete value of the subunit's or individual's contribution to present and future organizational success.

Often measures are chosen to appraise each unit's results primarily with respect to their reliability (number of patents registered or number of patients served), not necessarily because they measure the right things (economic value added). Thus the ease of finding a reliable measure often overshadows the difficulty of developing a truly valid one – which raises the possibility that numerous performance measures may be rooted in a false assumption: If it can be measured easily, it must be valid.

Participants in the reward system track, drawing from their updated understanding of accurate measures and their continuing interaction with participants in the strategy–structure track, now experience a fundamental insight: When there are interdependent task flows among subunits, it is virtually impossible to establish an accurate measure of results – one that is both reliable and valid – other than for the organization as a whole (for example, productivity, net cash flow, or return on capital). Appreciate the case in which subunits are structured according to functional specialties: Every subunit is so interrelated with other subunits that results cannot be measured for any one subunit; each one's true value to the organization is completely intermingled with its task flows to and from other subunits. Thus each work unit's output may have actual *measurable* value only when it is interconnected – sequentially and reciprocally – with the task flow of other units. A research and development (R&D) subunit has limited value, for example, unless its outputs are designed into commercial products by engineering, which next are produced by manufacturing, and which then are sold and distributed to customers by sales. (Perhaps this is one reason why *reliable* measures are chosen to appraise these subunits even though such measures may not be *valid* indicators of performance results.) When several interrelated subunits are formed into a more encompassing unit, however, it is much easier to construct accurate measures of results – such as arranging all the functions that provide one product line into one SBU, which then becomes a cash-flow center (as long as the other SBUs in the organization remain operationally separate from one another, even if they are strategically interconnected via core competencies).

Now participants in the reward system track comprehend how the successful completion of the strategy–structure track sets the stage for the accurate measurement of results as close to the subunit level as possible – given the nature of task flows. The more the organization is structured to contain the most vital task flows within subunits, the more that accurate measures of results are relevant to these *autonomous* subunits. These valid and reliable assessments of performance outcomes can then be related to extrinsic rewards within each subunit that can be rationally defended and therefore openly shared throughout the organization. Moreover, the more each job has been designed to contain a complete set of tasks under the internal control of each member, the more that results can be accurately measured at the individual level (for example, reductions in process costs and cycle time for a self-contained part of a value–added process) – which also provides the basis for distributing extrinsic rewards to the members of each subunit. These *justifiable* rewards-for-performance distributions to members can then be made public within the appropriate domains of the organization – as long as the prescribed boundaries of individual privacy (for example, individual salaries) are not violated.

DESIGNING JOBS PARTICULARLY FOR SELF-MOTION MONADS As we observed previously in the chapter, deploying strategy–structure involves three key interfaces: the *strategic interface* (translating a strategic architecture into the right strategic objectives), the *structural interface* (designing subunits to contain the interdependent tasks that are needed to achieve objectives), and the *job interface* (designing jobs to encourage all members to spend the right amount of time on the right tasks according to the right objectives). The job interface is another key area in which the strategy–structure track must be coordinated with the reward system track – since it is possible to do more than merely design jobs whose task flow can be self-controlled by subunit members. Other *meaningful job characteristics* within each subunit can further motivate members to achieve high performance. Additionally, enabling members to set job-specific performance goals that are based on their subunit's strategic objectives, referred to as *participative goal setting*, can intensify the motivational potential of job design. Encouraging members to become actively involved in setting their own individual performance goals, including all the relevant behavior and results that could possibly contribute to organizational success, can significantly increase motivation and job performance. The goal–setting process is particularly inspirational when goals are established to go far beyond the previous achievements of subunit members – as in *stretch goals* – as long as they are attainable.

Regarding *meaningful job characteristics*, Hackman and Oldham (1980) have developed a practical framework for designing jobs that, in essence, is ideally suited for self-motion monads. According to their research, the presence of three key psychological states generates internal motivation: experienced meaningfulness, experienced responsibility, and knowledge of results. These *internal mental states* potentially reside in all people: (1) the desire for self–expression that makes a difference in other people's lives, (2) the need to self–control a basic portion of the work that contributes to a useful product or service for others, and (3) the wish for self–knowledge about what others actually experience from either a portion or the whole product or service. The more a job's key characteristics can be designed to satisfy these profound desires, needs, and wishes for *self-referencing behavior*, the more that members will be motivated to generate high performance. According to Hackman and Oldham, there are five job characteristics that will satisfy the three mental states: (1) jobs that embrace a self-contained piece of work that has a coherent theme; (2) jobs that encourage freedom, responsibility, and autonomy while doing the work; (3) jobs that require a great variety of skills and abilities for self-expression; (4) jobs that affect the lives and well–being of other people within the organization as well as around the world; and (5) jobs that receive regular and useful feedback about how others are being affected by value–added processes, products, and services.

The first two characteristics were addressed in the strategy–structure track by containing the sequential and reciprocal task flows within (versus between) self-managing subunits. The last three characteristics, however, provide additional qualities that can readily be designed into jobs as the strategy-structure track's concern with the job interface joins the reward track's focus on job motivation. Moreover, the *three process tracks* (Chapter 5) also offer valuable guidelines for all five job characteristics defined above and therefore must be joined with the *two system tracks* – through ongoing, cross–track discussions. Essentially, the distinctive methods of total quality management, business process reengineering, and organizational learning are used for establishing value–added processes that satisfy the needs of internal and external customers. With the intention of achieving strategic objectives, the organization's customers will regularly be asked to provide feedback to members who can then gradually and radically improve their value–added processes – and subsequently spread this useful knowledge throughout the organization. Touching other people's lives and receiving feedback about it, while using a great variety of skills and abilities in the process, enhances the motivation of self–motion monads.

With respect to *participative goal setting*, Locke and Latham (1990) have demonstrated that encouraging members to set specific goals that support their strategic objectives increases motivation and performance. Building on the old notion of management by objectives (MBO), Locke and Latham argue that participative goal setting creates focus, purpose, and meaning. They show that setting goals (1) directs a member's attention to the most important tasks that must be completed – both effectively and efficiently; (2) regulates a member's effort among different tasks – according to their distinct contributions to the goals; (3) increases a member's persistence in working on very difficult tasks (*because* they are linked to goals) – instead of automatically completing easy tasks when goals have not been set; and (4) encourages a member to formulate specific strategies and action plans to achieve his goals – which otherwise would have produced impulsive, unfocused, and misguided efforts. Similar to what was advocated for MBO, individual goals must be directly tied to strategic objectives – and should be specific, measurable, time–stipulated, achievable, challenging. Specific goals that have roughly a 50% chance of being achieved in a certain time period will certainly be a challenge to members: first to develop effective strategies and action plans to accomplish these goals, then to focus their energy and abilities toward implementing their plans – and to persist in their goal–directed efforts even when unforeseen obstacles threaten their mission. Goals that have a greater than 90% chance of success will never motivate members to stretch themselves – such goals seem easy to attain without really trying. But goals with less than a 10% likelihood of success will be viewed as not only unrealistic but also disheartening – definitely not challenging.

After exploring these motivational concepts, the participants in the reward system track agree that all members should be introduced to the same material. As a result, all jobs can be self–designed to incorporate all five characteristics of meaningful jobs and all four benefits of goal setting. By applying these two approaches to job design, self–motion monads will stretch themselves to their quantum limits.

ACCURATELY MEASURING BEHAVIOR As discussed before, *performance* is defined by all the behavior and results that embody the eight tracks of the completely integrated program and, consequently, all the interrelated attributes of a quantum organization. Furthermore, accurately measuring performance (via reliable and valid assessments of productivity, positive cash flow, and economic value–added contributions) is made possible by the successful completion of the prior tracks – notably strategy–structure. Accurately measuring *behavior*, however, will appear especially subjective in any situation. On the one hand, measuring net cash flow is much like measuring inert objects: It is easy to apply formulas, rules, and laws when addressing a well-established economic phenomenon. On the other hand, measuring human behavior is similar to measuring nuclear particles: It is difficult to be precise when there are uncertainties regarding the position and momentum of quantum waves and particles. This does not mean we should abandon performance measures for behavior; it only means that "soft judgments" will never have the same credibility as "hard facts" (such as productivity or net cash flow). But behavioral measures are still needed for measuring the true and complete contribution of each organizational member to strategic objectives.

Many types of rating scales have been developed and used to assess behavior. The typical rating scales have response categories that vary from "poor" to "excellent," from "well below average" to "well above average," or from "strongly disagree" to "strongly agree." Each response on the scale is also assigned a number that can then be used for numerous calculations and purposes. But rating scales differ in many ways: (1) who develops the scales; (2) how many response categories are designated for each scale; (3) how behaviorally specific each response category is for each scale; (4) who responds to these scales; and (5) how these responses (as an average or a total score) will be used for performance evaluation and feedback.

One approach, called *behaviorally anchored rating scales* (BARS), seems to provide the most accurate – reliable and valid – rating scales for assessing performance behavior (Smith and Kendall, 1963). Briefly, in answer to the above questions, it is the members themselves, aided by the participants in the reward system track (with inputs from other key stakeholders), who develop their work unit's rating scales. The members also determine how finely to distinguish the response categories along each scale (for example, choosing a range of scale numbers from 1 to 5 or 1 to 7). Most important, *the members themselves develop the specific behavioral descriptions that will correspond to a number for each response category on every scale.* These elaborated behavioral anchors not only reduce several response biases that can occur when the meaning of response categories is either obscure or nonexistent, but also provide effective feedback: The behavioral descriptions that are anchored to each number make it easy to identify the *specific behavior* that establishes the high end of the response scale – which will help improve a member's performance in a specific domain (such as enacting certain cultural norms or facilitating certain task flows across subunit boundaries).

But who should complete these behaviorally anchored rating scales for each subunit member in an organization? Performance evaluation and feedback seem to be most believable when 360° – *full-circle* – responses are provided by significant suppliers, customers, subunit members, members from other subunits, other representatives in collateral structures, and any other relevant persons who are able to observe and measure a member's behavior. Given the wide range of behavior that defines performance and the great variety of exchanges that take place in a quantum organization, full-circle measurement is often necessary for evaluating the performance behavior of organizational members (London and Beatty, 1993).

Naturally, several subjective ratings of performance *behavior* can be combined with a number of accurate measures of performance *results* – at levels of aggregation (individuals, subunits, SBUs, strategic clusters of SBUs, organizations as a whole, and networks of organizations). Eventually, the holistic performance formula that an organization will use for evaluation and feedback must differentially weigh the various components of results and behavior. In this way, the performance formula can focus everyone's attention on what is mandatory for success: achieving strategic objectives today while realizing the strategic architecture tomorrow.

Developing and Deploying Reward Practices

The three stages of developing and deploying reward practices are outlined here (and shown in Figure 4.7, page 152, as the *right* three waves):

DEVELOPING REWARD PRACTICES Just as soon as the participants in the reward system track have absorbed all the foregoing principles, they generally agree that an organization with SBUs in a variety of markets will not be best served by one centralized reward system. While there should be some shared policies and procedures across all subunits – in order to attain some measure of equity and to aid in human resources planning – each work unit may need to have a somewhat different reward system to match its unique challenges. Nevertheless, a creative synthesis between a corporate reward policy and subunit–by–subunit reward practices can be developed for the organization.

If some members of the organization are unionized, a special effort can be made to remove the constraints imposed by collective bargaining agreements. If this is not feasible, then some parts of the organization will be directed by union contracts (typically a *non*-performance–based reward system), while other parts can design performance–based reward systems. But the existence of union membership should not rule out the possibility of gaining union/management cooperation.

Now the participants in the reward system track are asked to devise alternative reward systems for their organization – in the form of general approaches, not the detailed reward practices that will be developed and implemented by each subunit. Each radically different proposal addresses these important questions: What is motivation? What is a reward? What is performance? What is measurement? And, accordingly, how should the organization motivate high performance – measured accurately – with its extrinsic and intrinsic rewards? In several C–groups, the participants then surface and classify their assumptions in order to support their proposed reward systems. Following the debate on assumptions across all C–groups, an S–group resolves any remaining differences.

Based on revised assumptions, the S–group develops a synthesized approach to a new reward system that most often includes the following characteristics: The organization as a whole will be governed by a unified corporate reward policy that includes accurately measuring performance and equitably distributing rewards to all members based on performance. Typically this policy requires a more open reward system than previously was in place so members are given the specific information comparisons that support the credibility of the new reward system. Further, the policy expresses a genuine commitment to do whatever it takes to keep the link between rewards and performance exceedingly clear in everyone's mind. Moreover, the policy requires that each member's performance evaluation include an exhaustive and accurate measurement of results and behavior (thereby including all relevant performance dimensions for success in the present and future) – and use a variety of inputs for behavioral measures whenever possible (from peers, customers, clients, and so on).

Staying within the guidelines of this corporate reward policy, every *autonomous* subunit (including strategic business units, product lines, and profit centers) has the freedom to design the specific reward practices that are expected to achieve high performance. The participants in the reward system track will facilitate this process – subunit by subunit – so that the whole membership is guided by the same knowledge of reward systems that the participants themselves have acquired. Human resources experts from either inside or outside the organization can also be used to ensure that all technical guidelines and legal requirements are fully understood and taken into account in the development and use of reward practices.

Although different combinations of reward practices are offered for different subunits, many share similar features. The performance formula that determines a member's overall evaluation might look rather complex on the surface. But closer inspection will reveal that it attempts to capture the true and complete (accurate) value of the member's performance. The formula might include individual, work group, departmental, divisional, and organizational assessments of *results* – with more weight given to the results that are closest to the individual. The formula might also integrate quarterly, annual, and five-year ratings of *behavior* – with more emphasis given to behavior that promotes future success.

Each subunit offers a wide variety of extrinsic and intrinsic rewards to satisfy different member needs and desires. Typically, a cafeteria-style benefit package is presented to members so they can modify their health insurance, life insurance, pension plans, and other fringe benefits – based on their changing needs. Numerous educational and career development programs are also included in the total package of rewards provided to members. When consistent with the demands of the job, flexible working hours and work-at-home privileges are additional options that might be made available. In certain cases, a skill-based portion of pay is provided both to reward those who acquire additional expertise and to develop a multiskilled workforce that can adjust quickly to changing circumstances. In various situations, an all-salaried workforce is implemented in order to treat members as self-reliant professionals (self-motion monads). In some cases, members are offered stock options so they can invest in their own efforts in their own organization.

The size of cash bonuses distributed to subunit members can vary tremendously, depending on the performance formula and the success of both individual and subunit efforts. Furthermore, annual bonuses may be a convincing incentive in a performance-based reward system, since they can easily range from 0 to 100% of salary. Spot bonuses, given for a short burst of effort or a particular outcome, are excellent reinforcements to the pay-for-performance link. Salary changes, while satisfying for the sake of security, are less effective for motivating high performance, since increases in salary for one year continue into the future.

IMPLEMENTING REWARD PRACTICES While the differentiated reward system that each subunit developed for itself might seem very promising on paper, the mystery, as always, is whether reward practices will be used as intended. Implementation, of course, is a complex problem, especially for a system that is designed to motivate and reward high performance.

The various plans for implementing new reward practices throughout the organization, therefore, should be developed very thoughtfully – utilizing assumptional analysis whenever participants in the reward system track propose very different approaches. Not surprisingly, however, the derived conclusion for implementing reward practices is often quite similar to the one deduced for implementing the new strategy–structures – which helps members to cope with change. The process takes time (several months to one year), and members' feelings about the process should be monitored regularly. Moreover, extensive participation should be encouraged so that special features of the new reward practices are understood and accepted by subunit members. And, naturally, portions of the earlier tracks should be conducted again – if further development of quantum infrastructures and strategy–structures is deemed necessary.

The quality of group process in every subunit plays a central role in implementing reward practices. It is mandatory that subunit members be able to engage in frank discussions on (1) the performance evaluation of each member, (2) the actual distribution of rewards to each member, and (3) performance feedback to each member. It is important to distinguish, however, the *evaluative* component (when performance outcomes, bonuses, and salary changes are first announced and subsequently discussed) from the *learning* component (when specific feedback is given on how behavior and results can be improved during the next work cycle). While these two components are usually blended together, they really need to be handled in separate group meetings – and separated in time as well. It is apparent that a person being evaluated by his peers can experience very sensitive feelings and underlying anxieties about self–worth and self–identity.

The participants in the reward system track frequently recommend that each subunit decide exactly how the two forums for group discussion (one for evaluation and one for learning) can be designed and scheduled to satisfy the organization's requirements and the desires of its members. Expectations about both meetings should be spelled out well in advance so that everyone will know how to prepare for these meetings – mentally and emotionally.

With respect to *performance evaluation*, these group discussions should be scheduled according to the rhythm and flow of work in each subunit. While it is usually convenient for an organization to schedule one formal evaluation each year, this plan may not be desirable if sbus, departments, and work groups have different varieties of jobs with different completion cycles. In a fast–paced work environment, it might be helpful to evaluate performance more frequently. If several performance cycles take place in a year, holding only annual reviews means that opportunities are missed to adjust performance during the year. Instead, a subunit might establish these agreements: A designated team leader will meet with each member at least once every month to examine performance results and behavior; the formal evaluation by the subunit will be conducted every six months; any member, upon request, can read his file; any member can request an appeals process, without receiving negative consequences, if he disagrees with his formal evaluation.

Regarding *performance feedback*, the members in each subunit usually agree to frequent face–to–face discussions in order to clarify expectations, offer suggestions for improvement, and give one another encouragement. These discussions focus on culture, skills, teamwork, cross–boundary task flow, participation in PMOs, and process improvement. The purpose is to provide a constant stream of emotional support and effective feedback so that members can improve their overall performance – in terms of both efficiency (the correct allocation of time and other resources on tasks) and effectiveness (completing the right tasks according to the right objectives). A subunit might establish these additional agreements: Each member can arrange a feedback session with his work group whenever he needs more information and guidance; the subunit can initiate a discussion with any member (as a whole group or via a designated representative) whenever it seems necessary to address problematic behavior or results.

IMPROVING REWARD PRACTICES   After the first exhaustive round of implementing new reward practices subunit by subunit, the mission shifts to improving job design, extrinsic rewards, measurement, evaluation, and feedback – hence improving all reward practices within all subunits. The participants in the reward system track can survey subunit members on their motivational experiences and study results for performance trends. Subunit by subunit comparisons (and benchmarking other organizations) with regard to motivation and performance will likely suggest numerous opportunities to improve actual reward practices or their implementation. It is also essential to establish how performance formulas can be adjusted in any work unit – to improve both reliability and validity. Furthermore, there should be a procedure that allows for negotiation and change in a formula – not as an excuse for failing to achieve a realistic goal but as an acknowledgment of a quantum cosmos. At some point, the participants in the reward system track should reexamine the progress made in the prior tracks and recommend improvements, since quantum infrastructures and strategy–structures significantly affect reward practices.

④⑤ THE MIDDLE TWO TRACKS

Ideally, the participants in the strategy–structure and reward system tracks will join together to ensure that all formal systems are completely aligned and fully deployed. This ideal is evident when all subunit members have internalized a crystal–clear message of what specific behavior and results are needed for the present and future success of their organization.

The participants in these two middle tracks also interact with their counterparts in the last three tracks of the completely integrated program (the process tracks), since systems and processes are so highly interrelated: Processes become value–added only when they significantly contribute to strategic objectives; value–added processes – hence task flows – take place within and across subunit boundaries; and value–added processes will be self–managed successfully only if members receive the intrinsic/extrinsic rewards they desire and deserve.

What connects the active participants of all eight tracks, however, is how to improve infrastructures, systems, and processes *better and faster* than any other organization in the world. Such a distinctive vision may be the ultimate stretch goal for any quantum organization. Realizing this vision, however, means that process management must be completely integrated with quantum infrastructures and all formal systems.

PROCESS MANAGEMENT

Improving Core Processes
Within and Across Subunits

> Business process innovation, despite its promise of radical
> competitive benefit, is a rare phenomenon in the corporate
> world. Growing numbers of executives are aware of it,
> but not many have undertaken serious process innovation
> initiatives. The reason for this is simple – business process
> innovation requires abandoning comfortable ways of
> doing business. It necessitates thinking about organizations
> and organizational boundaries in new ways that involve
> major, large-scale organizational change. In short, business
> process innovation involves radical change, and individuals
> and organizations cannot always be expected to embrace
> such change.
>
> *— Thomas H. Davenport (1993, page 167)*

The position and movement of inert objects in the Cartesian–Newtonian universe can be predicted exactly by applying eternal laws – expressed in mathematical terms – with complete certainty. Indeed, mathematics gives definitive predictions in the old paradigm to the nth degree. The position and movement of self-motion monads in a quantum–relativistic universe, however, can only be designated as probabilities – expressed in statistical terms – of possible locations within a wave function (which is similar to a statistical distribution of data points). *Probability theory and statistical concepts make up the quantitative language for the new paradigm — versus mathematical laws for the old.* And counting discrete particles in the quantum world replaces continuous mathematical functions in the Newtonian universe. Statistical analysis of discrete particles is thus apropos to quantum phenomena.

Determining the movement of people and the flow of work within a quantum organization similarly requires the application of statistics – for assessing the efficiency and effectiveness of members' efforts. Basically, statistical tools and techniques provide a universal language for receiving useful feedback from customers, providing effective feedback to suppliers, and generating useful self-feedback for every organizational member – so that the flow of work can be consciously described, statistically controlled, and purposely improved. The language of statistics thus enables members to achieve (1) their performance goals, (2) the strategic objectives of every subunit, (3) the strategic architecture of their organization, and (4) intrinsic and extrinsic rewards – *by statistically charting the task flow that is created by their own seeing, thinking, and behaving.*

During the 1980s, many organizations leaped on the bandwagon to have their members learn and apply statistics under the rubric of quality management, companywide quality, and total quality management (TQM). These related efforts all propose continuous improvement in the flow of work in order to improve the desired attributes of products and services, minimize cycle times and process costs, and increase customer satisfaction (Deming, 1986; Juran, 1991; Crosby, 1979). This *process view of work* relies on a unique collection of quality tools – most of which use data collection and statistical techniques for managing processes. It is important to note that these quality tools/techniques for continuous improvement are not part of the skill development in the prior five tracks. Nor were these statistical tools actively promoted in corporate training and development programs before the 1980s (except in Japan and a few select companies elsewhere).

The great disappointment in the quality movement, however, is the high failure rate of *implementing* quality programs – consistently estimated to be about 75% (Ernst & Young, 1992; Spector and Beer, 1994). As a result, the quality movement has gradually but unequivocally developed a bad reputation, and, like other change initiatives that have been implemented in a quick-fix manner, quality programs are now viewed as a passing fad. Unfortunately, "the baby has been thrown out with the bathwater" – not because there is anything wrong with the intentions, principles, and tools of quality management per se, but because the implementation of quality programs generally overlooks the deficient infrastructures and misaligned systems that undermine most efforts at improvement and transformation. Because of the quality movement's quick-fix history and growing faddish reputation (particularly in the United States and Europe), I decided to use the more neutral term *gradual process track* for labeling the most distinctive concepts and statistical methods provided by TQM.

By the early 1990s, after many organizations and the popular press had tainted TQM, a second process-driven approach arrived on the scene: business process reengineering, process innovation, or, simply, *reengineering* (Hammer and Champy, 1993; Davenport, 1993). Besides seizing advantage of TQM's demise, proponents of reengineering organizations argued that quality programs achieve only modest – gradual – process improvement. Yet the need for most organizations (playing catch-up in the competitive, global economy) is dramatic – radical – process improvement. And this is the principal goal of reengineering programs that focus on restructuring work units around core business processes – enabled by recent advances in information, communication, and production technologies (hardware, software, databases, tracking systems, electronic communications, and so forth). With this greater potential for process improvement, however, the failure rate of radical improvement programs is even higher than that of gradual improvement programs (Hall, Rosenthal, and Wade, 1993). Again it seems that implementing radical change has little hope of success when an organization is distracted by unhealthy infrastructures and misaligned systems. And because of the rather ambivalent reputation associated with reengineering programs, I chose to use the more neutral term *radical process track* for naming the noteworthy principles and practices for reengineering business processes.

At the same time that reengineering was receiving attention, a third process-based approach was gaining momentum: organizational learning and knowledge-creating organizations (Senge, 1990; Nonaka, 1991; Garvin, 1993). While seemingly not relevant to the other two process approaches (TQM and reengineering), organizational learning is in fact very concerned with elaborating the processes by which knowledge is created, acquired, interpreted, stored, retrieved, shared, and used – within and between all organizational boundaries. By *improving* these knowledge-based processes, an organization can significantly improve its own efforts at implementing gradual and radical process improvement: Each subsequent effort at TQM or reengineering will then be implemented better and faster than before. Naturally, an explicit learning approach can also be applied to quantum infrastructures and formal systems – by capturing what was learned from attempts to improve these attributes so they can be improved even better and faster during the next round of self-transformation. Furthermore, this learning perspective can also be utilized for developing and introducing new products and services, implementing radically new information and communication technologies, creating strategic alliances and partnerships, and managing other complex, strategic challenges. The *learning process track,* therefore, concentrates on seeing *learning processes* so they can be described, controlled, and improved – while quality focuses on *functional processes* and reengineering focuses on *business processes*. Interestingly, many of the same methods and tools can be used for all three process tracks – which gives members a coherent understanding of *process management*.

This chapter starts with the underpinnings of the *gradual process track*: providing the essential concepts of quality management that reinforce the need for all members to see, think, and behave differently in a quantum universe – especially by seeing work flow (task flow) in an organization as value-added processes. Once core processes are seen in this way, they can be explicitly described, statistically controlled, and deliberately improved. All members actively participate in learning various process management tools in workshop meetings and then apply these methods in their work units – *before* the strategy–structure track implements the new operational structure and *before* the reward system track advocates new measures and rewards for continuous process improvements.

This chapter next presents the *radical process track*: the unique aspects of reengineering an organization into process–based (horizontal) subunits, which is enabled by information and communication technologies. A new collateral structure of twenty-five representatives is formed for this track (which interacts regularly with the members of the strategy–structure and reward system tracks) – so that *strategic processes* are used to form subunits in the new operational structure. These strategic processes are purposely selected and designed to achieve strategic objectives, which were derived from the strategic architecture. These core processes must also be aligned with each subunit's self-designed, performance-based reward system – so that all members will be self-motivated to work effectively and efficiently in their new horizontal subunits.

This chapter concludes with the *learning process track*: how the unique concepts and tools from TQM and reengineering can be used to describe, control, and improve learning processes within and between all subunits. A new collateral structure of twenty-five representatives is formed for this track in order to prioritize and then cultivate the core learning processes that flow across the new process–based subunits. Collaborating with the reward system track, these representatives also recommend incentives for capturing – and spreading – useful knowledge. As a result of managing its learning processes more explicitly, a quantum organization will be able to accomplish its strategy objectives and actualize its strategic architecture – better and faster – during each subsequent cycle of shaping its industry's evolution as well as actualizing its self-transformation.

⑥ THE GRADUAL PROCESS TRACK

Most people can see the immediate outcome of their efforts – particularly when it is packaged as a product (or labeled as a service) that is delivered to someone else. What is less obvious, however, is clearly seeing the *process* that was used to bring about the tangible outcome – because the process remains unconscious. It seems that new categories in the mind/brain are required for human beings to become consciously aware of their habitual ways of seeing, thinking, and behaving. Previously, quality programs have found that formal educational sessions must be provided in order for all members to become consciously aware of the implicit processes they use to produce explicit results. Recall the discovery of cultural norms, implicit assumptions, and group process in the first three tracks of the completely integrated program. Not until members are asked to discuss work flow or task flow – *out loud* – are new categories created in their minds/brains for seeing the process of their work as clearly as the results.

Identical to transformation itself, therefore, TQM is predominantly a particular way of seeing, thinking, and behaving – which amounts to a *process view of life*. Basically, the process of doing something is considered as more important than the results, simply because the process *determines* the results. And the desired or ultimate result – the prime reason for being – is satisfying and delighting *customers* according to their needs and wants (including quality products and services; zero defects, errors, and failures; short delivery time; and low cost/price). Other stakeholders (for example, governments, communities, employees, shareholders, suppliers, and trade unions) must also be satisfied in order to remain in business. But the key stakeholder is the ultimate customer who actually buys the organization's products and services. With regard to the fundamental ideology of TQM: *If all members continuously improve their processes, the results will also improve.*

A *process* is defined as a flow of tasks and decisions – which includes first receiving inputs from suppliers and eventually delivering outputs to customers. And all activity in an organization is meant to be a *value-added process* for both customers and other prime stakeholders (as introduced in Figure 4.12, page 170, and Figure 4.17, page 177). We now expand the use of the *process cell:* value-added processes (*P*) use inputs (*I*) from suppliers in order to provide outputs (*O*) to customers. After surveying basic material on quality management, we will organize the *gradual process track* into three categories: describing, controlling, and improving value-added processes. When all organizational members are experienced in managing processes *within* subunits, they will be ready for the challenge of radical change.

Employing the typical process cell, Figure 5.1 shows organizational members connected according to the specific outputs they *hand off* to one another. Three kinds of feedback provide opportunities to revise the work being done so that the ultimate customer is completely satisfied: (1) Each person in the *process chain* can assess the value of his own work and make the necessary mid–course corrections – before output is given or handed off to someone else; (2) each person can ask for feedback from customers in order to provide what they need/want; (3) each person can define what quality inputs are needed from suppliers – so that all processes add value down the process chain.

FIGURE 5.1
Defining the Process Chain

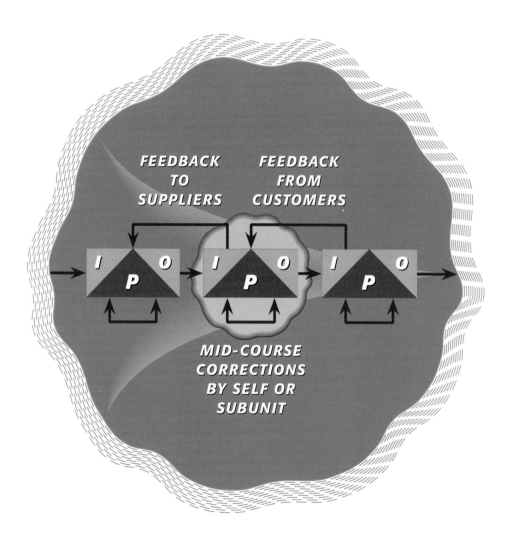

The process chain can extend far beyond the traditional boundaries of an organization: Comprehending the logic of quality handoffs and the role of different kinds of feedback should help all members see the kind of cross–boundary cooperation that is mandatory for success in a global marketplace, upstream and downstream. Note: The quantum circle in the center of Figure 5.2 symbolizes that every process chain begins and ends with the final customer – from anticipating customer needs to meeting or exceeding customer expectations. Besides *external* customers and suppliers (emerging from outside the organization), there are *internal* customers and suppliers defined as handoffs between members or subunits.

FIGURE 5.2
Extending the Process Chain

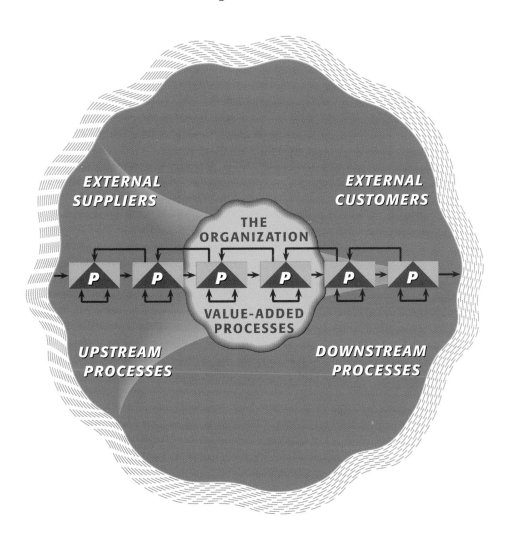

As shown in Figure 5.3, an error not caught upstream will cost more to correct downstream. Try to calculate the cost of repairs, returns, recalls, warranty claims, lawsuits, and, worst of all, lost customers. The *out-of-date assumption:* It costs more and more to provide better and better products and services. But this will only happen when an organization ensures the quality of its products by hiring scores of inspectors to check its outputs before sending them to the customer – which also includes hiring more inspectors to assess whether all the *other* inspectors are effectively doing their job! But the point is quickly reached where the cost of detecting and correcting errors becomes a large percentage of sales (Crosby, 1979).

FIGURE 5.3
Experiencing Quality Problems Downstream

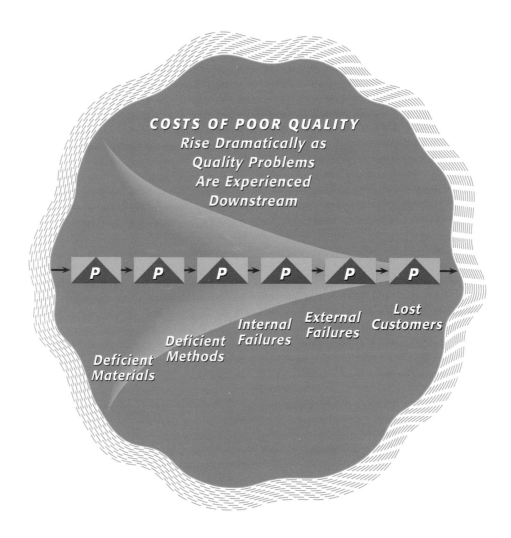

Addressing quality upstream will satisfy customers downstream. As pictured in Figure 5.4, just consider the benefits from shorter work cycles, less waste, lower production costs, reduced inventory, and, definitely best of all, more customers. The *up-to-date assumption:* If quality is built in at the start – upstream – because of all the feedback and mid-course corrections that catch errors before anything is sent downstream, better quality costs much less in the long run. Downstream inspectors are not necessary and customers receive exactly what they requested. Such a proactive approach to upstream quality, of course, demands that members be surrounded by quantum infrastructures, aligned systems, and value-added processes.

FIGURE 5.4
Addressing Quality Problems Upstream

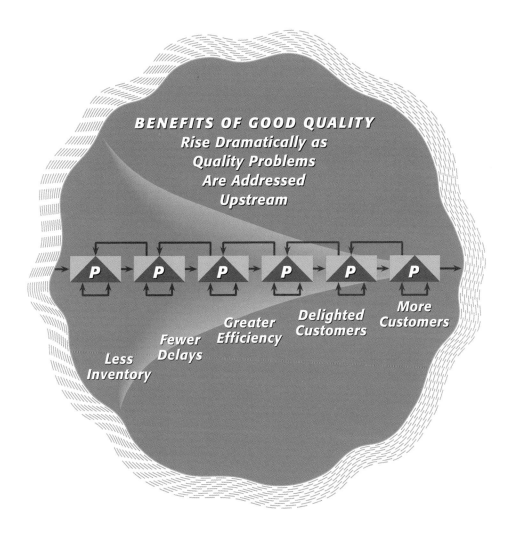

Customers are more concerned about the time it takes for them to receive a product or service than what it costs someone to provide it – as long as they pay a fair price. Organizations, however, are more concerned about cost than time, since net cash flow (at least in the short term) is cost driven. But for the long run, cycle time as well as process cost should be minimized for organizations to succeed and for customers to be delighted. As captured in Figure 5.5, only by describing their processes will members be able to assess time and cost – from the initial moment of request by a customer to the final point of receipt. Thereafter, they can reduce time and cost by statistically controlling and purposely improving their processes.

FIGURE 5.5
Experiencing Cycle Time

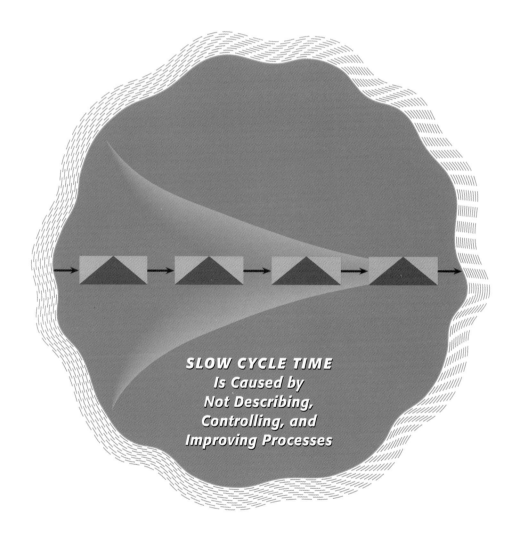

SLOW CYCLE TIME
Is Caused by
Not Describing,
Controlling, and
Improving Processes

A process chain of receiving inputs from suppliers *just in time to use the inputs* – and then supplying quality outputs to customers *just in time* for them to use the outputs – is the epitome of managing processes explicitly. The process cells in Figure 5.6 have been brought much closer together by reducing the time for handoffs from one person to another. Consequently, the cycle time for completing the process has been greatly reduced. Since everyone in the process chain is consistently reliable in providing inputs to the next subunit in the chain, there is no need to keep excess inventory *just in case* defective or tardy inputs are delivered: Everyone gets what they want just when they want it (Duncan, 1988).

FIGURE 5.6
Addressing Cycle Time

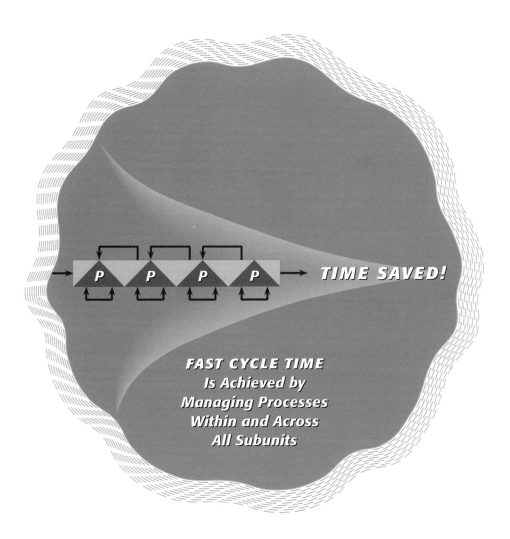

We can now put the separate pieces together: the prior emphasis on establishing quantum infrastructures and deploying formal systems with the current focus on managing processes for achieving success. Effective *infrastructures, systems, and processes must all be functioning in harmony* – to focus every member's attention on achieving customer satisfaction and delight. Without such a *holistic vision*, organizations will find it painfully difficult to achieve success in our competitive environment. This vision, incidentally, includes customer *delight* because mere satisfaction is no longer sufficient: Most organizations can satisfy their customers but are still losing them to competitors who provide products and services that altogether mesmerize people by *anticipating* their desires and giving them more than they could possibly have expected. Customers are delighted whenever organizations handle unusual or special requests in an effective and efficient manner – by *customizing* their products and services.

The rest of this section summarizes three basic stages for managing processes – describing, controlling, and improving processes – first within subunits before managing processes between subunits. These three stages are similar to the quality trilogy proposed by Juran (1991). In each stage, as we shall see, members must address a particular quality problem – each revealed by a significant gap between what is and what could or should be: (1) the gap exposing an unspoken, existing process versus a described, ideal process; (2) the gap signaling an out-of-control process vis-à-vis an under-control process; and (3) the gap detecting a deficient, under-control process versus an improved process that is under control. For every gap, the challenge is to determine what is *causing* the gap – so that the process can be better described, controlled, and improved in order to satisfy and delight the ultimate customer.

Deming's (1986) famous cycle (adapted from Shewhart, 1931) of Plan, Do, Check, Act (or PDCA) represents a comprehensive approach for solving quality problems that is similar to the steps of problem management. Just as a complex *problem* must first be sensed and correctly defined before it can be resolved, a complex *process* must first be described and streamlined before it can be controlled and improved. Similarly, deriving solutions to a quality problem is different from implementing a solution. Finally, it is vital to monitor the results of efforts to control and improve processes – and to learn from these efforts. Cycles of problem management (or PDCA) proceed as group members work at continuous improvement. In the next subsections, I not only show when the steps of problem management are applicable but offer additional tools for better describing, controlling, and improving value-added processes.

Describing Value-Added Processes

One of the most illuminating encounters during the gradual process track is when members experience their implicit processes face–to–face for the first time. It is one thing for group members to discuss how they get their work done – using the usual terms in their vocabulary. It is quite another thing, however, for group members to draw a flowchart of particular tasks and decisions – including the inputs they receive from various suppliers and the outputs they deliver to customers. Occasionally I ask members to draw detailed flowcharts of their work – individually – before they share their descriptions with one another. But when the group sharing begins, the differences among members – who are trying to accomplish the same goals – are disconcerting. Openly seeing and discussing these flowcharts, however, enables members to investigate why the *identical* process is being performed differently. They are then in the best position to dissolve these unfavorable differences.

Even more basic, there may be very different views in a work group about who the customer actually is and what the customer really needs. Again, it is surprising for group members to discover that they have been making vastly different assumptions about their customers – assumptions that significantly affect how they perform their tasks and decisions. Or as some members recognize: "No wonder our customers regularly complain that they receive our daily services differently – depending on who in our department happens to answer the phone!"

Not only is it imperative for subunit members themselves to draw flowcharts of their core processes. It may also be essential to include key customers and suppliers. Primary suppliers will be able to provide quality inputs if they have a rational understanding of what processes take place downstream. Prime customers can be given an opportunity to clarify and explain their special requirements. Recall: Actively involving all members and key stakeholders in describing processes is an important attribute of a quantum organization. When an external source prepares and delivers a process to members, they become passive jobholders.

Drawing flowcharts self–stimulates members to clarify, simplify, and streamline processes – leading to a more efficient and effective sequence of tasks and decisions (which is more likely to delight customers). In fact, using flowcharts as the *standard operating procedure* for selecting which tasks and decisions should be performed, and in what order, enables members to add value to the whole process chain in a reliable manner (no matter who in the subunit or organization performs the process).

It is helpful for members to use a universal convention for drawing flowcharts in order to have a common language for describing processes. Inputs from suppliers and outputs to customers are shown as ovals; tasks are shown as rectangles (and numbered as well); decisions (checkpoints for making mid-course corrections) are shown as diamonds with yes (go) and no (no-go) loops to move forward or backward – depending on the outcome of the decision. If members use the symbols shown in Figure 5.7, it will be much easier to manage processes – especially across boundaries. Note: These basic symbols are derived from the conventions established by ANSI, the American National Standards Institute.

FIGURE 5.7
Basic Symbols for Drawing Flowcharts

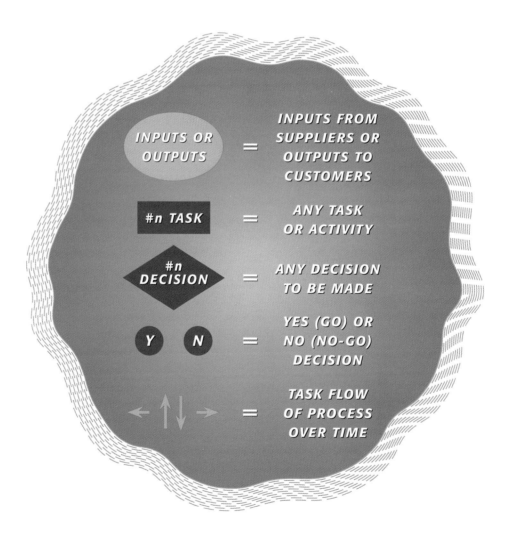

Additional symbols have been developed for identifying the nature of tasks and decisions – so that flowcharts can capture more information. Figure 5.8 gives special symbols for moving, waiting, preparing, checking, writing, explaining, and storing. While many more symbols are available (or can be designed), at some point, too many special symbols can get in the way of clearly communicating the task flow of a process – especially when a process cuts across several subunits. As a result, it is usually best to use extra symbols only if they provide value–added benefits for those members who are managing the process. The same value–added principle should be applied, of course, to all other quality tools.

FIGURE 5.8
Special Symbols for Drawing Flowcharts

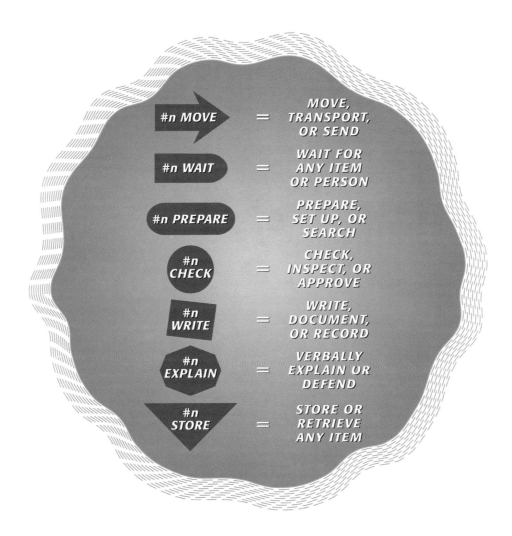

Figure 5.9 presents a flowchart. In most circumstances, there would be many more steps in the process. While drawing flowcharts, it might be useful to write comments on the side – especially when the definition or meaning of a task or decision is not clear or some further explanation is necessary for other members to understand the process. In some cases, a *process dictionary* can be prepared that defines all the tasks and decisions – and inputs and outputs – alphabetically. Since it may be useful to identify who is responsible for performing each task and decision in the process, work groups usually include the name of the assigned person inside each symbol on the flowchart, as well as the time and cost of the step.

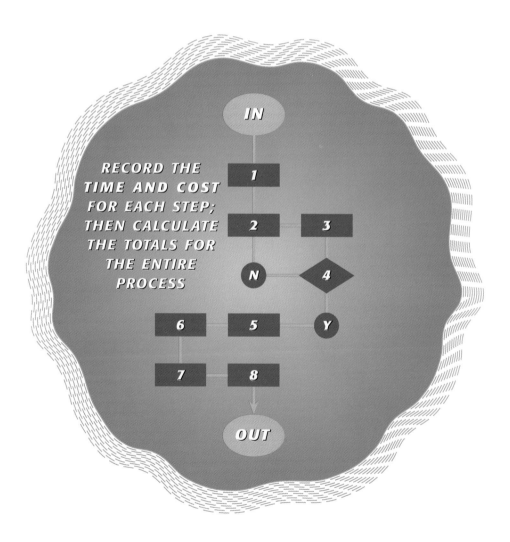

FIGURE 5.9
Describing Processes with Basic Symbols

An eye–catching approach for enhancing flowcharts is to highlight three salient distinctions: *customer value-added* (CVA) activities are tasks and decisions that the ultimate customer would gladly pay for; *other value-added* (OVA) activities are those that other stakeholders (including stockholders, regulatory agencies, and local communities) require members to provide; *no value-added* (NVA) activities are those that no stakeholder desires to pay for or requires members to provide. Illuminated in Figure 5.10, customer value–added activity is emphasized as *green* for go; other value–added is highlighted as *yellow* for caution; no value–added is accentuated as *red* for stop. These colors tend to stimulate appropriate action (Harrington, 1991).

FIGURE 5.10
Three Types of Value-Added Activities

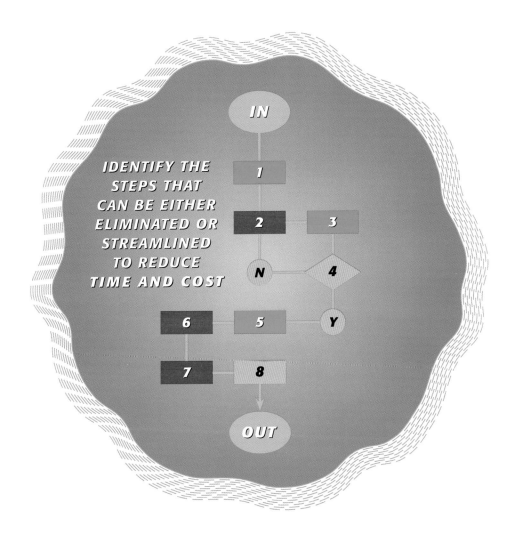

Besides revealing the nature of every task in the process (preparing, waiting, writing, and so forth), the flowchart illustrated in Figure 5.11 also signifies whether a task is CVA (green), OVA (yellow), or NVA (red). Showing the estimated time and cost next to each task in the process (and adding the totals) would provide the necessary information for members to learn how they are wasting their time and resources on tasks and decisions that no one wants (shown in red). Moreover, since some activities are for *other* stakeholders, perhaps these can be minimized – since the final customer does not want to pay for these requirements (yellow). The prime activities (green), however, must be performed to delight the customers.

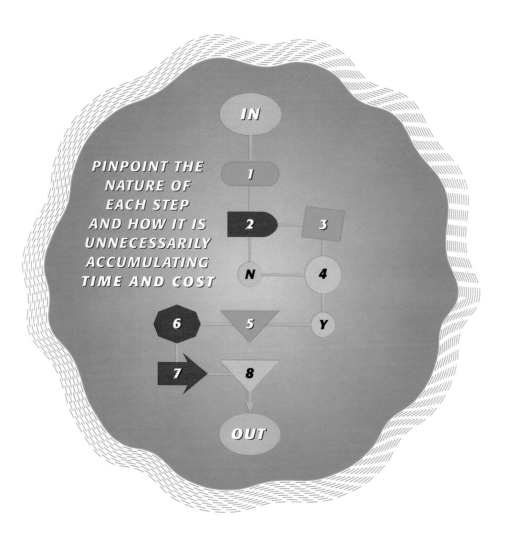

FIGURE 5.11
Describing Processes with Special Symbols

Figure 5.12 demonstrates how members were able to streamline the process by eliminating NVA (red) tasks and minimizing OVA (yellow) tasks. The flowchart shows a revamped process that addresses CVA (green) tasks and decisions to the delight of the final customer. Once this new process has been performed a number of cycles, it will be immensely beneficial to assess the average time and cost of every step in the process, calculate the totals, and then compare these to what was recorded with the old process. Substantial savings in time and cost are often realized just from members explicitly – and consciously – describing a process and then removing the barriers that prevent them from effectively using the process.

FIGURE 5.12
Redesigning the Old Process

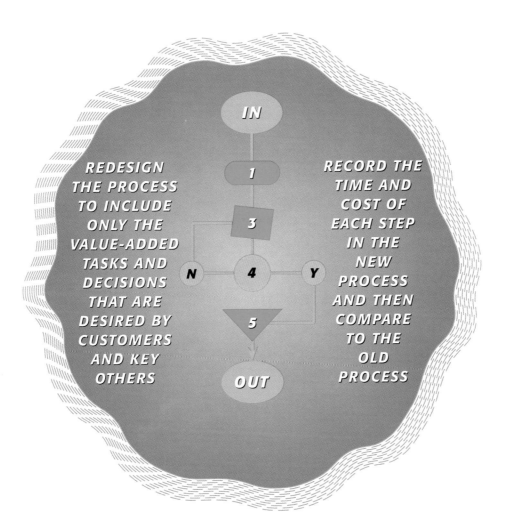

Figure 5.13 summarizes the new process – using renumbered steps and only the basic symbols. This makes it easier to compare with the old process (Figure 5.9, page 218). Yet members must use their new processes as *standard operating procedures*. Why wouldn't members do this? They might misunderstand them, not know about them, not be properly trained to do them, have been trained to do them differently, not have the resources to do them – or someone might have told them to apply these procedures differently. There are more reasons not to follow the established operating procedures than to do what is essential for satisfying customers. But these *description barriers*, once conscious, can be removed (Harrington, 1991).

FIGURE 5.13
Describing the New Process

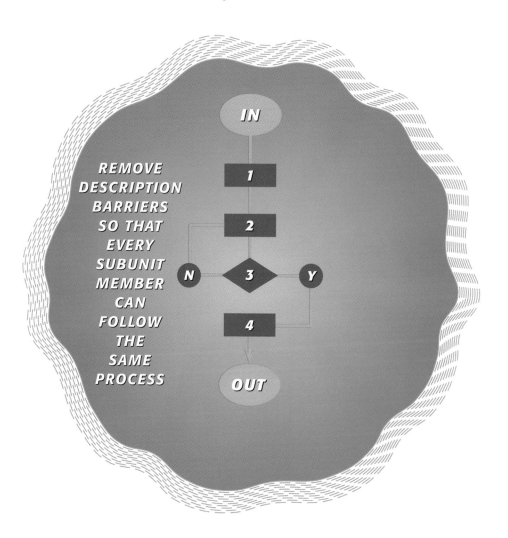

Members often wonder which of the many processes they perform in their subunits they should flowchart – in order to identify and remove description barriers. One important distinction is between a core process that flows *within* subunits (which is a prime candidate for *gradual* process improvement) and a process that still flows *across* subunits (which will be a potential candidate for subsequent *radical* process improvement).

A core process within subunits is defined by certain characteristics: (1) the process can be completed with little coordination of other groups, since the subunit itself primarily controls the outcome; (2) the process is performed every day or at least several times a week; (3) several members in the subunit are involved in performing the process; (4) the process is a major responsibility of the subunit and therefore contributes to strategic objectives; and (5) the process needs improvement. If several processes fit these characteristics, they should be prioritized according to their relative importance to strategic objectives and their need for improvement.

A core process that flows across work units, however, should not be addressed until the strategy–structure track (collaborating with a collateral structure in the radical process track) has redesigned the organization into more autonomous subunits (for example, each horizontal unit is formed to contain a whole business process). The members of these new subunits, therefore, will have much greater control over the outcome of their work: They will be able to redesign and then streamline the business processes that were previously fragmented across several functional subunits.

It is worthwhile to reiterate: A major benefit of drawing flowcharts for core processes is becoming altogether conscious of the three types of value–added processes – rather than members incorrectly assuming that all stakeholders (and all tasks and decisions) are of equal value. *Customer value–added* refers to the ultimate or end customer who is external to the organization – as formally expressed in the strategic objectives. CVA thus considers whether this end customer would directly pay for a specific task or decision – if given the chance. Most customers would refuse to pay for the preparation of an organization's income taxes or what they define as unnecessary paperwork. They only want to pay for activities that directly give them exactly what they want.

But in order to stay in business, every organization is still required (by law or social pressure) to satisfy other stakeholders in addition to the end customer. In most cases, however, the objective is to do only what is absolutely essential to satisfy these others, so that scarce resources are not diverted away from the organization's strategic objective: to satisfy – and delight – the ultimate customer. Thus members try to *minimize* OVA.

No organization, however, can afford to squander limited resources on tasks and decisions that no one wants or requires. The source of many NVA tasks is derived from Newtonian bureaucracy: quick fixes, shortcuts, patch-up jobs, and work-arounds from the past – including many efforts to control employees (resulting from outdated assumptions about human nature). But by making processes explicit with flowcharts, members have an opportunity to take a conscious look at what adds value for customers and other stakeholders versus what no one wants at all. If these NVA tasks are really helping nobody, they should be eliminated.

Another approach to minimize OVA tasks and eliminate NVA tasks is for members to start with a clean slate and describe an *ideal process* – using the various symbols for flowcharts. Recognizing that there is no substitute for conducting market research (whether through surveys about customer needs or by paying special attention to what customers suggest), subunit members list what they believe to be the most crucial needs and wants of final customers as well as the requirements of other primary stakeholders. Next members establish the specific *targets* they must achieve in order to satisfy and delight their external and internal customers. As we shall see, it is essential to translate each target into a number (for example, respond to each customer within twenty-four hours versus "as soon as possible"). Numbers will enable members to assess how well they are achieving their targets, as long as these targets are verified by their customers.

Members must also stipulate what they require from either internal or external suppliers (including information, materials, tools, instructions, forms, and any intermediate products and services) in order to add value. Again, members should emphasize the ideal: what they need, when they need it, where it should be delivered, how it should be delivered to them, and so forth. These ideal inputs should also be translated into numbers.

Using the basic symbols (and possibly using the special symbols as well), members draw a flowchart to show the *ideal* way their core process should be performed in order to delight the end customer (and satisfy the other key stakeholders). Then, using the same symbols, members draw a flowchart to describe the *actual* process by which work is currently being done. If there is a significant gap between the ideal and the actual process, members continue with the steps of problem management: defining root causes and choosing a solution. Since members began by describing their ideal process, their new solution likely minimizes OVA tasks and excludes NVA tasks. But no matter how well the new process has been captured by a flowchart on paper, members must still *implement* – hence *use* – this new process as their standard operating procedure.

Controlling Value-Added Processes

The primary reason for translating customer needs into specific targets (as numbers) is to be able to measure (rather than guess) how well members are performing their processes. Collecting data is a way to assess whether a process is under control and, if it isn't, to proceed with corrective action. Using a *quantum target* to signify any desired attribute, Figure 5.14 defines the center – the bull's–eye – as the customer's needs or requirements. For convenience, we will use a ten–point scale to represent all the numbers of a target (as a modified dartboard with one dividing line in the middle).

FIGURE 5.14
Defining a Quantum Target

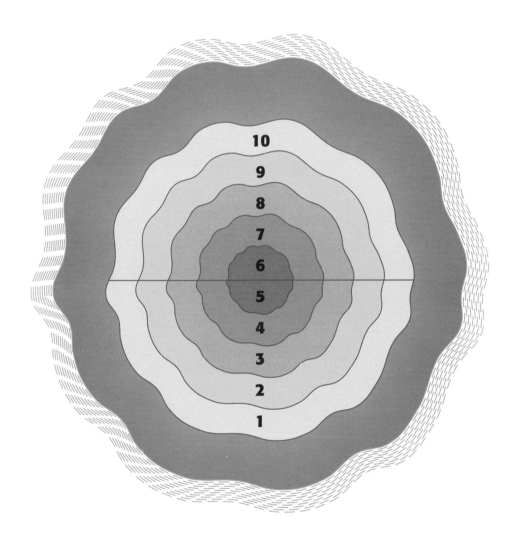

Any numerical scale can be used in place of 1 to 10. But for ease of presentation, we will use this scale on the following figures. (Members can determine the proper numerical scale for measuring how close they come to *their* targets.) For now, we'll get used to setting our sights on a number that, if obtained, would result in customer satisfaction. Take the case of a customer who always expects to receive a specialized product within five or six hours of ordering it. As shown in Figure 5.15, each white dot at the center of the target represents a "hit" for the customer at a different point in time. The concentration of white dots on the bull's-eye suggests perfect on-target performance: every "hit" is *within customer specifications*.

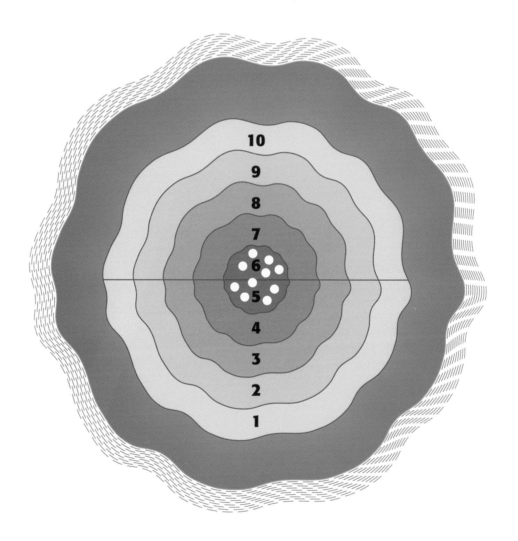

FIGURE 5.15
Perfectly On-Target

The distribution of white dots in Figure 5.16 explicitly demonstrates inconsistent performance: A customer cannot depend on the performance of the product or service from one moment to the next. On any given day, just about anything can happen – other than what is desired. Somewhere in between perfectly on–target and completely off–target performance, we encounter what is normal: Many hits at the center – with some misses on other regions of the target. In a quantum world where not everything can be entirely explained, predicted, or controlled (or measured with perfect precision), there will be some normal variation in providing any product or service. *Understanding variation is the key to controlling processes.*

FIGURE 5.16
Completely Off-Target

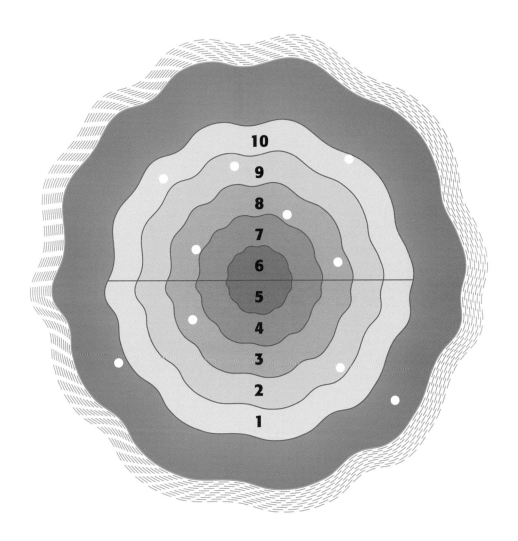

If you try to hit the same target numerous times – and the process is under control – most of your hits will be at the center, while a few hits will occur at the outer bands, as shown in Figure 5.17. If you don't do your best and aren't skilled at your job, of course, the outcomes will materialize all over the place. In these cases, it is still important to collect many data points to know with certainty if your process is either *under control* or *out of control*. When only a few data points are registered, it's hard to know if the first few hits are just due to luck or if the process that produces the hits is something a customer can rely on – repeatedly. *Only a dense spread of dots can reveal the wave function of potential particle locations.*

FIGURE 5.17
Normal Random Variation

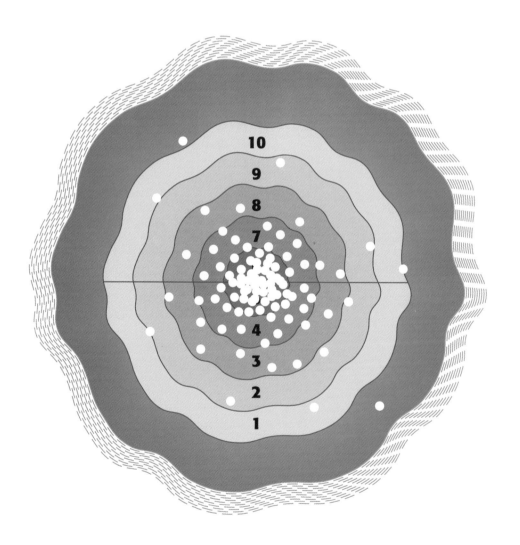

In Figure 5.18, the pattern of hits on the target can be rearranged to depict a *normal distribution of data points*. If there is any doubt that a process is normal, however, compute the average of several hits (between two and ten) – a "subgroup" of data points. Actually, the more hits you include in each subgroup, the more the *distribution of the averages* will correspond to a normal distribution – which is well known as the Central Limit Theorem (Montgomery, 1991). Be sure to assemble enough data so you can compute the averages of at least twenty–five subgroups. When the process is under control, the distribution of these averages will exhibit normal variation – easily recognized as a "bell–shaped" curve (or a quantum wave).

FIGURE 5.18
From Target Practice to a Normal Distribution

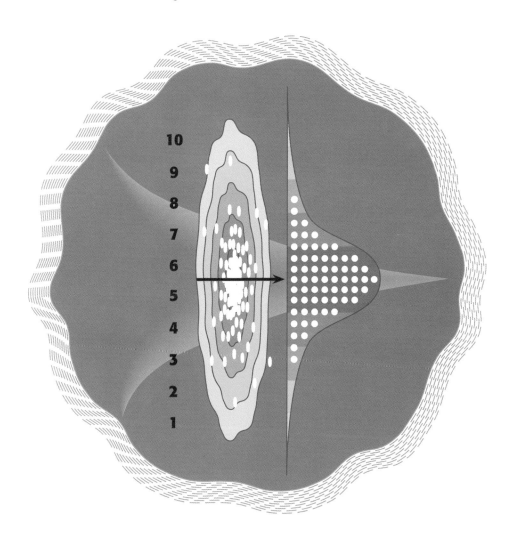

The five terms defined in Figure 5.19 will be used repeatedly while we review the methods for controlling value–added processes. Our focus, however, is on understanding the key concepts for managing processes – not on making statistical calculations or analyzing actual samples of data. The statistical formulas and procedures for managing quality are readily available (Amsden, Butler, and Amsden, 1991). As suggested in the figure, *variation* displays the actual spread of data points (hits) around the target. In the next figures, we'll say more about collecting data points, averaging subgroups, and then plotting them to learn if our processes for providing products and services to customers are on–target, with normal variation.

FIGURE 5.19
Standard Terms for a Normal Distribution

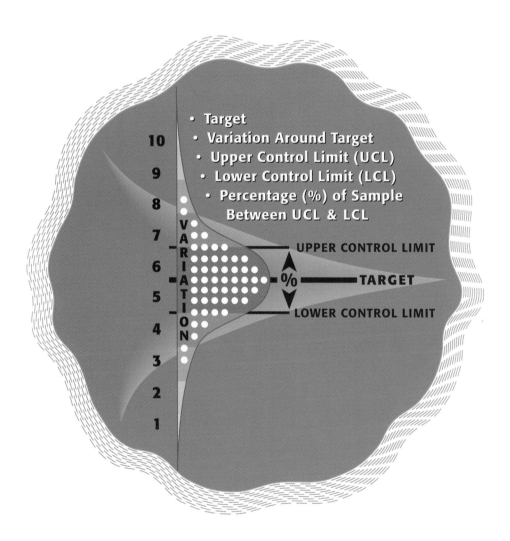

An important attribute of a normal distribution is the percentage of data points that fall within the upper control limit and the lower control limit – depending on how many "bands" of the distribution are included. The percentages that define the first, second, and third band of a normal distribution are 68.26%, 95.46%, and 99.73%, respectively. As portrayed in Figure 5.20, virtually all efforts at managing processes use the third band of the distribution for sensing if a process is actually out of control. Thus if data points show up outside the third band more than .27% of the time (100 – 99.73), which is often rounded up to 1%, the process is identified as out of control (Montgomery, 1991).

FIGURE 5.20
The Control Limits for the Third Band

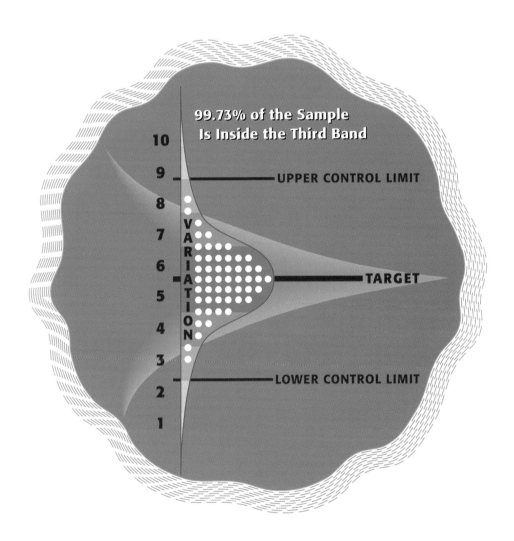

Collecting and averaging samples of data take place over time. As a result, Figure 5.21 now shows the data points (which at first were carefully arranged inside the normal distribution to reveal its shape) to include the dimension of *time*. From this moment forward, we will use this time–based graph of a normal distribution to display a process in motion. Remember, however, that every point on the chart represents an average of two to ten data points – to ensure that the process, if under control, will appear as a normal distribution. Only if you are utterly convinced that the underlying process is indeed normal will it be safe – and appropriate – to plot single data points (Juran, 1988).

FIGURE 5.21
From a Static to a Dynamic Picture of Data Points

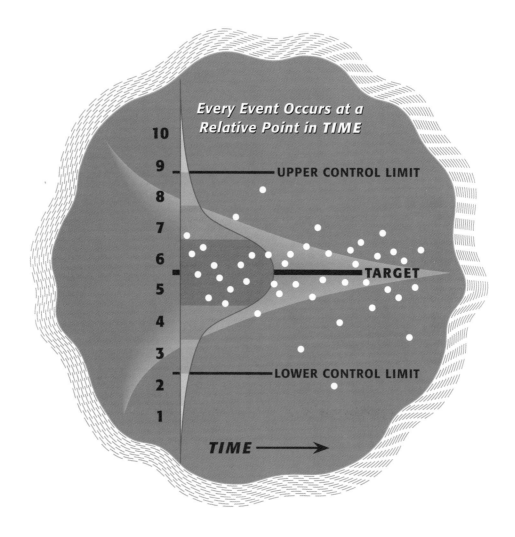

Figure 5.22 presents one of the classic tools of process management. When few, if any, calculations are made to determine the target line and the UCL and the LCL, the outcome is called a *run chart*. While it's easy to get carried away with statistical calculations (especially for organizations that have a technical orientation), a value–added perspective should always be taken: Are the time and effort to make the calculations worth the gain in precision? Much can be deduced from run charts – by eyeballing the data points – after connecting the dots. Several other process control charts are available for different kinds of variables. For a helpful overview of process control charts, see Ishikawa (1986).

FIGURE 5.22
The Process Control Chart

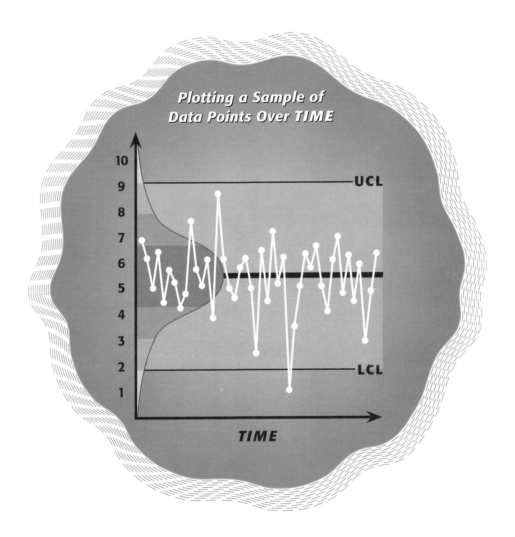

Merely by eyeballing the distribution of data points in Figure 5.23, you can see that this process is out of control (what we previously called completely off-target). Consider some of the causes that would prevent a process from taking place as intended: not following standard operating procedures as described by the subunit's flowchart; not properly training members to perform their work; not monitoring the process and making mid-course corrections; and not appropriately using all *available* resources. Thus processes become out of control by not applying members' energies and abilities on the right objectives and tasks – and not using incentives, training, tools, methods, information, and flowcharts to guide behavior.

FIGURE 5.23
An Out-of-Control Process

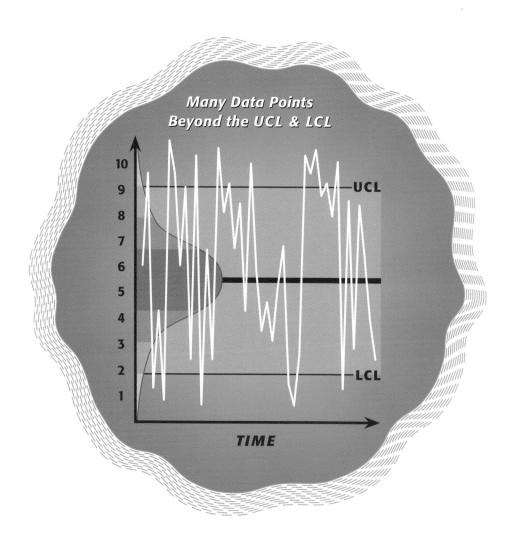

The prime challenge: If a process is out of control (hence a problem has been sensed), define the *special causes* of the problem and proceed with the steps of problem management. If no errors are committed, the process will come under control. With practice, everyone can learn to differentiate random variation from trends and spikes that are nonrandom – as shown in Figure 5.24. These trends and spikes derive from special causes that can be identified and removed, especially since the process control chart gives the time the gap occurred (and thus who was responsible for the process). But step 1, of course, is sensing a gap between an out–of–control process and what should be: *normal random variation.*

FIGURE 5.24
Nonrandom Trends and Spikes

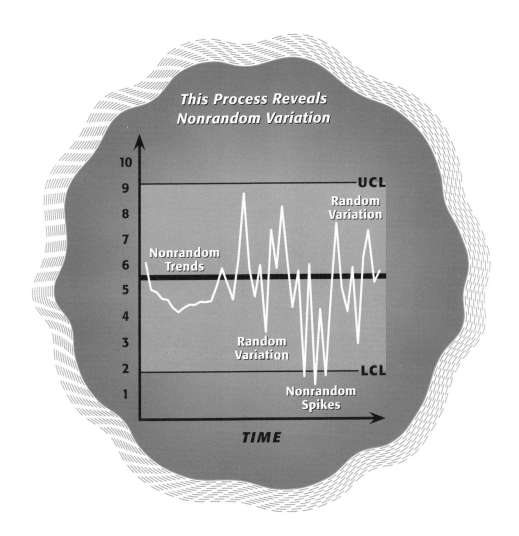

As a result of applying the steps of problem management, members can remove the *special causes* (or control barriers) that prevent their process from functioning as intended. Figure 5.25 captures the desired transition – from a process that was originally out of control to one that is now under control. Customers will now get reliable results between the two control limits – no matter which member performs the process. But we now must ask some difficult questions: Is this consistent performance good enough? What if customers require *less variation* around the target than this process is capable of providing – even when under statistical control? Basically, an under-control process that cannot satisfy customers must be improved.

FIGURE 5.25
From Out of Control to Under Control

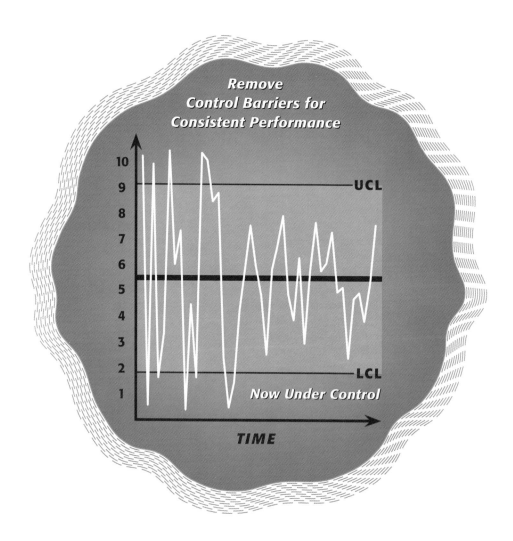

CHAPTER 5

Improving Value-Added Processes

It is tempting to try to improve a process by being more and more careful about how it is performed. If a process is already under control, however, its variation cannot be reduced further – it is random. And trying to undo what is random is only going to make matters worse. Members, therefore, should not tinker around with random variation. Instead, they should try to change the resources that determine targets (and the variations around targets) in the first place.

Remember that *controlling* processes takes the "factors of production" or resources as a given and focuses all attention on making the best use of what is currently available. Now with the switch to *improving* processes, almost nothing is fixed (let alone sacred). On the contrary, each subunit is expected to achieve even better targets with less variation – by modifying the combination of resources that shape how a process behaves when it is under control. In essence, the only real constraints arise from short–term resource limitations that each subunit must accept for the time being. In the long term, of course, anything is possible – by transforming industries and leveraging resources. This greater freedom will be apparent once the radical process track has restructured resources into autonomous units – but first members must learn to improve core processes *within* subunits.

When we speak of resources that determine (cause) the target and its variation, we specifically mean the major "factors of production," which can conveniently be classified into six categories: people (behavior, skills, abilities, and self–aware consciousness); technology (machines, computers, tools, and equipment); policies (guidelines, procedures, rules, regulations, and societal laws); materials (tangible inputs from suppliers); information (intangible inputs from suppliers); and flows (the velocity of physical and electronic movements of resources within and across subunit boundaries). Once every core process is under control, members can distinguish which of these *common causes* (or improvement barriers) are holding back process improvement and thus must be removed – along with any dysfunctional infrastructures and misaligned systems.

A caution: Members should first try to improve the resources they already have (training current employees), before they consider acquiring new resources (hiring new employees). Often organizations do not spend much time and effort finding creative ways to get more out of their "old" resources before they search for something new. If members have not yet learned how to improve the use of available technology, for example, why would it be any easier for them to use newer, more elaborate technology?

Members often switch technology only to discover that the problem was never with the technology itself, but rather with how it was implemented or used by untrained people. Members must define the root cause of their resource constraints (by analyzing assumptions) *before* they generate a new resource-based solution and, once again, implement it unsuccessfully.

It is worthwhile highlighting two key statistical principles that have been advocated by Shewhart (1931) and Deming (1986). The first principle emphasizes that all outcome variables (for example, product and service specifications, process costs, and cycle times) must be clearly defined and operationalized into accurate measures *before* a described process can be brought under statistical control – and then improved. Specifically, if the process of *measuring* some aspect of quality is not under statistical control (including the instrument, the context of measurement, and the members participating throughout the entire measurement process), all subsequent attempts to control and improve the process for producing quality will be futile. Rather than making general exhortations about improving quality, therefore, it is vital to establish what *specific* outcome variable is of interest (for example, cycle time) and then indicate precisely how this variable will be measured, by whom, and under what distinct conditions – so that the measurement process remains under statistical control.

A second principle of statistical variation concerns the fundamental division between special causes and common causes (Deming, 1986; 1993). *Special causes* (which drive processes out of statistical control, usually called control barriers) can often be removed by the subunit itself (for example, by ensuring that a described process is being followed by members as the standard operating procedure). But *common causes* (which render processes incapable of meeting customer specifications, usually called improvement barriers) can only be removed by those who have the necessary resources and the authority to redesign – or reengineer – the process itself. It seems very unreasonable, therefore, to hold the persons who *perform* the process accountable for various deficiencies in the *design* of the process (which is evident if the process is not capable of meeting customer specifications – even when it is under control – yet cannot be improved by the subunit). Practically (ethically) speaking, members should be held responsible only for keeping a process under control – especially when sources external to the subunit have, in essence, set the performance limits of the process. As a result, members can be expected to make only modest improvements to processes within their subunits by renewing and changing the resources that have been made available to them. They should not be expected to improve processes whose resources are controlled by other work units.

We now encounter another key principle. Any process that is under *statistical* control (according to the UCL and the LCL) may not be within the *specification limits* defined by the customer: the USL and LSL (the upper and the lower specification limits). The process in Figure 5.26 is not presently capable of consistently producing a "hit" between 3 and 8, with 5.5 as the target. Notice that several points on the chart are outside the USL and the LSL despite being inside the UCL and the LCL. This process, therefore, must be improved. Note: A *capability index* can be calculated to see the difference between statistical control and customer specifications. More information about this index is provided in Amsden, Butler, and Amsden (1989).

FIGURE 5.26
A Noncapable Process

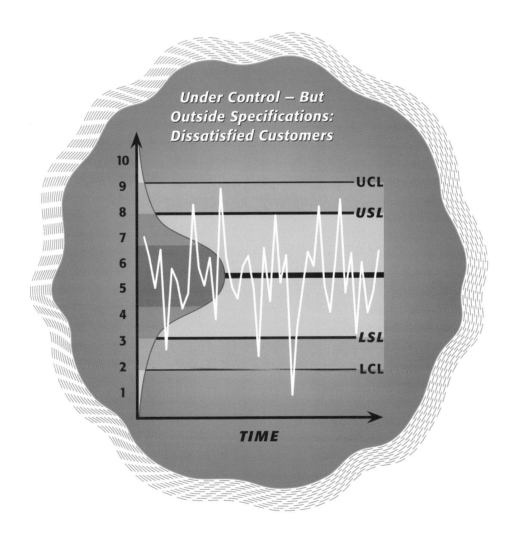

Figure 5.27 illustrates a capable process: one that is under statistical control and, at the same time, within customer specifications. In this case the customer, as before, wants a quality feature to range between 3 and 8, with 5.5 as the target. The improved process is now able to deliver. Note: If specification (USL/LSL) *and* control (UCL/LCL) limits are shown on the same process control chart, it is necessary to plot every data point individually. Using subgroups to ensure a normal distribution does not reveal whether one or more data points are beyond the specification limits – even if each subgroup of data points is under control. Customers want *every* product or service to meet their specifications, *every* time.

FIGURE 5.27
A Capable Process

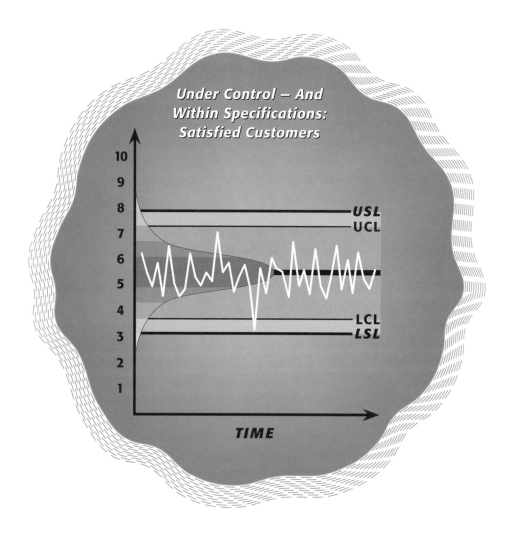

The popular term *zero defects* generally signifies that no data point is outside the specification limits. But variation around the target still causes headaches for customers – especially in the case when they may have to accept a product or service that is near the edge of acceptability (near the USL or the LSL) yet is "far away" from their target. This flawed concept led Taguchi to create a *quality loss function:* to identify the *increasing distance from the target* as the true indicator of defects – and loss to society (Taguchi and Clausing, 1990). Figure 5.28 *approximates* loss (in red). To minimize this loss, variation can be further reduced so that six (not three) bands of a normal distribution fall within specifications; this is called *six sigma quality.*

FIGURE 5.28
The Quality Loss Function

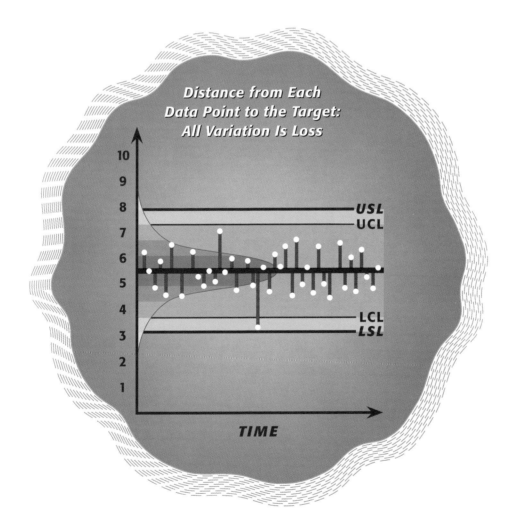

Here we revisit the epitome of quality management: fast cycle time based on minimal variation around the specified target for each process – as displayed in Figure 5.29. Therefore, it is not enough to reduce variation (improve processes) within the formal boundaries of an organization. The members of every subunit must collaborate with their upstream suppliers and their downstream customers. Why? To inspire them to actively renew and generate additional resources (people, technology, policies, materials, information, flows) in order to continuously improve their core processes by continually reducing their variation. Such collaboration stimulates the economic success of industries, nations, and the world (Porter, 1990).

FIGURE 5.29
Another Look at Fast Cycle Time

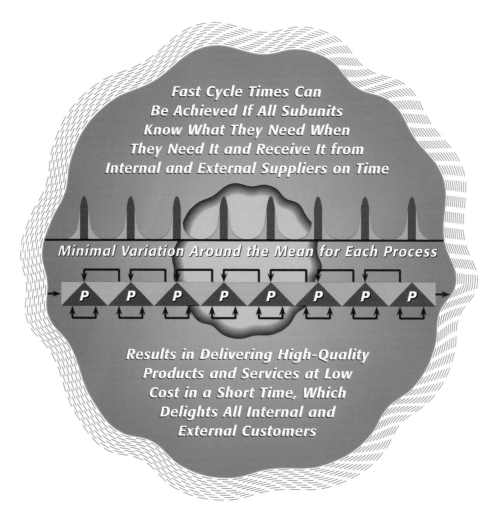

The control chart shown in Figure 5.30 presents the before, during, and after stages of improving a process. First, the familiar process is under control; then, a change in resources is implemented; next, the new process is out of control; eventually, the improved process is under control – with a better target and less variation than before (Juran, 1991). Most often, it is easier to improve a process by shifting its *target* (when the midpoint of the distribution is the ideal, not either endpoint) than to decrease its *variation*, which is the result of many interrelated "factors of production." As noted previously, however, reducing variation around the target – and thereby reducing loss to society – is the prime objective for improving a process.

FIGURE 5.30
Improving a Process

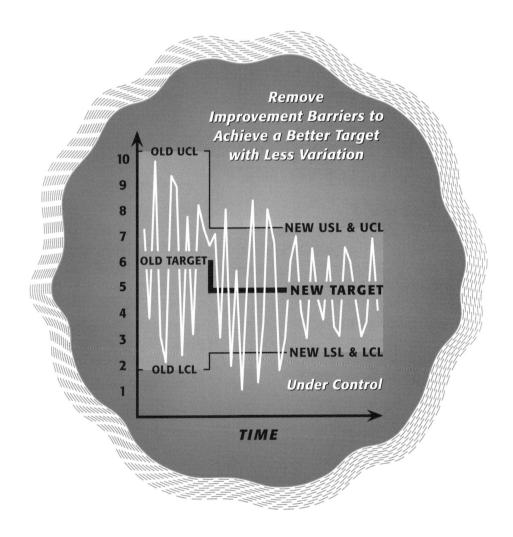

Continuous process improvement is helped out by *seven quality tools*. Although the names of the quality tools vary from one author to the next, there is still considerable overlap and thus agreement about their nature and use. Probably the best discussion is by Ishikawa (1986). Basically, the seven tools help members to see the underlying relationship between two or more variables with greater insight than a table of numbers. Combined with assumptional analysis, members have a powerful – and easy to use – *tool kit for managing their core processes*, as pictured in Figure 5.31. The decision to use these statistical tools, as always, should be based on a value-added assessment. For an additional set of *seven new tools*, see Mizuno (1988).

FIGURE 5.31
Seven Quality Tools for Process Improvement

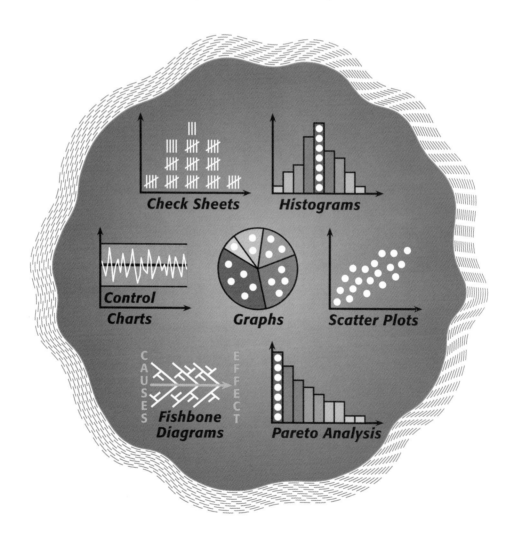

❼ THE RADICAL PROCESS TRACK

The primary reason why improving processes within functional subunits can achieve only gradual improvement is that each work unit, on its own, has few degrees of freedom to modify the "factors of production" (people, technology, materials, information, policies, and flows). Fundamentally, a narrowly focused subunit does not have the formal authority to change the *common causes* behind a long process chain. Stated differently, the level of improvement for functionally based subunits is severely limited when significant task flow crosses functional boundaries: It is hard for members to manage the "white space" between subunits from *within* their subunits. Although established standards do not exist, process improvement *within functions* is limited to 5–15% (whether the focus is on reducing cycle time, process cost, errors, defects, and failures – or meeting product and service specifications).

But when a core process can be managed *across* pertinent functional boundaries (referred to as a cross–functional or cross–boundary process), it becomes possible to alter the "factors of production" that are allocated across all the relevant work units – in order to streamline cross–boundary task flow. By specifically managing what had been left to fall between the cracks, process improvement may generate gains between 25 and 50%. To reach this higher level of improvement, however, it is necessary to involve a lot of members in *cross-functional teams* – in order to describe, control, and improve cross–boundary processes – above and beyond their other efforts to improve core processes within functional subunits.

But when cross–boundary task flows are superabundant, numerous cross–boundary teams must be established. In particular, many members may spend too much time on various cross–functional teams addressing ever–increasing cross–boundary task flow rather than doing their primary work *within* subunits. In the extreme cases, members may be assigned to three or more cross–functional teams – concurrently. Such multiple team involvement can certainly confuse members as to the relative priority of every process and, not surprisingly, encourages the commentary: "He who dies with the most teams wins." Such extravagant use of cross–functional teams for managing significant cross–boundary task flow is self–defeating in the long term: Resources are depleted, members get confused, subunits can't self–manage – and the underlying task flow problem is neglected. To achieve dramatic improvements, a radical approach is required – one that redirects the time and cost of *cross-boundary teams* to value–added tasks and decisions that are contained within *newly formed subunits*.

Reforming subunit boundaries around the most strategically salient cross-boundary processes (also called *strategic processes*) – supported by the use of information and communication technologies – can achieve radical improvement. Indeed, the potential level of radical improvement is in the range of 100–1,000% or higher! Essentially, by restructuring and leveraging available, renewed, and additional resources across longer process chains, more "factors of production" will then be under the jurisdiction of truly comprehensive, self-managing subunits. Radical process improvement is therefore entirely in sync with the attributes of a quantum organization.

For the moment, let's define two types of cross-boundary processes subject to radical process improvement. *Business processes* are process chains that cut across at least two functional domains and add value for external customers (cva). Typical business processes include (1) customer order to delivery, order handling, and order fulfillment; (2) customer facing across marketing, sales, service, billing, credit, and warranty administration; (3) manufacturing merged with distribution; (4) enterprise logistics planning; (5) materials management – assimilating procurement, warehousing, and delivery; (6) partnering with upstream suppliers; and (7) new product and service development, introduction, and redevelopment. All these business processes serve external customers.

Management processes are process chains that cut across two or more functional areas and add value for other stakeholders (ova). Examples of management processes include (1) establishing and maintaining quantum infrastructures; (2) formulating strategic architecture and deriving strategic objectives; (3) arranging strategic alliances and networks; (4) aligning and deploying strategic objectives through structural forms; (5) organizing and coordinating radical process improvement; and (6) motivating, measuring, monitoring, and rewarding performance. All these management processes are designed to satisfy other key stakeholders more directly than external customers. If these management processes are performed well, of course, external customers will eventually benefit. But customers do not want to pay for these management activities. Incidentally, for convenience we will often use the term *business process* to refer to both types of cross-boundary processes. Sometimes, however, it is helpful to make the subtle distinction between business and management processes – so that cva activities can be treated differently from ova tasks and decisions.

The essential material for understanding the radical process track is presented in four parts: distinguishing gradual and radical improvement; redesigning structure for radical improvement; using economic criteria for process management; and mobilizing pmos for radical improvement.

Distinguishing Gradual and Radical Improvement

Let's examine the crucial differences between gradual and radical process improvement. Figure 5.32 uses the "Newtonian house" (first introduced on page 142) to illustrate the core distinctions. Notice the functional subunits that are being coordinated by – external – management. Gradual process improvement takes place within these vertical bars – subunit by subunit. The horizontal bars of "empty space" that lie in between these functional areas represent what falls between the cracks or what is passed over the walls (Rummler and Brache, 1990).

FIGURE 5.32
Gradual Improvement Within Management Functions

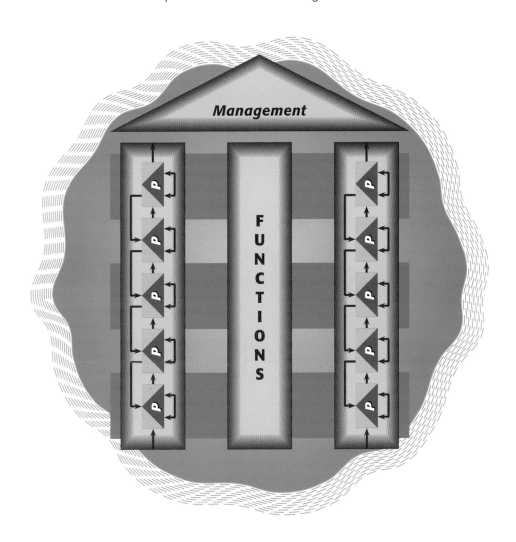

In Figure 5.33, it is essential to recognize that the wholly overlooked areas of "filled space" are exactly what boosts cycle time and process cost in a vertical organization. The special symbols for describing processes are for moving, waiting, preparing, checking, writing, explaining, and storing. Such task flow usually occurs between functional areas – representing the filled space on the organization's chart. Further, no matter how well each function performs its processes, the organization still can't perform to its potential if cross–boundary task flow nullifies the excellent efforts of the isolated functions. *Quality function deployment* is inefficient as well whenever excessive task flow cuts across functional subunits (Ernst & Young, 1990).

FIGURE 5.33
The Filled Space Between Management Functions

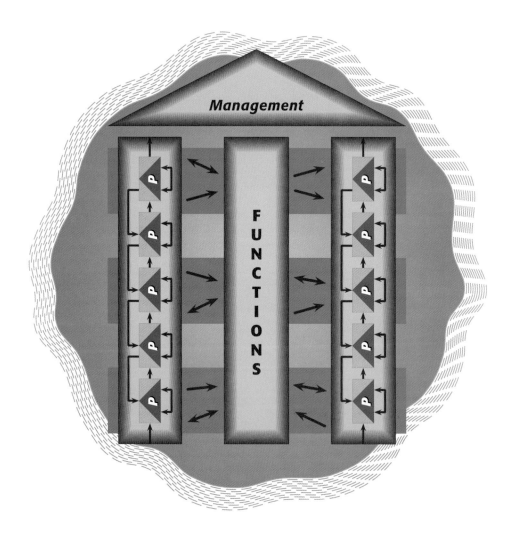

Now we examine an organization in which subunits are structured around business processes. The result? A horizontal organization emerges with horizontal bars representing business and management processes, as displayed in Figure 5.34. Moreover, these subunits are self-managed teams that control most of their work flow. But the horizontal organization still has "open space" – as depicted by the vertical bars on the chart. While the terms *silos* and *chimneys* have often been used to nickname the functional subunits within a vertical organization, the process-based work units of a horizontal organization might be nicknamed *highways*, *tunnels*, or *bridges* – implying that even these units have finite access across their boundaries.

FIGURE 5.34
A Horizontal Organization of Business Processes

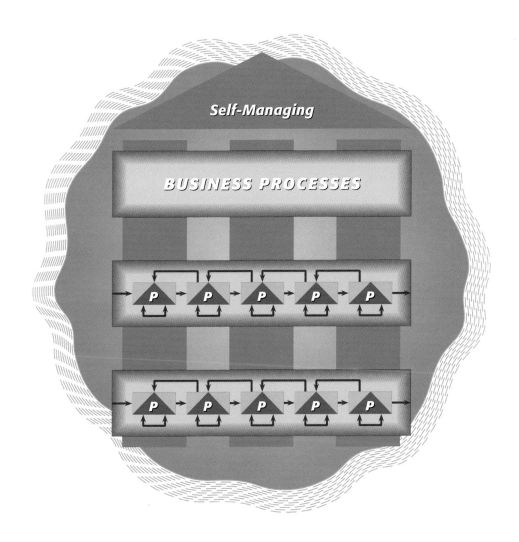

Even after describing, controlling, and improving every business (or management) process, the organization will not achieve its full potential unless the filled space between its process–based work units is addressed explicitly. This space, pictured in Figure 5.35, could result from functional expertise or technical skills that have not been fully applied. Some of the benefits of technical specialization might have been lost by concentrating too much on the business. Or this filled space could stem from important interfaces among processes that were overlooked but are essential to the accomplishment of strategic objectives (for example, how order fulfillment collects market information that feeds into new product development).

FIGURE 5.35
The Filled Space Between Business Processes

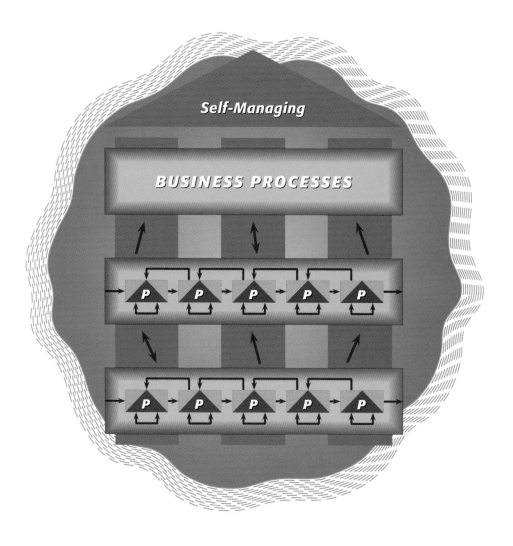

Being explicit about describing, controlling, and improving business processes within horizontal subunits as well as processes (task flows) that fall between boundaries – this is exactly what a quantum organization is self-designed to do! As shown in Figure 5.36, most task flow for achieving strategic objectives can be self-contained by business processes. Through teamwork and cooperation across boundaries (as supported by quantum infrastructures), *cross-business* processes can be explicitly managed. Further, cross–business process teams can be established – if extra help is needed. But if it takes many such teams to handle the excessive task flow between subunits, it's time to take another systematic look at strategy–structure!

FIGURE 5.36
Self-Managing Processes Within/Across Subunits

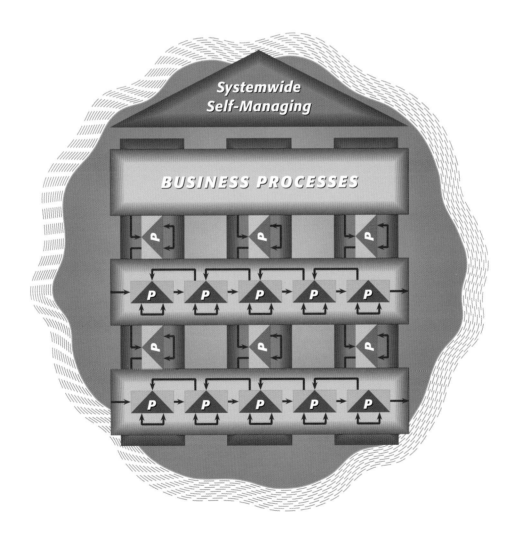

Redesigning Structure for Radical Improvement

Figure 5.37 revisits the difficulty of achieving radical improvement when formal subunits are organized by management functions. Taking the case of four functional spheres (sales, credit, manufacturing, shipping), all these subunits are intimately involved when a customer places an order. Yet not one subunit, by itself, can manage all the task flow. Instead, excessive time must be wasted interacting with other subunits in order to satisfy the end customer. Although cross-functional teams can help manage the task flow to some extent, their extra efforts add to cycle time and process cost.

FIGURE 5.37
Extensive Cross-Functional Task Flow

The basic symbols for flowcharts can also be utilized for describing cross-functional processes. Figure 5.38 shows (as a closed loop) the process that begins with a customer request and ends when the order is received by the customer. The darker lines pinpoint the boundaries that divide the four functional subunits. Notice that tasks and decisions are distinguished according to the three types: customer value–added (green), other value–added (yellow), and no value–added (red). One new symbol is introduced: a thick line around two or more tasks or decisions indicates that they are unnecessarily *duplicating* work – a classic symptom of fragmented subunits that don't communicate, collaborate, or trust one another.

FIGURE 5.38
Describing Cross-Functional Processes

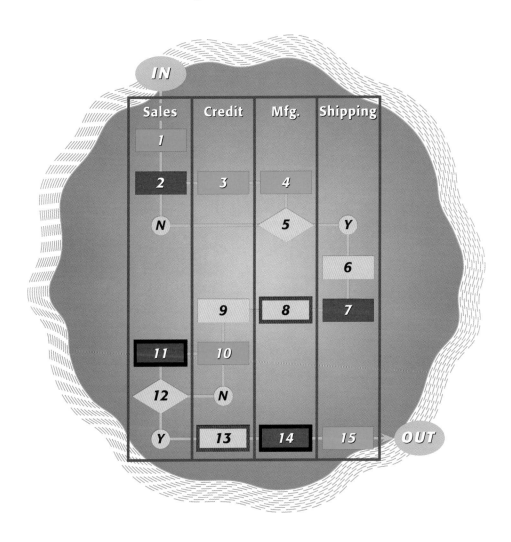

If the darker lines between the four functions are eliminated (NVA), the process chain, shown in Figure 5.39, can be radically improved. What were fragmented functions can now be integrated as a business process: the *order fulfillment process*. Instead of negotiating across kingdoms, fiefdoms, turfs, and chimneys, one whole subunit enables psychological bonds and physical proximity among group members – supported by cultural norms and the reward system – to manage all task flows from beginning to end. *A self-managing subunit fosters process management. After all, mid-course corrections are easier to coordinate (each member becomes his or her own customer) than requesting and receiving feedback between customers and suppliers across formal boundaries.*

FIGURE 5.39
From Fragmented Functions to One Business Process

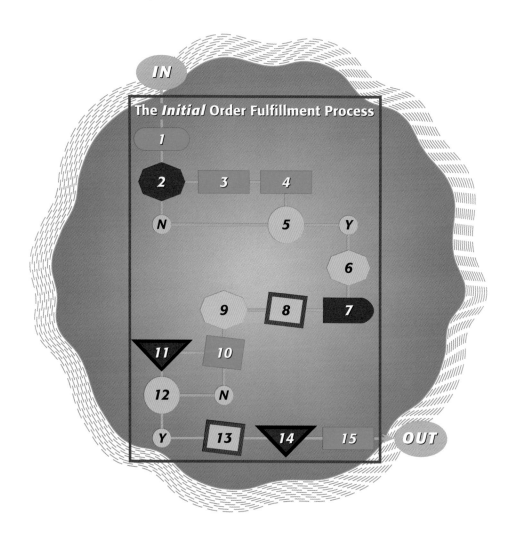

Perhaps the single factor of production or *common cause* that defines radical change is technology: communication and computer technologies that *eminently transform and speed up task flow.* Not only should organizations keep up with innovations (such as the rapid progression of *e-business*); they must also play a proactive role in designing new technologies. As a result, organizations can establish new operational structures that will radically reduce cycle times and process costs – while increasing customer delight. As depicted in Figure 5.40, such radical change is enabled by technologies that transform task flow (at light speed via fiber optics and wireless forms) around the globe (Tapscott and Caston, 1993; Keen, 1991; Wriston, 1992).

FIGURE 5.40
Global Technologies That Transform Task Flow

Technology can either speed up an existing mess (consisting of NVA) or it can allow members – previously affiliated with different functions in different locations – to reengineer and manage task flow electronically. As shown in Figure 5.41, the order fulfillment process has now been radically improved by minimizing OVA and eliminating NVA. All the remaining CVA tasks are handled by *one subunit* that promptly connects with all external customers, quickly initiates their orders, seamlessly brings their orders to completion, and then rapidly delivers these finished products to the right customers. One subunit can do it better and faster – by fully integrating computer, communication, production, and transportation technologies.

FIGURE 5.41
Reengineering a Business Process

Recall three interfaces for strategy–structure (pages 175–176). Figure 5.42 shows how the process view must be addressed at each interface: (1) to make sure that *strategic processes* for achieving strategic objectives (2) are designed into *horizontal structures* so that (3) members are able to perform a large piece of their process chains – and continuously improve processes. But if every subunit has not evolved into a *self-managing team* (enabled by information technology), cycle time, process cost, and product and service features will remain off-target – in spite of the right horizontal structures being designed for the right processes. *Policy deployment* means translating a process vision into desired results (Ernst & Young, 1990).

FIGURE 5.42
Three Interfaces for Process Management

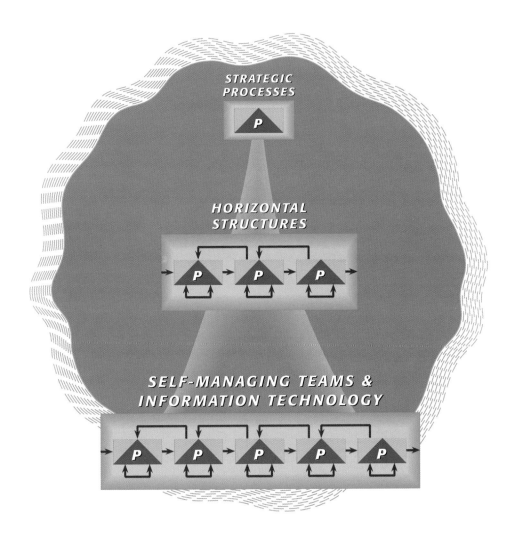

Using Economic Criteria for Process Management

Distinctive use has been made of the term *value-added*. Whether for noting what customers or other stakeholders want (CVA or OVA, respectively), the term has been used to underscore that all tasks, decisions, processes, and stakeholders are not of equal value. Moreover, we have acknowledged the importance of conducting a cost/benefit comparison whenever the use of a tool or technology is being considered: Do the benefits of using the tool or technology offset the related costs? Processes should not be improved – and tools should not be used – just because they are familiar (or popular) or happen to be available. Even more important: Time and energy should not be diverted by conducting value–based assessments if there is no gap between what the process actually delivers and what customers want. But it is essential to proceed with value–added and cost/benefit assessments if sizable gaps have been sensed – and thus processes need improvement.

Whenever a value–based perspective is used, we have assumed that members are able to correctly assess the priority of their tasks, decisions, and stakeholders – in order to make the best selections concerning which core processes to describe, control, and improve (what we have labeled as *strategic* processes). But for this important assumption to be true, members must clearly see the links from their *performance goals* (at the job interface) to the short–term *strategic objectives* of their SBU (at the structural interface), and, further, they must also see the links from the former to the long–term strategic architecture of the organization (at the strategic interface). But if formal systems have not been effectively aligned or deployed (Chapter 4), a genuine desire to make value–based decisions and cost/benefit analyses will be thwarted by members not having the "line–of–sight" information they need. Further, if quantum infrastructures have not been established in all work units throughout an organization (Chapter 3), a genuine desire to make value–based assessments and cost/benefit analyses will doubtless be blocked by dysfunctional cultures, inadequate problem–solving skills, and insufficient teamwork for obtaining the information and cooperation required for choosing the best options. A completely integrated program, therefore, is needed to materialize a *value-conscious organization*.

Even if quantum infrastructures and formal systems are established and functioning well, members still need knowledge on how to prioritize value–added processes and make cost/benefit selections – knowledge that has not been provided in any previous tracks of the completely integrated program and may not be conveniently available within the organization. But, at the very least, all members should know what creates value for an organization (Rappaport, 1986). Moreover, it is important that all members appreciate the main differences between economic value–added (EVA) and accounting profitability.

EVA offers an *economic model* for making decisions that is predicated on generating positive cash flow after capturing all the direct and indirect costs and benefits. Simply stated, EVA is the net cash flow that results from an investment after the cost of capital for that investment has been fully recovered (Stewart, 1991). Profitability derives from the *accounting model* for making clear decisions and paying corporate taxes; it is postulated to be a convenient and fairly arbitrary system of rules for determining costs and benefits. For example, using an arbitrary formula for allocating overhead costs across subunits (or processes) will not provide an accurate picture of *actual* process costs. Consequently, a profitability analysis using traditional accounting data could be seriously misleading – resulting in an inefficient allocation of resources. Using activity–based costing (ABC) to supplement traditional accounting rules provides a more accurate measurement of the direct and indirect *expenses* per process, but it does not recognize the direct and indirect *capital* tied up in each process (for example, employee hiring and training; computer hardware, software, and support services that are actually used to support each business process).

Keen (1997) provides a useful framework that can sensitize members to the crucial distinctions between economic value and paper profitability. Although it is virtually impossible to obtain precise assessments of *all* the true costs and benefits of a complex process or technology, especially in a quantum world, an approximate guess with EVA principles is much better than being precisely wrong with accounting rules. But the worst situation, according to Keen, is when members see only the benefits while selecting which core processes to describe, control, and improve. A typical example would be improving a process to gain faster cycle time but neglecting the fact that the costs to improve the process exceed the savings produced by an improved process. Even though the tangible benefits are meaningful, the improvement effort – as a whole – is a losing proposition. And what if this process is unimportant to customers and aimless to shareholders? To improve processes that are inconsequential to an organization's strategic objectives is to create liabilities, not assets.

Keen proposes two basic dimensions on which to rate each process: salience and worth. *Salience* is determined by the extent to which a process is expected to help members achieve strategic objectives and materialize the strategic architecture. Salience, therefore, is generally the same as CVA (benefits that customers are willing to pay for). But it might still be useful to assess (1) what percentage of the organization's customers are touched by each core process (or what percentage of total revenue these customers contribute to the organization) and (2) how meaningful each process is to these major customers – relative to other CVA processes. *Worth* is assessed according to EVA: the net cash that is expected to result from improving a process – above the cost of capital that is allocated to the process. Worth, therefore, requires an estimate of the cost of capital for each process along with the increases in cash flow (or budget allocations and so on) that the process is expected to generate. Accurate information on both dimensions (salience and worth), however, must also be combined with the size of the gap between the capability of the process in question and what customers want. The process with a larger gap has more *potential* for adding value to the organization – as long as (1) the process in question is high on both worth and salience and (2) there is at least one cost–effective solution that can be implemented successfully in the organization.

Thus another key factor in choosing processes to improve (or tools to use) concerns the costs of improving the process (or using the tool). Of the many ways to reduce cycle time for external customers, which are the most cost–effective? Alternative process solutions, therefore, are not equal. But if members are fully aware of decision trees in problem management, they will recognize that each tree has many branches (decision solutions), which generate different costs and benefits for the organization (including different challenges and costs throughout implementation). Undoubtedly, picking the first approach for reducing cycle time that comes to mind or using the first tool that happens to be available does not ensure the most cost–effective solution was chosen in comparison to all other branches on the decision tree. *All implemented solutions should be value-added.*

Remember: In a quantum world, precise numbers are displaced by statistical distributions. Thus accounting rules (developed for Newtonian organizations) may be inaccurate – and misleading. Statistical accounting principles for quantum organizations are yet to be developed or accepted. Consequently, we must continue to advocate a deep appreciation for the new economics of interdependence – and holism (Milgrom and Roberts, 1992; Deming, 1993). Capital investment decisions must acknowledge the quantum infrastructures that nurture systems and processes (Baldwin and Clark, 1992). These capital investment decisions should then be guided by an economic value–added analysis (Stewart, 1991; Rappaport, 1986) as well as cost/benefit methods (even if intuitively estimated versus information driven) for picking one infrastructure, technology, or process over another. The result? All members' efforts will continue to add *economic* value.

Mobilizing PMOs for Radical Improvement

Now that the major concepts about business and cross–business processes have been examined, we switch back to action. The shadow track (about twenty–five representatives) has established leadership for the completely integrated program – from *initiating the program* (see page 93). The shadow track now develops a method for listing – and prioritizing – all business and cross–business processes based on value–added to strategic objectives and their need for improvement. Next, the shadow track establishes one or more PMOs in order to describe, control, and improve the high–priority business (and cross–business) processes. Then the shadow trackers choose twenty–five members from relevant work units (and their key customers and suppliers) to become a problem management organization for every business process. Members of each PMO are formed into C–groups and an S–group. One person in the S–group is assigned the role of *process owner.*

All PMO members are chosen because they are directly involved in performing some portion of the business or cross–business process. They have learned the skills for process management, endorse desired cultural norms and the use of assumptional analysis, are team players, and will be rewarded for their contributions to the PMO.

Each C–group will be asked to design a radically different business process – using assumptional analysis. Once a radically improved process is synthesized by the S–group, each C–group proceeds to describe, control, and improve its segment of the process, coordinating its efforts with those of the other C–groups and the members who perform the new process.

The S–group, as always, consists of one or two representatives from each C–group. It is responsible for coordinating the key task flows among C–groups and synthesizing all remaining differences. It must also ensure that other relevant stakeholders are properly represented in the redesign of the business process and kept informed of all issues.

The process owner coordinates the S–group and reports directly to the shadow track. This person has a formal position that covers the entire process; has the resources, energy, and skills to foster radical change; can see the big picture and all the core interfaces among business processes; enjoys complex challenges and is willing to take necessary risks; and will gain rewards and satisfaction if the business process is radically improved.

The shadow track continues to coordinate the PMOs that have been mobilized. It ensures that every business process is designed to attain the strategic objectives of the organization, and it monitors and improves the key interfaces among all business and cross–business processes.

Figure 5.43 presents an overview of the interlocking roles of those involved in the PMOs: (1) The shadow track assumes strategic control over the entire array of business and cross-business processes and ensures that the strategy–structure and reward system tracks coordinate their missions with the radical process track; (2) each PMO retains structural control over designing its business or cross-business process; and (3) every work unit retains managerial control over performing its business process – which, of course, includes bringing this new process under statistical control and then gradually improving it. These three organizing levels correspond to the strategic, structural, and job interfaces, respectively.

FIGURE 5.43
Organizing for Radical Improvement

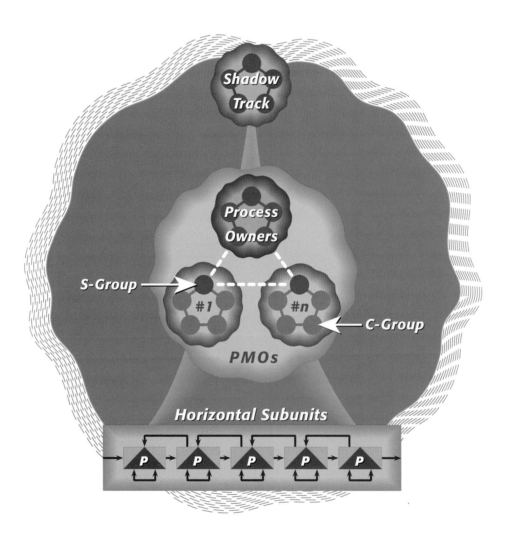

⑧ THE LEARNING PROCESS TRACK

Numerous authors have offered definitions of organizational learning that are intended to further the practice of developing learning organizations. The most frequently cited volume is Peter Senge's *The Fifth Discipline*, which is often credited with stimulating the surge of interest in this topic. Senge (1990, page 1) defines *learning organizations* as "organizations where people continually expand their capacity to create the results they truly desire, where collective aspiration is set free, and where people are continually learning how to learn together." While admiring the inspirational quality of Senge's definition, Garvin (1993) directs attention to its vagueness. And Garvin declares that we must be more specific about what organizational learning *means*, how to *manage* it, and how to *measure* it – the three Ms – if managers are to derive value from this new approach. Garvin (1993, page 80) then provides his own working definition: "A learning organization is an organization skilled at creating, acquiring, and transferring knowledge, and at modifying its behavior to reflect new knowledge and insights."

Garvin's perspective thus highlights what organizational learning is intended to produce: *better knowledge for better action*. This approach should help operationalize the learning concept for people who want to develop learning organizations. Argyris and Schön (1978) have already formulated this action–science, action–research, or knowledge–for–action perspective of organizational learning. An analogous approach has been captured by Nonaka's (1991, page 96) notion of the *knowledge-creating company*, which he introduces in this manner: "When markets shift, technologies proliferate, competitors multiply, and products become obsolete virtually overnight, successful organizations are those that consistently create new knowledge, disseminate it widely throughout the organization, and quickly embody it in new technologies and products."

Nonaka conjectures that knowledge creation involves transforming what is currently *implicit* (such as an idea that has not been proclaimed or shared) into something *explicit* (by expressing, documenting, and sharing it widely all around an organization). An ongoing cycle of shifting back and forth between implicit and explicit knowledge (between individuals, work units, and organizations) is what the acquisition and use of knowledge are all about. Knowledge is thus created by restructuring previous – implicit – knowledge through extensive cross–boundary interaction.

But what exactly is knowledge? Anderson (1983) reexamines this age–old question and derives a key distinction: *Declarative knowledge* is a conceptual understanding of systems, dynamics, relationships, events, and facts (as in knowing why..., knowing about..., or knowing that...) – whether or not you can do anything with this category of knowledge. *Procedural knowledge* is having the skill to actually do something, mentally or physically (as in knowing how...) – whether or not you actually understand what you are doing. Integrating declarative and procedural knowledge creates the very best of both worlds: providing the "whys" behind the "hows" for informed decision making, action taking, and learning across all boundaries. Thus individuals and organizations can attempt to acquire and use declarative and procedural knowledge, to invent better technologies (and also design better organizations), and develop better products/services for customers in order to survive and succeed.

But where is knowledge located? Typically, organizations do make some of their declarative and procedural knowledge explicit – and then store it electronically (in various databases) or on paper (as official documents on operating routines, administrative procedures, and processes). But most of the knowledge acquired and used for organizational decisions and actions is located in the *minds of individuals* (Kim, 1993). Interestingly, the literature on "schema theory" presumes that every person's knowledge is stored as mental categories and relationships among these categories (Markus and Zajonc, 1985), identical to paradigms (see Figure 2.9, on page 63). And two types of schema are proposed: *declarative schemas* are networks of meaning for understanding the "whys," and *procedural schemas* are networks of action for performing the "hows." Moreover, there are numerous ways of making changes in these schemas: (1) assimilating data within existing schemas – either to verify knowledge or gain confidence; (2) gradually restructuring schemas – by adding a few new categories or changing some relationships between categories; and (3) radically restructuring schemas – by changing whole schemas and their relationships with other schemas (Bartunek and Moch, 1987; Vosniadou and Brewer, 1987). To enhance learning and build learning organizations, therefore, we must be able to use and restructure the declarative and procedural schemas in every person's mind.

But where is the mind located? As discussed (see pages 32–36), the debate rages whether the brain contains all of a person's mind and consciousness or if the brain is a conduit for the collective mind that exists "out there" in the universe (Grof, 1993). Explorations with the latest technologies reveal, nevertheless, that the brain's organic structures and biochemical networks store both the long–term memory and short–term memory of declarative and procedural knowledge (Petri and Mishkin, 1994). The cerebral cortex and cerebellum amass long–term – implicit – memory in *automatic* neural networks. The hippocampus and surrounding cortical structures, however, use *conscious*, short–term – explicit – memory to (1) retrieve schemas from long–term memory; (2) use these schemas to collect data, make inferences, or take action; and (3) *gradually or radically restructure* these schemas before they are stored in long–term memory (Carter, 1998; Squire, 1987; 1992).

Without delving further into this exciting new research on learning, knowledge, and memory, suffice it to say that the effective functioning of a global learning organization parallels the dynamic functioning of neural networks in the brain – and networks of meaning and action in the mind. To thrive, according to this learning perspective, a quantum organization must function as a *collective brain* that has continual access to its declarative and procedural schemas – and can restructure its schemas gradually and radically (see pages 63, 64, and 68). Developing a collective mind/brain of *shared schemas* (including a shared paradigm) thus represents the epitome of creating and applying knowledge across all organizational boundaries. Keep in mind, however, that developing shared schemas (from individual schemas) necessitates considerable interaction among people (Kim, 1993), intensive reflection or a "mental dialogue" within each individual (Harris, 1994), and quantum infrastructures as well as formal systems to store this collective knowledge as organizational memory (Walsh and Ungson, 1991). Recognizing the mental and neurological processes that allow individuals to learn (via schemas and neural networks) makes it easier to understand the corresponding *organizational processes* by which knowledge is acquired, distributed, interpreted, and used (Huber, 1991).

What about interconnecting the foregoing perspectives? I find that knowledge (defined as declarative/procedural schemas of individuals and organizations) and learning processes (how schemas can be gradually and radically improved) offer the most practical ways to capture the essence of organizational learning. I propose the following definition as the basis for creating learning organizations: *A learning organization describes, controls, and improves the processes by which knowledge is created, acquired, distributed, interpreted, stored, retrieved, and used – for the purpose of achieving organizational success.*

This definition has several advantages in comparison to those noted earlier. Most important, the predominant theme of describing, controlling, and improving processes is, as we have seen, derived from the literature on quality management (Deming, 1986; Juran, 1991; Harrington, 1995). Not surprisingly, many tools from TQM can easily be applied to organizational learning. Total quality management, therefore, provides for organizational learning what Garvin (1993) recommends: (1) operational definitions that give practical *meaning* to the substance of process management; (2) specific guidelines, principles, and tools for *managing* processes effectively; and (3) suitably developed instruments for *measuring* process improvements (Ernst & Young, 1992; Harrington, 1995; Imai, 1986; Ishikawa, 1986; Juran, 1988; Montgomery, 1991). Reengineering also relies on the process approach for achieving its purpose: radical improvements in cycle times, process costs, and customer satisfaction. Leading books and articles clearly express what reengineering *means*, how to *manage* it, and how to *measure* improvements (Davenport, 1993; Keen, 1997; Hammer and Stanton, 1999). Correlating the process view of quality and reengineering to a process view of *knowledge*, therefore, provides the basics for developing learning organizations.

Specifically, members can learn to describe the processes by which they learn – how they create and use knowledge – especially focusing on the primary knowledge that contributes to the strategic objectives of their organization. This pursuit of both declarative and procedural knowledge may require subunits to interact with internal and external stakeholders. But it is precisely these interactions across organizational boundaries (and self-reflections within individuals) that allow these schemas to coalesce in the first place and then be gradually and radically improved thereafter.

Let's take a moment to consider how subunits can describe, control, and improve learning processes – and thus make their implicit knowledge more explicit – by effectively using the tools and principles for managing quality. With regard to *describing learning processes*, imagine asking subunits to flowchart (1) how they learn (create or acquire knowledge) about their customers' needs, (2) how they can satisfy those needs and wants, and (3) how they can identify and remove "description barriers": making incorrect assumptions regarding how to acquire valid and useful knowledge about their customers – and not agreeing on which learning processes must be followed by all members at all times (Harrington, 1995). Thus, by drawing flowcharts, members would be making their learning processes, the steps by which they acquire and use knowledge, explicit.

With regard to *controlling learning processes*, imagine asking work units to assess (1) how regularly and consistently they follow their processes for learning about customer needs, (2) how frequently and continuously they apply what they learn to satisfy customer needs, and (3) how they identify and remove the "special causes" that prevent them from performing their learning processes frequently and consistently. (These three questions can be answered either verbally or statistically, depending on what precision in analysis is desired and what kind of data is collected.)

With regard to *improving learning processes*, consider asking work units to assess (1) how they can generate knowledge *better and faster* than before, (2) how they can apply this knowledge *better and faster* in order to radically reduce the cycle time and costs needed to delight their present and future customers, and (3) how they can define and remove the "common causes" that prevent them from radically improving their learning processes (by changing the resources that constrain the performance of these processes). All the resources that are applicable to reengineering (people, technology, policies, and so on), can thus be used to improve learning.

Exemplars of *learning processes* include (1) facilitating cross–boundary exchanges among key stakeholders; (2) extracting useful knowledge from past failures as well as successes; (3) gaining knowledge through strategic alliances, ventures, mergers, and acquisitions; (4) conducting experiments on radical organizational structures and networks; (5) capturing members' knowledge in shared databases; (6) inventing ways to increase the rate of developing quantum infrastructures and formal systems; and (7) finding ways to increase the rate of gradual and radical improvement.

These learning processes involve capturing implicit knowledge and then intentionally using it to achieve organizational success. Information technology is expeditiously being developed to improve both the quality and velocity of value–added knowledge. Several software packages make it exceedingly practical to improve existing processes within and between all organizational boundaries. Allen Systems Group (ASG), headquartered in Naples, Florida, provides a variety of systems and services for aligning processes with information technology. But these solutions should never be used simply because they are available. Rather, a value–added estimate should always determine whether it is worthwhile to use any process tool (including information technology). In addition, computer–based systems allow users to become deeply engrossed in incredible detail, possibly far beyond what is required to describe, control, and improve processes. It is also important, therefore, to estimate what level of detail will generate the most value–added information for process innovation (Davenport, 1993).

Basically, ASG presents a quantum view of information technology: transforming out–of–date, incoherent legacy systems into fully integrated solutions for the rapidly evolving e–business environment. *This problem in reengineering software is identical to the problem of speeding up process improvement.* Computer–aided systems engineering (CASE) tools can therefore be used to identify poorly documented, fairly jumbled business and management processes and redesign them into streamlined, value–added processes that radically reduce cycle time, process cost, and excess inventory. These CASE tools can then be used to restructure subunits – to contain core processes within (versus across) boundaries. Competent users of these sophisticated software tools can quickly and easily redesign processes – on–screen – to see how changes in assumptions impact cycle times, process costs, defects and errors, and product or service specifications. Thereafter, processes can be described, controlled, and radically improved (Andrews and Leventhal, 1993). Using *design tools* enables members not only to capture this process knowledge, but also to spread it rapidly throughout an organization. After several cycles of managing processes with computer technology, members can *improve* their use of this technology – based on what they learned.

Another computer–based tool for organizational learning has been derived specifically from the mind/brain's learning processes: Knowledge Bridge™ by ServiceWare, Oakmont, Pennsylvania. Users create categories that pertain to any problem situation (including the relationships among these categories), thereby capturing their experiences. As new experiences are encountered, they are entered into the computer's database – and the relationships and the categories are gradually and radically restructured to reflect new knowledge. This software program, equivalent to the neural networks in the brain and the schemas of the mind, is capable of learning: All the declarative and procedural knowledge that has been captured can not only be quickly spread to members throughout an organization, but also be immediately adjusted – in real time – as members experience and record new events.

While learning processes usually focus on the organization, it is also meaningful to manage the processes that develop *within* every individual. Continual pressure for gradual and radical improvement can take a great toll on the human mind, soul, and spirit, because most people experience change as loss – and as a potential threat to who they are and what they have accomplished. As a result, a key feature of the learning process track (which recognizes the *personal* transformation that must complement any *organizational* transformation) is to ask members to describe, control, and improve their self–aware consciousness. As they proceed, they will be able to absorb gradual and radical change – faster and better – without losing themselves in the process. The next chapter addresses the development of self–aware consciousness – the central theme in this book – in detail.

Once members have learned to describe, control, and improve their learning (and self–awareness) processes within their subunits, the shadow track establishes a new PMO for this eighth track. The mission for another twenty–five members is to manage the learning processes that flow across boundaries. Capturing all value–added knowledge and making it instantly available in customized forms for all work units in the organization – the prime goal of organizational learning – is enabled by computer hardware and software for knowledge management.

Figure 5.44 displays the intricate thread that is woven when explicit attention is given to all horizontal and vertical task flows – by describing, controlling, and improving all *business processes* and *cross-business processes* in a *strategic business unit*. This thread is considerably strengthened when SBU members also describe, control, and improve their *learning processes*. In fact, SBU members can speed up the rate at which they gradually and radically improve their business processes – in order to delight their customers and other key stakeholders. And by capturing what they learned, they do not have to reinvent the wheel every time they experience a similar problem or process. They can also share this knowledge with other SBUs.

FIGURE 5.44
An SBU's Tapestry of Value-Added Processes

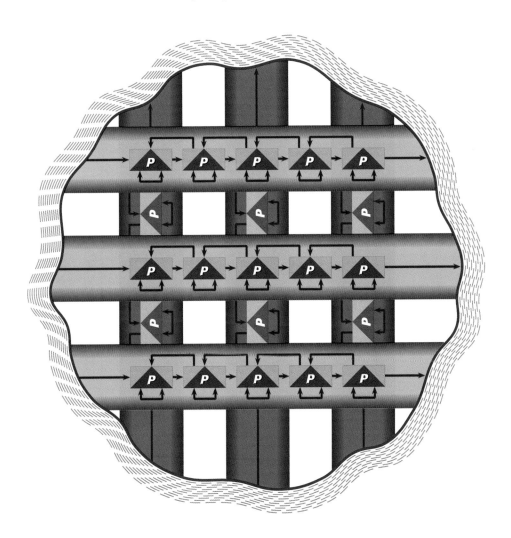

Now let's consider all the SBUs that make up a global organization. What if every SBU has established quantum infrastructures throughout its work units and has effectively aligned/deployed all of its formal systems? And what if all members in every SBU have acquired the skills to conduct gradual – and radical – improvement for their business *and* cross–business processes? The progression continues: What if the members in every SBU are also able to describe, control, and improve all core learning processes within and across subunits? Figure 5.45 suggests that such an integration of SBUs, coordinated by the *core*, has the best chance of achieving strategic objectives and the strategic architecture – with e–business and more.

FIGURE 5.45
The Core and SBUs of a Quantum Organization

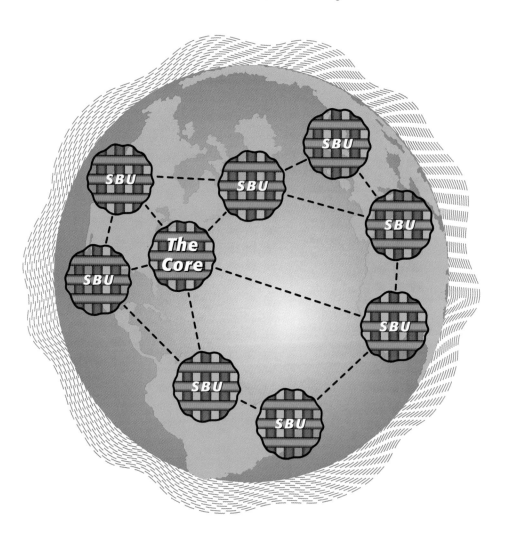

In sum, the eight tracks of the completely integrated program have valuable consequences. Each track accelerates *self-aware consciousness* for all members. Whether the present focus of concern is cultural norms, implicit assumptions, group processes, strategic architecture, task flow, or learning processes, members discover the obscure quantum waves that shape how they see, think, and behave. During this journey, their latent potential to contribute meaningfully to *organizational success* becomes fully challenged. Through collective action, members corroborate what gives them *meaning*. Figure 5.46 shows the eight tracks as deliberately shifting the paradigm in everyone's mind/brain – so that these aspirations can be realized.

FIGURE 5.46
The Valuable Consequences of Self-Transformation

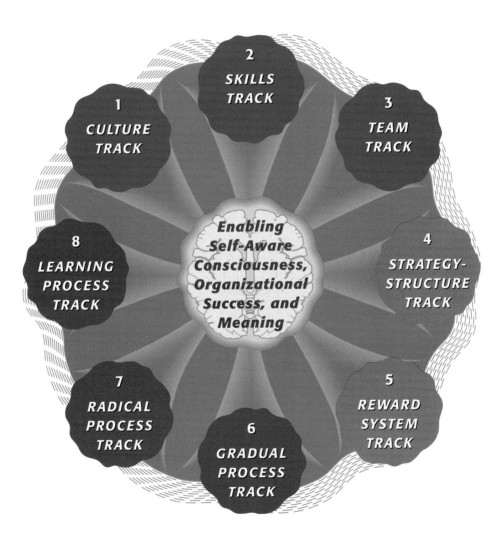

Self–transformation has been defined as fundamentally changing the way all members see, think, and behave. These *internal processes* circulate within everyone's mind/brain – although very few people are consciously aware of how they see, think, and behave. The same holds true for all aspects of process management. Unless a deliberate effort is undertaken to describe, control, and improve the flow of tasks and decisions, all *external* processes remain out of mind – and out of sight. The purpose of the process tracks, however, is to make all these internal and external processes explicit – so they can be self–managed more efficiently and effectively. Consequently, the artificial split between internal and external processes disappears: The flow of organizational tasks and decisions can be gradually and radically restructured along with the categories and relationships in every person's mind/brain. And managing learning processes more explicitly is identical to examining self–awareness: how we learn about "out there" is the same as how we learn about "in here." Descartes' dualistic split of the human mind as being completely separate from the physical world has, therefore, no place in quantum theory, let alone quantum organizations.

Gradual process improvement takes place within the boundaries of subunits – usually organized by management functions. The structure of the organization is considered as fixed – at least for the moment. But this temporary constraint provides an excellent environment for members to learn the basic principles and tools for process management.

Radical process improvement, however, takes very little for granted. While reengineering is often associated with information technology, the essence of this perspective is challenging the implicit assumptions behind old structural boxes. As a result, vertical subunits organized according to management functions are giving way to horizontal subunits designed for business processes. Although information technology can fundamentally change and dramatically speed up task flow, radical process improvement can still take place without newer technologies. *The prime challenge is creating holistic categories to replace specialized categories in everyone's mind/brain.*

Learning process improvement is being self–reflective: How did we improve our processes – and how can we do this better and faster during the next round? The same learning perspective, of course, can be applied to anything: enhancing quantum infrastructures, aligning formal systems, and developing self–aware consciousness. It is this latter theme, which has been pervasive throughout our discussions, that will be further explored in the final chapter of the book.

CHAPTER 6

CRITICAL SUCCESS FACTORS

Enabling Self-Aware Consciousness, Organizational Success, and Personal Meaning

> The *ultimate depth* is an ultimate oneness with the All, with the Cosmos. But this realization is not given equally to all beings, even though all beings are equally manifestations of Spirit. This *realization* is the result of a developmental and evolutionary process of growth and transcendence.... Maybe the evolutionary sequence really is from matter to body to mind to soul to spirit, each transcending and including, each with a greater depth and greater consciousness and wider embrace. And in the highest reaches of evolution, maybe, just maybe, an individual's consciousness does indeed touch infinity – a total embrace of the entire Cosmos – a Cosmic consciousness that is Spirit awakened to its own true nature.
> – *Ken Wilber (1996, pages 39, 42)*

At the start, I defined self–aware consciousness as getting acquainted with your paradigm (including how it differs from other paradigms) and then consciously changing it to be more adaptive for today's world. In the four preceding chapters, we have learned how self–aware consciousness can be cultivated and advanced through the eight tracks of self-transformation. But a deeper understanding of this principal concept is needed: Not only does consciousness materialize particles out of waves, but consciousness also enables the evolution of the universe. In the same way, the continued development of quantum organizations depends on attracting, retaining, and motivating self–aware members so they can actualize their quantum potential. Self–aware consciousness, therefore, is the crucial integral in the evolution of the universe and its organizations.

As we shall see, self-aware consciousness exists in the *interior depth* of self-motion monads – as opposed to being visible on the *exterior surfaces* of material forms. And just as all living forms respond to their surroundings, self-aware consciousness evolves so that people can discover more about themselves as well as their universe. Ultimately, the interior and exterior manifestations of the universe – called *Spirit* – can be integrated into one holistic experience for all self-aware, self-motion monads. Becoming one with the universe and therefore knowing oneself *as the universe* represents the ultimate depth of human enlightenment.

Spirit is the life-force of the universe – the energizing principle that propels matter and consciousness toward greater complexity, variety, and life. For many people, Spirit is equivalent to God, Allah, Buddha, or other gods and goddesses. But for other people, Spirit is the supreme principle – devoid of any denomination – that propels the evolutionary unfolding of nature and life. Because Spirit is usually appropriated by different leaders of organized religion, national policies have been established to keep the religious worship of Spirit entirely separate from the human expression of Spirit in other types of organizations – such as business and government. It is not my intention here to debate the purpose of organized religion in society. My point is simply this: *Whether organized or not, whether named or not, whether widely accepted or not, Spirit is defined as the absolute mystery that creates all that is, all that was, and all that will be.*

As universes and organizations evolve, some human beings become aware they are manifestations of Spirit – concerning how they see, think, and behave – and their physical, chemical, and biological forms. As they achieve this threshold of self-aware consciousness, Spirit begins to know itself: *Passive observers become active participants.* Enlightenment is the next key threshold in the evolution of self-aware consciousness. Active participants can evolve far beyond their skin-encapsulated minds by becoming aware that all visible forms – and all invisible forces – throughout the universe are dynamic manifestations of that same Spirit: *Active participants thus become enlightened participants.*

Once the transpersonal realms of Spirit are experienced, self-motion monads can feel authentic compassion for people, groups, organizations, Earth, and the cosmos. In even higher stages of enlightenment, people can experience the universe vacant of any material forms whatsoever (termed complete *emptiness*) and, at that moment, feel oneness with all forms in the universe (termed *nondualism*). Now people can see, think, and behave with a universal – spiritual – perspective. As this engaging paradigm becomes shared among its members, a quantum organization materializes its quest for self–aware consciousness, organizational success, personal meaning – and the eternal evolution of Spirit (Schwartz and Russek, 1999).

This chapter begins by examining self–aware consciousness in three levels of depth – from passive observers to active participants and then to enlightened participants. In this discussion, we will see that self–designing and self–managing quantum infrastructures, formal systems, and process management (all three components of transformation) is specifically what enables the evolution of self–aware consciousness (with some additional assistance from ego–defining activities, interpretive therapies, meditative practices, and Holotropic Breathwork™). After giving us a deeper notion of Spirit, the chapter then summarizes twenty critical success factors that can transform a Newtonian organization of primarily passive observers into a quantum organization of enlightened participants. Our book culminates by recognizing the *primordial search for meaning* as the mystical origin of ego energy and spiritual enlightenment. But also considered is the follow–up question of what human beings desire *after* they have actualized personal meaning – which sets the stage for the further evolution of organizations and the universe.

ENABLING SELF-AWARE CONSCIOUSNESS

Consistent with the Cartesian–Newtonian Paradigm, passive observers do not need much self–awareness while performing their programmed jobs. Nor are they particularly aware of their own paradigm in the first place (and how it affects their seeing, thinking, or behaving). Passive jobholders are only authorized to follow official procedures, engineer well–structured problems, and refer anything else to their unconscious administrators. In the framework of human development, passive observers in a Newtonian organization can do their jobs with an *egocentric* orientation: They assume that others see the world just as they do. Indeed, passive jobholders have trouble envisioning the many different perspectives of their stakeholders (including external customers and members in other departments in the same organization) – let alone considering how perspectives evolve. But when faced with the realities of a quantum world, egocentric jobholders with little self–awareness cannot mobilize the intellectual and emotional capacity to adapt to change – or inaugurate a change process themselves. Passive jobholders look to somebody else, invariably senior management, to take the lead for change and improvement. And, not surprisingly, these passive observers automatically expect others to accept full responsibility for the success of the organization.

For a Newtonian organization, a sufficient mass of senior managers must first mobilize the necessary courage, conviction, and commitment to put in motion a completely integrated program (unlike adhoc or shotgun approaches). Senior managers must also rely on their traditional authority to *demand* the participation of all members in the transformation process. Without this corporate-wide requirement, most passive jobholders (at any level in the organization) would not volunteer to become acquainted with their paradigms and then purposely change the way they see, think, and behave. It appears that passive observers must first achieve a threshold of self-awareness before they will intentionally continue with their personal transformation along with their organization's transformation (without an external push from senior management).

As discussed in Chapter 3, the first three tracks require all members to participate in workshops (pictured in Figure 2.19, page 89). During this period, members discuss cultural norms, implicit assumptions, and group process – all of which requires them to examine how they see, think, and behave. These monthly discussions gradually open everyone's eyes to the perceptions, expectations, stereotypes, prejudices, and perspectives (hence the categories in their minds/brains) that determine how they assimilate information, make decisions, and engage in action. In addition, there are many workshop sessions in which members receive detailed feedback on how they affect other members in their work group and how their work group, as a whole, is experienced by other work units in the organization. Having frequent opportunities to receive feedback, discuss what it means, and decide whether to change how every member (or subunit as a whole) sees, thinks, and behaves – *all this activity creates and sustains the vital threshold of self-awareness to self-transform passive observers into active participants.* Quantum infrastructures thereby become infused throughout the organization with the goal of further enhancing the self-aware consciousness of members – the premier attribute of a quantum organization.

As discussed in Chapter 4, once the twenty-five participants in the strategy-structure track have formulated the strategic architecture, derived the strategic objectives, and then reorganized the structure of subunits, all members throughout the organization proceed to self-design the detailed charters for their subunits as well as the general parameters of their jobs. And once the participants in the reward system track have developed the organization-wide reward policies, all members proceed to self-design the specific reward practices for their subunits and the detailed characteristics of their jobs – which includes the setting of performance goals. Thereafter, members are entirely responsible for self-managing their new work units on an ongoing basis. Such wide–scale participation in their organization's strategy–structure and reward systems (not including the many additional activities that take place for the participants in these two tracks) prepares all members to further strengthen their self–aware consciousness. Because quantum infrastructures have already been created, members are entirely capable of designing their subunits to maximize their self–motivation and personal meaning. Apparently it is by self–designing their formal systems during the middle two tracks that members become even more self–aware of what they need and want – and, therefore, who they are.

As elaborated in Chapter 5, all members are encouraged to become actively involved in applying the tools of process management during the last three tracks of the completely integrated program: initially for gradual process improvement within their subunits; secondly for radical process improvement across all boundaries; thirdly for extracting what they learn and then making their newly acquired knowledge promptly accessible to other members and subunits throughout the organization. Previously the organization's business (and learning) processes were mostly implicit. But *self-reflection about process management further enhances self-aware consciousness by focusing attention on what it means for members to provide value-added contributions to other people – both inside and outside the organization.*

By actively participating in all eight tracks of the program, therefore, passive jobholders are self–transformed into *active participants.* By receiving and responding to feedback on a wide variety of behavioral dynamics, by self–designing and self–managing their formal systems, and by managing value–added processes within (and across) subunits, all members become significantly more aware of themselves. Because several of these activities occur in groups, the egocentric orientations of passive jobholders become sociocentric orientations of active participants: As all members learn more about themselves, they can relate to other souls in the world much more effectively. Particularly for organizations that have a diverse membership (in terms of gender, race, age, religion, nationality, and so forth), members are exposed to a great variety of cultures, assumptions, perspectives, and hence categories via effective dialogue. Consequently, *members' minds/brains undergo gradual and radical restructuring just by frequently engaging in meaningful interactions about difficult subjects with diverse others.* Furthermore, members are frequently challenged to examine their traditional (Cartesian–Newtonian) ways of seeing, thinking, and behaving. In the process, they discover that quantum–relativistic perspectives of reality better portray a global, living, evolving economy – and they see why their *active participation (versus passive compliance) is the key to self-transformation.*

Once members have experienced their self-discovery, they become hooked. Their appetite for enhancing self-aware consciousness does not subside with the eight tracks. Even before the first cycle of transformation has ended, members begin asking for more information about self-aware consciousness – including advanced theories and methods. For members who want more depth of understanding about themselves, therefore, it is necessary to journey the Western and Eastern paths to ego development (Freud) and spiritual enlightenment (Buddha), respectively.

Exploring Ego Energy and Ego-Defining Processes

Becoming *self-aware* of one's paradigm (and then consciously altering it) is only one of many *self-concepts* that have been studied by psychiatrists and psychologists in the Western world. Since the work of Sigmund Freud in the nineteenth century, a variety of terms have been used to describe the personal ego – including self-esteem, self-regard, self-respect, self-worth, self-confidence, self-appraisal, and self-efficacy (Bandura, 1986; Branden, 1994; Brockner; 1988). These self-perceptions usually remain unconscious when people keep their true opinions of themselves – from themselves – which is called *self-deception*. Yet people can become entirely aware of their self-concepts and, thereby, revise their opinions of themselves to be more accurate and adaptive for today's world. Such self-discovery followed by self-improvement recognizes that the *interior* self is a worthwhile area for study similar to any *exterior* object in one's environment.

It is now important to recognize what takes place during a person's efforts to discover (and then change) his or her self-concepts: *A vast amount of psychic energy is generated inside people who are actively exploring their self-concepts.* This *ego energy*, as we will call it, is similar to what Young (1976) considered the primary source of the internal energy within self-motion monads. For human beings, this ego energy is what stimulates and motivates members to see, think, and behave in quantum organizations. Specifically, *ego energy* is defined as each person's primordial struggle to know, both consciously and accurately, their

1 IDENTITY: Who am I? What makes me special or unique? What emotional attachments (ego investments) should I make?

2 COMPETENCY: How effective am I at being who I am? Are my decisions, actions, and attachments ethical?

3   VALUE: Have I contributed what others need or want?
    Is my organization benefiting from my decisions, actions,
    and attachments?

4   WORTH: Am I a good or bad person? Do I deserve to
    be happy?

5   RESPONSIBILITY: Who controls who I am, what I do, what
    emotional attachments I make, and whether I am good
    or bad, happy or sad?

Most ego psychologists agree that the original source of ego energy is basic anxiety from the infant's first separation from its mother and the added anxiety that derives from a generalized fear of further separations throughout life (Freud, 1960). The conflicting fears of *abandonment* (being completely separate from others) versus *suffocation* (being completely fused with others and, hence, not being separate) bring about ego development: Who am I? What makes me unique? What makes me valuable? Moreover, the fear of not being in control (when, for example, other people are in a position to make decisions that can lead to separation and abandonment) creates even more anxiety. It seems that ego energy is engendered by an intrapsychic chain reaction: the ongoing tension between the ego and its separateness/fusion with the rest of the world; the additional anxiety that a person experiences from not being in control of this endeavor; and the biochemical, neurological, and biomechanical energy that the ego taps in order to manage this anxiety.

People may differ significantly with respect to the potential amount of ego energy available to them – due to various environmental, genetic, and developmental factors that create different reservoirs of biochemical, neurological, and biomechanical energy. Allcorn (1992), for one, suggests that different kinds of family pathology – stemming from parents who are physically, sexually, or emotionally abusive; cold, unpredictable, uncaring, unnurturing, and unavailable – determine the level of anxiety that people experience and therefore can utilize for ego energy. Family pathology also affects each person's repertoire of psychological defenses (such as denial, splitting, projection, suppression, regression) and interpersonal behavior (overly aggressive, passively hostile, withdrawing from the situation) that people use to cope with their anxiety (Horney, 1950). But it would be mere speculation to suggest the extent of such differences in the potential ego energy among the members of a given organization. One thing, however, is entirely inescapable: *The more that people use psychological defense mechanisms and dysfunctional interpersonal behavior to cope with their anxiety, the less ego energy is available for using their knowledge and skills for making value-added decisions and taking the most effective courses of action.*

Consider two familiar experiences in a Newtonian organization that can stimulate excessive anxiety during externally managed restructuring, downsizing, redeployment, and job abolishment. To begin with, members can easily feel out of control, since these corporate decisions are generally out of their hands and little formal communication is provided as senior managers make these decisions secretly and devise their implementation. Further, major structural change severely shatters the psychological bonds among members of former work units – as old jobs are eliminated while new jobs and departments are formed. In most large-scale change efforts, members feel significantly violated on both counts: (1) their self-identity, competency, value, worth, and responsibility are being negatively affected (or certainly threatened) by someone else and (2) their familiar emotional attachments to the organization are being torn apart without anything (at least for the time being) to replace them – a powerful replay, perhaps, of abrupt separations at birth and thereafter.

Actually, when members are victims of external, unannounced, and severe disruptions to their ego attachments (which undermine the essence of who they are and what makes them unique, valuable, and worthwhile), they may expend a large amount of their ego energy taking care of their anxiety with various psychological defenses – which prevents them from *seeing* reality. To handle this unsettling anxiety, members may also rely on dysfunctional behavior – which prevents them from effectively *managing* reality. The sad outcome? If the underlying ego/organization relationships have not been properly established and sustained, day-to-day decisions will be based on personal preferences and office politics – the classic case of psychological sensitivities and self-protecting behavior in a Newtonian organization. Alternatively, when members are able to examine as well as control their self-concepts, they will be free to see and manage reality in a nondefensive and effective manner. Members will thus be able to devote their energy and skills to complex problems and business processes.

While the eight tracks provided many opportunities for members to discover their paradigms, only introductory material was included on the engaging topic of ego psychology. But if members are given the chance to become even more conscious of their own self-concepts (and then be able to improve them), more ego energy will be available for the attainment of both personal goals and strategic objectives.

In another workshop setting, members of intact work groups (using their evolving skills for problem management, assumptional analysis, and group process) can be asked to discuss the following questions:

1. IDENTITY: What is my essence? To what "objects" (thoughts, things, and people) do I attach myself? What attachments do I use to define who I am? Can I redefine my essence so that I am not vulnerable to losing the very things that are "taken away" during change and transformation — such as job titles, office locations, parking spaces, assigned tasks, objectives, people, and familiar practices?

2. COMPETENCY: How skilled am I at detaching my ego from objects and reattaching myself to new thoughts, things, and people? How resilient am I during organizational change and transformation? Am I able to accept loss and move on? How can I enhance my capacity to switch my ego attachments more quickly and with less pain?

3. VALUE: How do I add value to others? Am I secure enough as a person to supply what others need and want? Can I put myself in other people's shoes so that I can genuinely experience their worldview? Do I feel less valuable the more I give to others — or can I add value to myself while I give wholeheartedly to others?

4. WORTH: Am I a happy person? Do I have any regrets? Can I make sure that I won't have regrets in the future? What makes me happy? Is it things, thoughts, people, or some spiritual essence inside me? Do I want to change what makes me happy so that my sense of well-being is deep and secure?

5. RESPONSIBILITY: Do I live unconsciously? How can I be more aware of my thoughts, feelings, and emotions? Do I accept the consequences of my decisions and actions? Do I avoid or deny the role I play in what happens to me and others? How can I face life head on and not hide from what is or what could be? How can I ensure that I won't deceive myself — especially when reality hurts?

I have witnessed numerous group sessions on these key questions. Especially when members are proficient at holding in–depth discussions on difficult problems and have reached threshold levels of self–awareness and self–confidence, they proceed to share their essence with other group members. As long as cultural norms support such personal sharing of the self–concepts, members are often amazed at how much they learn about each other – and not just about themselves. In fact, group members often feel emotionally closer to one another as a result of these discussions and then experience greater trust and goodwill. Interestingly, members often acknowledge that they have never discussed such questions beforehand – not even with their dearest friends – and vow to discuss these questions from now on with their spouses and children.

Appropriate to this discussion are *seven stages* for working through a significant loss – derived from research on death and dying (Kübler–Ross, 1969). But any change in a person's life, not just the death of a loved one, can be experienced as loss: a person can become emotionally attached to things, thoughts, companions, and a work life. Following a significant *loss*, the first reaction is *shock*. People may experience a physical and emotional numbness; they usually have trouble eating, sleeping, concentrating, and remembering. Then *denial* is used to ward off anxiety: "It didn't happen; it couldn't have happened; I'm only dreaming." Next, denial turns to *anger*: "Why me? This should never have happened! It's not fair! How dare they do this to me!" Eventually, deep–felt *sadness* may be experienced: "It really happened. I lost an important aspect of my life. I miss what I had before." Then sadness turns to *acceptance*: "I must surrender to reality. I can't change it. That's just the way it is." Ultimately, acceptance leads to *adaptation*: "It's time to move forward. I have to get on with my life. It's time for action." In our dynamic world, however, it's only a matter of time before another loss occurs and the process of coping with loss continues.

Some people have great difficulty moving through the seven stages of loss – effectively and efficiently. Perhaps their self–concepts have been damaged by prior experiences (including early abandonment) – and then repressed. When these people face another traumatic loss, they get stuck in shock, denial, or anger. Prolonged agony in these early stages is termed the *doom cycle*. Some people remain bitter for years (or even decades) after a loss and never get over it. But with sufficient self–awareness, emotional support from others, and help for consciously working through the loss, people can counteract the self–defeating entanglement of the doom cycle. They can work through the stages of sadness, acceptance, and adaptation: the *growth cycle*.

Figure 6.1 illustrates the seven stages of loss. The amount of time in each stage is influenced by the amount of ego energy that is available to a person – versus being diverted (and drained) by psychological defenses and dysfunctional behavior. Recall that ego energy is produced by a chain reaction in the mind/brain struggling to make sense of the self-concepts: identity, competency, value, worth, and responsibility. If you haven't spent much effort defining your self-concepts, however, you are inclined to get stuck in the *doom cycle:* somewhere in shock, denial, or anger. But if you've developed self-awareness about your self-concepts and have deliberately worked at improving them, you are more likely to reach the *growth cycle.*

FIGURE 6.1
Ego Energy and Coping with Loss

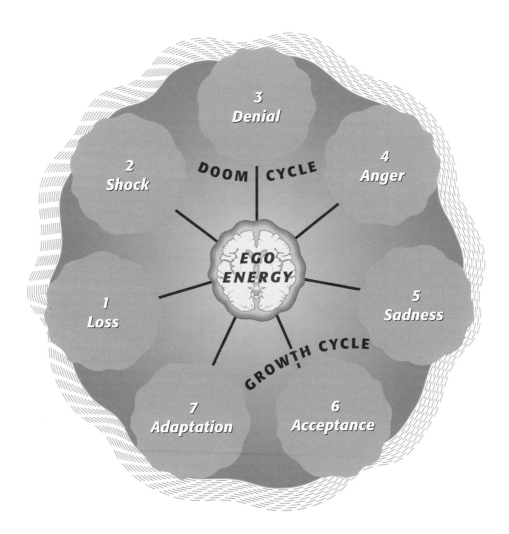

As members first discuss and then internalize the seven stages (and the two cycles) for coping with loss, they gain self-awareness about their emotional attachments. They are then better able to make more conscious decisions about what attachments are long lasting (intimate relationships, reliable avenues for aesthetic creations and self-expression, and spiritual commitments that are internally maintained) – versus what attachments are capricious (job titles, office locations, and other external fashions that are under the direct control or whim of distant others). Members will be more adaptive during ensuing transformation (and loss) if they are more attached to what cannot be taken away and less attached to momentary forms and fleeting arrangements.

A provocative approach for developing self-aware consciousness in an organization is to apply the various principles and practices of process management. Since *defining self-concepts* can be viewed as *managing processes*, the self-concepts can be specifically described, controlled, and improved. In additional workshop sessions, members can address five key questions that will enable them to become more conscious of the implicit processes they use to manage their self-concepts:

1   What is the process by which you define your essence and what makes you special and unique? (IDENTITY)

2   What is the process by which you develop skill and consistency at being who you are? (COMPETENCY)

3   What is the process by which you create value for yourself and contribute value to other people's lives? (VALUE)

4   What is the process by which you judge whether you are a good or bad person and whether you deserve to be happy? (WORTH)

5   What is the process by which you control who you are, what you do, and whether you are good or bad, happy or sad? (RESPONSIBILITY)

In terms of process management, a person's answers to these crucial questions can be called *ego-defining processes*. In fact, each self-concept may be produced by a different process. The ego–identity process to establish the essence of "who I am," for example, may be totally different from the ego-investment process by which members first detach themselves from a familiar work environment and then reattach themselves to a new job, department, and location (during structural change). And if organizations wish to enhance their members' self-concepts so there is more ego energy available to achieve strategic objectives, the ego–defining process for each of the five self-concepts must be described – made self-conscious – before it can be controlled and improved. Directives to increase ego energy (the results) are no more effective than pronouncements or slogans to improve quality. Since the process causes the results, the only way to improve the results (such as more meaningful, productive, and satisfying self-concepts) is to improve ego–defining processes.

DESCRIBING EGO-DEFINING PROCESSES What would it be like for members to describe their ego–defining processes – under the conditions of free choice, psychological safety, and guidance by qualified facilitators? Every member would first be asked to write conscientious answers to the questions about each self-concept – to establish a baseline for subsequent improvement efforts. Then every member would be asked to describe the process he implicitly uses to define each self-concept: What is the process by which you establish your self–identity, competency, value, worth, and responsibility? Just as with business processes, of course, members would not be asked to describe all their ego–defining processes: only those that are most value–added (to members and their organization) and in need of improvement.

We can only imagine what an eye–opening experience it would be for members to flowchart the *ideal* value–added processes they should use to approach the five questions about their self-concepts. They could then examine the ideal next to their *actual* (implicit) ego–defining processes and then close the gap between them – which would clarify what they know and feel about themselves. Of course, they would first have to address the TQM basics: Who is the final *customer* and who are the primary *suppliers?*

Every member's ultimate customer should ideally be himself – with family, friends, and the organization as the other key stakeholders. Every member's primary supplier should ideally be himself as well – with only a few others, carefully chosen, who provide authentic feedback, emotional support, or role models. Recalling the key distinction between special and common causes of statistical variation, members would also be attentive to the key implications of *responsibility:* Who controls who I am, what I do, what ego attachments I choose, and whether I am good or bad, happy or sad? If members inadvertently permit multiple suppliers to prescribe who they are and what makes them special and unique, then, by default, some of the common causes of their ego–defining processes are not under their control (and hence responsibility). They are thus at the complete mercy of others for determining – and later improving – their self–concepts. But if members describe their ideal ego–defining processes so that they are fully responsible for who they are and what affords them value and self–worth, both the special and common causes are under their command. For better or worse, they are at their own mercy. *An ideal ego-defining process, therefore, is when each person is his own primary supplier of identity, competency, value, worth, and responsibility and purposely decides who has a say in defining his self-concepts.*

Using the flowchart symbols displayed on pages 216–217 and noting whether a task is customer value–added (CVA), other value–added (OVA), or no value–added (NVA) could reveal some fascinating insights. Imagine the case in which most of ego–defining activities are NVA or OVA – rather than being customer value–added (CVA) for the self. The worst thing (from the position of later encouraging members to improve their self–concepts) is any process that discloses (1) unreliable, multiple suppliers of information and support for defining the self–concepts, (2) numerous customers other than the self as the prime beneficiaries of the available ego energy, and (3) many steps in the process being NVA or OVA (not CVA). Members defined as experiencing *chronically low self-esteem* are probably living unconsciously according to dysfunctional ego–defining processes, to the disadvantage of themselves and their organizations. Once ego–defining barriers are clearly defined, however, they can be removed – thereby closing the gap between actual and ideal process.

CONTROLLING EGO-DEFINING PROCESSES   Once each member has described the processes that should be used at all times to determine his self–concepts (analogous to using an agreed–upon business process as the standard operating procedure), focus shifts to checking that each process is under control. One might wonder whether a person's self–concepts are stable and reliable if they regularly fall outside the statistical control limits and thus indicate an out–of–control process – for example, when a person feels exceptionally good one moment, fine the next, and then completely worthless.

While measuring self–concepts is most certainly a difficult task, it is nevertheless an essential step in controlling and subsequently improving one's self–concepts. And if the same member is defining his self–concepts and also assessing them under similar conditions, the measuring process itself is likely to be under statistical control.

This is not the place to discuss the assortment of methods by which the self-concepts can be measured, but it's natural to intrigue the reader with some interesting possibilities: Just imagine what it would be like for each member to develop a concise operational definition for his identity, competency, value, worth, and responsibility, and then, on a seven-point scale (from extremely low to extremely high), to assess each self-concept with a specific number (position) on the scale. Regarding the self-concept of responsibility, as an example, each member could ask himself: To what extent do I determine how good I feel about myself? To what extent do I determine whether I am happy or sad? To what extent do I determine my emotional attachments to my career? The person would then respond to each question on a seven-point scale (adjusting the endpoints of the scale to fit the nature of the question – for example, from "completely" to "not at all"). You can imagine just how problematic it would be to feel attached and secure in an organization if this crucial ego-defining process were left implicit – which would thus prevent it from being measured, controlled, and improved. The lessons learned from process management are clear: A process that is neither described nor controlled cannot be improved; and, worse yet, an implicit process cannot possibly satisfy the changing needs and rising expectations of the customer (the self).

In line with the principles and practices of TQM, it is important for members to measure their self-concepts on a recurring basis (once every day, as a guideline, or at least once a week) by responding to the identical questions on the same scales. Then process control charts can be used to discover if the process for determining each self-concept is under control. For any process that is out of control, the standard set of quality tools can be used to pinpoint the special causes, to see where and how the process of defining a self-concept has broken down. And finally, action steps can be planned and implemented in order to remove the identified control barriers (special causes). But even if the processes for defining the self are brought under control, they may not be capable of satisfying the person or the organization. A process that is under control but not capable must therefore be improved.

IMPROVING EGO-DEFINING PROCESSES Now let's contemplate how people can actually improve their self-concepts so they feel more unique, valuable, and better about themselves. Naturally, some self-concepts (and their ego-defining processes) may be more important to individuals and their organizations than others – depending on the person's goals, what is in most need of improvement, and the challenges facing an organization.

It may be beneficial, therefore, to prioritize the importance of improving each self-concept. Nevertheless, we'll proceed assuming that one or more self-concepts have been selected for process improvement.

Imagine what it would be like for members to set new targets – by stretching themselves to experience improved self-concepts beyond their earlier baseline definitions. With regard to each self-concept, each person would ask: How much better do I want to be – as assessed by my answers to the same questions on the same scales? How much do I want to reduce the variation around my self-targets – so I experience less variation about who I am and what makes me valuable on a daily or weekly basis? Once improvement goals have been stated (guided, perhaps, by benchmarking what other people have accomplished with respect to their self-concepts), members can be asked to list improvement barriers and then develop and implement action plans to remove them.

Recall: The more you are your own supplier (and purposely choose whether to use other people's views for defining your self-concepts), the more you can eliminate common causes (improvement barriers) as well as special causes (control barriers) – without relying on outside sources. But the more you rely on multiple suppliers, the more the common causes of your ego-defining processes will be determined by others – which limits the extent to which a person can improve himself by himself.

Process control charts can also be used to see if each new target has been achieved (with less variation around the target). When a person first attempts to define himself differently, his new ego-defining process might initially be out of control (as in regressing to dysfunctional feelings about the self, since the improved process is still unfamiliar). Gradually, however, control barriers can be pinpointed and removed with the various quality tools, which then brings the improved process under control. The result? Members have improved their self-concepts (identity, competency, value, worth, and responsibility) – so that there is more positive and reliable ego energy to unleash, mobilize, and channel in desirable ways.

Note: While we have employed TQM literally, it is vital to recognize that the philosophy and concepts of TQM can be applied *qualitatively* – and not just quantitatively. Instead of using flowcharts, we can write a simple narrative that illustrates the steps for an ego-defining process. The key, of course, is making the process explicit and, therefore, open for inspection. Similarly, it may not be necessary to use control charts or other statistical methods for the self-concepts; the fundamental concern is whether each ego-defining process is taking place regularly and consistently. Moreover, processes can often be improved without engaging in rigorous statistical analyses. Perhaps a subjective assessment can be done to establish which ego–defining processes are worthy of analysis and whether that analysis should be qualitative or quantitative: whether numbers would stimulate a more probing dialogue or, instead, would get in the way.

But it is important to see that process management gives members valuable tools for self–development. Indeed, discussing one's self–concepts with supportive others (whether or not augmented by numbers on scales to stimulate discussion) creates new categories about the self–concepts in members' minds/brains. Members can thus improve themselves as long as they have (1) achieved a threshold level of self–awareness (via actively creating and maintaining their quantum infrastructures), (2) learned the concepts and tools of process management, and (3) successfully managed business processes within and across their subunits. With this foundation, dialogue among members about their self–concepts will continue to focus on probing the *interior depths* of their ego–defining processes.

Although this discussion has been especially speculative, its logic is incontrovertible: If a business process cannot be improved unless it is first described and controlled, what does it really mean to empower members to enhance their self–aware consciousness? And knowing what it takes to make dramatic improvements in business processes, why would it be any different (let alone easier) to make order–of–magnitude improvements in the self–concepts? In either case, business process or ego–defining process, implicit assumptions are the basis for improvement barriers, particularly when radical improvement is necessary in our dynamic, global economy. Although the focus of TQM has been on the work–related processes *outside* members, it may now be imperative to explore the ego–defining processes *inside* every person.

Besides using TQM concepts/tools for improving ego energy, people can further increase their self–awareness and reality–based functioning by actively participating in one–on–one interpretive therapies with an expert psychotherapist. Regardless of which particular approach to therapy they choose, people with the desire can gradually work through traumas and conflicts that took place in their lives (particularly during childhood and early adulthood), which may have undermined their ego development. By removing psychological distortions and ineffective behavior, most people can indeed enhance their self–acceptance, self–knowledge, and self–aware consciousness. Their ego energy will then be fully available for authentic self–expression and personal meaning. Such people will therefore be able to contribute genuinely and energetically to a quantum organization that offers meaningful opportunities for their reality–based behavior.

Exploring Spirit and Spiritual Enlightenment

Holding open discussions on the self-concepts or systematically applying process management to improve ego-defining processes (and interpretive therapies on a personal basis) can heighten the self-aware consciousness of active participants. This rational outcome achieves the Western world's dream of promoting the reality-based functioning of the human ego. But there is more to the evolution of consciousness than simply being aware of oneself and contributing most of one's energy reservoir to what is and what could be (instead of warding off anxiety or acting out psychic pain on others). Indeed, higher levels of consciousness have been explored by the Eastern world – under the name of Spirit (acknowledging the supreme principle of the universe) and enlightenment (experiencing oneness with Spirit and all manifestations in the universe). By confronting these deeper degrees of self-aware consciousness, active participants become *enlightened* participants. As a result, quantum organizations will be able to tap higher degrees of feeling and creativity since their members will be more in tune with the universal manifestations of Spirit.

The Eastern world has proposed as many as eighteen distinct stages of spiritual enlightenment that are notably deeper than the stages of ego development that have been so extensively studied in the Western world. Wilber (1996) defines four comprehensive stages that capture the different depths of transpersonal experience: the psychic, the subtle, the causal, and the nondual. The key feature of these four stages is that they transcend a person's mind: Consciousness extends above and beyond the rational ego states or the "skin-encapsulated ego."

During the *psychic stage*, a person feels one with the physical cosmos and can deeply partake in all physical forms in nature – what Wilber calls *oneness with the physiosphere*. In this beyond-ego stage, there is no distinction between the self and physical designs of Spirit. In the *subtle stage*, a person encounters immeasurable happiness, love, and compassion for the living universe – what might be called *oneness with the emotiosphere*. Here there is no distinction between the self and all emotional manifestations of Spirit. Primordial archetypes, including gods and goddesses, are experienced in this realm of divine emotions and feelings.

Added enlightenment occurs during the *causal stage*. In this stage, no physical manifestations or emotional archetypes emerge in consciousness. Instead, the self experiences complete *emptiness* of form – and yet fullness with the wholeness of Spirit. According to Wilber, this stage is associated with such trans-ego experiences as formless absorption, classical nirvana, or, simply, a dreamless sleep. Perhaps for the first time, the self recognizes that it is itself an object that has been looked at just like all other subjects and objects in the cosmos. *But who or what is seeing the self?* Whatever it is, it is not an object; otherwise it would have been seen as such during a prior stage of transpersonal enlightenment. Therefore, when a person begins to experience the void of Emptiness, a highly provocative question arises in consciousness: *Who is the I, the observer, vis-à-vis the self that is being seen?* If the "I" that sees the self (and all other forms in the universe) is not an object, what is looking at all those objects and subjects? The answer, it appears, is that the "I" is entirely invisible and formless – a pure energy of self-aware consciousness for seeing and knowing the All.

Ultimate enlightenment comes during the *nondual stage*. In this stage, the "I" is all that is and can be witnessed. Since all forms in the spacetime continuum are created by means of pure consciousness, *pure consciousness is everything*. Nondual means there is no longer any real distinction between the witness itself and what is witnessed, between mind and nature. Thus there is no longer a witness and an object or a seer and a seen. Essentially, when you see an object, you are also looking at yourself – simultaneously. In Wilber's words, you are no longer trapped in your body; the separate self is nowhere to be found. Since additional forms are perpetually being created in the universe, these will now be known in their pure – *nondual* – nature for any person who can experience this depth of enlightenment.

Note: Just as the reader might be having some trouble in identifying with the four stages of enlightenment, so is the writer! It is still very rare for members to achieve these deeper levels of self-aware consciousness – especially in the West, where the main focus has been on ego psychology, not spiritual enlightenment. But people thoroughly immersed in the old Eastern practices of meditation have established considerable agreement about the stages of enlightenment (similar to the degree of agreement in the West about the different stages of ego development). For an excellent book that covers a variety of meditative practices, see Kornfield (1993). As presented in Chapter 1 (page 35), Grof's (1993) Holotropic Breathwork™ is a fusion of East and West that provides opportunities for ego development and transpersonal experiences. Although members can be encouraged to investigate these methods for further developing self-aware consciousness (including psychotherapies), these spiritual paths should only be pursued in a voluntary manner. Their success significantly depends on participants making a full commitment to self-inquiry (Gangaji, 1999) – a commitment that cannot be mandated by any organization. But, *organizations can actively encourage and support the self-discovery of their members.*

For the purpose of first clarifying and then advancing the engaging topic of spiritual enlightenment, again I rely on artwork to illuminate the key themes. Figure 6.2 symbolically represents the initial manifestation of *Spirit*: the commencement of the spacetime continuum by which all other material objects form – and move – through space and time. Beforehand, we held this station for *first light* (Figure 2.2, page 56), which subsequently materialized nuclear particles, atoms, inorganic/organic molecules (inert molar objects), plants, animals, and people (Young, 1976). Now *first light* is preceded by the word *Spirit* as revealed in Genesis when God created the universe: "Let there be light: and there was light."

FIGURE 6.2
Spirit as the Creation of Spacetime

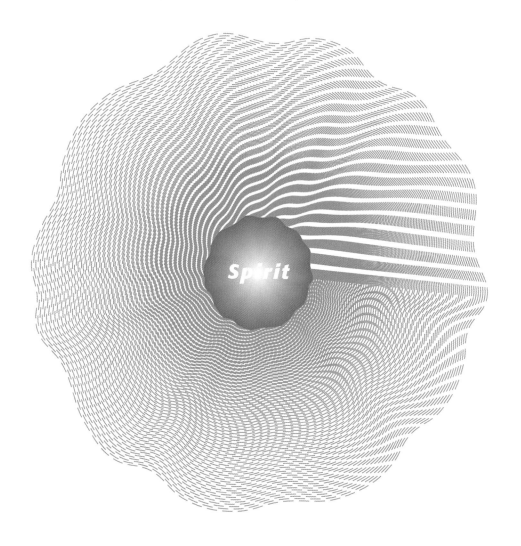

Before Spirit personalizes itself as material forms, there is essence in emptiness: the great void of Spirit in spacetime. As Figure 6.3 displays, this background of emptiness is precisely what has been graphically portrayed in virtually all the figures illustrated throughout this book. Although the word *Emptiness* may be misleading, it is not meant to convey nothingness. Emptiness, instead, simply means devoid of material substance and forms. Actually, in the deeper stages of enlightenment (the causal stage), a person can experience this great void of Spirit and thereby get in touch with the spiritual context for all forms in the cosmos. This awareness shepherds the journey from egocentric to worldcentric consciousness (Wilber, 1996).

FIGURE 6.3
Spirit as Formless Emptiness

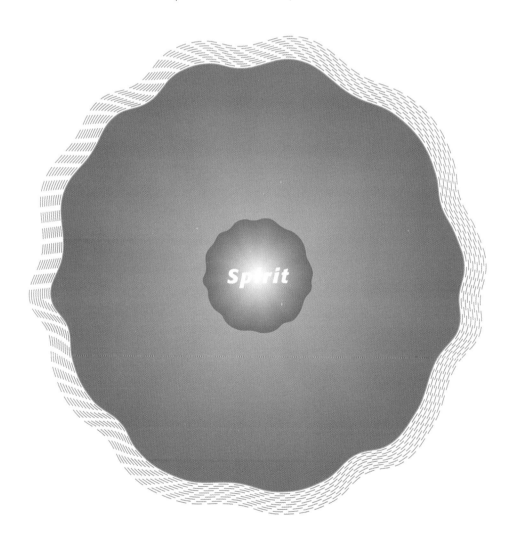

The evolution of matter to human form generates the potential for Spirit to know itself. As shown in Figure 6.4, a human being first interacts with the universe as a *passive observer* – reacting to external forces but not self-aware of her own mind. By realizing and defining her self-concepts, however, a person reaches the vital threshold of self-awareness. This inner competition for self-identity, competency, value, worth, and responsibility is what generates ego energy – which can transform *a passive observer into an active participant*. With continued ego development and progress in spiritual enlightenment, *a person self-transforms into an enlightened participant*. Now she is able to feel oneness with all other forms in the universe.

FIGURE 6.4
Human Forms Evolve to Know Spirit

Ego development and spiritual enlightenment are the two paths to self-aware consciousness. First, psychological defenses and dysfunctional behavior must be removed so that a person is free to use his ego energy for actually seeing and managing reality. He can then initiate his journey far beyond his skin-encapsulated ego to transpersonal realms – including the psychic, the subtle, the causal, and the nondual (Wilber, 1996). During the deepest experiences of spiritual enlightenment, a person sees himself as an object of study – but is sufficiently enlightened to ask this intriguing question: *If I see myself, who or what is doing the seeing?* Figure 6.5 provides the answer: *Spirit* – that which created spacetime and evolved to see itself.

FIGURE 6.5
Human Forms as Self-Aware Spirit

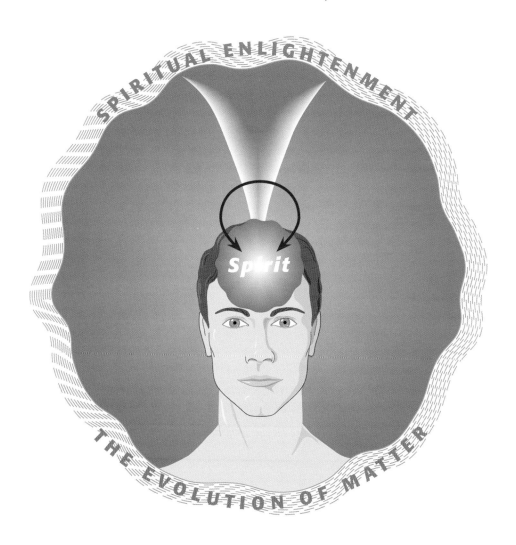

Now we examine ego development and spiritual enlightenment in a larger context. Wilber (1995) created a valuable framework for integrating both Eastern and Western philosophy/science. One dichotomy recognizes the *exterior surfaces* of physical objects versus what is experienced through the *interior depths* of consciousness. But a second dichotomy emphasizes an *individual* manifestation of Spirit (as a unique experience) versus a *collective* manifestation of Spirit (entirely shared among people). Merging these two distinctions results in four categories. Figure 6.6 broadens Wilber's model to include the Quantum–Relativistic Paradigm and the self-transformation of people and organizations. *Spirit is known through these forms and experiences.*

FIGURE 6.6
The Four Manifestations of Spirit

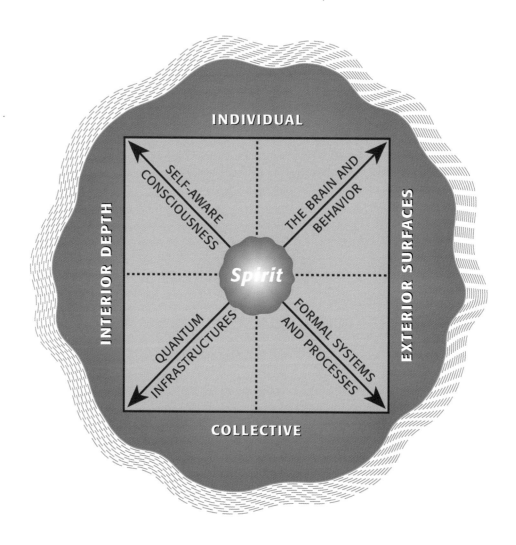

The conscious evolution of exterior forms and interior experiences is accelerated by passive Newtonian organizations self-transforming into enlightened quantum organizations. Active participation in self-designing and self-managing systems and processes brings about personal meaning and organizational success. As a result, members receive intrinsic rewards from their continued growth in self-aware consciousness along with their interpersonal encounters through quantum infrastructures. Members also receive extrinsic rewards for their behavioral contributions to the strategic architecture and strategic objectives. As displayed in Figure 6.7, all signs of Spirit spread and become known through self-transformation.

FIGURE 6.7
Spirit Becomes More Aware of Itself

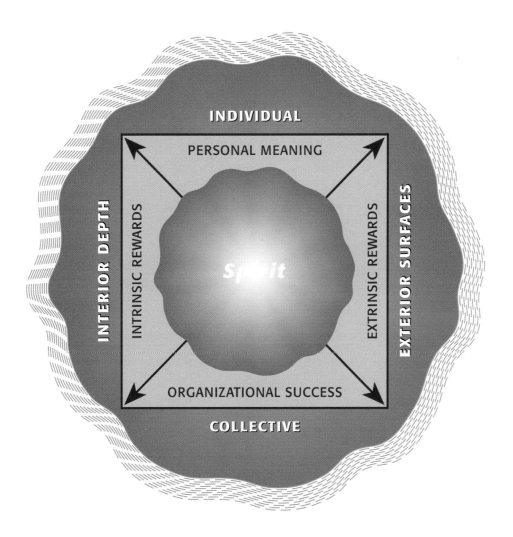

The eight tracks of the completely integrated program are portrayed in Figure 6.8 with the four signs of Spirit. The first three tracks (1, 2, 3) are implemented to enhance the interior depths of members and their shared infrastructures – even though interpersonal and group behavior is visible as exterior surfaces. The middle two tracks (4, 5) then redesign the exterior surfaces of an organization – its formal systems. Consequently, the neural networks in members' brains are rewired when implicit assumptions and task flow create new categories for industries, markets, subunits, and jobs. The last three tracks (6, 7, 8) also redesign the exterior surfaces (and minds) by formally documenting processes within and across all boundaries.

FIGURE 6.8
Spirit and Self-Transformation

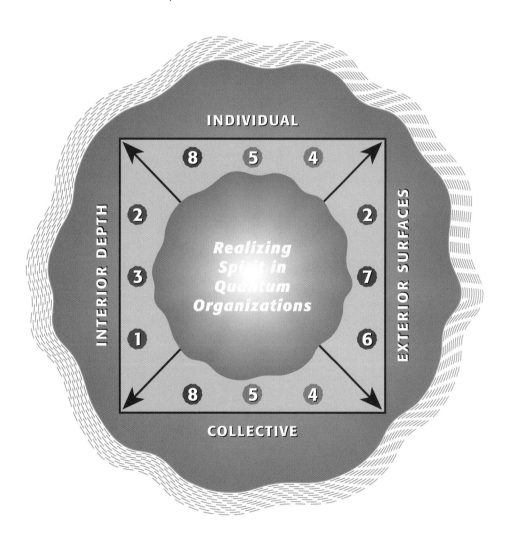

Enabling Organizational Success

I have used *eight tracks* to illuminate a completely integrated program. But there is nothing magical about the digit 8 or the particular way in which the tracks have been formulated. Numerous other tracks, trails, paths, and avenues could have been used for helping members self–transform their organization. Whether a program actually *succeeds* at its mission, however, does depend on several critical factors that must be addressed – whether there are twelve steps, six stages, or four paths to organizational success. For example, the prescribed sequence of first developing an infrastructure so that all members have the prerequisite skills and a functional culture – *before* discussing new strategic directions in group meetings – is a critical success factor regardless of the specific nature of an *n*–path program. And the need to develop reward practices that will actively challenge members to achieve strategic objectives in the short term – while materializing the strategic architecture for the long term – is another critical success factor regardless of the labels used to denote ends, means, and incentives. In the following discussion, therefore, while we will continue to make use of the completely integrated program of eight tracks (since it is familiar to me), there are twenty critical success factors (CSF #1 to CSF #20) essential to all organizations that are prepared to transform themselves into enlightened quantum organizations.

> **CSF #1** A critical mass of senior managers should be very knowledgeable about all principles and practices of the program — including the two dueling paradigms, the attributes of a Newtonian versus a quantum organization, the eight tracks and their prescribed sequence, the five stages of self-transformation, and these twenty critical success factors.

The core decision makers in a Newtonian organization, the powers–that–be, must become fully aware of a completely integrated program in contrast to adhoc and shotgun approaches. They should also be informed about the details of the program and what is required of their energy and time as well as organizational resources. Ideally, there should never be big surprises concerning what to expect if the completely integrated program is implemented. Indeed, perhaps the best indicator of having provided all the relevant information up front to a critical mass of senior managers is when no one could ever say: "Why didn't I know about this beforehand?"

CSF #2   Senior managers should be advised on how their behavior and attitudes will express active support for the program rather than send signals that will kill it.

It seems to be a universal dynamic in Newtonian organizations that passive jobholders look to their managers and supervisors to learn if they are really serious about following through on a decision – or a program. If a program for transforming the organization is given just lip service by senior managers (whether it is an adhoc, shotgun, or integrated program), members quickly learn to focus on more important activities. Since many senior managers may be particularly unaware that subtle aspects of their behavior are sending very telling signals to others, managers often need coaching on their nonverbal communication. Indeed, when managers are consciously aware of how other people read them, it becomes an explicit act of sabotage to continue sending the very signals that will undermine the success of the program. In most cases, it is helpful providing the same coaching on nonverbal communication to all members!

CSF #3   All managers' performance assessments should include their active involvement in the program.

If senior managers are entirely genuine about following through on transformation, they should use the current reward system to support it – even if it will be revised sometime later. In one organization, for example, it was made known to every member that 25% of the annual bonuses of all managerial personnel would be judged by the extent of their support and participation in the completely integrated program. If the percentage had been 5% or 10%, this announcement would not have had a big effect on members. And a 5% or 10% amount might not have had much impact on managers either. But twenty-five percentage points clearly delivered a resounding, organization-wide message: There will be active participation throughout the program – or it's going to cost you dearly. At this moment, no one had any inkling how active participation would be measured. But a strong signal was sent nonetheless: The members sensed that something very different was about to happen (relative to all the prior approaches to change and improvement).

CSF #4   Changes in key management positions should be made to actively support the principles and practices of the program.

During the length of a program – especially self–transformation that proceeds for a number of years – key managers come and go. Sometimes the senior managers who initiated the program leave the organization (or are transferred to different locations) for credible reasons. What members usually agonize about, however, is *who* is going to replace these managers. Consider the early stages of the program: Changes in senior management personnel can have an adverse effect on the continuation and success of transformation. A clear signal (with a lot of substance) is to replace these managers with persons who have the abilities and inclinations to become actively involved in supporting self–transformation – and setting the best example for others. If key management positions are staffed with persons who have the *opposite* characteristics, however, the success of the program might be jeopardized – first, by the members who take these decisions as a signal that senior management does not really know what it is doing (or is not interested in seeing the whole effort through); second, by the actual *damage* caused by the new managers when they thwart member initiatives that are intended to improve the organization. All signals, decisions, and actions by management, therefore, must be in sync with transformation.

CSF #5   A comprehensive, organization-wide diagnosis of the dysfunctions in infrastructures, systems, and processes should be conducted by experts — and then discussed by all organizational members.

It is essential to obtain a comprehensive, in–depth diagnosis of the organization's *deficient* infrastructures, systems, and processes because two questions arise again and again: (1) Why are we doing this program? (2) Is this program really that important – relative to all the other business and technical problems we have to address right now? If the diagnostic report is well done, it provides a deep, penetrating look into the tangled web of dysfunctions that will continue to thwart all efforts at resolving business and technical problems in the organization – especially the problems that flow across subunit boundaries (which usually account for the majority of problems that organizations face in today's global economy).

One way to tell if the diagnostic report was professionally done is if it evokes *pain* among members when it is first shared with them. A valid diagnosis is not an easy thing to see and appreciate, for example, when it is brightly projected on a large screen in a darkened room. Just imagine a large auditorium where the following cultural norms – which have never been spoken or written of previously – are presented to members of the organization: "When things go wrong, punish and blame others. Ridicule people from other work groups and departments. If you don't trust other departments to give you what you need, duplicate their work. Don't trust senior managers' motives – they lie. Don't trust members' commitment – they loaf. Don't speak to those who arrived from 'the merger' (which took place ten years ago). Don't be the bearer of bad news – you'll be shot on the spot. Don't disagree with your boss – any disagreements will be held against you." Even this abridged sample of cultural norms cannot convey the depth of analysis provided by a demonstrative narrative in an actual diagnosis. But an essential point must be made: Such a probing diagnostic report helps answer the two recurring questions regarding the program. In essence, it is the dysfunctions in infrastructures, systems, and processes, as presented in the diagnostic report, that justify "why we are doing this program" and "why we won't be able to accomplish anything else that is crucial and complex unless we eliminate these dysfunctions." (Sometime later, for purposes of evaluating the results of transformation, it is usually prudent to conduct another diagnosis – to see if the various dysfunctions in infrastructures, systems, and processes that were identified in the first diagnostic report were actually removed.)

> **CSF #6** A steering committee (representing all levels, areas, and locations in the organization) should accept full responsibility for the program's success.

Responsibility for scheduling and implementing the program – and evaluating the results – is neither delegated to consultants nor assigned to some staff group. Alternatively, a steering committee of about twenty–five members – sometimes labeled the shadow track (operating parallel to all eight tracks) – is mobilized after the diagnosis is sanctioned by the senior managers. This steering committee accepts complete responsibility for the success of the program. Its members – comprising essential managers and an identical number of employees representing all levels and areas in the organization – are carefully picked by the senior management group. (But the criteria and process of selection are made public to foster acceptance of the steering committee.) Essentially, the members of the shadow track meet regularly to monitor the impact of the program on the functioning of the organization and to discover or invent methods for improving the implementation process. Furthermore, the shadow track also develops the process for selecting the participants in the other collateral structures – for example, the strategy–structure, reward system, and radical process tracks.

CSF #7 Since process improvement creates excess capacity, an ethical plan to redeploy human resources should be developed in order to gain financial returns and economic efficiency for the organization.

Both reengineering and TQM assume that an improved process will lead to improved results. But such a premise should not be taken on faith. Just consider the case in which an organization achieves a 100% reduction in cycle time and a 50% reduction in costs – by eliminating many process steps and thereby reducing the direct involvement of numerous members who had performed these particular steps in the antiquated process. Are these members just standing around and doing nothing? Actually, if they are *not* redeployed to other activities that generate economic value for the organization (by either expanding the customer base for current products and services or inventing new products and services for the future), then their employment should be terminated (divested) from the organization (compassionately, of course). If not, they persevere as idle capacity that, if neither redeployed nor removed, *prevents the organization from translating its process improvements into financial returns* (Kaplan and Norton, 1992). Failing to redeploy idle capacity, therefore, entirely undermines the economic value of process management, let alone self–transformation.

Before an organization attempts to make major system and process changes, the steering committee (or shadow track) should develop a plan that outlines the corporate–wide policies and procedures for handling the excess capacity (human resources) that results from process improvement. Specifically, the plan should include how resources will be redeployed to take full advantage of excess capacity (thereby creating additional value) and how idle capacity will be removed to reduce operating expenses (as another way to improve financial returns). Developing such a plan well in advance of dramatically improving systems and processes (and sharing it with the membership) may not only avoid very painful decisions (such as layoffs) but also outline equitable procedures if such unpopular decisions prove necessary. Thus a good understanding of economic value–added is needed in order to recognize the importance of managing excess capacity in a proactive – and compassionate – manner.

CSF #8 All members should be required to attend all workshop sessions (tracks 1, 2, 3, 6, and 8) and should be fairly represented on all redesign and reengineering projects (tracks 4, 5, 7 and 8).

It would be nice if all members acknowledged that transformation is essential for organizational survival and success – and knew they had to change their familiar ways of seeing, thinking, and behaving. In reality, most people believe that it is the *others* who need to improve. Moreover, change involves some risk of embarrassment and failure and evokes some pain or, at the very least, some inconvenience in having to do customary things differently. Asked to go through uncertainty, pain, and deprivation voluntarily, most people will probably say no (or wait for everyone else to change before they commit to the change process themselves). Given ego development within the context of Newtonian organizations, therefore, it is essential to *require* all members to participate in the program – to attend all workshop sessions (about one day per month) and any assigned team in a PMO (about five to ten hours a week). Senior management may have to make modifications in members' other assignments, of course, so they are not overwhelmed with work. But if transformation has a high priority (as it must if it is to succeed), it should not only be required for everyone but also take priority over some other work. Voluntary participation in a change process will only succeed *after* self-transformation.

I recall one organization that seriously questioned whether to make the workshop meetings (tracks 1, 2, 3, 6, 8) required for all members and, further, whether to schedule these workshops for one day per month for an entire year. Senior managers agonized over whether they could add all this extra work onto the organization. I reminded them of the diagnostic report. It had clearly disclosed significant dysfunctions in infrastructures, systems, and processes, which, in essence, made it exceedingly difficult to accomplish their work. Still they maintained: "But one day a month for all members is just too much time! Couldn't we make the program *voluntary* and schedule it on the last Saturday of *every other month?*" I then asked the senior managers to itemize the ways in which they waste time now – and calculate how much time they waste every month. Their own lists of time wasters shocked them; in fact, they actually re-created many parts of the diagnostic report! They also estimated that they waste from three to five days every month *because of* the numerous dysfunctions in infrastructures, systems, and processes. As a result of this revealing exercise, these senior managers came to the logical conclusion that investing the required one day per month for every member would quickly recover the three to five days a month that were currently being wasted. The awakened managers decided to proceed with what they now judged to be a good investment in self-transformation since they now conceded the daily consequences of various dysfunctions.

CSF #9 All members should attend monthly workshop sessions in their intact — natural — work units.

The primary danger for most educational programs is that the skills and knowledge learned in the off–site workshop setting will not transfer back to the workplace. I call this common experience the *three-day washout effect*: only three days after participants have returned to their jobs, it's as if the workshop never took place! Even when they ask their supervisors to consider modifying something, based on what was learned, members are often faced with: "Get back to work. We'll talk about it later." But "later," of course, never comes. Instead, it's back to business as usual – just as before. And if what is acquired in a workshop is not transferred back to the job, there is little hope of transforming an organization.

One way to overcome the three–day washout effect is for members to attend off–site workshops in their *natural work units* (with or without the immediate boss present – depending on the diagnostic results concerning what would work best for learning and changing). If the material is *learned* as a group, it is more likely to be *used* as a group – if for no other reason than members can remind one another of what was learned and provide emotional support for trying to do things differently and better. Another way to neutralize the infamous three–day washout effect is to conduct the workshops on a recurring basis – month after month – to reinforce what is being learned and applied on the job. Nothing complex and important can possibly be learned and put to use in just one workshop session.

CSF #10 Homework should be assigned in every workshop session in order to continue the learning process during the month, in between these sessions.

A series of monthly workshops in natural work units is essential to develop – and then encourage – the social momentum of transformation. A difficulty arises, however, if the members don't keep the process going *in between* these monthly workshops. To counteract the propensity to talk transformation during the workshops but revert right back to business as usual in the workplace, each session concludes with a *homework assignment*: to complete the exercises and discussions that were introduced during the day. The primary reason is to keep the process going between the formal workshop meetings. And by documenting what was learned, each subunit can move ahead in a very efficient manner rather than wondering, "What were those cultural norms and implicit assumptions we analyzed during the last session?" And while doing the homework, group members begin discussing many other things: "What did you do about that problem you had? It would help me to know." Thus there are many by-products from doing the homework – captured by this slogan: "It hurts, but it works!"

CSF #11 **The many logistical aspects of the program should be managed efficiently and effectively by a team of dedicated professionals.**

Scheduling and implementing a completely integrated program can be a logistical nightmare if the improvement effort has not been planned, organized, and managed with special care and extreme attention to detail. Besides scheduling members for different tracks, workshops, and sections, there are numerous types of materials to distribute to the right members at the right time – with the necessary reminders. Furthermore, managing conference facilities for the workshops is a major responsibility in its own right – especially since so many things can go wrong (traffic, food, service, equipment, weather, and so forth).

Even an improvement program for a few hundred members always requires a full-time logistics coordinator as well as a part-time assistant. Programs that involve several hundreds or thousands of members would always need a logistics team: an overall coordinator with a few subgroups to focus on maintaining a database of all members, managing audiovisual equipment/supplies, and providing clerical assistance (Kilmann, 1992). The primary mission of the logistics team is to enable all members to focus on learning, not complaining.

CSF #12 **All members should learn the identical concepts, tools, and techniques, enabled by the consistent use of expert facilitators and workshop materials.**

When hundreds or even thousands of members are participating in a program, due to logistical constraints and pedagogy, there will be many sections of members attending various workshops (approximately fifty to one hundred persons per section). Consistency in what is learned during the workshops is vital – since members from different work units will be working together on numerous cross-boundary teams and, subsequently, may be assigned to new subunits (after reengineering business processes into a horizontal organization). If there is great variation in what people learn, it will be a headache attempting to solve cross-boundary problems and processes (which necessarily requires both a common language and a shared understanding of how to use complex analytic techniques such as assumptional analysis). And if there is a perception that some sections of members are actually receiving *better* (and not just different) presentations and information, bad feelings of mistrust, inequity, and frustration might spread – reinforcing the exact dysfunctions the program is attempting to remove. But using equivalent materials for all sections of members, using the same facilitators for the workshop sections (or skillfully coordinating the presentations of all facilitators), and monitoring potential consistency problems from session to session (and making adjustments, as necessary, to enhance consistency) will help members *receive* the same knowledge – and *perceive* this to be so.

> CSF #13 All members should be encouraged to enhance their self-aware consciousness by managing their cultural norms, implicit assumptions, and group process. Thereafter, they should be encouraged to further define their self-concepts and meditate on the stages of spiritual enlightenment.

During the program, members should frequently – and genuinely– be encouraged to gain self–aware consciousness. First they are exposed to the formal workshop sessions, in which they are introduced to topics that have not been discussed previously. If members become involved in these discussions (as initially encouraged by their managers), they will gain the necessary threshold of self-aware consciousness to make the switch from passive observers to active participants. Thereafter, all members should be encouraged to develop themselves further via optional discussions on the self–concepts and the stages of spiritual enlightenment. Naturally, further work on self–aware consciousness can be addressed by members in other settings. But the essential action step involves members encouraging one another to continually enhance their self–aware consciousness – and thus become more valuable to themselves and their organization.

> CSF #14 Each work group should self-design as well as self-manage its own sanctioning system in order to celebrate victories and penalize violations.

It is not until the fifth track – the reward system track – that formal incentives will be available to all members for behaving according to the principles and practices of the program. Before the *formal* reward system is designed and implemented, therefore, an *informal* reward system must be developed and utilized within every work unit. Essentially, if there are no penalties for continuing in old ways and no rewards for engaging in new behavior, *why would anyone want to change?* Naturally, after a vital threshold of transformation is attained, intrinsic rewards will help members to focus their self-motion on self-aware consciousness, organizational success, and personal meaning.

Each work unit is therefore asked to develop a *sanctioning system* that monitors and enforces the skills and behavior learned in the workshops. Specifically, each work group is asked to reach a consensus on what will be done if any member acts out dysfunctional behavior (referred to as a violation) or engages in desired behavior (referred to as a victory). As long as the informal reward system is ethical and legal, every work group can be encouraged to be as creative as possible in rewarding desired behavior while penalizing outmoded habits. Ironically, those members who profess they don't need such a system are usually the first to be sanctioned!

CSF #15   Work groups should use a process observer in every meeting — in the workshops and in the workplace.

Much of organizational life occurs in groups (both formal subunits and cross-boundary teams). Groups are also the major vehicle for trying new behavior, receiving feedback, adjusting behavior, and so on. For the dual purpose of improving group functioning both in the workshops and in the workplace, it is important to appoint one member as the "process observer" at the start of every group meeting. This member is responsible for monitoring how well the group is applying what has been learned. At the end of each meeting, he summarizes what the group did particularly well and in what ways the group fell short. A different member should be appointed to this role every time the group meets. Over a period of a few months, every member will thus have the opportunity to develop group observation skills and practice giving effective feedback. At some point, it will no longer be necessary to appoint a process observer; the ability and responsibility for improving group process will have become fully shared among all members.

CSF #16   Surveys and instruments should be used to provide effective feedback to individuals and work groups on their seeing, thinking, and behaving.

When people try to change their behavior on the job, let alone the behavior of their whole work unit, they need information and feedback. There are a variety of ways of providing useful information so members can (1) assess where they are now, (2) decide where they need to go, (3) do something to close the gap, (4) reassess where they are, and so forth (Plan, Do, Check, Act and the steps of problem management). Instruments that give feedback about a person's style of managing differences (or conflicts) are exceedingly helpful, as are surveys that capture how groups manage their time or attempt to solve their recurring problems. These quantitative assessments also enable repeat comparisons over intervals of time (every three months) to see what improvements have taken place and what still needs to be done. Since the workshop sections are organized according to natural work groups, not only will members remind one another of what was assessed on personality and behavior instruments, but each subunit is readily available to calculate group profiles and discuss the implications of the results for improving the organization. It is important to recount a typical experience: *Deriving a number* from responses to a paper–and–pencil instrument always seems to stimulate a lively discussion as long as exact numbers are not taken too seriously (Thomas and Kilmann, 1974).

CSF #17 Work groups should regularly deliver — oral — progress reports to other groups on "what we have done differently" since the program began.

CSF #18 Individuals should regularly receive — oral — feedback on "what I have done differently" since the program began.

Feedback given in public (in front of one's own work group or in front of several other work groups) can motivate fundamental changes in behavior – because people are deeply affected by the presence of others. Of course, these public exchanges should be done effectively (as learned in the skills track) and members should also be open to learn from these exchanges (which does develop as the program unfolds). But even when members or work groups are utterly sincere in their efforts to change and improve, they may still demonstrate a large gap between what they *want* to do differently and their actual behavior on the job. Receiving feedback from other people (who can observe the person or work unit in question) is needed to close the habitual gap between knowing something (intellect) and really doing it (behavior). Imagine, for example, the following "public progress report" that should be conducted bimonthly *for each group* during the workshops (and conducted periodically *for each member*).

Each natural work unit first meets to discuss and answer this series of questions: "Since the program was initiated, what has improved, stayed the same, or become worse? And, by the way, what has *your* group done differently during this same period of time?" Then each group is asked to present its responses – publicly – to the rest of the community (the other work groups in the same section). During the early stages of the program, a few work groups report that "most things have stayed the same, nothing has improved, and some things have actually gotten worse" – followed in the same sentence by: "And we haven't had the time to do our homework assignments, we usually forget to appoint a process observer in our group meetings, nor have we bothered to sanction anyone's behavior. We're just too busy." A few other work groups, however, often report that quite a few things have already improved since the program began: more sharing of information, better listening, less interrupting, and increased cooperation across subunits. These same groups immediately add: "We completed our homework assignments during lunch and breaks, we assigned a process observer at every meeting, and we have given both positive and negative sanctions to one another based on our agreed–upon sanctioning system." As a result of these public progress reports, it gradually becomes obvious that there is a direct cause–and–effect relationship between doing things differently and situations actually improving in the organization!

Since these public reports are conducted at least every other month in a workshop session, it becomes increasingly difficult for work units to disclose publicly to their peers that "nothing has changed and we haven't done anything differently." Soon enough, community–wide sanctions (soft groans or mild laughter) are applied to those groups that seem unwilling to see the connection between learning and applying the principles of the program – and what happens in the organization as a result. After several months of these progress reports (publicly presented by every work unit in the organization), it becomes virtually impossible for any group to say that it could not do anything differently – when so many other groups *in the very same organization* were able to recognize so many ways to improve their organization (through their work units). Besides, most groups do not like to disclose feelings of helplessness; instead, they move into action.

> **CSF #19** Transformational changes in seeing, thinking, and behaving should be further stimulated by recurring discussions on ego strength and internal control.

If the public progress reports and group sanctions are not sufficient to convince members to change and to help them improve, there are two special topics (and work group discussions on these topics) that stimulate self-transformation: ego strength and internal control. During workshop sessions, group members are exposed to the impact of a person's ego on his capacity to adapt to loss and change. As noted earlier in this chapter, people with *low* self-esteem (or undefined self-concepts in general) have a greater difficulty in coping with loss in their personal and work lives than those with *high* self-esteem (Figure 6.1, page 285). The relevant implication is that people who have trouble adapting to change *must have low opinions of themselves*. Whether this implication is true or not for any *individual* case is beside the point: No one wants to acknowledge that he may have low self-esteem and definitely does not want this possibility to be known (or believed) publicly. Consequently, when people discuss how to change and improve, the mere mention of the debilitating impact of low self-esteem seems to induce the desired shift in seeing, thinking, and behaving for all group members.

The second topic is internal control: whether people take personal responsibility for their transformation. Rotter's (1971) distinction between internal and external locus of control is especially helpful in challenging members to examine themselves – rather than pointing fingers at others. Briefly, *external control* is when a person believes that what happens to him is determined by outside forces (luck, politics, or other people's behavior). In contrast, *internal control* is when a person believes that what happens to him is determined by what he does or doesn't do (his decisions, attitudes, and behavior). Naturally, internal control helps people take responsibility for change. External control shifts all the attention to someone else; hence no personal responsibility for change is experienced.

Even after having participated in several workshops in the program, some members continue waiting for something to happen: "My boss still doesn't keep me informed of what goes on." "The other groups still don't cooperate with us." "My assistants still don't complete their assigned work on time." "When will this organization change?" But after group members have heard about internal and external control, such helpless complaints are met with public challenges: "You seem to have some strong beliefs in external control!" "Don't you recall that nothing will ever change around here if you continue to believe that someone else out there must change you?" "Don't you realize that *you* are the driver of organizational change – and that *you* must do something to improve things?" Most people would rather change their behavior than be subjected to these additional public sanctions! As a result, passive behavior (external control) self-transforms into active participation (internal control).

> **CSF #20** An organization-wide newsletter should regularly highlight success stories — how individuals and groups improved performance — and genuine celebrations should be held to recognize victories and encourage further improvements.

Another important way to reinforce change and improvement is to give organization-wide attention to key events and successful outcomes – beyond the workshop setting. One approach for reaching all members in the completely integrated program is through the use of formal channels: company newsletters or magazines, for example, and paper or electronic bulletin boards. More interactive – and involving – approaches, including rites, rituals, and ceremonies, can be very powerful reminders of what has been accomplished and can inspire members to strive for more dramatic change and improvement (self-transformation).

If these twenty *critical success factors* are seriously used for managing the completely integrated program (and if the program's other principles and practices are also applied), then members have an excellent chance to actualize the strategic architecture of their organization. Of course, there is always a possibility that some other organization might dream up a new technology that fundamentally reinvents the boundaries of the industry or significantly lowers the cost of producing its products and services. Or another organization might develop a more effective infrastructure with better systems and processes. Or the federal government might decide to revamp how organizations compete and whether particular technologies should be protected. *But if the members of an organization continuously monitor and improve their infrastructures, systems, and processes, they have an excellent chance of first determining and then adapting to their chosen network of external stakeholders.* In a quantum world, this is about as good as it gets – as long as (1) capital investments are made for the whole process of self-transformation and (2) economic value–added criteria are used for making all other decisions on designing systems and managing processes. While eventual survival and success cannot be guaranteed, the statistical probabilities are remarkably increased by all members seeing, thinking, and behaving according to the categories in the new paradigm. And besides economic criteria, there are also psychological criteria, such as the evolution of personal meaning.

ENABLING PERSONAL MEANING

People's need to make sense of the world and determine their place in it has been noted at several points in this book. When members formulate the strategic architecture, for example, they are, in essence, defining what their organization as a whole wants to contribute to a certain portion of society – and how it plans to do so. This search for meaning is also used by members to self-design their subunits and jobs – so they can see what they are adding to the well-being of others. And when members partake in the fundamental struggle to define who they are and what makes them unique and valuable (so they can better respond to loss and change), they are also trying to discover their personal meaning in this world. Only in a Newtonian organization have members evidently resigned themselves to following routine procedures while saving whatever ego energy remains for other settings (if they are still able to manage this split between work and life). But the more an organization can help its members to discover their reasons for being actively involved in life, the more that a win/win outcome will develop: What is good for an organization is also good for its members. Thus the traditional wall between individual and collective interests disappears – as did the dualistic split between mind and matter.

An exciting question, however, is whether the struggle for personal meaning is the ultimate – final – individual motive for evolution. What if personal meaning can be fulfilled in a quantum organization? What then? It might be worthwhile to imagine the basis of an organization's collective energy to continue evolving *if its members choose to discover the truth about who they really are – and live their lives as pure Spirit* (Gangaji, 1999).

It seems to me that the subsequent step in the evolution of people and their organizations is returning energy to the world community – so that others can also reach their spiritual fulfillment in an ecologically safe environment. The cycle seems to start with the evolution of Spirit toward material forms that become self-aware – to spiritual enlightenment where material forms no longer have meaning. The evolutionary cycle returns to its start by dematerializing the forms that once provided meaning. In the process, highly evolved persons use their accumulated forms (wealth) to supply what others need so that our whole community of beings evolves collectively. Such a philanthropic perspective emerges from a worldcentric orientation: seeing, thinking, and behaving according to a holistic web of all human (and living) beings in the world and, hence, knowing that the destiny of each one is the destiny of all. The Spirit of the universe achieves its original purpose: seeing itself through *all* forms in the universe.

Concluding Remarks

From the beginning of this book, the objective has been to see a different paradigm for people and their organizations. But merely seeing the new Quantum–Relativistic Paradigm (and how it differs in so many ways from the old Cartesian–Newtonian Paradigm) is not enough. The key challenge is *transforming a Newtonian organization into a quantum organization.* A program of eight tracks has been offered as one way to achieve self-transformation. Hopefully, this discussion will encourage others to create additional ways in which the new paradigm can generate new organizations – with a deep appreciation of all manifestations of Spirit.

I would like to conclude with a pertinent challenge by Mitroff and Denton (1999, page 7), who have conducted what is undoubtedly the first research study on spirituality in the workplace:

> We disagree strongly with the perilous path that most organizations have undertaken, that is, separating spiritual concerns from the workplace.... We believe that the workplace is one of the most important settings in which people come together daily to accomplish what they cannot do on their own, that is, to realize their full potential as human beings. For organizations to erect walls in the way of everyday spiritual development goes against the grain of deep human needs and puts an intolerable burden on individuals. This is precisely why organizations as wholes and not just individuals need to become more spiritual. Unless organizations become more spiritual, the fragmentation and ambivalence felt by individuals cannot be repaired. Unless organizations become more spiritual, they cannot reap the benefits of the full and deep engagement of their employees, their so–called most valuable resource. In the plainest terms, unless organizations not only acknowledge the soul but also attempt to deal directly with spiritual concerns in the workplace, they will not meet the challenges of the next millennium.

Allcorn, S. 1992. *Codependency in the Workplace*. Westport, CT: Quorum Books.

Amsden, D.M., H.E. Butler, and R.T. Amsden. 1991. *SPC Simplified Workbook: Practical Steps to Quality*. White Plains, NY: Quality Resources.

Amsden, R.T., H.E. Butler, and D.M. Amsden. 1989. *SPC Simplified: Practical Steps to Quality*. White Plains, NY: Quality Resources.

Anderson, J.R. 1983. *The Architecture of Cognition*. Cambridge, MA: Harvard University Press.

Andrews, D.C., and N.S. Leventhal. 1993. *FUSION — Integrating IE, CASE, and JAD: A Handbook for Reengineering the Systems Organization*. Englewood Cliffs, NJ: Prentice–Hall.

Argyris, C., and D.A. Schön. 1978. *Organizational Learning: A Theory of Action Perspective*. Reading, MA: Addison–Wesley.

Aristotle. 1958. *The Pocket Aristotle*. Edited by J.D. Kaplan. New York: Simon & Schuster.

Baldwin, C.Y., and K.B. Clark. 1992. "Capabilities and Capital Investment: New Perspectives on Capital Budgeting." *Journal of Applied Corporate Finance*: 67–82.

Bandura, A. 1986. *Social Foundations of Thought and Action: A Social-Cognitive View*. Englewood Cliffs, NJ: Prentice–Hall.

Barton, S. 1994. "Chaos, Self–Organization, and Psychology." *American Psychologist* (January): 5–14.

Bartunek, J.M., and M.K. Moch. 1987. "First–Order, Second–Order, and Third–Order Change and Organization Development Interventions: A Cognitive Approach." *Journal of Applied Behavioral Science* 23 (4): 483–500.

Bateson, G. 1979. *Mind and Nature: A Necessary Unity*. New York: Dutton.

Beer, M., and B. Spector. 1993. "Organizational Diagnosis: Its Role in Organizational Learning." *Journal of Counseling and Development* (July–August): 642–650.

Bohm, D. 1980. *Wholeness and the Implicate Order*. London: Routledge.

Bohr, N. 1958. *Atomic Theory and Human Knowledge*. New York: Wiley.

Branden, N. 1994. *The Six Pillars of Self-Esteem*. New York: Bantam Books.

Briggs, J., and D. Peat. 1984. *Looking Glass Universe: The Emerging Science of Wholeness*. New York: Simon & Schuster.

Briggs, J., and D. Peat. 1989. *Turbulent Mirror: An Illustrated Guide to Chaos Theory and the Science of Wholeness*. New York: Harper & Row.

Bringhurst, R. 1992. *The Elements of Typographical Style*. Vancouver: Hartley & Marks.

Brockner, J. 1988. *Self-Esteem at Work: Research, Theory, and Practice*. Lexington, MA: Lexington Books.

Bushe, G.R., and A.B. Shani. 1991. *Parallel Learning Structures: Increasing Innovation in Bureaucracies*. Reading, MA: Addison–Wesley.

Capra, F. 1991. *The Tao of Physics: An Exploration of the Parallels Between Modern Physics and Eastern Mysticism*. Boston: Shambhala.

Carter, R. 1998. *Mapping the Mind*. Berkeley: University of California Press.

Chopra, D. 1989. *Quantum Healing: Exploring the Frontiers of Mind and Body Medicine*. New York: Bantam Books.

Clark, R. 1971. *Einstein: The Life and Times*. New York: Avon.

Crosby, P.B. 1979. *Quality Is Free*. New York: McGraw-Hill.

Darwin, C. 1986. *The Origin of the Species by Means of Natural Selection or the Preservation of Favored Races in the Struggle for Life*. London: Penguin Classics.

Davenport, T.H. 1993. *Process Innovation: Reengineering Work Through Information Technology*. Boston: Harvard Business School Press.

Davies, P. 1999. *The Fifth Miracle: The Search for the Origin and Meaning of Life*. New York: Touchtone.

Davies, P., and J. Brown. 1988. *Superstrings: A Theory of Everything?* Cambridge, United Kingdom: Cambridge University Press.

Deming, W.E. 1986. *Out of the Crisis*. Cambridge, MA: Massachusetts Institute of Technology.

Deming, W.E. 1993. *The New Economics: For Industry, Government, Education*. Cambridge, MA: Massachusetts Institute of Technology.

Descartes, R. 1969. *Philosophical Works*. London: Cambridge University Press.

Duncan, W.L. 1988. *Just-in-Time in American Manufacturing*. Dearborn, MI: Society of Manufacturing Engineers.

Dyer, W.G. 1977. *Team Building: Issues and Alternatives*. Reading, MA: Addison–Wesley.

Eccles, J.C. 1966. *Brain and Conscious Experience*. New York: Springer Verlag.

Eccles, J.C. 1989. *Evolution of the Brain — Creation of the Self*. New York: Routledge.

Einstein, A. 1961. *Relativity: The Special and the General Theory*. New York: Bonanza Books.

Einstein, A. 1979. *The World As I See It*. Secaucus, NJ: Citadel.

Einstein, A. 1983. *Sidelights on Relativity*. New York: Dover.

Einstein, A. 1988. *The Meaning of Relativity.* Princeton, NJ: Princeton University Press.

Ernst & Young. 1990. *Total Quality.* Homewood, IL: Business One Irwin.

Ernst & Young. 1992. *International Quality Study: Best Practices Report.* Cleveland, OH: Ernst & Young and American Quality Foundation.

Euclid. 1956. *The Thirteen Books of the Elements.* New York: Dover.

Frank, A. 1997. "Quantum Honeybees." *Discover* (November): 80–87.

Freud, S. 1960. *The Ego and the Id.* New York: Norton.

Frolov, V.P., M.A. Markov, and M.A. Mukhanov. 1989. "Through a Black Hole into a New Universe?" *Physical Letters* B216: 272–276.

Gangaji. 1999. *Freedom & Resolve: The Living Edge of Surrender.* Novato, CA: The Gangaji Foundation.

Garvin, D.A. 1993. "Building a Learning Organization." *Harvard Business Review* (July–August): 78–91.

Gell-Mann, M. 1994. *The Quark and the Jaguar.* New York: Freeman.

Genz, H. 1999. *Nothingness: The Science of Empty Space.* Reading, MA: Perseus Books.

Gleick, J. 1987. *Chaos: Making a New Science.* New York: Penguin.

Goswami, A. 1993. *The Self-Aware Universe: How Consciousness Creates the Material World.* New York: Tarcher/Putnam.

Greene, B. 1999. *The Elegant Universe: Superstrings, Hidden Dimensions, and the Quest for the Ultimate Theory.* New York: Norton.

Gribbin, J. 1998. *The Search for Superstrings, Symmetry, and the Theory of Everything.* Boston: Little, Brown.

Grof, S. 1993. *The Holotropic Mind: The Three Levels of Human Consciousness and How They Shape Our Lives.* San Francisco: HarperCollins.

Hackman, J.R., and G.R. Oldham. 1980. *Work Redesign.* Reading, MA: Addison-Wesley.

Hall, G., J. Rosenthal, and J. Wade. 1993. "How to Make Reengineering *Really* Work." *Harvard Business Review* (November–December): 119–131.

Hamel, G., and C.K. Prahalad. 1994. *Competing for the Future.* Boston: Harvard Business School Press.

Hammer, M., and J. Champy. 1993. *Reengineering the Corporation: A Manifesto for Business Revolution.* New York: Harper Business.

Hammer, M., and S. Stanton. 1999. "How Process Enterprises *Really* Work." *Harvard Business Review* (November–December): 108–118.

Harrington, H.J. 1991. *Business Process Improvement.* New York: McGraw-Hill.

Harrington, H.J. 1995. *Total Improvement Management.* New York: McGraw-Hill.

Harris, S.G. 1994. "Organizational Culture and Individual Sensemaking: A Schema-Based Perspective." *Organization Science* 5 (3): 309–321.

Harrison, M.I. 1987. *Diagnosing Organizations: Methods, Models, and Processes.* Newbury Park, CA: Sage.

Hawking, S. 1996. *A Brief History of Time: The Updated and Expanded Tenth Anniversary Edition.* New York, Bantam Books.

Heisenberg, W. 1958. *Physics and Philosophy.* New York: Harper.

Heisenberg, W. 1971. *Physics and Beyond: Encounters and Conversations.* New York: Harper & Row.

Herbert, N. 1987. *Quantum Reality: Beyond the New Physics.* New York: Anchor Books.

Herbert, N. 1993. *Elemental Mind: Human Consciousness and the New Physics.* New York: Plume.

Hooper, J., and D. Teresi. 1986. *The 3-Pound Universe.* New York: Dell.

Horgan, J. 1994. "Can Science Explain Consciousness?" *Scientific American* (July): 88–94.

Horgan, J. 1999. *The Undiscovered Mind: How the Human Brain Defies Replication, Medication, and Explanation.* New York: Free Press.

Horney, K. 1950. *Neurosis and Human Growth.* New York: Norton.

Huber, G.P. 1991. "Organizational Learning: The Contributing Processes and the Literatures." *Organization Science* 2 (1): 88–115.

Imai, M. 1986. *Kaizen: The Key to Japan's Success.* New York: Random House.

Ishikawa, K. 1986. *Guide to Quality Control.* Tokyo: Asian Productivity Organization.

James, W. 1902. *The Varieties of Religious Experience: A Study in Human Nature.* London: Longmans.

Jantsch, E. 1980. *The Self-Organizing Universe.* New York: Pergamon.

Jung, C.G. 1960. *Synchronicity.* In *Collected Works,* Volume 8. Bollingen Series XX. Princeton, NJ: Princeton University Press.

Jung, C.G. 1961. *Memories, Dreams, Reflections.* New York: Pantheon.

Jung, C.G., and W. Pauli. 1955. *The Nature and Interpretation of the Psyche.* New York: Pantheon.

Juran, J.M. 1988. *Juran's Quality Handbook.* 4th ed. New York: McGraw-Hill.

Juran, J.M. 1991. *Juran's New Quality Road Map: Planning, Setting, and Reaching Quality Goals.* New York: Free Press.

Kaplan, R.S., and D.P. Norton. 1992. "The Balanced Scorecard – Measures That Drive Performance." *Harvard Business Review* (January–February): 71–79.

Kauffman, S. 1993. *The Origins of Order: Self-Organization and Selection in Evolution.* New York: Oxford University Press.

Kaufman, L., and I. Rock. 1982. "The Moon Illusion." *Scientific American* (July): 120.

Keen, P.G.W. 1991. *Shaping the Future: Business Design Through Information Technology.* Boston: Harvard Business School Press.

Keen, P.G.W. 1997. *The Process Edge: Creating Value Where It Counts.* Boston: Harvard Business School Press.

Kilmann, R.H. 1977. *Social Systems Design: Normative Theory and the MAPS Design Technology.* New York: Elsevier North-Holland.

Kilmann, R.H. 1983a. "A Dialectical Approach to Formulating and Testing Social Science Theories: Assumptional Analysis." *Human Relations* 36 (1): 1–22.

Kilmann, R.H. 1983b. "The Costs of Organization Structure: Dispelling the Myths of Independent Divisions and Organization-Wide Decision Making." *Accounting, Organizations and Society* 8 (4): 341–357.

Kilmann, R.H. 1984. *Beyond the Quick Fix: Managing Five Tracks to Organizational Success.* San Francisco: Jossey-Bass.

Kilmann, R.H. 1989a. *Escaping the Quick Fix Trap: How to Make Organizational Improvements That Really Last.* San Francisco: Jossey-Bass Audiobook.

Kilmann, R.H. 1989b. *Managing Beyond the Quick Fix: A Completely Integrated Program for Creating and Maintaining Organizational Success.* San Francisco: Jossey-Bass.

Kilmann, R.H. 1991. *Workbook for Implementing the Tracks: Volumes I & II.* Pittsburgh: Organizational Design Consultants.

Kilmann, R.H. 1992. *Logistics Manual for Implementing the Tracks: Planning and Organizing Workshop Sessions.* Pittsburgh: Organizational Design Consultants.

Kilmann, R.H. 1993. *Holographic Quality Management: Workbook for Continuous Improvement.* Pittsburgh: Organizational Design Consultants.

Kilmann, R.H. 1995. "A Holistic Program and Critical Success Factors of Corporate Transformation." *European Management Journal* 13 (2): 175–186.

Kilmann, R.H., T.J. Benecki, and Y.M. Shkop. 1979. "Integrating the Benefits of Different Efforts at Management Consulting: The Case of Human Resources, Organization Development, and Organization Design." In G. J. Gore and R. G. Wright (eds.), *The Academic/Consultant Connection.* Dubuque, IA: Kendall/Hunt.

Kilmann, R.H., and T.J. Covin. 1988. *Corporate Transformation: Revitalizing Organizations for a Competitive World.* San Francisco: Jossey-Bass.

Kim, D.H. 1993. "The Link Between Individual and Organizational Learning." *Sloan Management Review* (Fall): 37–49.

Kornfield, J. 1993. *A Path with Heart: A Guide Through the Perils and Promises of Spiritual Life.* New York: Bantam Books.

Kübler-Ross, E. 1969. *On Death and Dying.* New York: Macmillan.

Kuhn, T.S. 1962. *The Structure of Scientific Revolutions*. Chicago: University of Chicago Press.

Lawler, E.E., III. 1990. *Strategic Pay: Aligning Organizational Strategies and Pay*. San Francisco: Jossey-Bass.

Leahey, T.H., and R.J. Harris. 1993. *Learning and Cognition*. 3rd ed. Englewood Cliffs, NJ: Prentice-Hall.

Levy, S. 1994. "Dr. Edelman's Brain." *The New Yorker* (May 2): 62–73.

Limerick, D., and B. Cunnington. 1993. *Managing the New Organization: A Blueprint for Networks and Strategic Alliances*. San Francisco: Jossey-Bass.

Locke, E.A., and G.P. Latham. 1990. *A Theory of Goal Setting and Task Performance*. Englewood Cliffs, NJ: Prentice-Hall.

London, M., and R.W. Beatty. 1993. "360-Degree Feedback as a Competitive Advantage." *Human Resources Management* (Summer-Fall): 353–372.

Lorentz, A., A. Einstein, H. Minkowski, and H. Weyle. 1952. *The Principles of Relativity*. New York: Dover.

Lovelock, J. 1979. *Gaia: A New Look at Life on Earth*. New York: Oxford University Press.

Lovelock, J. 1988. *Ages of Gaia*. New York: Norton.

Mackenzie, K.D. 1986. *Organizational Design: The Organizational Audit and Analysis Technology*. Norwood, NJ: Ablex.

Mackenzie, K.D. 1991. *The Organizational Hologram: The Effective Management of Organizational Change*. Boston: Kluwer.

MacLean, P. 1985. "Brain Evolution Relating to Family, Play, and the Separation Call." *Archives of General Psychiatry* 42 (April): 405–416.

Markus, H., and R.B. Zajonc. 1985. "The Cognitive Perspective in Social Psychology." In G. Lindzey and E. Aronson (eds.), *The Handbook of Social Psychology*, vol. 1. 3rd ed. New York: Random House.

Mason, R.O., and I.I. Mitroff. 1981. *Challenging Strategic Planning Assumptions*. New York: Wiley.

McGrath, J.E. 1984. *Groups: Interaction and Performance*. Englewood Cliffs, NJ: Prentice-Hall.

Milgrom, P., and J. Roberts. 1992. *Economics, Organization, and Management*. Englewood Cliffs, NJ: Prentice-Hall.

Mitroff, I.I., and E.A. Denton. 1999. *A Spiritual Audit of Corporate America*. San Francisco: Jossey-Bass.

Mizuno, S. 1988. *Management for Quality Improvement: The Seven New QC Tools*. Cambridge, MA: Productivity Press.

Montgomery, D.C. 1991. *Introduction to Statistical Quality Control*. New York: Wiley.

Mook, D.E., and T. Vargish. 1987. *Inside Relativity*. Princeton, NJ: Princeton University Press.

Motz, L., and J.H. Weaver. 1989. *The Story of Physics*. New York: Avon Books.

Newton, I. 1934. *Principia*. Berkeley: University of California Press.

Newton, I. 1960. *Mathematical Principles of Natural Philosophy*. Berkeley: University of California Press.

Nonaka, I. 1991. "The Knowledge–Creating Company." *Harvard Business Review* (November–December): 96–104.

Ornstein, R.E. 1968. *The Nature of Human Consciousness*. San Francisco: Freeman.

Pais, A. 1982. *Subtle Is the Lord: The Science and the Life of Albert Einstein*. Oxford: Oxford University Press.

Parker, G.M. 1990. *Team Players and Teamwork: The New Competitive Business Strategy*. San Francisco: Jossey–Bass.

Peat, F.D. 1987. *Synchronicity: The Bridge Between Matter and Mind*. Toronto: Bantam Books.

Peat, F.D. 1988. *Superstrings and the Search for the Theory of Everything*. Chicago: Contemporary Books.

Peat, F.D. 1991. *The Philosopher's Stone: Chaos, Synchronicity, and the Hidden Order of the World*. New York: Bantam Books.

Penrose, R. 1989. *The Emperor's New Mind*. Oxford: Oxford University Press.

Petri, H.L., and M. Mishkin. 1994. "Behaviorism, Cognitivism, and the Neuropsychology of Memory." *American Scientist* 82: 30–37.

Planck, M. 1936. *The Philosophy of Physics*. New York: Norton.

Porter, L.W., and E.E. Lawler III. 1968. *Managerial Attitudes and Performance*. Homewood, IL: Irwin–Dorsey.

Porter, L.W., E.E. Lawler III, and J.R. Hackman. 1975. *Behavior in Organizations*. New York: McGraw–Hill.

Porter, M.E. 1980. *Competitive Strategy*. New York: Free Press.

Porter, M.E. 1990. *The Competitive Advantage of Nations*. New York: Free Press.

Prigogine, I., and I. Stenger. 1984. *Order Out of Chaos: Man's Dialogue with Nature*. New York: Bantam Books.

Rank, O. 1929. *The Trauma of Birth*. New York: Harcourt Brace.

Rappaport, A. 1986. *Creating Shareholder Value: The New Standard for Business Performance*. New York: Free Press.

Rotter, J.B. 1971. "External Control and Internal Control." *Psychology Today* (June): 37–42, 58–59.

Rummler, G.A., and A.P. Brache. 1990. *Improving Performance: How to Manage the White Space on the Organization Chart*. San Francisco: Jossey–Bass.

Schmalensee, R., and R.D. Willig. 1989. *Handbook of Industrial Organization*, vol. 1 and 2. New York: Elsevier Science.

Schrödinger, E. 1969. *What Is Life? and Mind and Matter*. London: Cambridge University Press.

Schwartz, G.E.R., and L.G.S. Russek. 1999. *The Living Energy Universe.* Charlottesville, VA: Hampton Roads.

Searle, J. 1984. *Minds, Brains, and Science.* Cambridge, MA: Harvard University Press.

Senge, P. 1990. *The Fifth Discipline: The Art and Practice of the Learning Organization.* New York: Doubleday/Currency.

Sheldrake, R. 1981. *A New Science of Life.* Los Angeles: Tarcher.

Sheldrake, R. 1988. *The Presence of the Past: Morphic Resonance and the Habits of Nature.* New York: Random House.

Shewhart, W.A. 1931. *Economic Control of Quality of Manufactured Product.* New York: Van Nostrand.

Shlain, L. 1991. *Art and Physics: Parallel Visions in Space, Time, and Light.* New York: William Morrow.

Singer, J. 1972. *Boundaries of the Soul: The Practice of Jung's Psychology.* New York: Doubleday.

Smith, P.C., and L.M. Kendall. 1963. "Retranslation of Expectations: An Approach to the Construction of Unambiguous Anchors for Ratings Scales." *Journal of Applied Psychology* (April): 149–155.

Smolin, L. 1997. *The Life of the Cosmos.* Oxford: Oxford University Press.

Spector, B., and M. Beer. 1994. "Beyond TQM Programmes." *Journal of Organizational Change Management* 7 (2): 63–70.

Squire, L. 1987. *Memory and Brain.* New York: Oxford University Press.

Squire, L. 1992. "Memory and the Hippocampus: A Synthesis from Findings with Rats, Monkeys, and Humans." *Psychological Review* 99: 195–231.

St. Augustine. 1958. *City of God.* Garden City, NY: Anchor/Doubleday.

Stewart, G.B., III. 1991. *The Quest for Value: The EVA Management Guide.* New York: Harper Business.

Taguchi, G., and D. Clausing. 1990. "Robust Quality." *Harvard Business Review* (January–February): 65–75.

Talbot, M. 1991. *The Holographic Universe.* New York: Harper Perennial.

Tapscott, D., and A. Caston. 1993. *Paradigm Shift: The New Promise of Information Technology.* New York: McGraw-Hill.

Tart, C. 1975. *States of Consciousness.* New York: Dutton.

Taylor, J. 1973. *Black Holes: The End of the Universe?* New York: Random House.

Teilhard de Chardin, P. 1965. *Building the Earth.* New York: Discus Books.

Thomas, K.W., and R.H. Kilmann. 1974. *The Thomas-Kilmann Conflict-Mode Instrument.* Palo Alto, CA: Xicom.

Thompson, J.D. 1967. *Organizations in Action: Social Science Bases of Administrative Theory.* New York: McGraw-Hill.

Thorne, K. 1994. *Black Holes and Time Warps.* New York: Norton.

Trice, H.M., and J.M. Beyer. 1993. *The Cultures of Work Organizations*. Englewood Cliffs, NJ: Prentice–Hall.

Von Neumann, J. 1955. *The Mathematical Foundations of Quantum Mechanics*. Princeton, NJ: Princeton University Press.

Vosniadou, S., and W.F. Brewer. 1987. "Theories of Knowledge Restructuring in Development." *Review of Educational Research* 57 (1): 51–67.

Vroom, V.H. 1964. *Work and Motivation*. New York: Wiley.

Walsh, J.P., and G.R. Ungson. 1991. "Organizational Memory." *Academy of Management Review* 16 (1): 57–91.

Wheatley, M.J. 1992. *Leadership and the New Science: Learning About Organization from an Orderly Universe*. San Francisco: Berrett–Koehler.

Wheeler, J.A. 1990. *A Journey into Gravity and Spacetime*. New York: Scientific American Library.

Wigner, E. 1967. *Symmetries and Reflections*. Bloomington: University of Indiana Press.

Wilber, K. 1979. *The Spectrum of Consciousness*. Wheaton, IL: Theosophical Publication House.

Wilber, K. 1980. *The Atman Project: A Transpersonal View of Human Development*. Wheaton, IL: Theosophical Publication House.

Wilber, K. 1995. *Sex, Ecology, Spirituality: The Spirit of Evolution*. Boston: Shambhala.

Wilber, K. 1996. *A Brief History of Everything*. Boston: Shambhala.

Wolf, F.A. 1981. *Taking the Quantum Leap: The New Physics for Non-Scientists*. San Francisco: Harper & Row.

Wolf, F.A. 1988. *Parallel Universes: The Search for Other Worlds*. New York: Simon & Schuster.

Wriston, W.B. 1992. *The Twilight of Sovereignty: How the Information Revolution Is Transforming Our World*. New York: Scribners.

Young, A.M. 1976. *The Reflexive Universe: Evolution of Consciousness*. Cambria, CA: Anodos Foundation.

Zand, D.E. 1981. *Information, Organization, and Power*. New York: McGraw–Hill.

Zohar, D. 1990. *The Quantum Self: Human Nature and Consciousness Defined by the New Physics*. New York: William Morrow.

Zohar, D. 1997. *Rewiring the Corporate Brain: Using the New Science to Rethink How We Structure and Lead Organizations*. San Francisco: Berrett–Koehler.

Zuckav, G. 1979. *The Dancing Wu Li Masters: An Overview of the New Physics*. New York: William Morrow.

RALPH H. KILMANN is George H. Love Professor of Organization and Management at the Joseph M. Katz Graduate School of Business, University of Pittsburgh. He earned both his B.S. degree and M.S. degree in industrial administration from Carnegie Mellon University in 1970 and a Ph.D. degree in management from the University of California at Los Angeles in 1972. Since 1975, he has been president of Organizational Design Consultants – a firm specializing in quantum transformations.

Kilmann is an internationally recognized authority on systems change. He has consulted for numerous corporations throughout the United States and Europe, including AT&T, Kodak, IBM, Ford, General Electric, General Motors, Lockheed, Olivetti, Philips, TRW, Westinghouse, Wolseley, and Xerox. He has also consulted for numerous health–care, financial, and government organizations, including the U.S. Bureau of the Census and the Office of the President. He is profiled in *Who's Who in America* and *Who's Who in the World*.

Kilmann has published more than one hundred articles and fifteen books on such subjects as organizational theory, organizational design, and change management. He is the developer of the MAPS Design Technology® and coauthor of diagnostic instruments, including the *Thomas-Kilmann Conflict Mode Instrument* and the *Kilmann-Saxton Culture-Gap® Survey*.

Kilmann's significant books include *Social Systems Design* (1977), *Beyond the Quick Fix* (1984), *Escaping the Quick Fix Trap* (1989), *Managing Beyond the Quick Fix* (1989), *Gaining Control of the Corporate Culture* (1985), *Corporate Transformation* (1988), *Making Organizations Competitive* (1991), *Workbook for Implementing the Tracks* (1991), *Logistics Manual for Implementing the Tracks* (1992), *Holographic Quality Management* (1993), *Managing Ego Energy* (1994) – all unified in *Quantum Organizations* (2001).

Kilmann's hobbies include running, mountain biking, scuba diving, golf, photography, fine art, enjoying many types of music (by attending opera, symphony, and rock concerts), and fine dining. He has a passion for home theater – a setting that integrates science, art, music, and intimacy. Yet his long–term hobby, since childhood, is printing.

To learn more about the author's research and consulting practice, visit his web site at **www.kilmann.com**.

TWO FLAGGED ENTRIES, •defined, •pictured, ARE LISTED FIRST.

brain. *See also* consciousness; mind/brain
  •pictured, *60*
  correlated brains, *46–47*
  description, *43–44*
  evolution, *44–45*
  hemispheres
    corpus callosum, *44–48, 50, 53, 60*
    evolution, *47–48, 53*
    interacting, *45–48, 50, 60–61*
    left/right brain, *44–48, 53, 60, 121*
  neural connections
    adding/losing/rewiring, *61–64, 72, 76, 98, 118, 277, 298*
    rapidly firing, *45–46, 60–61*
  organic structures, *264–265*
  quantum functioning, *45–48*
Branden, N., *278*
Brewer, W.F., *264*
Briggs, J., *39, 46*
Bringhurst, R., *2*
Brockner, J., *278*
Brown, J., *27*
Buddha, *xix, 274, 278. See also* Spirit
Bushe, G.R., *141*
business processes. *See* process management; processes: types: business; structure: according to: business processes
Butler, H.E., *230, 239*

C

C-groups (conclusion groups). *See* problem management organization (PMO): structure: C-groups/S-group
Capra, F., *50–51*
Carter, R., *44, 265*
Cartesian-Newtonian Paradigm (old), *xv, 14, 15–19, 34–36. See also* categories; objects (inert); paradigm
  •pictured, *67*
  complete certainty, *203*
  deficient for explaining
    light, *19*
    particles/people, *48, 76, 275*
  effective for explaining
    billiard balls, *17, 18, 42, 48*
    molecules/moons, *41, 43*

Cartesian-Newtonian... *(continued)*
  origin, *15–16*
  perspectives on
    ego energy, *275*
    process management, *215, 224*
    reward systems, *185–186*
    strategy, *155–156*
    structure, *167–168*
  seven categories, *17–19*
cases
  American Gas & Electric (AGE), *100–107*
  Good Foods, *180–182*
  InfoTech, *162–163*
  other examples
    assumptional analysis, *132–135*
    change management, *132–135*
    problem management, *119–120*
Caston, A., *255*
categories. *See also* mind/brain; paradigm
  creating new, *45–48, 64, 118, 180–182*
    information technology and, *268*
    stored in mind/brain, *264–265, 289*
  rigid set of, *xiv, xv, 13, 16, 66, 151*
  types
    contradictory, *14, 64–65*
    fragmented, *xiii–xiv, xvi, xvii, 16, 17, 253–254*
    holistic, *xiii–xiv, xv, xvii, xxii, 79, 140–141, 150–154, 214, 272*
    Newtonian, *17–19, 51, 66–67*
    quantum, *48–51, 69, 156–157*
    specialized, *xiii, xv, 112, 117–119, 132–135, 150*
Catholic Church, *15–16*
Champy, J., *205*
change initiatives. *See also* program, completely integrated; programs, fragmented; transformation
  disciplines/specialties, *132, 133–134, 149, 150*
  popular, *75, 119*
  types
    nontransformational, *77, 78, 91*
    transformational, *75–78, 80–81*
chaos theory, *46*
  edge of chaos, *13, 64*
  strange attractors, *46–48, 61, 64*
Chopra, D., *43*

Christ, J., *15*
Clark, K.B., *159, 260*
Clark, R., *22*
Clausing, D., *241*
completely integrated program. *See* program, completely integrated; transformation
consciousness, *30–33, 47–51. See also* matter; self-aware consciousness; universal consciousness
    bonding electrons, *31, 32, 46*
    materializing matter, *31, 32, 41, 55, 157*
    mind/matter interplay, *36, 47*
    nonordinary states, *34–36, 50, 58–59*
    ordinary states, *33–34, 50, 59*
    transpersonal journey, *36–37, 40*
control (internal/external), *78, 176–177, 194, 275*
    •defined, *311*
    discussing internal control, *310–312*
Copernicus, *16*
core competencies. *See* strategy: core competencies
cosmology. *See also* evolution; universe
    creation
        biblical, *20, 292*
        big bang, *38–39, 56*
    evolution
        life cycles of universes, *38–39*
        mind/matter, *xiv, xv, 39*
        self-transforming systems, *39, 41*
    natural selection (cosmological)
        black holes, *37–39, 56*
        stable atoms, *37, 38*
        supernovas, *37–39*
cosmos, *30–33. See also* universe
    Eastern philosophies, *51*
    Western philosophies, *15, 50*
Covin, T.J., *14*
critical success factors. *See also* economic value-added; organizational success; transformation
    •defined, *299*
    (1) a critical mass of support, *299*
    (2) self-aware senior managers, *300*
    (3) rewarding senior managers, *300*
    (4) supportive replacements, *300–301*
    (5) a probing diagnosis, *301–302*

critical success factors *(continued)*
    (6) a steering committee, *302*
    (7) an ethical plan, *303*
    (8) required attendance, *303–304*
    (9) workshops for work units, *305*
    (10) homework assignments, *305–306*
    (11) managing logistical aspects, *306*
    (12) consistent knowledge, *306–307*
    (13) enhancing self-awareness, *307*
    (14) self-designing sanctions, *307–308*
    (15) using a process observer, *308*
    (16) effective feedback, *308–309*
    (17–18) progress reports, *309–310*
    (19) ego and internal control, *310–312*
    (20) celebrating successes, *312*
Crosby, P.B., *204, 210*
culture. *See also* culture track
    •defined, *97*
    cultural norms
        •defined, *97–98*
        dysfunctional/unhealthy, *xviii, 98, 188–189, 301*
        functional/healthy, *9, 98, 137, 190*
    culture-gaps, *108, 109*
    diagnosing cultural norms, *98–100*
    Newtonian norms
        (1) do not trust, *101–102*
        (2) refuse to see, *102*
        (3) pick your favorites, *102–103*
        (4) play the game, *103*
        (5) do not confront, *103*
        (6) decide in a vacuum, *104*
        (7) do not listen, *104*
        (8) avoid problems, *105*
        (9) blame others, *105*
        (10) punish others, *105–106*
        (11) do not communicate, *106*
        (12) keep wounds open, *106*
        summary, *106–107*
    peer group pressure, *97, 188–189*
    sanctioning systems, *110–111*
        celebrating successes, *312*
        self-designing sanctions, *307–308*
    steps
        (1) surfacing actual norms, *107*
        (2) establishing desired norms, *108*
        (3) identifying culture-gaps, *108–109*
        (4) closing culture-gaps, *109–112*

culture track. *See also* culture; program, completely integrated: (1) culture track; quantum infrastructures
  active participation, *85*
  revisiting after restructuring, *179, 182*
Cunnington, B., *139*
customers. *See* process management: customers

Darwin, C.
  natural selection, *37, 38, 43*
Davenport, T.H., *203, 205, 266, 267*
Davies, P., *27, 41*
Deming, W.E., *204, 214, 238, 260, 265*
Denton, E.A., *314*
Descartes, R., *xv, 16, 36*
  dualism, *xv, 16–17, 28–30, 33, 272, 313*
diagnosing organizations. *See also* culture: diagnosing cultural norms; transformation: stages: (2) diagnosing the problems
  report/results (diagnostic), *96, 100, 101, 107, 146, 148, 149, 304*
    comprehensive (in-depth), *301–302*
dualism. *See* Descartes, R.: dualism
Duncan, W.L., *213*
Dyer, W.G., *136*
dysfunctions. *See also* transformation: stages: (2) diagnosing the problems
  defense mechanisms, *35, 73, 279–280*
  dysfunctional
    behavior, *xix, 73, 279–280, 295*
    culture, *98, 188–189, 301*
    families, *12, 279–280*
    infrastructures, *91, 146, 162, 186, 188, 204–205, 237, 258*
    processes, *215, 220, 272*
    systems, *162, 176, 186, 188, 204, 258*
  symptoms of, *87–88*
  tangled web of, *301–302, 304*

Earth, *24, 25–26. See also* solar systems
  Gaia Theory, *39–41, 51, 68*
  transpersonal journey, *40*

Eastern civilization, *xxi, 50–51, 278, 290*
  focus on spiritual enlightenment, *291*
  integrated with the West, *296*
e-business/commerce, *xiii, 255, 267, 270*
Eccles, J.C., *43, 46*
economic value–added, *184, 242. See also* organizational success; processes: value–added (va)
  •defined, *259–260*
  barriers/dysfunctions, *258–259*
  cost/benefit analysis, *115, 217, 233, 244, 258, 267, 285*
  linked to strategic objectives, *170, 312*
  present value analysis, *156, 159*
  redeploying idle resources, *303*
  versus accounting practices, *259*
effectiveness. *See* organizational success
efficiency. *See* organizational success
ego development. *See also* ego energy; self-aware consciousness; Spirit; spiritual enlightenment
  commitment/desire, *73, 289*
  coping with loss, *86, 178, 268, 311*
    seven stages, *282–283*
  path to self-awareness, *295, 307*
  practices
    interpretive therapies, *275, 289, 290*
    managing attachments, *284*
    removing distortions, *289, 295*
  stages
    (1) egocentric, *275, 277, 293*
    (2) sociocentric, *277*
    (3) worldcentric, *293, 313*
ego energy. *See also* ego development
  •defined, *278–279*
  amounts available, *279–280, 283*
  attributes (healthy)
    adaptive to change/loss, *284, 311*
    person as own customer, *285–286*
    person as own supplier, *286, 288*
    seeing/managing reality, *280, 288, 290, 295*
  attributes (unhealthy)
    drained by defenses, *280, 283, 295*
    implicit/noncapable self, *286, 287*
    satisfying other customers, *286*
    using many suppliers, *285–286, 288*
  discussing ego strength, *310–312*

Jung, C.G., *32–33, 34*
Juran, J.M., *204, 232, 265–266*
    quality trilogy, *214, 243*

Kaplan, R.S., *303*
Kauffman, S., *38, 39, 43*
Kaufman, L., *41*
Keen, P.G.W., *255, 259–260, 266*
Kendall, L.M., *196*
Kepler, *16*
Kilmann, R.H., *14, 93, 94, 112, 134–135,*
    137, 146, 174, 180–181, 306, 309
Kim, D.H., *264, 265*
Knowledge Bridge (software from
    ServiceWare), *268*
knowledge management. *See* learning;
    program, completely integrated:
    (8) learning process track; structure:
    types (of organization): learning/
    knowledge
Kornfield, J., *291*
Kübler-Ross, E., *282–283*
Kuhn, T.S., *xiv, 13*

language of organizations, *65–66*
    common across all subunits, *307*
Latham, G.P., *195*
Lawler, E.E., III, *185, 188, 189–190*
Lawrence, A., *28*
laws (of nature)
    general, *21, 23, 25*
    special, *23*
leadership for transformation. *See also*
    critical success factors; shadow
    track; transformation: stages:
    (1) initiating the program
    critical mass, *299*
    effective, *78, 182*
    ineffective, *5, 163*
    in Newtonian organizations, *276, 304*
    paradigmatic roots, *13*
    quantum thinking, *45*
    shared among members, *146–147*
Leahey, T.H., *xx*

learning. *See also* critical success factors;
    learning process track
    •defined, *70, 86, 263*
        an integrated definition, *265–266*
    gap (knowing/doing), *309–310*
    knowledge (why/how)
        computer technology for, *267–268*
        declarative/procedural, *263–265, 268*
        gradually/radically restructuring,
          264–265, 266, 268, 272
        implicit/explicit, *263, 266, 267*
        retrieving/storing, *264*
        rewiring brains, *61–62, 76, 265*
    spacetime (where/when)
        across boundaries, *161, 264, 265, 266,*
          267, 270
        inside individuals, *263, 265, 266, 270*
        off-site workshops, *112, 135*
        transfer to workplace, *85, 86, 96, 135,*
          305–306
    summary, *272*
learning process track. *See also* learning;
    process management; program,
    completely integrated: (8) learning
    process track
    active participation, *86*
    forming a PMO, *268*
    learning processes, *265–268*
    links to other tracks, *86, 97, 206*
    origin, *205–206*
Leventhal, N.S., *268*
Levy, S., *46*
light (radiant energy)
    •pictured, *56, 57*
    electromagnetic spectrum, *20, 21*
    first instant of, *20, 56, 292*
    mass/energy and, *22, 49*
    photons, *20, 29, 41–42, 81–82*
    speed of
        absolute, *21, 22–23, 25, 31*
        actual, *21–23, 41*
        approaching, *20, 22, 23*
        relative, *21*
        transcending, *29, 31, 49*
    Spirit and, *292*
    transpersonal journey, *36–37*
    ultraviolet catastrophe, *19, 74*
    wave/particle aspects, *19, 28, 29, 37*

Limerick, D., *139*
Locke, E.A., *195*
logistics (of change). *See* program, completely integrated: workbooks; transformation: logistical aspects
London, M., *197*
Lorentz, A., *22*
Lovelock, J., *39–40*

Mackenzie, K.D., *150, 154, 174, 182*
MacLean, P., *44*
management functions. *See* gradual process improvement: management functions; structure: according to: management functions
Markov, M.A., *38*
Markus, H., *264*
Martinec, E., *28*
Mason, R.O., *112*
mass, *20, 22, 23, 29, 37. See also* energy large/dense/near light speed, *42*
matter, *27, 29–30. See also* consciousness creation of, *57–59*
    dark, *26, 39, 55*
    evolution of, *42, 294–295*
Maxwell, J., *20, 21*
McGrath, J.E., *136*
measurement. *See* quantum physics/theory: measurement; statistical theories/methods; validation: reliability/validity
mechanics, theories of
    Newtonian, *16, 17–19, 22, 43, 157, 203*
    quantum, *31, 41–48, 49*
    relativistic, *21, 41*
members. *See* participants; reward systems: members
Milgrom, P., *xx, 159, 260*
mind/brain. *See also* brain; categories; consciousness; paradigm
    •pictured, *59*
    conduit for consciousness, *264*
    creative potential, *61*
    evolution, *24, 63–64, 72*
    gradually/radically restructuring, *264, 265, 266, 272, 277*

mind/brain (*continued*)
    memory management, *64, 264*
    quantum thinking, *45–46, 52*
        •defined, *45*
        •pictured, *60–62*
        collective, *74, 96*
        creating new categories, *45, 64, 118*
        strange attractor, *46–48, 60–61, 64*
    seeing/thinking/behaving
        mental filters, *33, 59*
        new paradigm, *xiv, 48, 163, 204, 271*
        spirituality, *274–275, 313*
        transformation, *13–15, 272, 304, 308–309*
    source of energy, *278, 279, 283*
Minkowski, H., *22*
Mishkin, M., *264*
Mitroff, I.I., *112, 314*
Mizuno, S., *244*
Moch, M.K., *264*
monads, self-motion. *See also* motivation: source: internal spark; participants; quantum organizations
    •defined, *42*
    correlated/connected, *46–48, 50*
    particles/people, *42–43, 49–50, 155*
    self-designing/self-managing, *193–195*
    source of energy, *278*
Montgomery, D.C., *229, 231, 266*
Mook, D.E., *23, 25*
motivation, *183. See also* reward systems
    •defined, *186*
    expectancy theory, *188*
    source
        external force, *42–43, 48, 51, 186, 187*
        internal spark, *42–43, 49, 186–187, 194–195, 277, 278*
Motz, L., *16, 21*
Mukhanov, M.A., *38*

natural selection. *See* cosmology: natural selection (cosmological); Darwin, C.: natural selection; evolution
new organizations. *See* quantum organizations

problem management organization
(PMO), *85, 86, 141–149. See also*
assumptional analysis; problem
management; quantum
infrastructures; structure
•defined, *142*
•pictured, *142–145, 166*
assumptional analysis and, *142,
144–145, 198, 200*
examples
Good Foods, *180–182*
InfoTech, *162–163*
reward systems, *198*
forming, *143*
criteria, *146, 147, 149, 153–154*
participants in the PMO
(a) shadow track, *146–147*
(b) strategy-structure track, *147–148*
(c) reward system track, *148–154*
(d) radical process track, *261–262*
(e) learning process track, *268*
prerequisites, *145*
purpose/procedures, *140, 149*
structure
C-groups/S-group, *132–135,
142–145, 167, 183*
collateral/operational, *141–143,
145, 166, 183*
roles/responsibilities, *261–262*
variety of uses, *140, 179*
process management, *52, 70–71, 83. See
also* processes; program, completely
integrated: tracks: (c) last three;
statistical theories/methods;
technologies, reengineering;
strategy-structure track;
transformation
•defined, *80, 205–206*
active participation, *206, 215, 277, 297*
assumptional analysis and, *210, 211,
215, 244*
barriers
(1) description (implicit processes),
221–222, 224, 266
(2) control (special causes), *234–236,
238, 266*
(3) improvement (common causes),
237, 238, 267

process management (*continued*)
commandment, *52, 87*
customers
actively participating, *215*
downstream processes, *210–211, 242*
end/ultimate, *207, 209, 224*
external/internal, *209, 256*
identifying/quantifying needs, *224,
225–226*
quality function deployment, *248*
feedback
•pictured, *170, 208*
(a) from customers, *170, 194–195*
(b) to suppliers, *170*
(c) within self, *170, 254*
statistical language for, *204*
gaps
(1) ideal/actual process, *224*
(2) under/out of control, *235*
(3) capable/noncapable, *239, 258*
quality loss function, *241, 243*
summary, *214*
outcomes, *207*
assumptions about, *268*
customer delight, *184, 214, 215, 269*
cycle time, *212–213, 220–221, 242*
excess capacity, *303*
potential improvement, *245–246*
process costs, *212–213, 220–221*
six sigma quality, *241*
zero defects, *241*
prerequisites, *52, 140, 206*
problem management and, *214, 224,
235–236, 238*
Spirit and, *298*
stakeholders (other), *207, 219, 220*
steps
(1) describing processes, *215–224*
(2) controlling processes, *225–236*
(3) improving processes, *237–244*
for ego-defining processes, *285–289*
for learning processes, *266–267*
suppliers
actively participating, *215*
external/internal, *209*
stipulating requirements for, *224*
upstream processes, *210–211, 242*
process observer, *137, 308. See also* teams

Roman civilization, *15*
Rosenthal, J., *205*
Rotter, J.B., *311*
Rummler, G.A., *168, 247*
Russek, L.G.S., *33, 56, 275*

S

S-group (synthesis group). *See* problem
    management organization (PMO):
    structure: C-groups/S-group
schema theory. *See also* categories; mind/
    brain; paradigm: schema (mental)
    •defined/pictured, *63–64*
    transforming schemas, *264–265, 266*
Schmalensee, R., *156*
Schön, D.A., *263*
Schrödinger, E., *28, 31*
Schwartz, G.E.R., *33, 56, 275*
science, *36*. *See also* experiments
    evolution of, *38, 49*
    integrated theories, *xxi, 37, 49*
Searle, J., *43*
self-aware consciousness, *33–36,*
    47–51. *See also* consciousness;
    universal consciousness
    •defined, *xiv, 273*
    applying, *57, 70, 161*
    brain
        dialogue/location in the, *47–48*
    collapsing waves, *30, 41, 55, 157*
    enhanced by
        all eight tracks, *271, 273, 277, 280*
        first three tracks, *111, 121, 136, 276*
        last three tracks, *207, 272*
        middle two tracks, *276–277*
        summary, *277, 307*
    evolution
        active to enlightened, *275, 290, 294*
        passive to active, *275–277, 294, 312*
    revolution, *xiv–xv*
    self-concepts (core)
        five definitions, *278–279*
        five discussions, *281*
        five processes, *284*
        prerequisites, *281, 282*
        using process tools, *284–285*
    self-concepts (other), *3, 50, 60, 194, 278*

self-designing. *See* quantum
    organizations
self-managing. *See* quantum
    organizations
self-motion monads. *See* monads
self-transformation. *See* transformation
Senge, P., *205, 263*
ServiceWare, *268*
shadow track. *See also* leadership for
    transformation; program,
    completely integrated
    forming, *146–147*
    mission/plans, *93, 303*
    mobilizing (other PMOs)
        (a) strategy-structure track, *147–148*
        (b) reward system track, *148–154*
        (c) radical process track, *261–262*
        (d) learning process track, *268*
Shani, A.B., *141*
Sheldrake, R., *33*
Shewhart, W.A., *214, 238*
Shkop, Y.M., *134–135*
Shlain, L., *xxi, 15, 44–45, 53*
Singer, J., *33*
skills track. *See also* assumptional
    analysis; problem management;
    program, completely integrated:
    (2) skills track; quantum
    infrastructures
    active participation, *85*
    learning quantum thinking, *96, 118,*
        121, 130
    revisiting after restructuring, *179, 182*
Smith, P.C., *196*
Smolin, L., *xxi, 37–41*
solar systems, *16, 19*
    moons, *43*
    planets, *19, 25*
    sun, *16, 40*
soul, *8–9*. *See also* Spirit
space, *18–19, 32*. *See also* spacetime
    continuum; time
    Christian
        disjointed, *15*
    Einsteinian
        curved, *23–24, 25, 28, 55*
        energy/matter, *39*
        relative, *22, 25*

statistical theories/methods (*continued*)

teams *(continued)*
 types
  cross–boundary, *96, 135, 142, 245,*
   251, 252
  project groups, *96*
  steering committees, *96, 135, 142*
  task forces, *101, 135*
  work units, *136, 169, 305*
technologies, reengineering. *See also*
  processes; structure
 communication/information, *xiii, 157,*
  162–163, 205, 246, 255–256
 computer-aided systems engineering
  (CASE tools), *267–268*
 MAPS Design Technology, *180–182*
 production/transportation, *160, 256*
Teilhard de Chardin, P., *32*
Teresi, D., *43, 44*
theories. *See* chaos theory; cosmology;
  mechanics, theories of; Newtonian
  physics/theory; quantum physics/
  theory; relativity, theories of;
  schema theory; statistical theories/
  methods; superstring theory
thermodynamics. *See* cosmology;
  Newtonian physics/theory
Thomas, K.W., *137, 309*
Thompson, J.D., *170*
Thorne, K., *37, 39*
thought experiments. *See* Einstein, A.:
  thought experiments
time, *20, 32. See also* space; spacetime
  continuum
 absolute (Newtonian), *23*
 disjointed (Christian), *15*
 relative (Einsteinian), *22, 25*
total quality management (TQM).
  See process management
tracks. *See* change initiatives; program,
  completely integrated;
  transformation
transformation. *See also* change
  initiatives; paradigm: shift
  (transformational)
 •defined, *13–14, 76, 272*
 active participation, *277, 300*
 big picture, *89–91, 202*
 challenge, *51–52, 74, 314*

transformation *(continued)*
 change initiatives
  choosing, *77–79*
  sequencing, *77, 81–84*
 components (three), *52, 79–80, 83–84*
 consultants (expert), *93, 98–100, 119,*
  147, 148, 149, 306–307
 critical success factors, *299–312*
 fall/rise of systems/processes, *83–84*
 gap, *76, 92–93, 140*
 logistical aspects, *112, 146–147, 306*
 potential outcomes, *xix, 52, 54, 312*
 quantum thinking, *45*
 Spirit, *296–297, 298, 314*
 stages
  •pictured, *92*
  (1) initiating the program, *92–93*
  (2) diagnosing the problems, *92–93,*
   96, 140, 148, 149
  (3) scheduling the tracks, *92–93*
  (4) implementing the tracks, *92–93,*
   94, 146, 160, 182, 199–201
  (5) evaluating the results, *92–93, 146*
transpersonal journeys, *31–34. See also*
  spiritual enlightenment
 The Cosmic Tree, *36–37*
 Descartes' dreams, *36*
 Einstein's thoughts, *35*
 The Living Earth, *40*
 The Ultimate Encounter, *3–11*
trees (decision). *See* problem
  management: trees (decision)
Trice, H.M., *97*

U

uncertainty. *See* assumptional analysis;
  quantum physics/theory
unconscious organizations, *xvii, 3.*
  See also Newtonian organizations
 on autopilot
  organizations, *66*
  people, *7, 8, 33, 70*
Ungson, G.R., *265*
universal consciousness, *34–36, 58–59.*
  See also consciousness; self-aware
  consciousness
 •defined, *32–33*

universal consciousness (*continued*)
  dialogue within brain, *48*
  Eastern philosophies, *50–51*
  reservoir of knowledge, *74, 264–265*
  across space/time, *35, 43, 50*
  transcending light speed, *29, 31–32*
universe. *See also* cosmos; Spirit
  •pictured, *55*
  dimensions
    consciousness (one), *31–33, 35, 49*
    space (three), *24, 25, 29, 32, 49*
    spacetime (many), *22, 23–25, 32, 49, 55–56*
    time (one), *24, 30, 32, 49*
  foundation
    consciousness, *48*
    matter, *18, 31*
    strings, *26–28, 41, 49, 56*
  self-organizing/self-transforming, *39, 43, 49, 50*
  types
    absolute (one), *18–19*
    relativistic (many), *23–26, 36–41, 49*

validation
  Einstein's theories, *25–26*
  experience as proof, *xxi–xxii*
  pudding as proof, *xxi–xxii*
  reliability/validity, *192*
value-added. *See* economic value-added;
    processes: value-added (VA)
Vargish, T., *23, 25*
Von Neumann, J., *30*
Vosniadou, S., *264*
Vroom, V.H., *188*

Wade, J., *205*
Walsh, J.P., *265*

waves, *19, 41. See also* particles
  particles
    collapsing into, *29–30, 32*
    as potential for, *29, 31, 228*
    reverting to, *29*
  string-based, *55–64, 68*
  vibrating/oscillating, *27, 56*
Weaver, J.H., *16, 21*
Western civilization, *xiii, xxi, 15, 17, 36, 278*
  difficulty with new paradigm, *31–33, 34, 50*
  focus on ego development, *291*
  integrated with the East, *296*
Weyle, H., *22*
Wheatley, M.J., *xvi, xxi, 17*
Wheeler, J.A., *24, 28–29*
Wigner, E., *46*
Wilber, K., *xxi, 34, 273, 290–291, 293, 295, 296*
Willig, R.D., *156*
Wolf, F.A., *28, 39*
workbooks for implementing the tracks, *306–307. See also* learning; program, completely integrated: workbooks; transformation: logistical aspects
workshops (sessions), *304–307. See also* learning; program, completely integrated; transformation: logistical aspects
  first three tracks, *107, 112, 135, 276*
  last three tracks, *86, 281, 284*
worldview. *See* paradigm
Wriston, W.B., *255*

X Y Z

Young, A.M., *xx, xxi, 20, 42–43, 81–82, 278, 292*
Zajonc, R.B., *264*
Zand, D.E., *141*
Zohar, D., *xvi, xxi, 13, 31, 45, 95*
Zuckav, G., *28*